Modernizing China

Investing in Soft Infrastructure

Edited by
W. Raphael Lam
Markus Rodlauer
Alfred Schipke

INTERNATIONAL MONETARY FUND

Cover design: Jesse Sanchez

Cataloging-in-Publication Data
Joint Bank-Fund Library

Names: Lam, W. Raphael | Rodlauer, Markus. | Schipke, Alfred, 1959- | International Monetary Fund.
Title: Modernizing China : investing in soft infrastructure / edited by W. Raphael Lam, Markus Rodlauer, Alfred Schipke.
Description: Washington, DC : International Monetary Fund, 2017. | Includes bibliographical references.
Identifiers: ISBN 9781513539942
Subjects: LCSH: Infrastructure (Economics)--China. | China—Economic conditions. | Corporate governance. | Fiscal policy--China. | Monetary policy—China.
Classification: LCC HC430.C3 M63 2017

ISBN 978-1-51353-994-2 (Paper)
978-1-47555-849-4 (ePub)
978-1-47555-852-4 (Mobipocket)
978-1-47555-854-8 (PDF)

Please send orders to:
International Monetary Fund, Publication Services
P.O. Box 92780, Washington, DC 20090, U.S.A.
Tel.: (202) 623-7430 Fax: (202) 623-7201
E-mail: publications@imf.org
Internet: www.elibrary.imf.org
www.imfbookstore.org

Contents

State-Owned Enterprise Frameworks

Macroeconomic Statistics for Policymaking

Foreword

China's economic growth over the past 35 years has sharply reduced poverty, created a large and rapidly growing middle class, and made its physical infrastructure a benchmark for countries around the world. Now the economy has embarked on its next transformation toward higher-income and advanced economy status.

In line with the proverb in the Chinese *Book of Odes (Shijing)*, "pursuing reform is a continuous mission regardless of the glorious past," China has launched comprehensive reforms to promote growth that is sustainable, inclusive, and environment friendly. This requires a more market-driven economy, based more on services and consumption than on industry and physical investment. It also requires investing more in "soft infrastructure," including frameworks for well-functioning markets and effective macroeconomic management.

Drawing on international experiences, this book provides guidance for a strengthening of fiscal, monetary, and financial sector frameworks. It encourages further reforms of state-owned enterprises, calls for policy actions to address the financial risks of local governments' funding practices, and highlights the need for better and more frequent macroeconomic statistics.

The recent inclusion of the Chinese renminbi in the IMF's Special Drawing Rights basket has recognized the significant reform progress achieved in many areas. Now is the time to build on these accomplishments. By expanding and deepening reforms, China will be able to support durable growth and stability at home and abroad.

The IMF remains a committed partner in China's transformation, offering policy advice, technical assistance, and training. We hope this book will contribute to the broader discussion about how best to achieve a successful transformation.

Christine Lagarde
Managing Director
International Monetary Fund

Acknowledgments

Modernizing China: Investing in Soft Infrastructure comprehensively analyzes the institutions and policies that govern important macroeconomic and financial areas in China, reviews reform progress, and—based on international experience—suggests ways to strengthen policy frameworks further.

The publication involved broad collaboration across many IMF departments, as well as contributions from Chinese colleagues. It also benefited from valuable inputs from James Daniel and other colleagues on the China team in the IMF's Asia and Pacific Department.

We express our strong appreciation for the continued support of ZHU Jun, AI Ming, and other colleagues at the People's Bank of China, as well as the IMF Executive Director JIN Zhongxia. Likewise, we benefited from invaluable comments and feedback of our Chinese and World Bank colleagues, and participants at the 2015 and 2016 Joint People's Bank of China/IMF Conferences.

We are indebted to the IMF's Editorial and Publications Division. Particular thanks go to Gemma Rose Diaz for working overtime and managing the production of the book, as well as Linda Long, Michael Harrup, and Patricia Loo for their many contributions. We also thank Jeremy Clift, Jeffrey Hayden, and Linda Griffin Kean for their unwavering support. Lesa Yee from the IMF China team went the extra mile in coordinating manuscript production.

We are very grateful to Eric Van Zant, Lucy Morales, and Katy Whipple for their outstanding editing of the manuscript and handling of the many updates and changes.

W. Raphael Lam, Markus Rodlauer, and Alfred Schipke
Editors

Contributors

Chikako Baba is Economist in the Monetary and Macroprudential Policies Division of the IMF's Monetary and Capital Markets Department. She has worked on a number of core policy papers related to capital flow management, macroprudential policy, and monetary policy. Ms. Baba holds a Ph.D. in economics from the University of Wisconsin-Madison. Since joining the IMF, she has also worked in the African Department.

John Brondolo is Senior Economist in the Revenue Administration 1 Division of the IMF's Fiscal Affairs Department. During his 25-year career at the IMF, Mr. Brondolo has assisted many IMF member countries in designing and implementing tax administration reform programs. Since the early 1990s, he has advised the State Administration of Taxation on a broad range of reform initiatives and is currently responsible for managing the IMF's technical cooperation activities with the administration. Mr. Brondolo has also published papers on tax administration topics, including *Collecting Taxes in an Economic Crisis: Challenges and Policy Options*. He possesses a Master of Public Policy degree from the John F. Kennedy School of Government, Harvard University.

Salim M. Darbar is Senior Economist in the Monetary and Macroprudential Policies Division of the IMF's Monetary and Capital Markets Department. In recent years, he has mostly worked on issues related to macroprudential policies, capital flow management, and foreign exchange regulations. Previously, he worked on emerging market and developing economies in the IMF's European Department, African Department, and Middle East Department. Mr. Darbar holds a Ph.D. in economics from Tulane University.

Ruud A. de Mooij is Deputy Division Chief in the Tax Policy Division of the IMF's Fiscal Affairs Department. Mr. de Mooij is responsible for much of the analytical work of the division, including recent work on fiscal policy and inequality, international spillovers from corporate taxation, and investment tax incentives. He also contributes to technical assistance on tax policy to IMF member countries. Before joining the IMF, Mr. de Mooij was Professor of Public Economics at Erasmus University Rotterdam in the Netherlands. He has published extensively on taxation issues, including in the *American Economic Review* and the *Journal of Public Economics*. Mr. de Mooij is research fellow at the Oxford University Center for Business Taxation, the University of Bergen, ZEW in Mannheim, and the CESifo network in Munich. He is also member of the Board of the National Tax Association.

Robert Dippelsman is Deputy Division Chief of the Real Sector Division of the IMF's Statistics Department. He previously worked in the Balance of Payments and Government Finance Divisions of the Statistics Department. Before joining the IMF, he worked in the Australian Bureau of Statistics.

David Gentry is Senior Economist in the Fiscal Affairs Department of the IMF. In this capacity he addresses public financial management issues relating to fiscal planning, budget preparation, and treasury management by leading technical assistance missions, organizing technical assistance carried out by external experts, and participating in the analytical agenda of Fiscal Affairs Department. His technical assistance work is concentrated in the Asia and Pacific region. In recent years he has participated in major Fiscal Affairs Department analytical efforts, including updating the Fiscal Transparency Code and Manual and conducting studies on the effectiveness of Group of Twenty countries' budget institutions and improving the efficiency of public investment. Prior to joining the IMF headquarters staff he served as resident budget adviser to ministries of finance in Albania, Georgia, and Mongolia under the auspices of the IMF and the U.S. Department of the Treasury.

Naomi Griffin is Senior Economist in the Monetary and Capital Markets Department at the IMF, managing the delivery of financial sector technical assistance to a number of countries worldwide. Ms. Griffin's previous assignments at the IMF include country surveillance on emerging markets in Latin America. Prior to joining the IMF in 2011, she worked at the U.S. Congressional Budget Office, analyzing the effects of economic policies during the global financial crisis. She holds a Ph.D. in economics from the University of Maryland and a Master of Arts in international relations from Johns Hopkins University's School of Advanced International Studies.

Sanjeev Gupta is Deputy Director of the Fiscal Affairs Department at the IMF and previously was in its African Department and European Department. Mr. Gupta has led IMF missions to some 25 countries in Africa, Asia, Europe, and the Middle East, and represented the institution in numerous international meetings and conferences. Prior to joining the IMF, he was a fellow of the Kiel Institute of World Economics, Germany; Professor in the Administrative Staff College of India, Hyderabad; and Secretary of the Federation of Indian Chambers of Commerce and Industry. Mr. Gupta has authored/coauthored over 150 papers on macroeconomic and fiscal issues, and authored/coauthored/coedited 11 books; the most recent books, all published by the IMF, are *The Economics of Public Health Care Reform in Advanced and Emerging Economies* in 2012, *Energy Subsidy Reform: Lessons and Implications* in 2013, *Equitable and Sustainable Pensions: Challenges and Experiences* in 2014, and *Fiscal Policy and Inequality* in 2015.

Karl Habermeier is Assistant Director in the IMF's Monetary and Capital Markets Department, where he leads the division responsible for monetary and macroprudential policies. His recent work has focused on the challenges for monetary policy after the crisis, the development of macroprudential frameworks, and the management of international capital flows. Mr. Habermeier holds a Ph.D. in economics from Stanford University.

Annamaria Kokenyne Ivanics is Lead Financial Sector Expert in the IMF's Monetary and Capital Markets Department. Ms. Kokenyne Ivanics' work has focused on crisis countries, capital flow management, and foreign exchange markets and frameworks. Before joining the IMF, she was the Head of the International Economic Relations Department in the Ministry of Finance in Hungary. Ms. Kokenyne holds a Master of Science in economics from Budapest University of Economics and a J.D. from Eotvos University, Hungary.

W. Raphael Lam is IMF Deputy Resident Representative in China. He comanages the office by providing policy advice and undertaking analytical work, and helps coordinate IMF-China technical assistance and training in China. Previously, he worked in the European Department, Finance Department, and the Asia and Pacific Department. He participated in the IMF's lending program to Iceland during the global financial crisis and Japan's Financial Sector Assessment Program, and was involved in IMF regional surveillance in Asia. He has written research papers on a wide range of issues on China, including real estate, the labor market, local government finances, and state-owned enterprise reform. Mr. Lam previously worked with the Hong Kong Monetary Authority and has a Ph.D. in economics from University of California, Los Angeles.

MA Jun is Chief Economist at the People's Bank of China's Research Bureau. Before joining the central bank in early 2014, he worked for 13 years at Deutsche Bank, where he was Managing Director, Chief Economist for Greater China, and Head of China and Hong Kong Strategy. Prior to joining Deutsche Bank in 2000, he worked as public policy specialist, economist, and Senior Economist at the IMF and World Bank from 1992–2000. From 1988–90, he was a research fellow at the Development Research Center of China's State Council. Mr. Ma has published 11 books and several hundred articles on the Chinese economy, global economy, and financial markets. His main research interests include macroeconomics, monetary and financial policies, and environmental economics. Mr. Ma received his Ph.D. in economics from Georgetown University in 1994 and a Master's in management science from Fudan University in 1988.

Malhar Nabar is Deputy Division Chief in the World Economic Studies Division of the IMF's Research Department. Previously, he worked on the China team in the Asia and Pacific Department and was Mission Chief for Hong Kong SAR. His research interests are in financial development, investment, and productivity growth. He has published in the *Journal of Development Economics*, *Economic Inquiry*, *Journal of Macroeconomics*, and IMF Working Papers. In 2013 he coedited the book of recent IMF research *China's Economy in Transition*. Mr. Nabar holds a Ph.D. in economics from Brown University.

Markus Rodlauer is Deputy Director of the IMF's Asia and Pacific Department. Among other leadership responsibilities, he heads the IMF's China team, which conducted the annual Article IV Consultations with China in recent years. His previous jobs at the IMF included Deputy Director of Human Resources; Deputy Director in the Western Hemisphere Department; Mission Chief for a number of countries in Asia, Europe, and South America; and IMF Representative to Poland and the Philippines. Mr. Rodlauer worked with the Ministry of Foreign Affairs of Austria before joining the IMF. His academic training includes degrees in law, economics, and international relations.

Alfred Schipke is IMF Senior Resident Representative for China. He provides policy advice, leads the analytical work of the office, and coordinates the IMF's training and technical assistance in China. Previously, he was Division Chief in the Asia and Pacific Department, where he coordinated the work on fast-growing low-income countries in southeast Asia (frontier economies) and led missions to Vietnam. He was a Division Chief in the IMF's Western Hemisphere Department in charge of the Latin Caribbean and Eastern Caribbean Currency Union divisions and negotiated a number of IMF programs. He teaches international finance at Harvard University, John F. Kennedy School of Government, and has authored and edited a number of books and articles. His research focuses on economic integration and the linkages between macroeconomics and finance.

Mauricio Soto is Senior Economist at the IMF, where he has assessed the fiscal impact of social insurance programs in advanced and emerging market economies (largely pensions and health). He has collaborated with the authorities of more than a dozen countries in analyzing fiscal issues over the past five years. Prior to joining the IMF, he worked as a researcher on retirement issues—first at the Center for Retirement Research at Boston College and most recently at the Urban Institute. He has authored and coauthored several papers on age-related spending, and his research has been published in *Labour*, the *Journal of Pension Economics and Finance*, and the *Journal of Financial Planning*.

Camilo E. Tovar is Senior Economist at the Strategy Division of the IMF's Strategy, Policy, and Review Department. Previously, he worked on Pakistan and in the Western Hemisphere Department. Prior to joining the IMF, Mr. Tovar worked at the Bank for International Settlements. He has served as Economic Advisor to the Executive Secretary of the United Nations Economic Commission for Latin America and the Caribbean in Chile, as well as Advisor to the Finance Minister of Colombia and to the Director of the National Planning Department in Colombia. Mr. Tovar holds a Ph.D. and M.Sc. in economics from the University of Wisconsin-Madison and an M.A. in economics from the University of Los Andes (Colombia). His research has been published in refereed journals, including the *BIS Quarterly Review*, *Journal of International Money and Finance*, *Journal of International Commerce Economics and Policy*, *Economic Review*, *Open Economies Review*, and *Economics e-Journal*.

Holger van Eden is Deputy Division Chief in the Public Financial Management II Division of the Fiscal Affairs Department of the IMF. He has worked extensively with ministries of finance in eastern Europe, Asia, Latin America, and the Caribbean. His focus areas range from budget preparation, public investment management, finance ministry institutional restructuring, and budget and fiscal responsibility laws to government treasury and cash management. Mr. van Eden has led and participated in more than 50 IMF technical assistance missions, including to China, as well as to Belgium, Bhutan, Brazil, Colombia, Estonia, Greece, India, Indonesia, Jamaica, Japan, Mexico, Mongolia, the Netherlands, and Thailand. Before joining the IMF, Mr. van Eden worked as team leader and project coordinator in international consultancy, as an economic journalist and editor, and as a financial consultant for a global accounting firm. He started his career in the Netherlands Ministry of Finance. Mr. van Eden is currently coeditor of the IMF's *PFM Blog*.

James P. Walsh is Deputy Chief in the IMF's Monetary and Capital Markets Department, focusing on issues related to monetary policy and financial stability, particularly in Asia and the Americas. He is also Deputy Mission Chief for the China Financial Sector Assessment Program. His analytical work has covered macro-financial linkages, inflation, financing infrastructure investment, and systemic financial risks. In 2014 he coedited *The Future of Asian Finance*. He has a Ph.D. in economics from the University of Chicago.

WEI Jianing is Director-General and Researcher in the Development Research Center of the State Council. He has had extensive experience in the center, specializing in macroeconomics. He first joined the center's Macro Economy Department in 1991 and became the Director-General (Inspector) in 2013. Mr. Wei has collaborated and written joint works with many distinguished and prominent economists, including Mr. Wu Jinglian and Mr. Sun Xiangqing. He has been prolific and has published on macroeconomic policies, financial risks and supervision, and fiscal issues on local government finances, which serve as inputs to the policy design. In 2014 he published a book on resolving the risks of local government debt and new municipal financing. He received his doctoral degree in economics from the China Academy of Social Science.

Philippe Wingender is Economist in the Tax Policy Division of the Fiscal Affairs Department at the IMF. Mr. Wingender joined the Fiscal Affairs Department after obtaining his Ph.D. in economics from the University of California, Berkeley. His research interests include labor supply responses to tax changes, the incidence of tax reform, taxation and informality, and the macroeconomic effects of fiscal policy. As an IMF economist, he has worked on several countries, including China, as well as on Bosnia and Herzegovina, Kosovo, Trinidad and Tobago, and Uganda.

ZHANG Zhiyong is former Deputy Commissioner of State Tax Administration (SAT) of China. During his 33-year career there, Mr. Zhang held a wide range of senior positions, including Director General of the International Taxation Department, Director General of the Large Business Taxation Department, Director General of the SAT's Beijing Municipal Tax Office, and Director of the Income Tax Division of the Foreign Investment Taxation Department. Through these positions, he has been deeply involved in many of China's tax policy and administration reforms and has worked closely with international organizations and revenue agencies of other countries. Mr. Zhang has a Bachelor of Arts in English from the Beijing Foreign Language Institute and has been a Visiting Scholar of Tax Laws at the Law School of Columbia University.

ZHAO Xiuzhen is Senior Economist in the Strategy, Standards, and Review Division of the IMF's Statistics Department. She previously worked in the Financial Institutions Division of the Statistics Department. Before joining the IMF, Ms. Zhao worked in the National Bureau of Statistics of China.

ZHU Ling is Economist in the Monetary and Macroprudential Policies Division of the IMF's Monetary and Capital Markets Department. Mr. Zhu holds a Ph.D. in economics from the University of Maryland. His research focuses on capital flows, capital flow management, and financial stability.

Viktoriya Zotova is Research Analyst in the Monetary and Macroprudential Policies Division of the IMF's Monetary and Capital Markets Department. She has worked in the areas of foreign exchange regulations and capital flows and has provided research and analytical support for a number of empirical and policy papers. Ms. Zotova holds a Bachelor of Arts in economics from St. Norbert College.

Abbreviations and Acronyms

AMC	asset management company
AREAER	*Annual Report on Exchange Arrangements and Exchange Restrictions*
BEPS	base erosion and profit shifting
BIS	Bank for International Settlements
BPM6	*Balance of Payments and International Investment Position Manual, Sixth Edition*
CBRC	China Banking Regulatory Commission
CDS	credit default swap
CIBM	China Interbank Bond Market
CNY	Chinese yuan (*renminbi*)
CPI	consumer price index
CSRC	China Securities Regulatory Commission
CTAIS	China Tax Administration Information System
DGI	Data Gaps Initiative
DSGE	dynamic stochastic general equilibrium
EBS	Electronic Broking Services
FDI	foreign direct investment
FSB	Financial Stability Board
FSI	financial soundness indicator
G20	Group of Twenty
GDDS	General Data Dissemination System
GFSM	*Government Finance Statistics Manual*
GTP	Golden Tax Project
IBS	international banking statistics
IMS	international monetary system
IRS	internal revenue service
JSCB	joint-stock commercial bank
LGFV	local government financing vehicle
LIBOR	London Interbank Offered Rate
MAP	mutual agreement procedure
MPS	Material Product System
MTBF	medium-term budget framework
MTEF	medium-term expenditure framework
MTFF	medium-term fiscal framework
MTPF	medium-term program framework
NBS	National Bureau of Statistics
NDRC	National Development and Reform Commission
NPC	National People's Congress
NPL	nonperforming loan
OECD	Organisation for Economic Co-operation and Development

P2P	peer-to-peer
PBC	People's Bank of China
PE	permanent establishment
PPI	producer price index
PPP	public-private partnership
QDII	Qualified Domestic Institutional Investor
QFII	Qualified Foreign Institutional Investor
RMB	renminbi
ROBEK	Register for Government Approval of Financial Obligations
RPPI	residential property price index
RQFII	Renminbi Qualified Foreign Institutional Investor
SAFE	State Administration of Foreign Exchange
SAR	Special Administrative Region
SASAC	State-Owned Assets Supervision and Administration Commission
SAT	State Administration of Taxation
SDDS	Special Data Dissemination Standard
SDR	special drawing right
SHIBOR	Shanghai Interbank Offered Rate
SME	small and medium-sized enterprise
SNA	System of National Accounts
SOE	state-owned enterprise
SVAR	structural vector autoregression
TCL	Tax Collection Law
TFP	total factor productivity
TSF	total social financing
UNCTAD	United Nations Conference on Trade and Development
URR	unremunerated reserve requirement
VAT	value-added tax
WMP	wealth management product
WTO	World Trade Organization

CHAPTER 1

China's Economic Success and Reforms: Investing in Soft Infrastructure

W. Raphael Lam, Markus Rodlauer, and Alfred Schipke

China matters as never before. It is now the second largest economy in the world—and the largest in purchasing power parity. Even at half its historical economic growth rate, it contributes nearly one-third to global growth. In addition, its global export share amounts to about 15 percent, and more than 120 countries count China as their largest trading partner (Figures 1.1 and 1.2) (Ministry of Commerce 2014).

Since the late 1970s, successive waves of reform have slashed poverty, raised the country to middle-income status, and spurred the building of enviable physical infrastructure. Now China is once again at a critical juncture in its economic history as it tries to transform a growth model that is generally seen as tired and in need of rejuvenation. The success of fresh reforms will be crucial not just for its own population, but will also have significant implications for the region and the world given China's economic size, trade links, and increasing financial integration.[1]

A unifying theme across reforms is the need to build a new set of policy frameworks for more effective markets. That is, transformation can no longer be achieved by increasing physical investment and allocating resources by government direction. This does not mean that markets should be unfettered; rather, they should be allowed to work efficiently and sustainably, in line with broad social and economic policy goals.

In a nutshell, China is aiming to build new *soft* infrastructure—that is, the institutional foundation that underpins and guides the functioning of markets—as the key organizing principle toward sustained economic and social progress. Such infrastructure includes, for example, an equitable and environment-friendly tax regime, price-based financial and monetary frameworks that help channel savings to the most productive users, and strong corporate governance that avoids waste and safeguards the legitimate interests of workers and consumers.

Premier LI Keqiang (2016) emphasized this new focus when he highlighted that "overcoming imbalances in the economy is to overcome institutional

---

We would like to thank QI Zhe for providing excellent support.

[1]See Annex 1.1 for selected economic indicators.

Figure 1.1. China's Share in Global Output
(Percent in purchasing power parity, 2015)

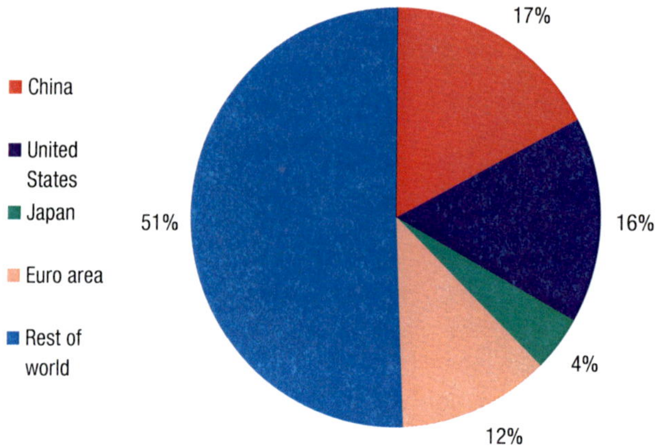

Source: IMF, *Regional Economic Outlook: Asia and Pacific*, April 2016.

Figure 1.2. China's Growing Share of Global Trade
(Percent of total global trade)

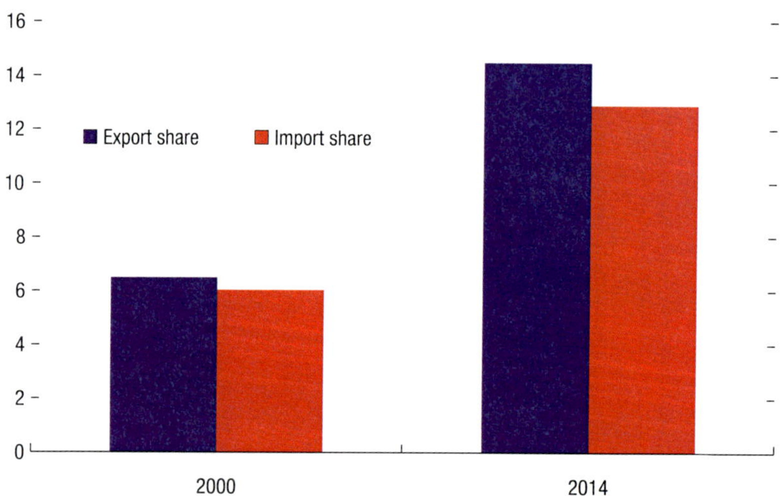

Source: United Nations Trade Statistics.

challenges," and "a greater emphasis will go beyond physical investment, centering on soft areas, including the provision of public services."

Unlike investments in physical infrastructure, however, the benefits of policy frameworks and institutions are often less well understood by the public and hence more difficult for policymakers to implement. Yet failure to modernize and strengthen policy frameworks would undermine growth potential, trap the country at the middle-income level, and leave the economy and financial system more vulnerable to domestic or external shocks.

This book reviews policies and institutions in China today, the road ahead, and key principles that can help navigate it. To set the stage, this summary chapter briefly discusses the country's development and its global footprint, followed by a review of reform progress and shortcomings. As in any other country, designing and implementing bold, far-reaching reforms faces opposition from the status quo; these are also highlighted in this chapter. Finally, the chapter summarizes the insights to be had from the chapters that follow.

CHINA'S DEVELOPMENT AND GLOBAL FOOTPRINT

Economic reforms and opening-up policies commenced with the vision of a moderate and prosperous *Xiaokang* society launched by DENG Xiaoping in 1978, laying the foundations for stellar growth (CPC News 2014). Average annual growth of about 10 percent since then has transformed the country, allowing it to reach middle-income status and spurring the rapid construction of an impressive array of roads, airports, bridges, high-rise buildings, and other infrastructure. China's high-speed rail system is now the largest in the world.

Significant structural transformation has accompanied economic development. During the first decades, the country transitioned from agriculture to manufacturing and moved up the value chain by diversifying into new sectors and improving the quality of goods produced.[2] Similar to the experience of other countries, it started to de-industrialize at an income level of about $9,000 (in 1990 international prices), with the output share of the industrial sector peaking in 2011. More recently, the services sector has become an increasingly important economic pillar.

During this process, some 250–300 million migrants moved from rural agricultural areas to cities for more gainful employment, and 600 million people escaped poverty. As living standards rose, they created a middle-class that now numbers some 150 million people, second in size only to the United States (World Bank and Development Research Center of the State Council 2014). Life expectancy and literacy jumped and the urban-rural income gap shrank, particularly in the decade after the turn of the century (see Annex 1.2).

Given China's strong trade linkages and critical role in the global economy, estimates suggest that changes in its growth outlook would have very large knock-on effects. A 1 percentage point growth shock in China, for example, would affect growth in other Asian countries by about 0.3 percentage point on average; even in

[2]See Henn, Papageorgiou, and Spatafora 2015 on China's diversification and quality upgrading.

Figure 1.3. Rising Spillovers from Shocks in China
(Percent change in GDP after one year for a median country for 1 percentage point negative GDP shock in China)

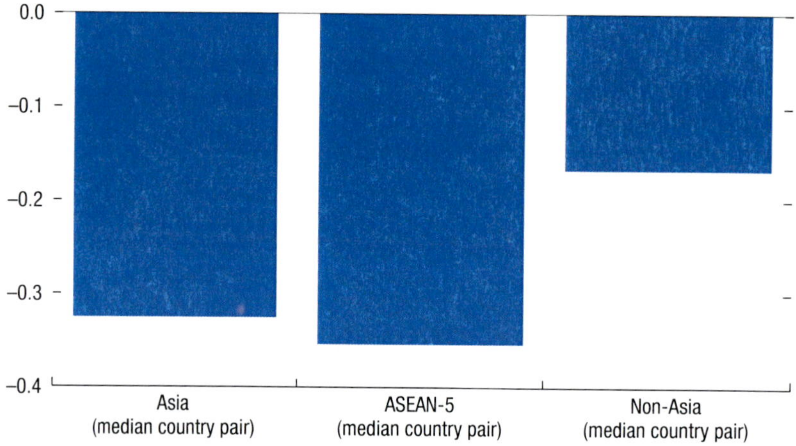

Source: IMF staff estimates based on Cashin, Mohaddes, and Raissi 2016.
Note: ASEAN-5 = Indonesia, Malaysia, the Philippines, Singapore, and Thailand.

the rest of the world the impact would be significant (Figure 1.3). Reflecting the close economic integration through global value chains, the strongest impact would be on countries such as Korea and Malaysia. As China is a major importer of commodities, changes in investment demand can account for up to half of changes in broad commodity prices, albeit with marked differences across countries and commodities (IMF 2016a). Despite the country's limited direct financial sector linkages to the rest of the world, volatility in equity and foreign exchange markets in 2015–16 has demonstrated that events in China are increasingly having an impact on equity prices in both emerging market and advanced economies.

China's successful transformation will thus reverberate at home and throughout the world, and warrant economic adjustments elsewhere. Commodity-exporting nations are likely to see permanently lower demand, while countries specializing in the production of consumer goods will benefit from China's growing middle class and its rising demand for consumer products. Other economies, especially in southeast Asia, will benefit from changing supply chains as China moves up the value chain.

REFORMS: ADDRESSING ECONOMIC IMBALANCES

As noted, the growth model is facing its limits, with growth slowing and vulnerabilities rising.[3] Successful development in the past relied on high investment,

[3]See IMF 2016a for a discussion of China's economic challenges and reform progress.

relatively inexpensive labor, productivity-enhancing foreign direct investment, and strong global demand. Along the way, the government played an important role in the allocation of resources, both through state-owned enterprises (SOEs) and local governments, especially in infrastructure.

The moderation of China's growth has been structural, in part reflecting natural convergence as income per capita reached middle-income levels. At the same time, slower growth reflects waning dividends from previous productivity-boosting reforms, such as the SOE reform at the end of the 1990s and accession to the World Trade Organization in 2001.

China, prior to the global financial crisis, had recognized the limits of its growth model and the growing imbalances inherent in it. Former Premier WEN Jiabao in March 2007 called for reforms to address *unsteady, unbalanced, uncoordinated, and unsustainable development.*[4] As the global financial crisis unfolded, reforms were largely put on hold, and the country embarked on massive economic stimulus amounting to 11 percent of GDP, mostly for infrastructure and social housing. This stabilized domestic demand and was a welcome shot in the arm for the global economy. But it also led to a further buildup in imbalances and increased vulnerabilities (see Figure 1.4).

The new leadership that took office in 2013 renewed the impetus for reforms with the comprehensive "Third Plenum Reform Blueprint" and with the approval of the 13th Five-Year Plan in 2016. Both documents comprehensively identify the challenges and spell out broad reform areas to be accomplished by 2020. Focusing on quality growth, they aim at boosting consumption, expanding the service sector, protecting the environment, further opening up the economy, expanding public services, and reducing poverty.

Reform progress has been strong in many areas, and it certainly stands out positively in an international context. Particularly strong advances have been made in improving monetary and fiscal frameworks and advancing urbanization (Annex 1.3). But progress has also been uneven, and the unfinished agenda is long and complex. Among others, the important SOE reform and opening up the service sector are lagging. The challenge is to implement reforms decisively in a number of critical areas. Steadfast implementation with the right priorities and appropriate sequencing put China on a sustainable, inclusive, and environment-friendly growth path that converges toward high-income levels.

Transformation and Rebalancing

China's economic challenges are unique in many dimensions, including scale, complexity, and impact on the global economy. What are the key areas that China needs to address? This is frequently dubbed *rebalancing*, that is, shifting the economy from:[5]

---

[4]Speech at the National People's Congress (Xinhua News 2007) and Consulate General of the People's Republic of China in San Francisco (2007).

[5]See IMF 2016a, Lipton 2016, and Zhang 2016 for a discussion of the rebalancing.

Figure 1.4. Diminishing Returns on Investment
(Percent)

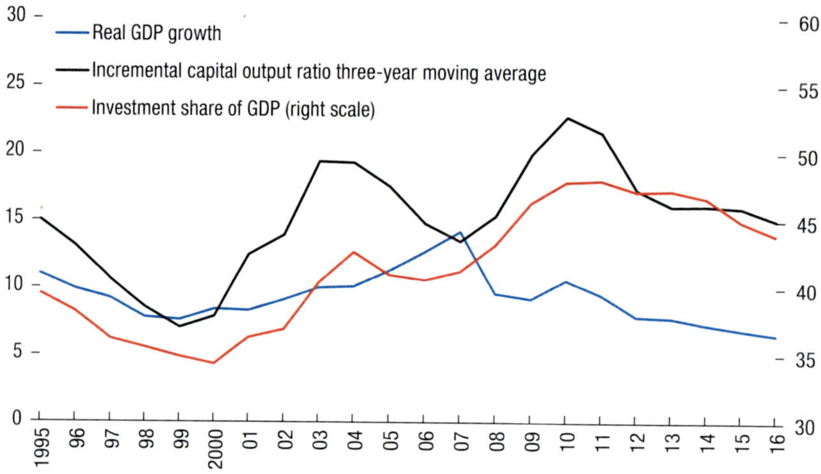

Source: CEIC.

- external to domestic demand
- investment to consumption
- industry to services
- state-led to more market- and private-sector-driven allocation of resources
- excessive corporate debt to sustainable leverage
- rising fiscal (especially local government) debts to medium-term fiscal sustainability
- financial sector liberalization to better governance
- increasing factor inputs to boosting productivity and innovation
- unequal growth to a more inclusive economy
- high pollution to greener growth with sustainable energy use
- old-style, infrequent government announcements to timely, market-friendly, transparent communication

In particular:

- *Domestic demand.* China's reliance on external demand prior to the global financial crisis was associated with large external imbalances reflected in a current account surplus that reached 10 percent of GDP in 2007. Since then, it has declined to about 2 percent in 2016, reflecting the rebalancing from exports to domestic demand (Figure 1.5).

Figure 1.5. Rebalancing from External to Domestic Demand
(Percent of GDP)

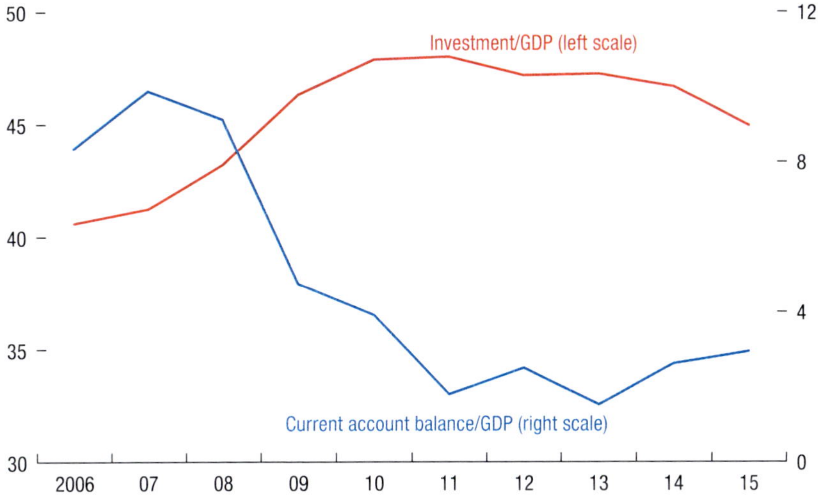

Sources: CEIC; and IMF staff estimates.

- *Consumption.* The growth model relied on a high investment (and savings) ratio, which reached 45 percent of GDP following the postcrisis stimulus. Although the stimulus contributed to the shift to domestic demand, it fostered growing domestic imbalances of weaker investment efficiency, more credit, and lower growth. More recently, there has been some progress in reversing this trend, reflected in a growing share of private consumption due to rising disposable household income. Investment has moderated along with the national savings rate, but it remained high at 43 percent in 2016—even by the standards of other previously fast-growing economies such as Korea. Moving further toward consumption will be paramount for China's rebalancing.
- *Services.* The economy has been transforming from agriculture to manufacturing, and more recently toward services. The latter now account for a rising share of GDP, growing faster than the industrial sector in real terms. The transition is mirrored in the labor market, where the service sector generates millions of jobs each year and now accounts for 40 percent of employment.
- *Productivity and innovation.* China's growth model relied on increases in factor inputs (capital and surplus labor from rural areas). With diminishing returns on investment and a declining labor force, fostering increased productivity will be critical for sustained growth.[6]

[6]See also World Bank and Development Research Center of the State Council 2013.

- *Sustainable leverage.* Credit growth since the global financial crisis has significantly outpaced nominal GDP growth, with nonfinancial sector (corporate and household) credit increasing from about 90 percent of GDP in 2008 to 160 percent of GDP in 2015 (Figure 1.6). International experience suggests that strong credit growth is often followed by sharp growth slowdowns and, in almost half of cases, financial sector stress (Figure 1.7). In China, while both households and the public sector have leveraged up, a key growth driver is corporate investment, especially in infrastructure and real estate. This in turn has fueled expansion in sectors that are now facing significant overcapacity (such as steel, coal, and cement). Rising leverage has gone hand in hand with weaker financial performance in the corporate sector—especially as it relates to SOEs—and deterioration of bank loan quality. This calls for comprehensive debt restructuring to address stock issues and a hardening of budget constraints to ensure that resources flow to viable projects.

  China's strong credit growth has been, in part, related to the practice of setting annual growth targets prompting policymakers to resort to short-term unsustainable stimulus measures. Apart from setting growth targets at more sustainable levels or downplaying them compared to other indicators (such as household income or employment), it is warranted to consider eliminating them altogether and instead—similar to other major advanced and emerging market economies—moving toward projections. This would alleviate the pressure to rely on low-quality, credit-financed investment to support growth.

- *Sound local government finances.* With a deficit of about 3 percent of GDP in 2015, China's general government deficit is relatively small; so is the general government debt of about 40 percent of GDP. But the picture changes when accounting for local government off-budget activities. Local governments provide significant public services and undertake sizable investment, but have structural resource misalignments since the revenue base is small (even after central government transfers) compared to spending obligations. Local governments have, therefore, a strong incentive to rely on nontraditional forms of resource mobilization, including from the sale of assets (land) and the establishment of special financing vehicles to borrow from banks and capital markets. As a result, local government off-budget deficits amounted to 6–7 percent of GDP in recent years. A broader definition of government that includes general government and estimates for off-budget activities hence shows an "augmented" deficit of about 10 percent of GDP (Figure 1.8; the corresponding augmented debt level was 60 percent of GDP in 2016). Putting local governments on a sound fiscal footing by resolving intergovernmental imbalances—and eventually stabilizing China's "augmented" debt over the medium term—is therefore paramount.

- *Financial sector governance.* Financial sector liberalization (such as interest rates and the elimination of loan-to-deposit ratios) has advanced significantly

Figure 1.6. Sharp Increase in Credit

(Percent of GDP)

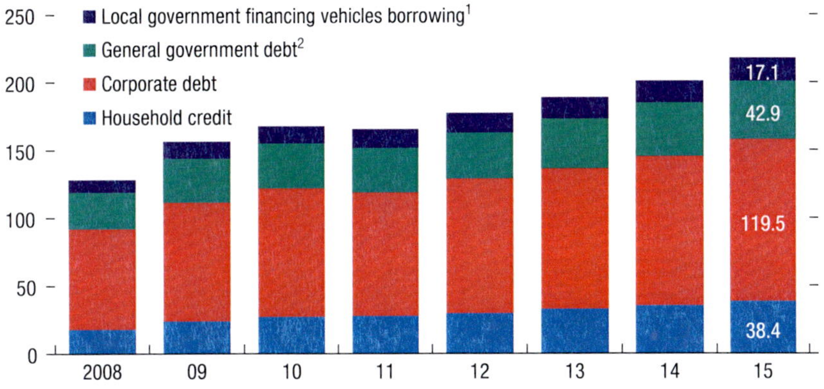

Sources: CEIC; and IMF staff estimates.

[1] Local government financing vehicle (LGFV) debt not classified as official general government debt. Total local government debt (official and LGFV debt not classified as official government debt) was about 40 percent of GDP in 2015.

[2] Includes part of LGFV debt that is recognized as official local government debt.

Figure 1.7. Global Credit Booms Tend to End Badly

(Percentage points)

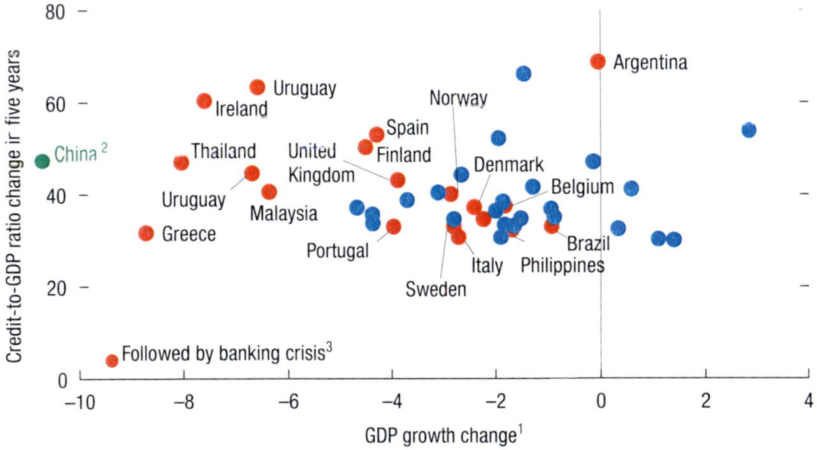

Source: IMF staff estimates.

[1] Average growth differential between five-year postboom and five-year preboom periods.

[2] No growth change as China's boom has not ended.

[3] Banking crisis (red dots) is identified following Laeven and Valencia 2012. Blue dots indicate no banking crisis.

Figure 1.8. Fiscal Deficit Remains Large, but More On-Budget
(Percent of GDP)

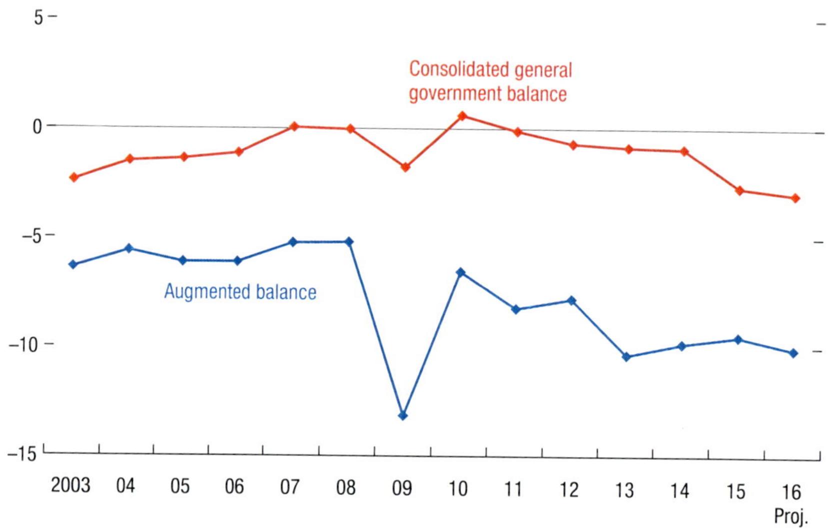

Sources: CEIC; Chinese authorities; and IMF staff estimates.

over the past few years. At the same time, a rapidly changing financial landscape, the mushrooming of new financial products—often cutting across regulatory agencies—and rising vulnerabilities imply that stronger financial sector regulation and better coordination and information sharing among regulatory agencies should top the reform agenda.

- *Private sector.* While the private sector has been growing as a share of the economy, the public sector continues to play an important role through SOEs, public investments—especially through local governments—and in general by directing resources, including through quantitative targets and moral suasion. Letting the market play a more decisive role will entail opening up the economy to competition and creating a level playing field for both public and private companies.
- *Green growth.* Past economic success has come at a significant environmental cost. Air, water, and soil pollution account for the largest share, including costs associated with pollution-related health damage, global climate change impacts, and resource depletion. Estimates by the World Health Organization suggest that air pollution accounted for 1.4 million premature deaths in China in 2010. Rationalizing fuel subsidies, a less factor-intensive growth model, and an environment-friendly tax system will help address environmental degradation. Progress has been made, and China has demonstrated its commitment to environmental sustainability, including by signing the Paris Agreement to reduce carbon emissions.

Figure 1.9. Asia: Change in Gini Index, Past Two Decades
(Gini points, since 1990)

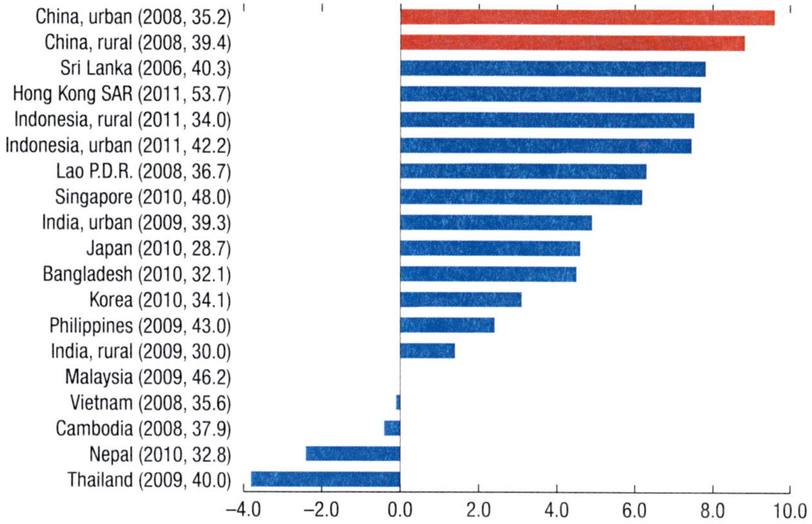

Sources: National authorities; World Bank; and IMF staff calculations.
Note: The latest available year and corresponding Gini coefficients are in parentheses.

- *Inclusive growth.* Remarkable growth has lifted millions out of poverty, but it has also been associated with rising income inequality, with the Gini coefficient now among the most unequal in the world (Figure 1.9). Alongside ensuring inclusive growth, China (and the other countries in the Group of Twenty [G20]) has identified mitigating inequality as an important area for reform. As international experience shows, inequality can in turn be a key driver for social and macroeconomic instability.

Market Allocation of Resources

Further liberalizing and opening up sectors to competition are critical if the market is to play a more decisive role. This does not mean unfettered markets, but markets that work efficiently, sustainably, and in line with broad social and economic goals.

An efficient market will require enforcement of rules and regulations, in particular, to allow for price discovery, which is critical for efficient resource allocation. Safeguards (such as social safety nets and resolution frameworks) can mitigate the adverse impact of greater market competition, including layoffs and bankruptcies. Despite the progress made on economic liberalization, China's hard budget constraints often still go unenforced, and public agencies tend to intervene and prevent the exit of nonviable firms and financial institutions

Figure 1.10. Insolvency Framework
(Number of cases, 2014)

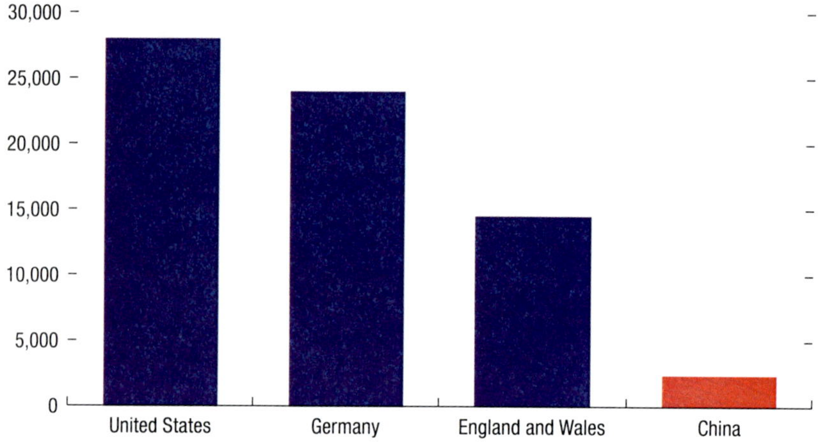

Sources: China Court; Credireform; Euler Hermes; Sinotrust; U.S. Trust Offices; and UK Insolvency Service.

(Figure 1.10). Yet such exits are part of the discovery process and, hence, of a dynamic and innovative economy. The still widespread perception that, ultimately, the government will step in to prevent losses undermines the effectiveness of market prices to play a decisive role.

Improved Communication and Transparency

Guiding markets and providing participants with clear policy direction reduce uncertainty and improve effectiveness. As the experience of advanced economies demonstrates, however, communicating effectively can be daunting and is sometimes more an art than a science. Furthermore, China's unique economic institutional setup creates additional challenges. Since most key economic decisions need approval by the State Council (equivalent to a government cabinet), the timing and outcome of policies of individual ministries and agencies—such as the People's Bank of China (PBC) and financial sector regulators—tend to be less certain at the time of submission, which constrains timely communication.

As mentioned, the broad economic reform objectives are laid out in key documents, such as the Third Party Plenum and the five-year plans. In addition, in December each year, the government puts forward a Work Program (approved by the National People's Congress in March the following year) about key policy priorities and annual economic targets. Respective ministries and public agencies prepare operational measures under the guidance and approval of the State Council. In formulating these policies, decision making is a two-way process in which ministries and local governments make proposals and political party members at corresponding levels provide input. In addition to the State Council, the

Communist Party can also provide direct policy guidance with, for example, input from the Office of the Leading Group on Economic and Financial Affairs.

The decision-making process has the merit of building policy consensus, but at times it can lead to mixed messages. Moreover, the dissemination of information is often indirect and opaque. For example, major policy changes are often signaled through speeches by officials at conferences and other not so well-known local events. In addition, media columnists, academics, and opinion leaders closely related to the government often serve to signal new policy changes. These leave significant room for multiple interpretations, which in turn can contribute to market volatility, at home and abroad.

Yet even within its unique setup, China still has significant scope to improve communication and transparency about policy objectives, including frameworks, and therefore to boost credibility and effectiveness at home and abroad. The government has recognized the importance of this; for example, ministerial heads were tasked to hold press conferences during the 2016 National People's Congress.

POLITICAL ECONOMY OF REFORMS AND INSTITUTIONS

Economic reforms in general, and strengthening policy frameworks in particular, are notoriously difficult in any country. Failing or delaying implementation often ends up with subdued growth, economic instability, policy setbacks, and, in the worst case, crises. At the same time, vested interest groups often resist change through their wide connections. To highlight the need to take on strong interest groups, President XI Jinping in September 2016 emphasized: "China's reforms have entered a crucial stage and the deep water area. Reforms will be resolutely carried out with forceful determination, daring to take on chronic problems and deep-seated vested interests and imbalances."

In the past, China has shown its determination to implement reforms. In some cases, the country overcame obstacles through reliance on external anchors, most notably the 2001 World Trade Organization accession, which was crucial to fostering competition and enterprise restructuring. Similar external anchors, such as trade agreements and investment treaties, could again foster competition and the unlocking of new growth poles.

Reform design and implementation require consensus within and across government agencies, including at subnational levels. Some local governments have been reform champions, for example, in initiating pilots, but others have resisted by circumventing rules or outright flouting them. It is therefore critical to create an incentive-compatible structure in line with national reform priorities.

Rapidly rising economic complexity and expansion of the financial system, deeper global integration, and the general push for reforms call for a constant upgrading of public institutions. The overall public sector is large, yet staffing is often thin at central ministries, regulators, and other agencies compared to public administrations in modern advanced economies, which are entrusted with the enormous task of upgrading policy frameworks, designing and implementing reforms, and monitoring and identifying new policies.

The IMF's 2011 Financial Sector Assessment Program, for example, had already called for a strengthening of staffing at key regulatory agencies. Since then, the financial system has almost doubled and become highly interlinked, but headquarter staffing at financial sector regulatory agencies and the PBC are still small and broadly unchanged.[7] The same is true at agencies such as the Ministry of Finance and the State Administration of Taxation (SAT). For example, while the SAT employs some 750,000 civil servants nationwide, its head office employs only 750. This ratio is very small compared to the staffing ratio of other effective tax agencies worldwide. Bringing the central staffing on par with these foreign tax agencies, the SAT's headquarters staffing would account for closer to 3–10 percent of the SAT system (see Chapter 3).

STRENGTHENING POLICY FRAMEWORKS: SUMMARY

China's transformation and rebalancing are challenging, but at the same time have significant consequences, particularly given the country's massive global footprint. As discussed above, a unifying theme is that the country needs to continue building a set of policy frameworks adaptable to the changing landscape, which will allow markets to function effectively. Stronger policy frameworks are crucial to effective macroeconomic management, addressing potential volatility and risks, and achieving sustainable growth.

Key priorities include halting high and rising corporate and public debts (in particular local government debt), imposing hard budget constraints, strengthening the resilience of the financial sector, and allowing markets to allocate resources efficiently.

As this chapter noted from the outset, more investment in soft infrastructure is needed, that is, the institutional plumbing that will run through and guide the convergence toward high-income status and integration into global markets. This will maximize the benefits of the reforms while avoiding crises. Nonetheless, the need for stronger policy frameworks, institutions, financial sector regulation and supervision, and macroeconomic statistics is less well understood publicly and often seen as less urgent—unlike investments in physical infrastructure. As a result, significant education and willingness to use political capital are needed.

This book looks at the key economic soft infrastructure issues that will be a determining factor in the transformation and rebalancing, including tax policy and administration, social security, SOE reform, medium-term expenditure frameworks, the role of local government finances, capital account liberalization, and renminbi internationalization. As China moves toward a more market-based

---

[7]The People's Bank of China (PBC) head office employs only about 750 people, the China Banking Regulatory Commission (CBRC) 600, and the China Securities Regulatory Commission (CSRC) some 730 staff.

allocation of resources, strengthening monetary policy frameworks and financial sector regulation will be particularly important in channeling credit and minimizing the risks of financial sector stress. In addition, statistical frameworks must be upgraded for macroeconomic policymaking.

FISCAL POLICY FRAMEWORKS

Modernizing the fiscal framework must accompany China's rebalancing from credit-financed and investment to consumption-led growth. In particular, stronger fiscal policy frameworks and social safety nets, in turn, will allow the country to contain rising vulnerabilities, manage over the business cycle, deal with rising health care and pension costs, address structural intergovernmental imbalances, and support more inclusive and environment-friendly growth.

Tax Policy

For tax policy, this implies deeper reforms to collect revenue more efficiently, facilitate more equitable income distribution, and foster an incentive structure that improves access to public services and puts local governments on sound fiscal footing.

The overall tax burden, at 20 percent of GDP, is lower than in the advanced economies and is broadly in line with other Asian members of the Organisation for Economic Co-operation and Development. More recently, the government completed extending value-added tax (VAT) to services, eliminating the cascading effects of turnover tax. The corporate income tax was reformed in 2008, providing more neutrality and revenue. Preparatory work is underway on the recurrent property tax, with efforts to strengthen housing registration and the legal foundation.

Among the remaining important challenges, the redistributive effects of taxes and transfers are still limited, while the revenue structure is heavily tilted toward indirect taxes and does not correct for environmental externalities. Moreover, local government revenue is not aligned with spending obligations.

Revenue reforms could partly address these issues. Reforms include gradually unifying current multiple VAT rates and the refund mechanism, bringing different sources of individual income to be taxed together, taking into account household income conditions and applying certain deductibles. The government also plans to reduce the already high level of social security contribution rates at an appropriate time and pace, provided sustainability is maintained. Greater use of environmental taxes will replace various fees levied for pollution, while a nationwide emission trading scheme will be introduced by 2017 (Parry and others 2016).

China's VAT reform is commendable. With respect to income tax, a dual income tax—based on the two main categories of labor and capital—appears to be more suitable for China for the individual income tax than a global income tax system, while there is room to improve the effective progressivity and widen the tax base. A gradual shift from indirect to direct tax can strengthen the redistributive power of tax policies, where China falls short relative to other economies. Reducing the social security contribution rate can support rebalancing, accompanied by other parametric changes to ensure sustainability. Finally, the shift to an ad-valorem environmental tax to replace various fees and surcharges is welcome.

Some of the tax policy reforms cut across ministries and, hence, call for inter-ministerial collaboration and will require strong top-level leadership.

Tax Administration

What are the main tax administration challenges? Tax administration reform can support China's economic reform agenda by mobilizing adequate revenue to pay for high-priority public sector expenditure and helping to promote the business climate. To do so, the SAT must address a range of *external* and *internal* issues facing the system as the economy moves toward a sustainable growth model that relies more on consumption and services.

On the external front, the growth slowdown in overcapacity sectors could lead to compliance issues emanating from distressed companies, while the new and growing service sector presents special tax collection challenges. At the same time, more complex financial instruments raise difficult tax issues as the financial sector develops. Increasing cross-provincial transactions challenge the decentralized tax administration because of the lack of information sharing across provincial tax bureaus.

Further unique tax challenges arise out of the strategy of "going global," as they have in other countries, with increased outward direct investment and the creation of multinational corporations. This includes companies' tendency to shift income to low-tax jurisdictions, taking deductions in high-tax jurisdictions and exploiting tax treaties. In addition, the SAT will need to implement a series of major tax policy reforms that are planned for the next few years, such as VAT, environment, property, and individual income taxes.

The tax system's increasingly complex external environment will put pressure on the SAT's internal administrative capacity. Potential vulnerabilities include its organizational structure, staff skills, and information systems. The SAT will need to strengthen its capacity in each of these areas while taking steps to reduce taxpayers' compliance costs. To address these challenges, the SAT has designed a five-year strategy for modernizing tax administration.

Medium-Term Expenditure Frameworks

China's strides in reforming its budget planning instrument in the past 15 years have included increasing the coverage of the State Budget through the joint presentation and approval of its various components (general budget, extra-budgetary funds, SOEs, social security funds). In addition, the revised budget law of early 2015 was important in putting fiscal and budgetary management on sounder footing and imposing harder budget constraints on local governments, the so-called "opening the front door" while "closing the back door" strategy.

Currently, the broad direction of fiscal policy is laid out in the five-year plans, while the national budget sets annual fiscal targets. The current arrangement, however, implies that the five-year plans do not usually account for resource constraints, while the annual budget is largely incremental, less attuned to changing policy priorities, and focused on recurrent expenditure and transfers. Adopting a medium-term fiscal framework in general and a medium-term expenditure framework (MTEF) in particular will ensure further fiscal discipline and harden budget constraints, identify fiscal risks at an earlier stage, and facilitate countercyclical fiscal policies.

Globally, more than 130 countries have already adopted medium-term fiscal frameworks or are doing so, and international experience suggests that China should do so gradually. An MTEF should (1) set medium-term fiscal policy targets consistent with fiscal stability and sustainability, (2) adopt top-down medium-term macroeconomic and fiscal forecasting, (3) develop a bottom-up baseline expenditure forecasting methodology, and (4) develop a strategic decision-making process in budgeting to decide on the use of available fiscal space.

The MTEF needs to take into account specific institutional circumstances. And as a medium-term framework, the Ministry of Finance needs to strengthen its macro-modeling and fiscal forecasting capabilities. Also, since local governments do a large part of fiscal spending (especially on infrastructure), it is paramount that the MTEF cover the scope of government as broadly as possible. As such, it must take into account that local governments have incentives to engage in off-budget expenditure, creative accounting, and public-private partnerships to avoid the MTEF constraints. Hence, the MTEF should define government (general government, including local government financing) vehicles and whether or not there is a fiscal rule. China has five-year plans, but a fully developed MTEF for such a long time horizon might be challenging. International experience suggests three year rolling plans are most feasible.

The success of the MTEF will require the highest political support, including from the State Council and the National People's Congress, and cooperation among key ministries such as the Ministry of Finance, the National Development and Reform Commission (NDRC), and the relevant spending ministries. Fully implementing an MTEF will be a multiyear effort, and appropriate sequencing will be paramount.

Social Security Reform

Population aging is a major challenge, with significant implications for employment, economic growth, and public finances. Health and social security outlays, in particular, will rise sharply. This phenomenon is not unique to China. But, in China, the population age 65 or older as a percent of the total population (dependency ratio) is increasing significantly faster than in other parts of the world, and is projected to triple from about 13 percent in 2015 to 47 percent by 2050. This would imply old-age dependency at about the level projected for advanced economies.

The current pension system has separate old-age schemes for (1) government employees, (2) salaried workers in the enterprise sector (both private and state owned), and (3) the rest of nonsalaried workers (including migrants). The schemes are "pay as you go," but they also include (with the exception of the one for government employees) a partially funded component. Combined, these schemes provide almost universal coverage for the elderly and relatively high coverage for the working-age population, although, for some groups, the level of benefits remains low and uneven.

However, the social security system faces challenges. These include the following:

- Population dynamics are at play, given that under current parameters the system faces significant imbalances. Absent reform, estimates suggest that pension expenditures will increase from about 3 percent of GDP in 2015 to 10 percent by 2050. The corollary of that is the sharp increase in the actuarial imbalance (discounted value of benefits minus contributions) to 120 percent of GDP by 2050, calling for urgent reform.
- China rapidly expanded transition rules to provide basic pensions for the current elderly who had never contributed, leading to very high contribution rates (27 percent of wages) for the current labor force. At the same time, benefits under the urban and rural resident scheme are still very low (with annual average pensions of about RMB1,000 [about $170] in parts of the system), resulting in pressure to increase pension benefits. This would make the system more equitable, but would put further strain on public finances.
- The system remains segmented, and since contributions, eligibility, and benefits differ across provinces and schemes, they impose significant restrictions on labor mobility, undermining urbanization-related productivity improvements.
- The underfunded pension system could not only undermine rebalancing but also threaten long-term fiscal sustainability.

As in other countries, there are no easy reform solutions. A menu of options will have to include parametric changes. Given the relatively low retirement age of 55 years for women and 60 years for men, extending retirement ages would significantly increase actuarial soundness. Since this would increase the labor force participation at older ages, it would also help growth. A change to pension indexation, that is, linking benefits to consumer prices instead of wages and prices, is another important reform. Yet little room exists to increase contribution rates. Instead, lower contribution rates can foster consumption and help rebalancing. To make this fiscally neutral, the legacy cost of providing pensions for the large segment that did not contribute should be put on the general budget, to be financed through general taxes rather than through a tax (pension contributions) on workers.

Local Government Finances

Besides providing basic public services such as education, health care, and social security benefits, local governments undertook sizable investment that has contributed to rapid growth. They carried out much of the large-scale fiscal stimulus since the global financial crisis, and local officials were often assessed based on the growth performance in the region. As a result, along with infrastructure investment, local governments have also been involved in land development and contributed to the real estate boom.

Yet local government finances have faced a structural misalignment. Their revenue base is small relative to spending obligations. This implies that local governments have to rely on transfers from the central government or resort to other financing. Until the revised budget law in 2015, local governments, with the exception of a few pilot programs, were formally prohibited from borrowing. Local government therefore had incentives to circumvent constraints by generating revenue from land sales and setting up financing vehicles to borrow from banks and capital markets to finance spending and achieve the growth target. This off-budget deficit is estimated to be large at about 6–7 percent of GDP in recent years, corresponding to the rapid buildup of debt of local governments and their financing vehicles by 24 percentage points of GDP between 2008 and 2015.

Recognizing the growing vulnerabilities in local government finance, the authorities have taken important first steps. National audits on local government debt were conducted, and a revised budget law was approved, effective in 2015. By formally allowing local governments to issue bonds, while prohibiting other forms of borrowing (open the front door while closing the back door), the budget law aimed to strengthen transparency and accountability of local government finances and addressed intergovernmental fiscal relationships. In that context, the government also rolled out a debt-swap program to facilitate the transition by converting existing financing vehicle debt to local government bonds, effectively reducing interest rates by 400 basis points and extending maturity.

While the budget law and related directives will help strengthen local government finances, key hurdles remain, and its success will rest on decisive implementation. As China still maintains an ambitious growth target, incentives remain for local governments to borrow in ways prohibited in the budget law. The local government bond market also remains underdeveloped despite its growing size, with limited liquidity and differentiation of risks.

Policy priorities therefore will be to further strengthen local government finances in the context of an MTEF. These include reining in possible circumvention, developing the bond market with greater liquidity and credit discipline, formulating a resolution framework for potential financial distress of local government, monitoring emerging risks and misuse of public-private partnership, and better aligning local government revenue and spending with a larger local revenue base and a larger share of social spending at the central level.

MONETARY AND FINANCIAL FRAMEWORKS

Continued transformation toward a market- and globally integrated economy implies moving further from quantitative and administrative to price-based allocation of resources. To maximize the benefits from increased liberalization and external opening, while minimizing vulnerabilities in financial or foreign exchange markets, a strengthening of monetary and exchange rate frameworks and financial regulation, together with a gradual further opening of the capital account, is needed.

Monetary Policy Framework

Greater exchange rate flexibility calls for, correspondingly, a modern monetary policy framework that focuses on domestic price stability. Although the legal framework does not provide the basis for such a target, Article 3 of the Law of the People's Republic of China on the PBC stipulates that "The aim of monetary policies shall be to maintain the stability of the value of the currency and thereby promote economic growth." Yet formally, the PBC targets multiple objectives, such as inflation, balance of payments, growth, and financial stability. Regarding tools, the government has relied on a quantitative monetary target (M2)—approved by the State Council—and a combination of quantity and price-based instruments, as well as moral suasion (Harjes 2016).

As in other countries, however, the relationship is weakening between quantitative targets such as M2 and inflation and growth. Hence, the question arises whether China should move toward a flexible inflation target with a price-based monetary policy framework. Indeed, empirical analysis shows that the correlation between M2 growth and inflation (lagged) declined sharply, as did the correlation between M2 and nominal GDP growth. The volatility of short-term interest rates tripled, suggesting that the demand for money became less stable and the money supply was not flexible enough to absorb the shock. Hence, moving toward a price-based monetary policy framework with interest rate as the primary instrument is advisable.

This raises two questions. How effective is the transmission mechanism from interest rates to bond yields and lending rates? What could be done to improve it? Evidence suggests that various institutional features have constrained the monetary transmission mechanism. They range from high reserve requirements on bank deposits and loan quotas to soft budget constraints, and regulatory arbitrage through shadow banking activity. The average bond yield sensitivity to changes in short-term interest rates is three-quarters that in the United States. The transmission through the banking sector, however, has been significantly less efficient, amounting to about ½ percent that in the United States. Removing institutional constraints could hence go a long way toward further improving the transmission mechanism.

China has taken additional important steps to build a foundation to move toward a market-based monetary policy framework. This includes—as mentioned above—formal interest rate liberalization, with removal of the deposit-rate ceiling and abolishment of the loan-to-deposit ratio for commercial banks, both in 2015. Operationally, the PBC also started to establish an effective interest rate corridor centered on the seven-day repo rate with limited volatility. Stabilizing the short-term interest rate, in turn, is crucial for the formulation of policy. Going forward, China should consider moving toward a flexible inflation target with the interest rate becoming the intermediate target (IMF 2016a, 2016b). Of course, this would imply that the current monetary M2 target needs to be phased out. More emphasis on communication and the operational independence of the central bank would support the transition to such a framework. Combined with greater exchange rate flexibility, with the aim to have an effective float in the next couple of years, this would allow monetary policy to respond more effectively to both domestic and external shocks.

Capital Account Liberalization

China first envisaged full capital account opening in 1993, aiming to reach this by 2000. This path was interrupted by the Asian financial crisis in the late 1990s. But the stated goal remains to achieve *managed capital account convertibility*, although without an official road map or target date.

Over the past decade, the authorities have significantly liberalized the capital account in a flexible manner, broadly consistent with the IMF's institutional view on capital account liberalization, which states that "countries with extensive and long-standing measures to limited capital flows are likely to benefit from further liberalization in an orderly manner." It highlights that there is "no presumption that full liberalization is an appropriate goal for all countries at all times" (IMF 2012).

How open is China's capital account, and how effective are existing controls? Formally (de jure), the IMF's *Annual Report on Exchange Arrangements and Exchange Restrictions* suggests that with 43 out of 53 categories having some degree of control, the capital account remains relatively closed. This is mirrored by the fact that when compared to its level of income, and measured by the sum of external assets—excluding foreign reserves—and liabilities in percent of GDP, China—together with India—is among the least financially integrated countries. The effectiveness of capital controls is also reflected in spreads between on- and offshore exchange rates and deviations from interest rate arbitrage. At the same time, there is evidence of greater de facto opening and circumvention—as the spillover from the turbulence in the Chinese stock market and the pressure on the exchange rate following the change in exchange rate policy in 2015 demonstrated—and hence financial sector integration might be more advanced than previously thought.

Reflecting residents' demand for portfolio rebalancing, some studies (for example, Bayoumi and Ohnsorge 2013) suggest that capital flow liberalization will lead to an increase in both gross in- and outflows, with net outflows dominating in the short term but becoming more balanced over the longer term. A gradual and well-sequenced capital account liberalization will therefore be critical for China and the world. In particular, liberalization needs to be coordinated with supporting macroeconomic, financial, and structural policies to create a virtuous cycle for continued safe liberalization (Table 1.1). Here the further strengthening

Table 1.1. Potential Sequencing of Capital Account Liberalization

Key Steps	Other Accompanying Reforms Needed	Specific Measures
• Gradual increase of quotas; relaxing qualification requirements (in- and outflow foreign direct investment and portfolio investment)	• Modernizing monetary policy framework • Implementing hard budget constraints • Reforming state-owned enterprises, addressing high corporate debt	• Deepening financial markets • Strengthening regulation and supervision • Building up capital and liquidity buffers • Adequate investment regulations (institutional) • Contingency plans
• Replacing quotas and qualification requirements with price-based controls (unremunerated reserve requirements or tax)	• Further strengthening monetary and exchange rate framework • Continued reform of state-owned enterprises and corporate sector • Enhancing monitoring of capital flows	• Continued financial market deepening • Introducing net stable funding ratio/liquidity charges on noncore funding • Higher risk weights on foreign exchange loans • Eliminating direct lending • Expanding the regulatory perimeter to shadow banking/corporate sector
• Gradual move from preapproval to registration and notification requirement followed by reporting requirement	• Continued improvement of monetary and exchange rate framework • Adequate capital flow monitoring framework	• Continued deepening of financial markets • Further strengthening of supervisory and regulatory framework
• Removal of most controls	• Track record of well-defined credible monetary policy and full exchange rate flexibility	• Adequate supervisory, micro-, and macroprudential framework

Sources: IMF, *Annual Report on Exchange Arrangements and Exchange Restrictions*; and IMF staff.

of monetary policy frameworks, fiscal reforms (to avoid fiscal dominance), strengthening the financial sector (proper risk pricing), and increased exchange rate flexibility are of the utmost importance.

Internationalization of the Renminbi

Growing global presence, implementation of policies and reforms, and increasing linkages have set the stage for a greater role for the renminbi (RMB) in the international monetary and financial system. The increasing use in transactions and wide trading of the RMB were recently recognized by the IMF's Executive Board decision to include the RMB in the IMF's special drawing right (SDR) basket of currencies. This decision, effective since October 1, 2016, constitutes a milestone in the integration of the economy into the global financial system and an acknowledgment of the progress made in reforming the domestic monetary and financial system.

How has RMB internationalization advanced? Trends across different indicators in the offshore use of the RMB confirm the increasing internationalization of the currency, in particular since 2009. This progress has been centered on the RMB's use for trade settlement and direct investment purposes; its use as an international funding and reserve currency, while growing, remains at an early stage. New evidence using high-frequency indicators from an electronic trading platform suggests, nonetheless, that the RMB is widely traded in offshore markets and that liquidity is comparable to that of other major currency pairs.

RMB inclusion in the SDR basket is not only a recognition of its increased global role, it also makes the SDR a more attractive reserve asset because of diversification and representation of another major currency. This should support raising the appeal of the SDR itself. Here China continues to play an important role by facilitating the issuance of an SDR bond by the World Bank in 2016 and taking important steps to facilitate the use of the SDR as a unit of account by publishing international payment statistics alongside the U.S. dollar.

While the internationalization of a currency is a market-driven process, policies and reform can facilitate the process. With this in mind, policy measures to promote RMB internationalization have covered three main areas: gradual opening of the capital account, steps to strengthen the domestic financial system, and offshore liquidity support through improvements to the cross-border payments infrastructure and central bank swap lines. Policies have been gradual, aimed at developing markets, moving to market-determined prices and interest rates, and implementing sound policy frameworks. Prospects for continued RMB internationalization remain strong, in particular as policies and reforms continue to support the process.

Financial Sector

The financial system has grown rapidly and undergone significant changes over the past decades. Today, four of the five largest banks globally, by total assets, are Chinese; the equity market ranks second only to that of the United States; and the bond market, where rapid growth has been more recent, is already the third largest in the world. In addition to its size, the structure of the financial system has changed significantly. While banks still account for the largest share of total financial system assets (about 80 percent), nonbank lending and financial products have mushroomed over the past decade. In addition, fully privately owned banks remain very small, even though the share of large state-owned banks has fallen to about 40 percent of the banking sector.

This rapid growth in nonbank financial activities has many causes. These include the credit-driven stimulus following the global financial crisis, return seeking intensified by a high rate of saving and restrictions on capital outflows, and a financial system that is both innovative and responsive to changing needs. They also include efforts to circumvent bank regulation, such as interest rate and quantitative controls, some of which have more recently been liberalized. This has led to a complex and opaque system linking borrowers and lenders. Banking sector risks have risen as a whole as financing has increased, loans have migrated into complex investment products, and off-balance-sheet exposures have risen.

Ensuring that financial sector frameworks are up-to-date in a fast-growing economy, especially with a financial system that grows much faster than nominal GDP, is challenging by any standard. The example of the fast growth of Alibaba's Internet-based money market fund highlights the speed at which financial innovations can take place: its establishment in mid-2013 saw a surge of more than 85 million customers within one year.

To ensure that China's savings are channeled to the most productive sectors of the economy—and to minimize vulnerabilities that could lead to financial system stress down the road—it is critical that regulation and supervision keep pace with the rapid growth and innovation in the financial sector. Regulators are aware of the risks, and recent measures have aimed to improve banks' risk management, limit the complexity of structured products and investment vehicles, and contain systemic risks.

STATE-OWNED ENTERPRISE FRAMEWORKS

Today, China is again at a crossroads that calls for ambitious SOE reform. Such reform can significantly improve resource allocation, contain excessive credit growth, facilitate other reforms, and unleash growth. Estimates suggest that reforms could increase GDP growth by 0.3–0.9 percentage point each year over a decade.

State-Owned Enterprise Reform

With over 150,000 in number, SOEs still play a critical role in the economy, despite their declining share of value added (falling from 40 percent to 16 percent) and urban employment over the past decades. SOEs still account for about half of total bank credit and 40 percent of total industrial assets. Also, they continue to benefit from implicit government support on factor inputs, including land and preferential access to credit, amounting to about 3 percent of GDP.

Easy access to financing has led to a significant buildup in leverage in SOEs, even though their financial performance has deteriorated. Much of the rise in aggregate corporate leverage (the ratio of total liabilities to owners' equity) since 2009 has taken place at SOEs. Their leverage ratios have risen to about 200 percent on average, mostly concentrated in overcapacity and heavy industries. At the same time, returns on SOE assets have deteriorated, and their productivity is just about 30–40 percent that of private enterprises (Hsieh and Song 2015). Moreover, the efficiency of Chinese SOEs appears to be lower than that in other developing economies, underscoring the urgency of SOE reforms.

SOE reforms feature prominently in the overall reform strategy, but objectives are competing, important details are still lacking, and implementation—as recognized by the government—has proven difficult. The 13th Five-Year Plan—before the 2013 Third Party Reform Blueprint—put SOE reform high on the agenda.

In addition, State Council directives about SOE reforms addressing overcapacity issues and "zombie" nonviable firms (most of which are SOEs) committed to cutting aggregate SOE losses by 2017 and expediting the exit of over 2,000 subsidiaries of central and nearly 7,000 local nonviable zombie SOEs. While reforms envisage "diverse forms of ownership and private participation in SOEs" and see the state as a capital investor rather than operator, they also emphasize the need for "making SOEs bigger and stronger to meet national strategies." Also, the leadership role of the Communist Party will be strengthened as key decisions will require party-member approval.

Experience in other countries suggests that China should (1) triage SOEs into the fundamentally sound, liquidate the nonviable ones, and establish a restructuring plan for viable but insolvent SOEs; (2) harden budget constraints by gradually resolving implicit guarantees through greater tolerance of defaults; (3) reduce barriers to entry and break up administrative monopolies; and (4) create a level playing field.

While these reforms are difficult to implement, the government has in the past been able to implement far-reaching reforms. For example, to deal with increasing inefficiencies, rising debt levels, and risks to financial sector stability, the 1998/99 reform led to a sharp decline in the number of SOEs, a temporary wave of layoffs (more than 30 million people), and debt resolution. Also, China has space to provide on-budget fiscal support to minimize economic hardship during the transition. The establishment of an RMB100 billion restructuring fund for the coal and steel industries in 2016 is an important step in this direction.

MACROECONOMIC STATISTICS FOR POLICYMAKING

While the economy is rebalancing, rapid structural changes pose significant challenges for the provision of comprehensive, timely, and reliable statistics, and require constant upgrading and investment in the statistical framework. Policymakers need reliable statistics to calibrate macroeconomic policies. Domestic investors and households also need them to make sound saving and investment decisions, and given an increasing global footprint and risk of spillovers, the same is true for international investors and policymakers.

Upgrading Macroeconomic Statistics

China has continuously upgraded its statistics and improved publicly available data, including subscription to the IMF's Special Data Dissemination Standard in 2015.[8] Particularly noteworthy is the progress in monetary and financial sector statistics, while in other areas (such as the real sector and government finance statistics) a redoubling of efforts is needed. For example, the National Accounts still lack a detailed breakdown on the expenditure side and the industrial sectors.

---

[8]The IMF's data standards are designed to promote the dissemination of timely and comprehensive statistics.

Having the granular breakdown will help explain the structural changes and the evolving relationship between conventional economic gauges and GDP growth. Another important area for improvement is the deflation methodology, where price indices are missing or are incomplete and frequently do not match the related activity or expenditure category. More high-frequency labor market data and indicators covering the rapidly growing new economy, such as services, can better calibrate short-term macroeconomic policies. Regarding government finance statistics, better tracking of the very large off-budget activities of local governments is needed (for example, local government financing vehicles). In the external sector, consistency among various trade data series should be improved.

Faced with an ever more complex economy and continued rapid change, some macroeconomic statistics have become less relevant while others, especially in the rapidly growing service sector, need to be expanded and added. Because China relies less and less on SOEs and instead fosters the development of entrepreneurship and small and medium-sized enterprises, it will be increasingly difficult to have direct access to source data. This calls, among other things, for the application of other techniques, such as sample surveys and data reporting. The G20 Data Gaps Initiative provides some guidance. Hence, the focus should be on reviewing the scope of data compiled, upgrading underlying methodologies, and improving dissemination further.

***

China has again reached a crossroads in its economic development. Ensuring a continued bright future requires steadfast implementation of the comprehensive reform agenda and, as the following chapters detail, greater investment in *soft* infrastructure.

ANNEX 1.1. SELECTED ECONOMIC INDICATORS, 2000–15

Annex Table 1.1.1. Selected Economic Indicators, 2000–15

Indicators	2000–07	2008–10	2011–14	2015
National Accounts				
Real GDP	10.5	9.8	8.1	6.9
Consumption	9.1	9.1	8.8	8.3
Investment	12.8	15.4	8.1	6.1
Net Exports (contribution)	0.8	–0.9	–0.1	–0.1
Gross National Saving (percent of GDP)	43.6	51.7	49.4	47.9
Labor Market				
Unemployment Rate (annual average)[1]	3.9	4.2	4.1	4.1
Prices				
Consumer Prices (average)	1.7	2.8	3.2	1.4
GDP Deflator	3.8	4.6	3.7	0.4
Financial				
Seven-Day Repo Rate (percent)	2.0	2.4	5.4	2.5
Ten-Year Government Bond Rate (percent)	3.6	3.4	3.8	2.9
Real Effective Exchange Rate (average)	–0.1	4.0	4.4	10.1
General Government (percent of GDP)				
Net Lending/Borrowing[2]	–1.8	–0.4	–0.6	–2.7
Revenue	15.9	23.6	27.6	28.6
Expenditure	17.7	24.0	28.2	31.3
Debt[3]	25.8	30.9	36.0	42.9
Balance of Payments (percent of GDP)				
Current Account Balance	4.4	5.9	2.1	3.0
Net International Investment Position	22.0	29.8	20.0	14.3
Gross Official Reserves (billions US$)	1,018	2,445	3,606	3,406
Memorandum Items				
Nominal GDP (billions RMB)[4]	16,466	36,018	56,812	69,630
Augmented Debt (percent of GDP)	40.4	43.3	48.9	55.8
Augmented Fiscal Balance (percent of GDP)	–6.0	–8.3	–9.0	–9.5

Sources: CEIC; IMF, Information Notice System; and IMF staff estimates and projections.

[1]Surveyed unemployment rate.

[2]Average selling prices estimated by IMF staff based on housing price data (Commodity Building Residential Price) of 70 large and mid-sized cities published by National Bureau of Statistics.

[3]Adjustments are made to the authorities' fiscal budgetary balances to reflect consolidated general government balance, including government-managed funds, state-administered state-owned enterprise funds, adjustment to the stabilization fund, and social security fund.

[4]Estimates of debt levels before 2015 include central government debt and explicit local government debt (identified by the Ministry of Finance and the National People's Congress in September 2015).

ANNEX 1.2. SELECTED SOCIAL INDICATORS

Annex Table 1.2.1. Selected Social Indicators

Indicators	1949–79	1980–2002	2002–12	2012–14	2015	United States	Japan	India	High-income Group	Middle-income Group	East Asia
GDP per Capita											
GDP per Capita (PPP, current US$)[1]	–	2,106	6,924	12,206	14,160	56,430	38,870	6,020	44,991	10,594	15,702
Population											
Life Expectancy at Birth (years)	56	69	74	76	76	79	84	68	81	71	75
Population Growth (percent)	2.0	1.5	0.6	0.5	0.5	0.8	–0.1	1.2	0.6	1.1	0.7
Dependency Ratio (percent of working-age population)	79	53	37	35	36	50	63	53	52	50	42
Education											
University and College Students (per 10th population)	6.3	37.3	183.3	241.4	252.4						
Pupil-Teacher Ratio in Secondary Education	21	17	16	15	15	15	–	31	12	18	16
Literacy Rate (percent)	71.6	93.0	95.1	–	–	–	–	69	99	83	95
Environment											
Freshwater Resources per Capita (cubic meters)	3,550	2,456	2,138	2,072	2,062	8,838	3,382	1,116	8,732	5,471	4,525
Pollutants PM2.5 air (average annual exposure in micrograms per cubic meter)	–	44	54	54	54	11	16	47	16	36	40
Infrastructure											
Railway Infrastructure (kilometers)	–	54,183	63,193	66,528	66,989	228,218	19,470	65,808	535,060	475,549	127,034
Internet Users (per 100 people)	–	3	20	46	49	87	91	18	83	35	47
Growth in Fixed Asset Investment (percent)	–	20	24	15	10						
Inequality											
Gini Coefficient	–	0.34	0.48	0.47	0.46	0.41	0.32	0.34	–	–	–

Sources: CEIC; and World Bank, World Development Indicators database.

Note: PPP = purchasing power parity.

[1]Data in 2015 are gross national income per capita adjusted with PPP in current U.S. dollars.

ANNEX 1.3. SELECTED ECONOMIC REFORMS, 2015–16

Reform progress has been wide ranging. Key reforms have been introduced to improve the monetary and fiscal frameworks and to promote urbanization.

Financial Sector Reforms

- Deposit insurance introduced (May 2015)
- Interest rates fully liberalized (October 2015)
- People's Bank of China launched the Macro Prudential Assessment mechanism (December 2015)
- Pilot programs initiated on securitization and debt-equity conversions to help address rising nonperforming loans (February 2016, April 2016)

Structural Reforms

- Capacity reduction targets (about 10–15 percent over the next 3–5 years) announced for coal and steel sectors (February 2016)
- A restructuring fund of RMB100 billion was established for social safety nets for layoffs in overcapacity sectors (February 2016)
- Published guidelines on SOE reforms, including the separation of some social functions from SOEs; 10 pilot programs were implemented (September 2015, February 2016, August 2016)
- Announced guidelines to enhance the pricing mechanism and reduce the number of prices set by central government (December 2015)
- Relaxed the one-child policy (December 2015)
- Property rights for rural land clarified, including use as collateral for securing agricultural loans (March 2016)
- Social housing program extended
- Majority of provinces announced guidelines on *hukou* (household registration) reforms (April 2016)

Fiscal Reforms

- Implementation of the new budget law (January 2015)
- Business tax fully converted to VAT for remaining services (May 2016)
- Twelve provinces have lowered the employer contributions toward social security payments (April 2016)
- New fiscal accounting framework (January 2016)
- Revised the price adjustment mechanism for oil products (January 2016)
- Tax cuts implemented for small and high-tech firms (September and November 2015)
- Carbon-emission trading scheme will be introduced (in 2017)

- Published guidelines in addressing intergovernmental fiscal imbalances (September 2016)
- Published directives on contingent measures to resolve local government debt issues (December 2016)

External Sector Reforms

- Mutual Recognition of Funds program introduced to allow mutual funds domiciled in mainland China and Hong Kong SAR to mobilize funds from the other jurisdiction (July 2015)
- Access to onshore fixed income and foreign exchange markets eased for official sector and qualified institutional investors (July 2015, October 2015, February 2016)
- RMB increasingly referencing a basket of currencies rather than solely the U.S. dollar; additional basket of currencies announced with weights (December 2015)
- RMB to be included in the SDR basket effective October 2016 (November 2015)
- Introduced the Shenzhen-Hong Kong Stock Connect program (December 2016)

REFERENCES

Bayoumi, T., and F. Ohnsorge. 2013. "Do Inflows or Outflows Dominate? Global Implications of Capital Account Liberalization in China." Working Paper No. 13/189, International Monetary Fund, Washington.

Cashin, P., K. Mohaddes, and M. Raissi. 2016. "China's Slowdown and Global Financial Market Volatility: Is World Growth Losing Out?" Working Paper No. 16/63, International Monetary Fund, Washington.

Consulate General of the People's Republic of China in San Francisco. 2007. "Premier Wen Jiabao's Press Conference." Press release, March 17, 2007.

CPC News. 2014. "The Eighth Five Year Plan (1991–1995): DENG Xiaoping's South Tour and Tides for Reform." Dangshi publication. http://dangshi.people.com.cn/GB/151935/204121/205065/12925938.html.

Harjes, T. 2016. "China: Shifting to a Modern, Market-Based Monetary Policy Framework." Selected Issues Paper, Country Report No. 16/271, International Monetary Fund, Washington.

Henn, C., C. Papageorgiou, and N. Spatafora. 2015. "Export Quality in Advanced and Developing Economies: Evidence from a New Data Set." World Trade Organization (WTO) Staff Working Paper, WTO, Geneva.

Hsieh, C. T., and Z. Song. 2015. "Grasp the Large, Let Go of the Small: The Transformation of the State Sector in China." Brookings Papers on Economic Activity, Spring 2015, Brookings Institution Press, Washington.

International Monetary Fund (IMF). 2012. *The Liberalization and Management of Capital Control Flows: An Institutional View*. Washington: International Monetary Fund.

———. 2016a. "Staff Report for the People's Republic of China 2016 Article IV Consultation." IMF Country Report No.16/270, International Monetary Fund, Washington.

———. 2016b. *World Economic Outlook.* Washington: International Monetary Fund, April.
Laeven, L., and F. Valencia. 2012. "Systemic Banking Crises Database: An Update." Working Paper No. 12/163, International Monetary Fund, Washington.
Lipton, D. 2016. Preparing the Ground. "China's Quest for Sustainable Growth Calls for Bold Fiscal Reforms." *Finance and Development*, March 2016, Washington.
Ministry of Commerce. 2014. "Press Conference by Minister of Commerce GAO Fucheng." March 2014. http://finance.ifeng.com/a/20140308/11836631_0.shtml.
Parry, I., B. Shang, P. Wingender, N. Vernon, and T. Narasimhan. 2016. "Climate Mitigation in China: Which Policies Are Most Effective?" Working Paper No. 16/148, International Monetary Fund, Washington.
Premier LI Keqiang. 2016. "Speech at the General Meetings of the State Council." September 2016. http://www.gov.cn/guowuyuan/2016-09/06/content_5105852.htm.
President XI Jinping. 2016. "Opening Remarks at the Business-20 Events Surrounding the Group of Twenty Summit." September 2016. http://news.china.com/focus/2016g20/11180309/20160903/23463997.html (in Chinese).
World Bank and Development Research Center of the State Council. 2013. *China 2030: Building a Modern, Harmonious, and Creative Society.* Washington.
———. 2014. "Urban China: Toward an Efficient, Inclusive and Sustainable Urbanization." Washington. https://openknowledge.worldbank.org/handle/10986/18865.
Zhang, L. 2016. "Rebalancing China—Progress and Reforms." Working Paper No. 16/183, International Monetary Fund, Washington.

CHAPTER 2

Modernizing the Tax Policy Regime

Ruud de Mooij, W. Raphael Lam, and Philippe Wingender

Fiscal reform is integral to China's broad reform plans and key for achieving more inclusive and sustainable growth. The 13th Five-Year Plan commits to deepening tax reforms to facilitate economic transition, and includes measures to collect revenues more efficiently, improve the fiscal framework, and strengthen local government finances. The authorities decided to establish the foundations of reforms by 2016 and modernize the fiscal framework by 2020.

Inefficiencies in the tax system are an important obstacle on China's path toward a new growth model. And although the overall tax burden is lower than the Organisation for Economic Co-operation and Development (OECD) average, fiscal policy plays a very modest redistributive role. This is reflected in a relatively heavy reliance on indirect taxes and the largely regressive design of direct taxation, especially in social security contributions. Local governments often rely on costly and inefficient revenue sources to finance spending, in part because their own sources are insufficient to cover their spending responsibilities. Tax policy reforms in the coming years should help better align them.

Some progress has been made in tax policy reforms in recent years (Table 2.1). In indirect taxation, for instance, the government in 2016 completed the extension of value-added tax (VAT) to services, replacing the distortive and cascading business tax. Fundamental reform of corporate taxation in 2008 created more neutrality and improved revenue performance. Legislative work is now underway to introduce a recurrent property tax that is expected to fund local government. Yet important challenges remain. For instance, considerable work is needed to make individual income tax more progressive and raise the revenue performance of such taxation. The actual implementation of a recurrent property tax and environmental tax is also challenging.

This chapter reviews the tax system and compares it with that of other countries. It elaborates on challenges in direct and indirect taxation, with the aim of identifying options that can help improve the efficiency and equity of taxation and contribute to a successful transition toward a model of sustainable and inclusive growth.

We are grateful for comments from the Ministry of Finance and State Administration of Taxation. CUI Lu and Sung Jung provided excellent research assistance.

Table 2.1. Recent Tax Reform Initiatives in China

	Transition from Business Tax to VAT	Corporate Income Tax	Personal Income Tax	Property Taxes
Current Tax System (2016)	- A rate of 3–5 percent on business tax based on turnover and 5–20 percent for entertainment services. A standard VAT rate of 17 percent was applied on goods and 6–11 percent on selected services.	- A profit tax of 20–25 percent for enterprises.	- Marginal tax rates on wage income range from 3–45 percent in seven progressive scales. Tax rates for other personal income are at about 20 percent.[1,2]	- Real estate taxes are levied in the form of urban land use, land appreciation, and properties other than privately owned residential units; property contracts are based on use and transactions. - Tax on privately owned residential property was rolled out in several pilot areas.
Tax Reform Measures and Initiatives				
2008		- Standardized tax rates between Chinese enterprises and foreign investment or enterprises.		
2010				- Pilots to introduce property taxes for residential property were approved.
2011	- The plan to establish pilots for the transition from business turnover tax to VAT was jointly approved by the State Council, Ministry of Finance, and State Administration of Taxation.		- The number of tax brackets was reduced from nine to seven with rates ranging from 3–45 percent.	- A tax rate of 0.5–1.2 percent was introduced for residential properties in Shanghai and Chongqing.[3]
2012	- Beginning in January, Shanghai was the first pilot area for the transition to VAT for transportation and modern services. - Pilot areas were extended to eight provinces from September to December.			
2013	- Transition to VAT was extended to the entire country for transportation and part of modern services in August.			

(continued)

Table 2.1. Recent Tax Reform Initiatives in China *(continued)*

	Transition from Business Tax to VAT	Corporate Income Tax	Personal Income Tax	Property Taxes
2014	- Beginning in January, transition to VAT was extended to railway transportation and the postal service. - Beginning in June, transition to VAT was extended to telecommunications.			
2015	- The plan of transition to VAT was extended to real estate, finance, and consumer services.		- Consolidated the social security system for public sector employees and corporations. - Strengthened portability of the pension systems between rural and urban residents.	- Registration of property ownership and transaction began. - Preparation for legislation on property tax was under consideration.
2016	- Completed the transition to VAT for remaining services.		- Initial consideration of individual income tax reform was submitted to the State Council.	

Sources: State Council; Ministry of Finance; and State Administration of Taxation.

Note: The 17 percent value-added tax (VAT) rate is levied on tangible goods, although some items are subject to a 13 percent rate. The 11 percent rate is levied on transportation services, and the 6 percent rate is levied on research and development, technological, cultural, logistical, and consultative services.

[1]Income from sole proprietorship and contractual work carries a tax rate of 5–35 percent in five progressive scales.

[2]Employees and employers also have social security contributions that range between 10 and 30 percent of employment income, respectively. Employment incomes are subject to a threshold between 60 percent and 300 percent of the previous year's local average income determined by local statistics departments.

[3]A tax of 0.5–1.2 percent was introduced for single-family houses and high-end apartments in Chongqing, while a property tax of 0.6 percent was levied on newly purchased properties for residents with two or more properties and newly purchased properties for nonresidents in Shanghai.

OVERVIEW OF CHINA'S TAX SYSTEM

The overall tax burden in China is comparable to those in other OECD economies in Asia, but it relies more heavily on indirect taxation. Tax revenue in China accounted for about 20 percent of GDP in 2015. This is much lower than the average 34 percent of GDP across the OECD but similar to Chile, Korea, and the United States. Indirect taxes on goods and services, including VAT and business turnover tax, account for more than half of tax revenue, compared with about one-third of revenue in other OECD countries (Figure 2.1). Direct taxes make up a relatively small percentage of tax revenue, especially for individual income tax, at 6 percent of revenue, much less than the 25 percent average across the OECD. China relies relatively heavily on nontax revenues, such as fees, fines, and income from state-owned enterprises. To make up for revenue shortages, local governments also frequently depend on revenue from land sales. Once adjusted for nontax revenue and net land sale proceeds (about 2¾ percent of GDP), the overall tax burden in China is similar to the tax-to-GDP ratio for other economies in the Asia and Pacific region, such as Australia, Japan, and Korea. Nominal revenue in China has grown about 20 percent year over year on average over the past decades. This exceeded nominal GDP growth for many years, although more recently—and as the economy is slowing—it has grown in line with nominal GDP growth.

The redistributive effect of taxes and transfers is relatively limited in China. In the mid-1980s, income inequality as measured by the Gini coefficient was low at around 0.3. Since then, it has continued to rise, in recent years to nearly 0.5.[1] This widening income inequality contrasts with the experiences of other middle-income countries, where inequality has largely remained constant over the same period (Cevik and Correa-Caro 2015). Fiscal policy also appears to contribute relatively little to reducing income inequality. For instance, if one looks at the difference between the Gini coefficients of market income (that is, before taxes and transfers) and disposable income (after taxes and transfers), there is virtually no difference. Hence, fiscal redistribution in China is mostly absent, unlike in other countries (Clements and others 2015). This reflects a near absence of progress in reforming direct taxes and transfers and great reliance on indirect taxes. On the spending side, quality and access to social services and the social safety net vary according to *hukou* (household residency) status, which reinforces the disparities and weakens the redistributive effect of fiscal policy.

Local government revenues and spending obligations are often misaligned. Broadly speaking, tax revenue in China is assigned in one of three ways (Table 2.2):

- *Central government taxes* used exclusively to finance central government spending. This includes taxes related to foreign trade, such as duties, VAT collected on imports, and taxes on luxury goods.

---

[1]Income disparities and limited redistribution are mirrored by the average income by group, with individuals in the highest-income decile earning more than 16–18 times those in the lowest decile, according to the World Bank and Development Research Center of the State Council (2013).

Figure 2.1. Revenue and Tax System

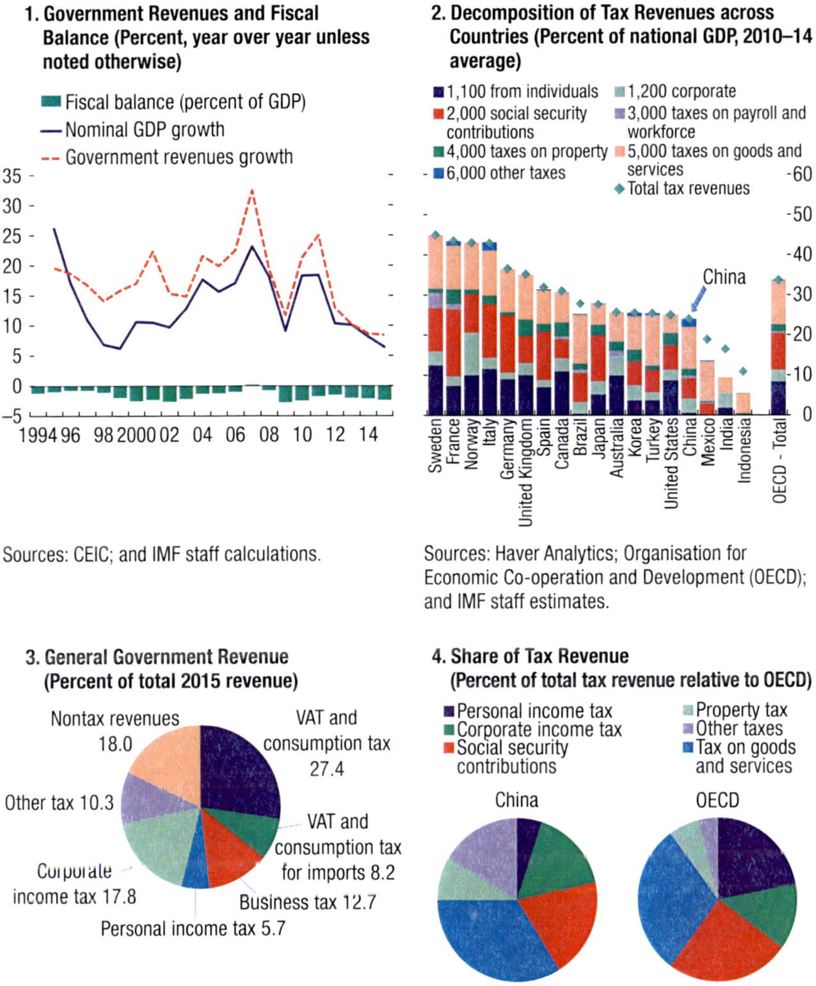

Panel 1 sources: CEIC; and IMF staff calculations.

Panel 2 sources: Haver Analytics; Organisation for Economic Co-operation and Development (OECD); and IMF staff estimates.

Panel 3 sources: CEIC; and IMF staff calculations.
Note: VAT = value-added tax.

Panel 4 sources: Haver Analytics; Organisation for Economic Co-operation and Development (OECD); and IMF staff estimates.

- *Local government taxes* under exclusive control of local governments, such as property-related taxes and business operation taxes.
- *Shared taxes between central and local government,* including direct taxes such as personal and corporate income taxes and VAT (excluding trade-related VAT). Revenue sharing can take various forms, but usually is based on prescribed revenue-sharing ratios.

Figure 2.1. Revenue and Tax System *(continued)*

5. Sources of Revenue for General Government (Percent of GDP)

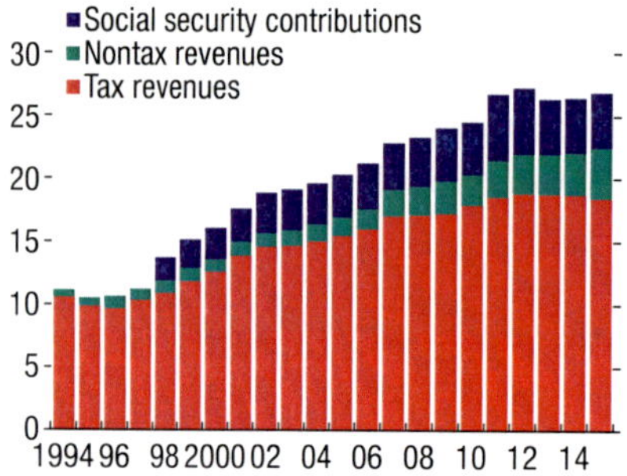

Sources: CEIC; and IMF staff calculations.

6. Redistributive Effect of Taxes across OECD Relative to China (Gini coefficient between 0 and 1)

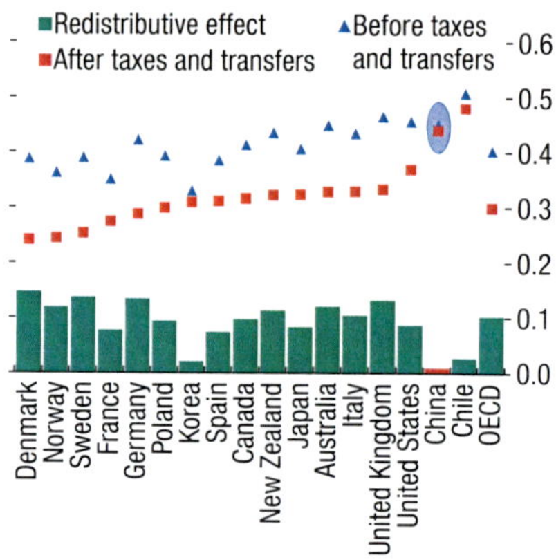

Source: Organisation for Economic Co-operation and Development (OECD).

Most local governments often face significant revenue shortfalls. Local government tax revenue, including shared taxes, accounts for nearly half of government revenue. In contrast, local government spending obligations account for roughly two-thirds of government expenditure (Wang and Herd 2013). This misalignment in revenue and spending is only partially corrected by transfers from the central to local governments and forces many local governments to rely on other sources of financing to meet spending obligations (Figure 2.2). For instance, in the past many sold land and engaged in off-budget borrowing through local government financing vehicles. Reform is therefore essential to better align local revenue and spending obligations.[2]

DIRECT TAX REFORMS

This section elaborates on reforms in the individual and corporate income tax system. It starts with a brief reflection on the current system, followed by an assessment of reform options. Income tax theory provides the conceptual underpinnings of the assessment (Box 2.1).

[2]Local governments can be broadly classified into provinces, prefectures, counties, and townships. Each administration is required to maintain a balanced budget and receives transfers from an upper level, while providing transfers to its lower levels of government. County governments typically have the highest spending obligations and are therefore the most dependent on transfers.

Table 2.2. Tax Sharing Arrangement between Central and Subnational Governments

As of 2014	General Government	Central Government	Local Government	In Percent of Total Tax Revenues and Social Security Contributions	Legal Sharing Rate	
		RMB Billions				
Tax Revenues	**11,918**	**6,004**	**5,914**	**80.4**		
Central Government Taxes						
Consumption	891	891		6.0	100	0
Consumption and Value Added of Imported Product	1,443	1,443		9.7	100	0
Tariffs	284	284		1.9	100	0
Refund of Tax for Export	−1,136	−1,136		−7.7	100	0
Cargo	5	5		0.0	100	0
Vehicle Purchase	289	289		1.9	100	0
Shared Taxes[1]						
Value Added	3,086	2,110	975	20.8	75/[50]	25/[50]
Enterprise Income	2,464	1,581	883	16.6	60	40
Individual Income	738	443	295	5.0	60	40
Stamp	154	65	89	1.0	97	3
Local Taxes						
Operation	1,778	7	1,771	12.0	1	99
Resource	108	. . .	104	0.7	0	100
City Maintenance and Construction	364	18	346	2.5	0	100
House	185	. . .	185	1.2	0	100
Use of Urban Land	199	. . .	199	1.3	0	100
Value Added of Land	391	. . .	391	2.6	0	100
Vehicle	54	. . .	54	0.4	0	100
Occupancy of Cultivated Land	206	. . .	206	1.4	0	100
Contract	400	. . .	400	2.7	0	100
Tobacco	14	. . .	14	0.1	0	100
Other	0	. . .	0	0.0	0	100
Social Security Contributions[2]	2,910		2,910	19.6	0	100
All Taxes and Social Security Contributions[3]	14,828	6,004	8,824	100	40	60

(continued)

Table 2.2. Tax Sharing Arrangement between Central and Subnational Governments *(continued)*

As of 2014	General Government	Central Government	Local Government	In Percent of Total Tax Revenues and Social Security Contributions	Legal Sharing Rate	
	RMB Billions					
Nontax Revenues						
Operating Expense in Administration Department	521	37	484			
Penalty Income	172	9	163			
Special Project Income	371	41	330			
Other Income	301	139	162			
Total Government Revenues (Including Social Security Contributions)	16,193	6,228	9,965		38	62

Sources: CEIC; and IMF staff estimates.

Note: . . . = not available.

[1]Following the completion of value-added tax reform, the tax sharing arrangement is temporarily split equally between central and local governments.

[2]Estimates based on social security contributions ratio to GDP.

[3]The sharing of tax revenues, if excluding social security contributions, will be about 50.4 percent and 49.6 percent, respectively, for central government and local governments.

Figure 2.2. Local Government Revenue and Tax Sharing System

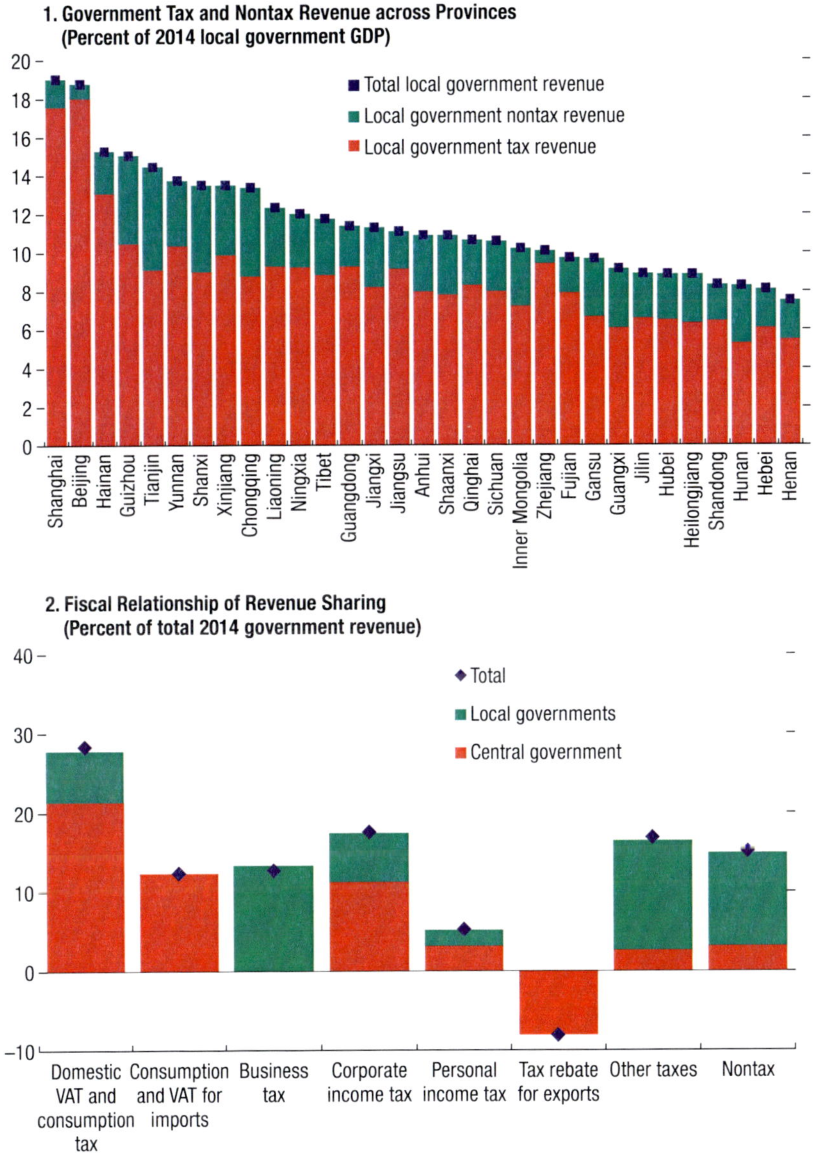

Sources: CEIC; and IMF staff calculations.
Note: VAT = value-added tax.

Box 2.1. Policy Guidance from Income Tax Theory

Optimal income tax theory seeks the most efficient way to collect revenue, taking into account distortions to behavior. A central result of the literature is that lump-sum taxes constitute the most efficient instrument because they do not involve any change in the marginal return to work. For obvious reasons, equity concerns have made this conclusion impractical; under a uniform lump-sum tax, all taxpayers are required to remit the same amount of taxes regardless of their ability to pay, which is viewed as unfair and politically unacceptable. In response to this lack of practical guidance, more detailed frameworks have been developed, and can be used to study tax policy in more realistic settings.

A key insight of the theoretical literature on optimal income taxes is that governments face a trade-off between equity and efficiency concerns. Equity concerns are typically addressed by assuming that the government values individuals' own welfare, but the social welfare weight placed on individuals generally decreases with ability and income. Society will therefore prefer, everything else equal, to redistribute after-tax income relatively more to those with less before-tax income. This requires that the tax system incorporate elements of progressivity. Efficiency concerns are typically modeled as a response of individuals' labor supply—and other margins of avoidance such as fringe benefits—to changes in marginal tax rates. The extent of the response is typically expressed as the elasticity of taxable income. This parameter is meant to capture the simple intuition that collecting revenue through increased marginal tax rates will generally lead people to work less and seek tax-favored forms of remuneration.[1] The optimal structure for the individual income tax usually involves marginal tax rates that follow a U-shaped pattern. Following the seminal work of James Mirrlees,[2] theoretical studies have found that the basic structure includes four main features: (1) a lump-sum amount guaranteed to all taxpayers; (2) high marginal tax rates at the bottom of the income distribution to ensure that only the low-paid benefit from the lump-sum amount; (3) low marginal tax rates for middle-income earners; and (4) increasing marginal tax rates for those with higher incomes. The prescription for high marginal tax rates at the bottom of the income distribution is perhaps a surprising feature of such a system since policymakers usually consider progressivity an important feature of any sound tax system. However, high marginal rates ensure that only the neediest benefit from the guaranteed amount provided under (1). The lump-sum amount combined with high marginal rates still ensures that *average* tax rates increase as incomes rise. Under such a stylized tax system, the redistribution achieved through the lump sum will strictly be targeted to the lowest earners.

These basic features have intuitive appeal. Such a structure ensures first that all taxpayers enjoy a minimum standard of living, which is guaranteed by a universal and refundable tax credit—or alternatively by welfare benefits provided outside the individual income tax. Maintaining well-targeted transfer payments in turn allows lower marginal tax rates across the board and smaller overall tax distortions. This feature of optimal tax policy can coexist with initially low and increasing headline marginal tax rates by relying on a phaseout of personal tax credit or through means-tested benefits. This combination then leads to higher effective marginal tax rates on low- to middle-income earners.

Low marginal tax rates for the middle-income group ensure distortions are minimized for most taxpayers. Income distributions are usually bell shaped, so that middle-income earners constitute by far the largest group of taxpayers. Efficiency considerations will

[1]An overview of the literature and a detailed presentation of the main results can be found in Piketty and Saez 2013.

[2]Mirrlees 1971.

Box 2.1. Policy Guidance from Income Tax Theory *(continued)*

therefore favor low marginal rates for most workers. Finally, the last main feature of the optimal structure is the progressivity of marginal rates after the modal income. Increasing marginal rates on the biggest incomes ensures that individuals with the highest earning potential will contribute relatively more to revenue collection.

Despite the inclusion of income heterogeneity among individuals in optimal tax models, their direct applicability is still limited. These models generally do not incorporate other dimensions of heterogeneity, such as family structure or other indicators of need, such as number of children or disability status. The general framework described above also considers individuals in a one-period static model. This precludes the study of life-cycle considerations in labor supply and other behavior such as saving and investment in education. It also implies that the model is most applicable to the taxation of income from labor, as opposed to capital income, where saving and intertemporal substitution of consumption introduce additional elements of complexity.[3]

[3]More on the optimal taxation of capital can be found in Diamond and Banks 2010.

Table 2.3. Individual Tax Rates Applicable to Annual Wages and Salaries

Range of Income (RMB)		Applicable Tax Rate (Percent)
0	18,000	3
18,001	54,000	10
54,001	108,000	20
108,001	420,000	25
420,001	660,000	30
600,001	960,000	35
Over	960,000	45

Source: International Bureau of Fiscal Documentation.
Note: A standard deduction of RMB42,000 is allowed in calculating taxable income.

INDIVIDUAL INCOME TAX

Current Situation and Issues

Individual income tax in China relies on a schedular system, where different sources of income are taxed according to varying structures and rates (Table 2.3). Income falls into 11 categories, including wages and salaries, unincorporated business income, income from personal services, interest, dividends and bonuses, and the leasing of property, among others. The tax unit of the individual income tax system is the individual. No provisions exist for couples to be taxed jointly, and tax credits are not available for specific family circumstances, such as the presence of dependents. The assessment period also differs across sources of income. Wages and salaries are assessed on a monthly basis, so that the tax withheld according to the rate schedule is final for most workers with only one place of employment. Individuals' business income is taxed annually after allowable costs, expenses, and losses have been deducted.

Table 2.4. Individual Tax Rates Applicable across Income Sources

Income Category	Applicable Tax Rates (Percent)
Wages and salaries	3–45
Unincorporated businesses	5–35
Labor services	20–40
Dividends (nonlisted and stock holdings less than a month)	20
From listed companies	
If held for more than a year	0
If held between a month and a year	10
Interest income	20
Royalties	16
Rental and leasing	10
Authors	14
Capital gains	20

Source: International Bureau of Fiscal Documentation.

The tax schedule for employment income is broadly progressive and comparable to those of OECD economies, but with wide tax brackets that start at higher incomes (Table 2.4). The highest marginal tax rate is 45 percent at the very top of the income distribution (about 35 times the national average wage, or 17 times the average urban wage) and applies to few income earners (Figure 2.3). In contrast, on average among OECD countries, top marginal tax rates are imposed on individual income at about four times the national average wage. Moreover, according to recent calculations based on household survey data, over 80 percent of workers are not liable to pay individual income tax (Lam and Wingender 2015). This is due to a high basic personal allowance of RMB42,000, twice the average national wage. In comparison, the average basic personal allowance in OECD countries is about one-quarter of the average national wage.

Individual income tax on unincorporated business activity and partnerships is also progressive, but with different rates than those on wages. Another income category defined in the legislation and taxed at different rates consists of income derived from labor service (such as medical, legal and accounting activities, consulting, and interior design). Dividends are taxable in general, although reduced rates apply to shares of companies listed on stock exchanges in China that are held for more than a month. Interest income is taxable, but interest from savings deposits and government bonds is exempt. Rental income is taxed at 10 percent after a 20 percent deduction. Capital gains are generally taxed at a 20 percent rate, although gains on the sale of shares of Chinese listed companies and houses that owners have occupied for two years or more are exempt.

Pensions and welfare benefits are exempt from taxation, and social security contributions are deductible. Since 2014, employee contributions to private company pension funds are deductible up to 4 percent of salary. Employer contributions are also exempt up to prescribed limits. Income derived from these tax-exempt contributions is taxable in retirement, although accrued gains are not. A pilot project launched in Beijing, Shanghai, and 29 other major cities on

Figure 2.3. Individual Income Tax

1. Social Security Contributions (Percent of GDP)

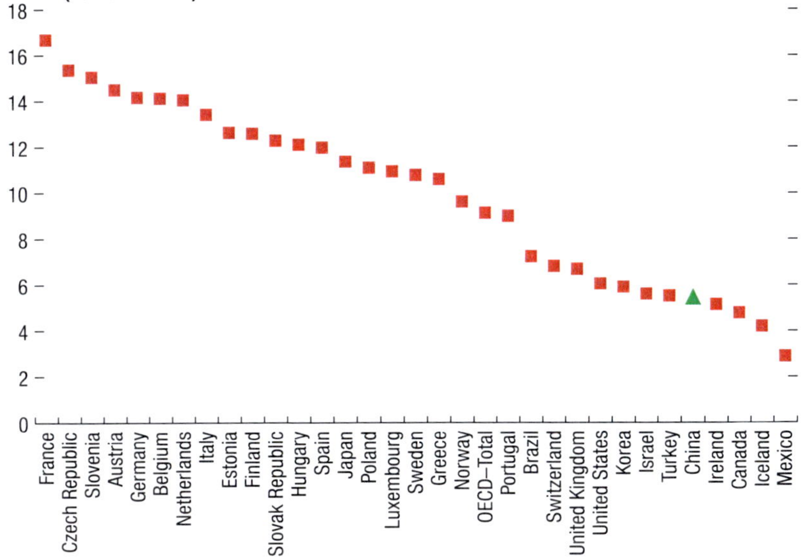

Source: Organisation for Economic Co-operation and Development (OECD) Tax Statistics.

2. Comparison of Average Tax Wedge by Income Level (Percent of gross income)

Sources: CEIC; Organisation for Economic Co-operation and Development (OECD); and IMF staff calculations.

Figure 2.3. Individual Income Tax *(continued)*

3. Average Tax Wedge by Income Level (Percent of gross income)

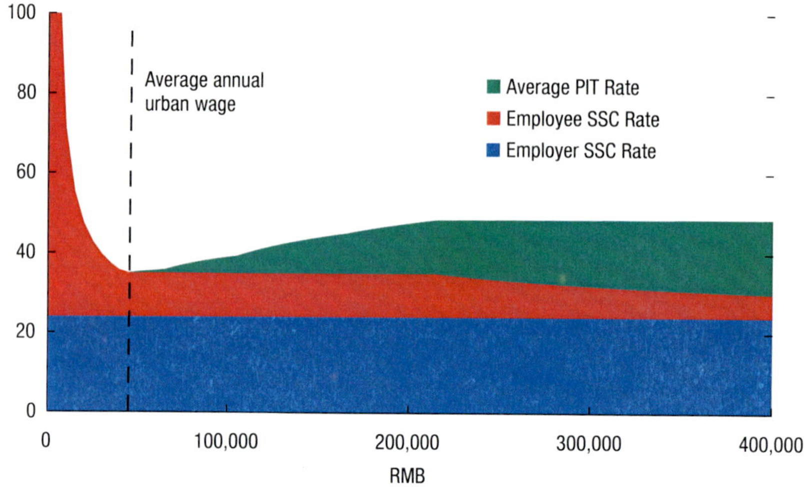

Sources: CEIC; International Bureau of Fiscal Documentation; and IMF staff calculations.
Note: PIT = personal income tax; SSC = social security contribution.

4. Individual Income Tax Marginal and Average Tax Rates and Income Distribution (Percent of gross income)

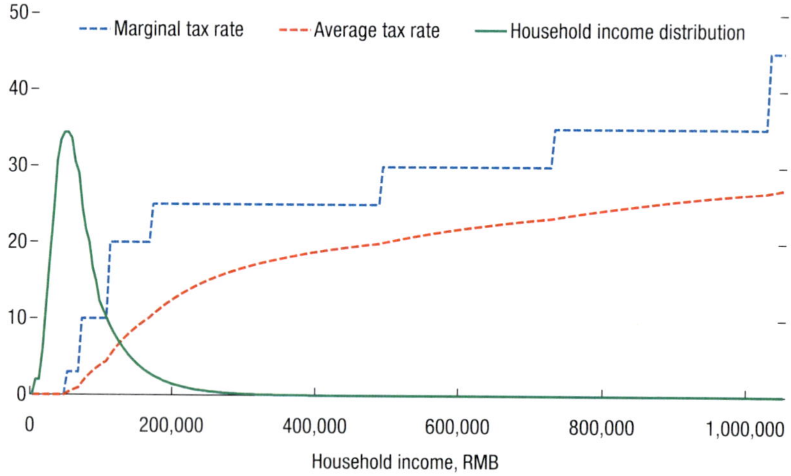

Sources: CEIC; International Bureau of Fiscal Documentation; and IMF staff calculations.

Figure 2.3. Individual Income Tax *(continued)*

5. Share of Total Income by Source (Percent, by income level, urban households, 2012)

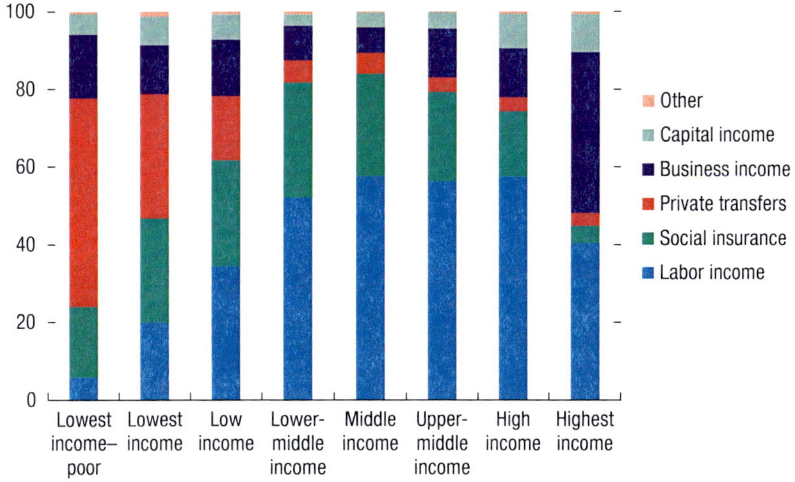

Source: China Household Finance Survey 2012.

6. Composition of Statutory Tax Burden (individual income tax and social security contribution) (Percent, by income level, urban households, 2012)

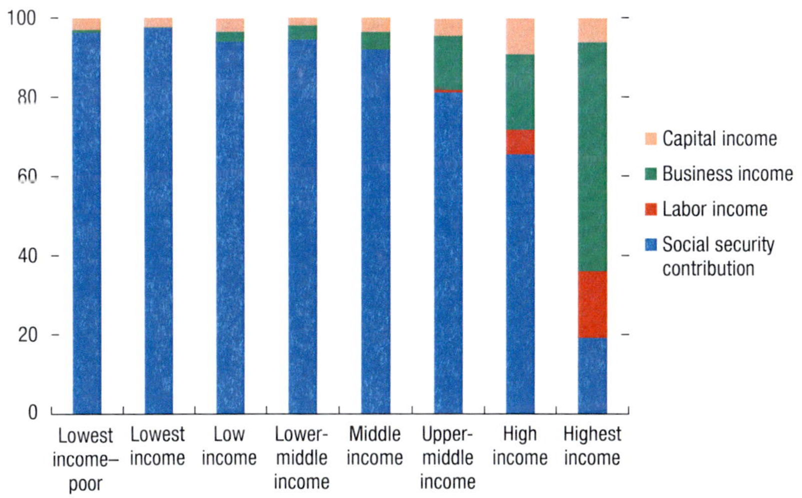

Sources: China Household Finance Survey 2012; and International Bureau of Fiscal Documentation.

Figure 2.3. Individual Income Tax *(continued)*

7. Statutory and Effective Average Tax Burden
(Percent, by income level, urban households, 2012)

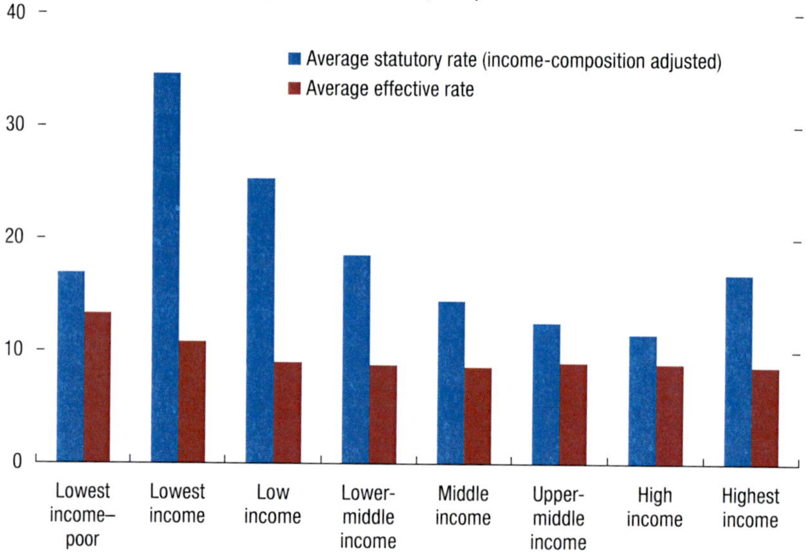

Sources: China Household Finance Survey 2012; and International Bureau of Fiscal Documentation.

8. Urban Household Income
(Percent, five-year average, year-over-year growth)

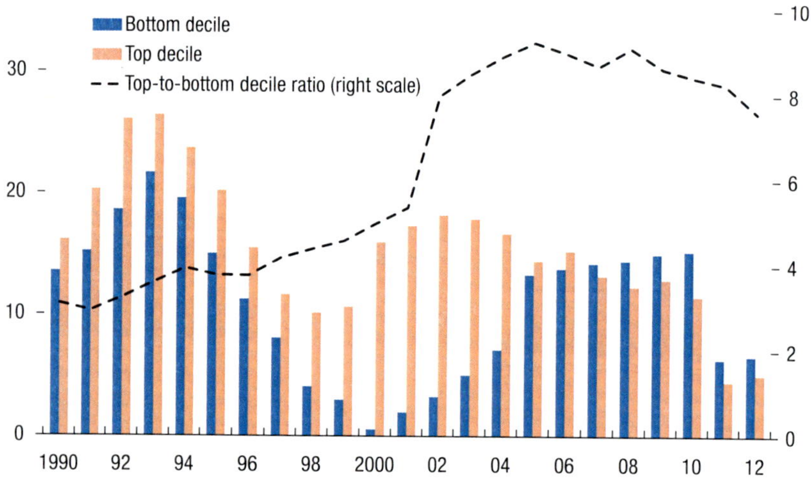

Sources: CEIC; and IMF staff calculations.

January 1, 2016, also allows employees, sole proprietors, and partners to deduct up to RMB2,400 annually for premiums paid to a qualified commercial health insurance scheme.

In addition to tax on wages and salaries, employees and their employers must contribute to social security for pensions, medical insurance, and unemployment insurance. Employee contributions are withheld from wages and remitted directly by employers, on average at about 11 percent of gross wages of employees (or net of income tax at nearly 9 percent) with the exact percentages varying between provinces and localities. Although a nominal flat rate is applied, a minimum employee contribution is also required and based on some imputed value of earnings. The imputed minimum earnings for workers, in turn, are set at 60 percent of the previous year's average wage in a locality. Estimates put the earnings of about 30 percent of the urban labor force in several large cities below the 60 percent threshold (Cai, Du, and Wang 2011). This feature of the schedule for social security contributions, along with a cap on contributions set at three times the average wage in a locality, implies that the effective contribution rate is very regressive in employee income (Brys and others 2013; World Bank and Development Research Center of the State Council 2013).

Proposed Reforms

The current schedular approach appears to be unfair and distortive. Taxing income under different categories creates considerable fragmentation and causes inequities that are often regarded as unfair. Distortions arise as individuals adjust their activities and report toward more tax-favored options. In that context, the Chinese authorities are discussing alternative models for income tax design, most notably global income tax and dual income tax systems.

The fragmentation of the present system for collecting individual income tax has led some to argue for the adoption of a global income tax system. This would mean that all 11 categories of income would be consolidated for each individual (or household) under a single tax base, and taxed using a marginal rate schedule based on ability to pay. A global income tax system is often viewed as the theoretical ideal for many countries. Many argue that it achieves both horizontal and vertical equity and avoids the tax arbitrage that can arise from different sources of income being taxed under different schedules. Despite its appeal, however, most advanced economies have moved away from a global income tax system over the past few decades. Indeed, even arrangements that closely resembled global income tax systems were often found to be inefficient and inequitable in practice.[3] For instance, high marginal tax rates on capital income were seen as highly inefficient because they distort decisions about savings and investment. The systems were also inequitable as evasion and

[3]Pure global income tax systems do not exist, even in countries that have tried to approximate them, such as the United Kingdom and the United States.

avoidance of taxes, especially by wealthy taxpayers, made the distribution of the tax burden much less progressive than it appeared in theory.

Global income tax systems were often costly to administer, as capital income is difficult to measure accurately, and all incomes had to be attributed to individuals (or households), necessitating large-scale filing of tax returns. To simplify their individual tax systems (reducing distortions and administrative complexity), many countries have therefore adopted a schedular approach to taxing labor and capital income.

A dual income tax system provides a more solid framework for a modernized individual income tax in China. Many OECD countries have adopted variants under which all types of income are allocated to one of two broad categories: labor or capital income. In China, this would be a significant step toward a fully integrated approach to taxing income, since the number of schedules would decline from 11 to two. Starting from the current individual system, a natural classification in China would allocate to a comprehensive labor income category all income from (1) wages and salaries; (2) the business of industrial and commercial operators; (3) business operations contracted or leased from enterprises; (4) labor service; (5) remunerations to authors; (6) royalties; (7) accidental income; and (8) other types of earnings. All of these income sources would be added together and taxed under a single comprehensive rate schedule. The remaining types of income identified in the individual tax legislation, including income from (9) interest, dividends, and bonuses; (10) leasing of property; and (11) transfer of property, would be classified as capital income.

The labor income tax schedule under a dual income tax system should include progressive marginal tax rates. Such a system would present many advantages from policy and tax administration perspectives. Income redistribution can be achieved by increasing marginal tax rates for high-income earners. Taxing all sources of labor income under the same schedule is also regarded as improving fairness. The design of the labor income tax schedule still leaves scope for many specific design options. These include the following:

- **Tax unit.** Economically and administratively it would be desirable to continue to tax individual income, as opposed to family income. Family-based taxation can be more equitable since households with the same incomes would be taxed the same, regardless of the distribution of income between spouses. Yet this approach is associated with important costs. First, under family-based taxation, individuals are taxed according to marital status, so the system is not neutral in that respect. Second, individual-based taxation is simpler to administer since withholding depends only on earnings and not on marital status, which the tax administration must verify. Third, high tax rates on secondary earners tend to discourage both labor-force participation and work effort, potentially undermining economic efficiency and growth.
- **Rate structure.** Labor income would be subject to a progressive marginal tax rate schedule but with scope for simplification. The number of mar-

ginal tax rates itself is not necessarily a source of added complexity, and reducing the number of rates can point to ways to simplify the system further. A schedule with marginal rates of 10, 20, and 35 percent, for instance, could strike a good balance between equity and efficiency. This schedule would raise the current minimum rate of 3 percent and reduce the top tax rate of 45 percent, which is higher than the average top rate in Asian countries. A somewhat higher rate at the bottom would efficiently expand the tax base—the first bracket collects revenue from all taxpayers with earnings above a certain level—while generating minimal efficiency costs on lower earners.

- **Threshold.** The current approach is to deduct a personal allowance of RMB42,000 a year—RMB3,500 a month—from taxable wages and salaries. While this shields the lowest-income earners from having to pay personal income tax, it also favors people with higher incomes, since the value of the allowance depends on marginal tax rates. The value of the basic personal allowance is, for instance, RMB1,260 for an individual in the first tax bracket (3 percent of RMB42,000), but RMB18,900 for individuals in the highest tax bracket of 45 percent—15 times more than for those with the lowest taxable incomes. An alternative approach that maintains favorable tax treatment for the low-paid group is to transform basic personal allowances from a deduction into a tax credit. This change would ensure that, for a given marginal tax rate structure, the allowance is constant across all incomes and does not benefit high-income earners disproportionately.
- **Targeted allowances.** The current individual tax system is simple to administer but difficult to tailor to the specific circumstances of taxpayers. It would in principle be possible to achieve more equity using selected targeted allowances that better reflect ability to pay. However, targeted allowances should be carefully considered: they often cause significant distortions, usually do not achieve their intended purpose, and are extremely difficult to repeal. Targeted allowances also often disproportionately benefit higher-income households, which would be especially true in China considering that only the highest-income individuals pay any tax under the current individual income tax system. To support equity considerations, China could consider introducing a targeted tax credit for children. This could be a sensible approach since the cost of raising children significantly affects the ability to pay tax, and a child tax credit would have few unintended consequences. It would not be advisable to introduce other allowances tied to spending on activities that are sometimes given preferential tax treatment (such as charitable giving, medical expenses, mortgage interest, and other expenditure), which are very easy to abuse and exceedingly costly to enforce.
- **Annual assessment.** Defining taxable labor income on an annual basis would result in a more equitable system. This would ensure a consistent

definition of taxable income, in particular between business and labor income, which would be consolidated as labor income under a dual income tax approach. It would also ensure equal treatment of workers with different earning patterns; for example, due to seasonal employment. Tax collection can remain largely based on monthly withholding, although end-of-year filing will increase somewhat for some taxpayers (such as professionals).

Under a dual income tax system, investment income is taxed uniformly at a flat rate. In principle, rates should be equal across all sources of investment income to maintain tax neutrality. In practice, however, several factors limit the desirability of this specific feature. Income from dividends, interest from deposits and government bonds, capital gains realized on real property, shares, and rental income would all be taxed at a proportional rate. The proportional tax rate on investment income should not differ too much from the top marginal tax rates applicable to labor income, taking into consideration any tax burden from corporate income tax. Lower effective tax rates on income from capital would create a strong incentive to recharacterize income from labor as income from capital, a problem that is especially relevant for small businesses. This incentive exists in many tax systems, especially when considering payroll or social security taxes that substantially increase effective marginal tax rates on labor income but leave the tax rates applied to income from capital unchanged. Moreover, given that investment income disproportionately accrues to the highest-income households in China, it would be appropriate to set this rate in relation to the top marginal rate on labor income. Maintaining a flat rate enables the continued use of final withholding, which ensures collection is administratively efficient.

- **Dividends.** Dividends are currently subject to individual income tax through final withholding from shareholders, after being paid out of profits already taxed as corporate income. The resulting double taxation of income from equity-financed investment is often an important source of nonneutrality because, unlike dividends, interest expenses can be deducted from corporate profits—and thus taxed only once. A simple way to mitigate these distortions is to impose lower withholding tax rates on dividends received. A reduced rate simply needs to ensure that dividends are taxed at the desired effective rate. A lower dividend tax rate of 10 or 15 percent, say, would be appropriate in China, given the double taxation of distributed corporate profits.[4] Since dividends disproportionately accrue to the top 10 percent of household incomes, this would imply broad consistency with a proposed top marginal tax rate of 35 percent on labor income. A slightly higher combined tax rate on dividends than on interest income would also achieve

[4]A statutory rate of 15 percent would imply that dividends are effectively taxed at a combined rate of 36.25 percent [0.25 + (1 – 0.25) × 0.15], given the regular enterprise income tax rate of 25 percent on corporate profits.

additional redistribution, since investment income of the lowest-income households is mostly composed of interest.

- **Capital gains.** Capital gains should in principle be taxed in the same way as other forms of investment income—on an annual accrual basis. In practice, however, taxing capital gains raises a number of practical problems. First, capital gains, especially gains from some forms of innovative financial instruments (such as derivatives), can be difficult to identify and measure. Second, compliance and enforcement in taxing capital gains from most assets on an accrual basis is difficult, and it would be undesirable from the perspective of investment neutrality to tax on an accrual basis only those assets where accrued gains would be easy to measure (for example, assets traded on public exchanges). For these reasons, virtually all systems across the world where capital gains are taxed do so upon realization. However, this can distort the decision of when to realize gains (or losses), which can result in inefficiencies and distort asset portfolios and risk sharing. As a result, taxes on capital gains typically make up only a small share of tax revenues—less than 1 percent on average in OECD countries. However, their taxation remains important to protect the revenue base of other sources, given the ease of transforming other forms of investment income (and in some cases labor income) into capital gains. A somewhat reduced tax rate can address several issues involved in taxing capital gains. It can mitigate the "lock-in" effect associated with the taxation of realized gains, decrease the potential tax advantage of realizing capital losses earlier than otherwise, and better reflect the taxation of the underlying appreciation over time. A lower tax rate also reduces the double taxation of enterprise profits—just as for dividends—since it is the after-tax profit that tends to be capitalized in share prices. Finally, taxing capital gains at a lower rate compensates investors for the nondeductibility of losses when collected under a final withholding regime.
- **Interest, royalties, and rental income.** These incomes could also be taxed at a rate of 20 percent, say. While this would be somewhat lower than the top marginal tax rate on labor income and the combined tax burden on dividends or capital gains, taxing incomes at much higher rates may not yield more revenue in light of their elastic base, which itself is in part due to international mobility. Exemptions for interest on government bonds and on deposit account savings with a Chinese bank should be repealed. Rental income should be taxed at about the same (effective) rate as other sources of investment income, following the neutrality principle. Currently, preferential treatment is given to gross rental income, which is taxed at a reduced individual income tax rate of 10 percent, with an additional cost imputation of 20 percent, making the effective tax rate on rental income 8 percent. This type of tax preference favors investment in real estate and can lead to distortions and overinvestment in the sector. Costs for the provision of rental services (such as financing or maintenance) might warrant a somewhat

lower rate than that applied to interest income. With the 20 percent cost imputation maintained, the effective tax rate on rental income could be brought to 16 percent to achieve rough neutrality.

Current Situation and Issues with Social Security Contributions

Social security contributions are strongly regressive in China. For most households, social security contributions constitute over 90 percent of direct tax liabilities. The average statutory tax rate across all sources of income, including business and capital income, also places a heavy burden on the poorest households. This is also reflected in the average effective tax rate (measured as the difference between gross market income and net disposable income after taxes and transfers) reported by households. As a result of both the imputed earnings base for social security contributions and the very high levels at which marginal tax rates on an individual's income start to be applied, the total tax burden on employment income is very high for the low-paid. Data from the household income survey suggest that households in the lowest income quartile pay a much higher effective tax rate than higher-income households (Lam and Wingender 2015). The effective tax schedule is regressive at the range of employment income below 70 percent of average wage income (in Figure 2.3, for example, the tax wedge in China is shown to be much higher than average OECD effective rates for single taxpayers and working couples with two children).

Proposed Reform of Social Security Contributions

Reform of social security contributions focuses on the efficiency, portability, and sustainability of the social security system (see also Chapter 5 on pension reform). The current structure and, in particular, the imputed taxable earnings for low-income earners reduce labor market flexibility and tend to favor informality and self-employment, which are not broadly covered by the contribution rules. This has probably led to significant numbers of low-income workers opting out of the system, since about a quarter of the urban labor force was not covered by social security contributions in 2010 (Hinz and others 2011). An important change would be to ensure that actual income is used in the calculation of insurance premiums, as opposed to the current system, which imputes a minimum level of earnings in the calculation of social security contributions. This change would avoid the sometimes extraordinarily high contribution rates for workers who earn below the minimum wage. Earnings of about one-third of the urban workforce in several major cities are well below the imputation threshold for social insurance contributions. Moreover, for about half of those workers the effective tax wedge in the formal sector (that is, the difference between gross and after-tax income) was in excess of 65 percent (Cai, Du, and Wang 2011). The authorities have committed to reducing the rate at a time and pace that ensure the sustainability of the social security system.

CORPORATE INCOME TAX

Current Situation and Issues

Before 2008, two parallel systems with different rates and incentives were applied to corporate income: one for domestic and another for foreign operations. The revision of the Enterprise Income Tax Law in 2008 eliminated this distinction and unified payments for all companies. It now operates a classical system, implying that a tax is applied on corporate profit, while distributed profit is taxed again on the individual and without relief. The law stipulates that taxes are due on the international business of the worldwide income of a resident company. Relief for double taxation is granted through tax credits for the foreign tax paid.

Between 2008 and 2012, corporate income tax accounted for 3.4 percent of GDP on average. This is somewhat higher than the 2.9 percent OECD average, but lower than in some other countries in the Asia and Pacific region (Figure 2.4). With a statutory rate of 25 percent, revenue productivity—measured as corporate income tax revenue in percent of GDP divided by the tax rate—is 0.14 percent; each percentage point of the corporate income tax rate generates about 0.14 percent of GDP. This is high compared to other countries. India and Japan raise almost the same revenue to output as China, but with much higher corporate income tax rates.

The Chinese statutory corporate income tax rate of 25 percent is competitive.[5] It is slightly higher than in some of the smaller countries in the region, yet similar to Indonesia and below the OECD average. It is also somewhat lower than in other large economies in the region, such as India and Japan. Large countries generally have higher tax rates than small countries—as witnessed by the Group of Seven's average corporate income tax rate of 31.3 percent in 2014 (Figure 2.4). That large countries set higher tax rates than small countries is a common feature of tax competition, as large countries have more to lose and less to gain from undercutting their neighbor's tax rates when competing for tax bases (Keen and Konrad 2013).

The effective tax rate on new investment in China is also lower than in other countries. Investment distortions do not depend strictly on statutory corporate income tax rates, but on effective tax rates.[6] The marginal effective tax rate is derived directly from the user cost, and it is a measure of the tax imposed on the marginal investment. A higher rate makes fewer investment projects worthwhile and will reduce investment. Tax rates can be calculated for different types of investment (buildings, equipment, intangibles) and alternative sources of finance (debt, retained

[5]A reduced rate of 20 percent applies to companies with annual income less than RMB300,000.

[6]Investment theory suggests that investment projects continue to be undertaken until the project that just breaks even. The price at this point is the user cost of capital, which depends not only on the corporate income tax rate but also on elements of the tax base, such as depreciation allowances, inventory valuation, interest deductibility, and investment tax credits.

Figure 2.4. Corporate Income Tax in China

1. Corporate Income Tax Revenue to GDP Ratio (Percent)

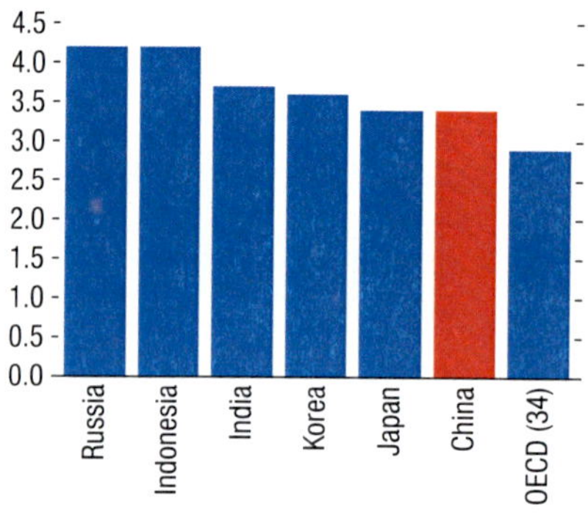

Source: Organisation for Economic Co-operation and Development (OECD).

2. Statutory Corporate Income Tax Rate across Economies (Percent)

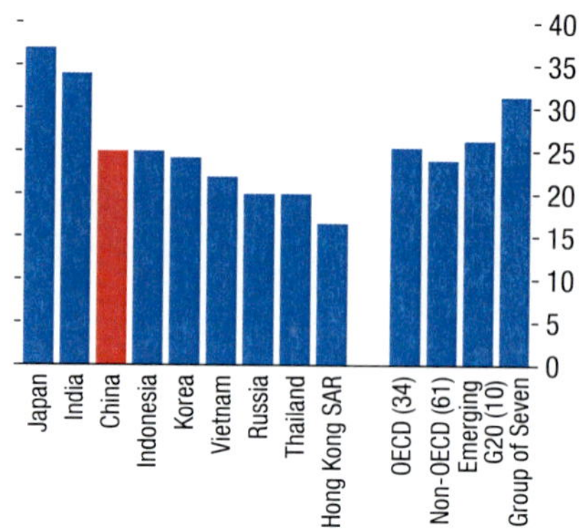

Source: Organisation for Economic Co-operation and Development (OECD).

3. Marginal Effective Tax Rate on Corporate Income (Percent)

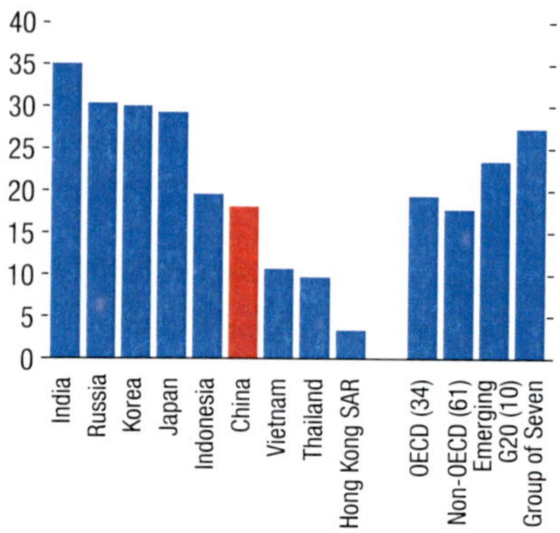

Source: Organisation for Economic Co-operation and Development (OECD).

4. Average Tax Burden along Income Distribution across Different Enterprises (Percent)

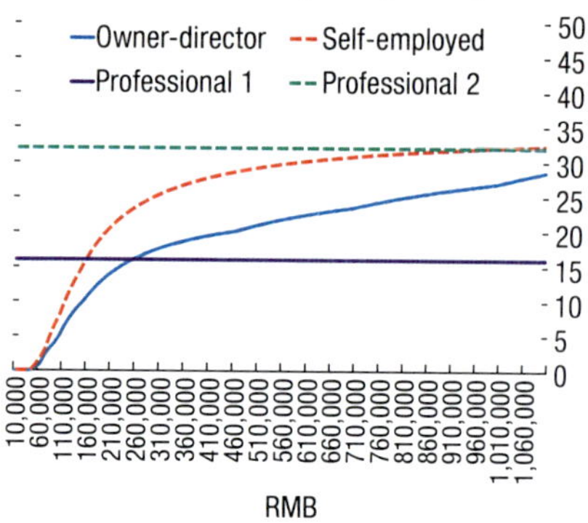

Source: IMF staff estimates based on statutory rates.
Note: Assumes taxable income of each business type is the same. The corporate business is assumed to distribute income as director renumeration to the point where it becomes tax preferred to distribute dividends. Professional 1 is assumed to receive all income subject to the 20 percent rate, while professional 2 is assumed to receive income in large payments exceeding RMB500,000.

earnings, new equity). The overall distortion of corporate income tax in China is modest compared to other countries, according to an international comparison of the weighted average of marginal effective tax rates (Chen and Mintz 2015). The rate in China is similar to the average in 61 non-OECD countries and slightly below the averages for the OECD and Group of Seven economies (see Figure 2.4).

Figure 2.4. Corporate Income Tax in China *(continued)*

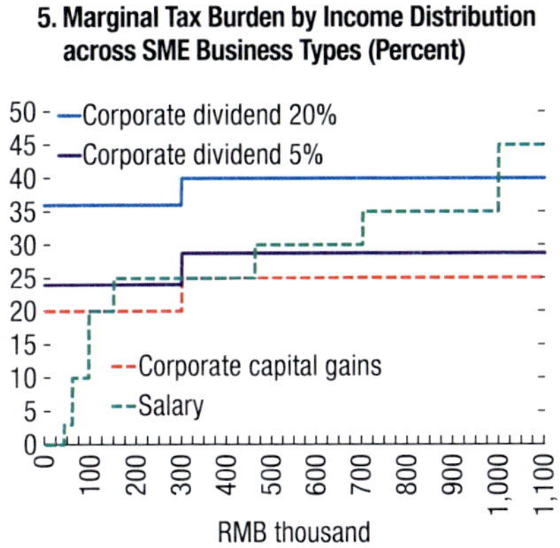

Source: IMF staff estimates.
Note: Assumes income of each business type is the same. The salary reflects a distribution of directors' remuneration. Corporate capital gains are only taxed by the Enterprise Income Tax. Dividend distributions considered here are taxed at either 5 percent or 20 percent. SME = small and medium-sized enterprise.

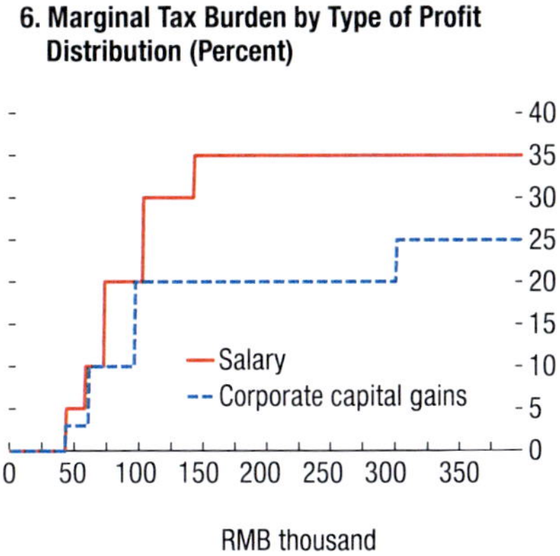

Source: IMF staff estimates.
Note: Assumes income of each business type is the same. Corporate capital gains are only taxed by the Enterprise Income Tax.

Rationalizing tax incentives in 2008 was a key step in the modernization of China's tax system. The elimination of tax incentives improved its neutrality and has contributed significantly to a more buoyant revenue base.[7] While having played a useful role in attracting foreign direct investment, tax incentives create significant distortions between industries, regions, and businesses when in place for too long. The abolishment of tax incentives in the 2008 reform might serve as an example for other countries wishing to boost revenue mobilization. The new set of tax incentives is much more limited in scope and scale, and some incentives are justified on the grounds that they support activities that generate positive externalities for other industries, such as super deductions for expenses on research and development.

Small and medium-sized enterprises are commonly hard to tax. Beyond tax evasion (understating income by underreporting receipts or overstating deductions), entrepreneurs often respond to opportunities for tax arbitrage, as they can easily choose to convert heavily taxed income into lightly taxed income (Saez

[7]Most tax incentives have been successfully phased out. Between the mid-1980s and mid-2000s, China introduced a range of industrial policy instruments, including tax incentives for special economic zones, reduced tax rates for foreign direct investment, and tax holidays for strategic industries. These schemes are regarded as having succeeded in achieving their objectives, including to attract foreign direct investment. Most tax incentives were phased out in the new Enterprise Income Tax Law, but some were retained, including a reduced rate for high-technology and research and development investment, new enterprises in the western region of the country, and selected services in the Shanghai free trade zones.

Table 2.5. Corporate Income Tax Schedule for Small and Medium-Sized Enterprises

From Renminbi	Up to Renminbi	Tax Rate on Business Income (Percent)
0	15,000	5
15,001	30,000	10
30,001	60,000	20
60,001	100,000	30
100,001	∞	35

Source: International Bureau of Fiscal Documentation.

2010). This makes it important to design an individual income tax system that provides for as much neutrality as possible in the taxation of entrepreneurial income, so that little room is left for entrepreneurs to engage in such arbitrage. Neutrality should be obtained in particular for decisions (1) to work as an entrepreneur or as an employee, which is especially relevant in sectors where tasks can be easily outsourced, as is the case in many service sectors; (2) to choose the legal form for a business, as either a separate legal entity (such as a limited liability corporation) or as a natural person (a sole proprietorship or partnership); (3) to distribute income earned by the entity or retain it in the company (so that it accumulates as an accrued capital gain); and (4) to distribute income from the legal entity to its owner(s) as labor remuneration, dividends, or a realized capital gain.

Currently, business income in China is taxed through a wide range of schedules. Sole proprietorships and partnerships are taxed under a special progressive rate schedule of the individual income tax system, with marginal rates of between 5 and 35 percent (Table 2.5). Closely held corporate businesses are taxed by the corporate income tax at a rate of 20 percent on annual income of less than RMB300,000 and at 25 percent for incomes above that. The distributions of closely held corporations can be taxed as wage income when paid as a director's remuneration (at the schedule for ordinary salary income), or as dividend income taxed at a flat rate of 20 percent. The combined burden of corporate income tax plus dividend tax therefore lies somewhere between 36 and 40 percent.[8] Several professional services are taxed at flat rates of 20, 30, or 40 percent on a per-payment basis—depending on the size of the payment—after a deduction of 20 percent for deemed expenses. Finally, micro businesses that are unable to keep books and records may be taxed on the profit they are deemed to have made.

Proposed Reform

The current regime creates horizontal inequities, distortions, and opportunities for tax avoidance. Some distortions are discrete in nature, such as the choice of legal form or decisions regarding entrepreneurial entry. Others affect marginal

[8]This reflects a 20 percent corporate income tax plus (1 – 0.2) × 20 percent dividend tax, and a 25 percent corporate income tax plus (1 – 0.25) × 20 percent dividend tax.

behaviors, such as the retention or distribution of income and the way in which income is distributed (see Figure 2.4).

- **Discrete distortions.** Average tax burdens vary for unincorporated business. For the corporate business that pays a salary to its owner-employee as long as it is taxed at a lower rate than dividends (the residual income is then paid as dividends), the tax rate will be different from those that pay above RMB50,000. Taxes on corporate businesses are always lighter than on noncorporate businesses in China, while professionals can be taxed more or less depending on their gross revenue and the size of payments.[9]
- **Marginal distortions.** The marginal tax burden also differs on corporate capital gains, corporate dividends (assuming a tax rate on dividends of either 20 percent or 5 percent), and salary payments, such as a director's remuneration (see Figure 2.4). Dividends are almost never tax preferred when taxed at 20 percent, but are charged at a lower marginal rate than is imposed on high salaries. Capital gains are least taxed at high incomes. Wages to low-income individuals accrue the lowest burden in light of the progressive structure of taxes on salaries.

Reforms to a dual-income-tax-inspired system would bring business income and various labor income under the same tax schedule. This would restore horizontal equity and eliminate distortions. For instance, applying the same schedule for taxable business income and salaries would eliminate differences in average tax burdens between employees, nonincorporated businesses, and corporate businesses that award a director's remuneration to the owner. Distortions in the choice between entrepreneurship and salaried employment would therefore be eliminated. Taxing professionals (and authors) on their annual income, rather than on a per payment basis, would also align the average tax burden with that of other businesses.

The overall tax burden on profit distributions for a closely held business would be roughly aligned at a dividend tax rate of 15 percent and a 35 percent top rate on salaries. If the top rate on salaries were 35 percent, a dividend tax rate of 13.3 percent would ensure complete neutrality for companies paying 25 percent corporate income tax; a dividend tax rate of 18.75 percent would achieve neutrality for companies paying 20 percent corporate income tax.[10] A dividend tax rate of 15 percent would therefore be "roughly" neutral for all entrepreneurs. Such treatment largely eliminates opportunities for tax arbitrage in the distribution of income by entrepreneurs between director's remuneration and dividend payments.

[9]Further differences in effective tax burdens between professionals can arise due to variation in actual costs incurred. For instance, if actual business expenses are 50 percent of revenue, the 16 percent tax on gross receipts is equivalent to an income tax rate of 32 percent.

[10]The formula to maintain neutrality between salary payments and dividends is TD = (TP – TC)/(1 – TC), where TD is the dividend tax, TP is the top personal income tax rate on salaries, and TC is the corporate income tax.

INDIRECT TAX REFORMS

This section elaborates on indirect tax reform and is guided by the conceptual framework shown in Box 2.2. The focus is mainly on options for reform of VAT and environmental taxation.

THE TRANSITION TO VAT

Current Situation and Issues

The transition to VAT for goods and services was completed in 2016. China applied VAT only to the supply of goods and imports before the transition to VAT beginning in 2012.[11] The standard VAT rate of 17 percent was complemented by a reduced rate of 13 percent for certain items. Small businesses became subject to a simplified VAT scheme, whereby they charge a reduced rate of 3 percent on sales but do not have the opportunity to claim refunds for input VAT.

Proposed Reform of VAT

The recent transition of business turnover tax into VAT is a very positive step toward raising the effectiveness and efficiency of China's tax system, but continued reform is needed. The transformation is expected to eliminate major distortions, yet important challenges remain that warrant ongoing reform. These cover the need to do the following:

- **Unify the refund mechanism.** Input tax on exports of all goods is currently not refunded in full. Refund rates vary between the full refund at the 17 percent VAT rate, to 5 percent or even to nothing for certain items. This violates an important principle of VAT as a destination-based tax, which requires full zero rating of exports with full crediting of input VAT. The practice in China imposes trade distortions that hurt the competitiveness of certain industries and distorts international trade.
- **Unify VAT rates.** The current VAT has four different rates: 6, 11, 13, and 17 percent. This departs from the widely accepted standard of a single VAT rate for all items—both to avoid distortions and to ease tax administration. Indeed, reduced rates forgo revenue and create compliance problems such as with how to classify certain items.

---

[11]The government started to extend the VAT to services as a replacement for the business tax in 2012. A pilot program was launched in Shanghai for transportation services (except railway transportation) and modern services industries. The pilot was extended to eight municipalities and provinces in August 2012. Two new VAT rates of 6 and 11 percent were added to the existing rates of 13 and 17 percent on goods. The Ministry of Finance and State Administration of Taxation extended VAT on these services to the entire country in August 2013. Beginning in January 2014, VAT for railway transportation and postal services was introduced nationwide. In June 2014, it was broadened to cover telecommunications services. The transition to the remaining services was completed in May 2016.

Box 2.2. Policy Guidance from Indirect Tax Theory

A comprehensive and uniform tax on consumption can be shown to be broadly equivalent to a tax on wages and profits. That is, lifetime consumption will match lifetime income for most individuals. So taxing them on either income or on consumption leads to similar revenue collection. However, beyond this observation, and based on very stylized models, a reform that replaces income-based taxation with consumption-based taxation can also effectively tax individuals' capital endowment. This constitutes an efficient lump-sum tax on endowments if the reform is unanticipated. Further extensions, such as on international trade, can break down this equivalence, with potential short-term benefits for terms of trade from the move to destination-based consumption taxes such as VAT, from origin-based labor and production taxes (de Mooij and Keen 2013).

The seminal contribution by Atkinson and Stiglitz (1976) established that under general conditions, an optimal collection policy will rely on both direct and indirect taxes. In a setting with heterogeneous agents, consumption tax will be used even when the government has access to a nonlinear income tax. The reason is that when consumption patterns differ systematically across people with different ability to earn income, these consumption patterns can be used to identify individuals' inherent ability. Moreover, when some goods are intrinsically related to either leisure or labor supply, varying tax rates can generate further gains in efficiency. However, the literature gives relatively little guidance about how to determine the specific composition.

Beyond these important theoretical considerations, the share of direct and indirect taxes is also a matter of administration. In particular, relying on both broad-based consumption taxes and income taxes reduces the risk of revenue leakage through evasion and noncompliance since it increases the opportunities to observe tax bases and collect taxes due. For example, taxes on wage income are effectively levied through withholding by employers. However, it is much harder to tax self-employed individuals through such schemes, so using indirect consumption taxes would be warranted to ensure some revenues are collected.

Individual commodity taxation should depend on the relative size of demand elasticities. This was shown in an early formulation of the problem of setting optimal tax policy by Ramsey (1927). Specifically, the ratio of the optimal ad valorem rates on two different commodities is determined by their cross-price elasticities with respect to the untaxed good (often assumed to be leisure for simplicity). Corlett and Haque (1953) also note this: a "second best" approach to indirect taxation is achieved by taxing goods and services that are most complementary to leisure. This also has the benefit of reducing distortions in labor supply incentives.

While recommendations from theory are straightforward, in practice the welfare gains of differential commodity taxation are not worth the higher administrative and compliance costs of more complex consumption tax systems (Crawford, Keen, and Smith 2010). Moreover, the distributional benefits of differential rates for certain necessities or luxury commodities are generally thought to be best achieved through income tax. The reason is that as long as the government uses an optimal nonlinear income tax, redistribution can be achieved without distorting the consumption choices of individuals, as would be the case with differential consumption tax rates.

Differential commodity tax rates may address externalities in consumption. A tax that accounts for the external effect incurred by other agents will cause the emitter to internalize the additional social cost of his action and choose the socially optimal level for his own private consumption (Pigou 1920).

Important examples are pollution, alcohol, and tobacco. Recent literature has also looked at how people's lack of consistency, self-control, or access to information may be grounds for using indirect taxes to encourage welfare-improving consumption. The case for correcting these "internalities" has been made for tobacco as well as for the overconsumption of sugar and fat.

- **Ensure neutral treatment of property and financial services.** Margin-based financial services are commonly VAT exempt, which creates inevitable distortions. To offset these, financial institutions may be taxed under a substitute Financial Activities Tax (IMF 2010). Newly constructed immovable property may be subject to full VAT, in lieu of tax on the added value that such property would generate over its lifetime.
- **Introduce a VAT registration threshold.** Businesses with sales below the threshold are not obliged to register and will no longer have to charge 3 percent VAT on their sales. They can be offered to register voluntarily, for example, if they mainly export goods that put them in a net refund position. Voluntary registration may be denied for very small traders, so as to avoid abuse of VAT refunds for items bought for personal use.

A key challenge associated with the transition to VAT is the revenue impact for local governments. Revenue from the business tax was exclusively allocated to local governments, while only 25 percent of VAT revenue is shared. By splitting domestic VAT revenues equally between the central and local governments, which is expected to slightly increase the central government's take, the reform has therefore reinforced the misalignment between local revenue and spending. This intensifies the need to reform local government financing more widely.

Environmental Taxation

Current Situation and Issues

China's economic success has come at a high environmental cost. The Chinese Academy of Environmental Planning estimates that the cost of environmental damage amounted to 3½ percent of GDP in 2010. The World Bank has reported an estimate of 9 percent of GDP, with air and water pollution accounting for the largest shares due to pollution-related health damage, global climate change impacts, and resource depletion (World Bank and Development Research Center 2013). The World Health Organization estimates 1.7 million deaths were attributable to ambient air pollution in 2012 for the Asia and Pacific region, the highest per capita rate in the world.

The authorities have taken steps to reduce the economy's reliance on natural resources and energy. The 13th Five-Year Plan built on environmental protection efforts adopted in 2011. The recent revision of the environmental protection law was also an important step toward setting a sound legal basis for further measures. However, the quantity-driven administrative approach has relied on targeted interventions, mandates, and regulations. Policy objectives are often pursued by mandating reductions in pollution and by setting targets without regard to current energy consumption and pollution. This can be especially burdensome for new plants and investments that already operate to the highest environmental standards.

China levies a variety of resource and vehicle taxes, and charges on air and water pollution (Figure 2.5). However, revenues are low compared to OECD countries and only a fraction of what is required to fully internalize the costs of

Figure 2.5. Environmental Taxes and Costs: China and the World

1. Effective Tax Rate on Fossil Fuels and Externality Costs (Percent of GDP, 2008–11)

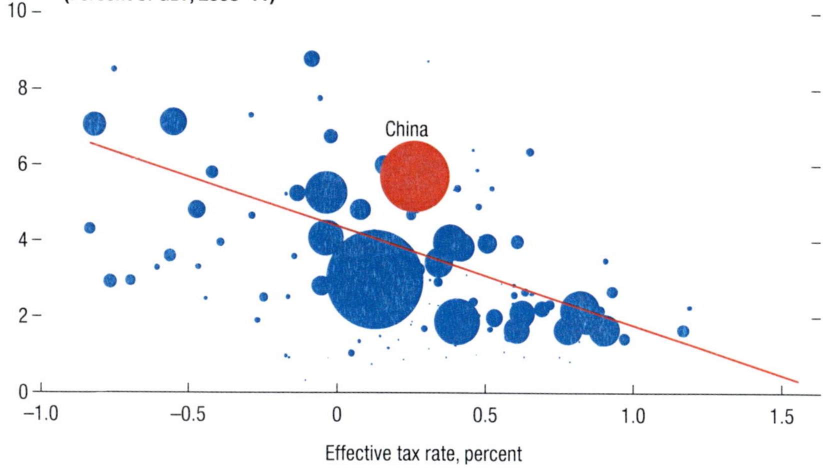

Sources: Getting Energy Price Right databases; and IMF Energy Subsidy Reform.
Note: The size of the circles indicates total externality costs in U.S. dollars.

2. Environment-Related Taxes in China (Percent of GDP, 2012)

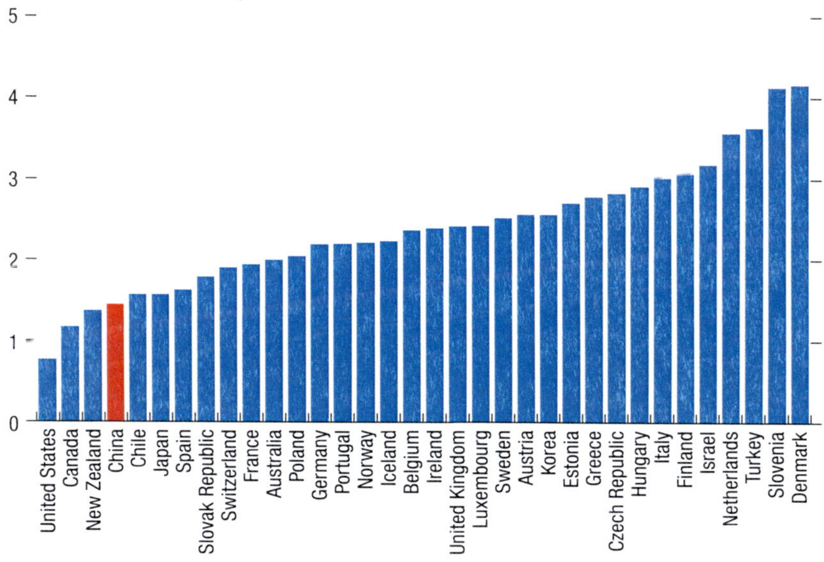

Source: Organisation for Economic Co-operation and Development Green Growth Indicators.

Figure 2.5. Environmental Taxes and Costs: China and the World *(continued)*

3. Coal Taxes to Correct Environmental Costs
(Corrective tax, U.S. dollars per gigajoule, 2010)

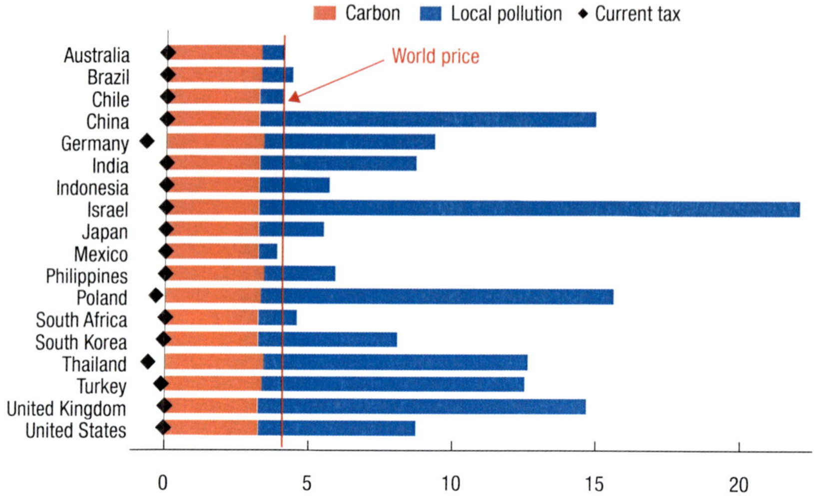

Source: Parry and others 2014.

4. Gasoline Taxes to Correct Environmental Costs
(Corrective tax, U.S. dollars per liter, 2010)

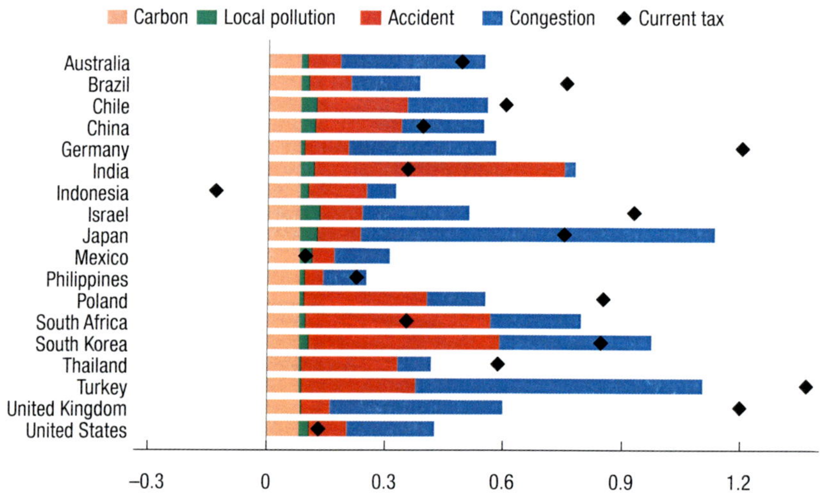

Source: Parry and others 2014.

climate change, local pollution, and congestion externalities. Energy prices are low, in particular for coal, which provides over 70 percent of the country's energy. Deregulation of prices for water, oil, natural gas, and electricity is ongoing; however, it is important that taxes are also employed to ensure prices reflect the full cost of externalities from energy and resource use.

A nationwide emission trading scheme will be introduced in 2017. It will build on seven regional pilot systems launched from 2011 to 2014 and will be the world's largest emission trading system, even as at the start it is still expected to only cover about half of all the country's emissions. The plan is to initially cover large entities in power generation, iron and steel, chemicals, cement, and paper. Small entities in these sectors, and those in road transportation, construction, and vehicle industries, representing about 50 percent of total emissions, will not be covered by the scheme, which means that low-cost emission reductions in these sectors will not be fully exploited. Beyond coverage issues, the specific design of the system will also be of great importance. It will be crucial that prices are sufficiently high and caps are stringent enough to support the country's mitigation plans. Given the considerable revenues at stake—potentially about 2 percent of GDP (Parry, Shang, and Wingender 2016)—initial allowances should be auctioned and not allocated for free.

Proposed Reform

Unlike targeted regulatory policies, taxes can be very effective at exploiting opportunities for improving energy efficiency and abating pollution; for example, by giving energy producers incentives to switch to cleaner fuel or by increasing prices of polluting fuels to reduce demand. Fiscal instruments can also provide especially strong incentives for power plants to install and operate emission control technologies. Countries with higher taxes on fossil fuels tend to incur lower externality costs such as local air pollution, greenhouse gas emissions, traffic congestion and accidents, and road damage.

While the national emission trading scheme is a key step in the right direction, several tax policy instruments can complement the reform. They include the following:

- **Carbon tax.** An upstream tax on fossil fuels based on carbon emission rates could be considered alongside the announced emission trading scheme (Parry, Shang, and Wingender 2016).[12] A tax on pollution at point of entry in the economy (coal mines, coal-powered energy plants, petroleum refineries, and the like) would reduce the administrative burden. It could also build on administrative structures already in place. A carbon tax on upstream production would provide the necessary incentives for emission-reducing behavior throughout the economy since energy prices would increase uni-

[12]The tax set on each fuel would equal the carbon dioxide coefficient (that is, the carbon dioxide produced by combusting a unit of the fuel) times the externality cost of climate change associated with the additional carbon dioxide emitted.

formly. A carbon tax and an emission trading scheme are not incompatible; they can be used in tandem to maximize tax arbitrage. Many countries have had successful experiences with carbon taxes.[13]

- **Tax on local air pollutants.** Current pollution levies on sulfur dioxide and nitrogen oxide emissions and small particulates could also be significantly increased. The revision to the Environmental Protection Law expected in 2016 will upgrade their legal status to full-fledged taxes. This will facilitate enforcement and ensure they provide the necessary incentives to reduce emissions as the current rates of taxes—about $200 per ton of sulfur dioxide for example—are only a fraction of the estimated health costs of local pollution (Parry and others 2014). The current direct subsidies and preferential pricing policies for the use of emission-control technologies could also be integrated into the tax system through a credit mechanism. The onus of reporting reductions in emissions through continuous monitoring would remain with the operator. This should be facilitated by the recent mandate for 15,000 plants to monitor and report their air-polluting emissions in real time.

China would need a relatively high corrective tax rate to fully internalize all costs (Parry and others 2014). The estimate is about $15 per gigajoule on energy produced from coal, which includes a carbon tax of around $35 per ton of carbon dioxide and additional taxes of approximately $20,000 for each ton of emitted sulfur dioxide, nitrogen oxides, and fine particulates. While the global costs of carbon dioxide emissions on climate change are roughly equal across countries, local pollution costs from the elevated risk of premature mortality are significantly higher in China, mainly due to the location of coal-intensive industries, the current low level of abatement among emitters, and high population density in exposed areas. Current taxes on coal are very low across all countries and, like many others, China's industrial and pricing policies in effect subsidize the use of coal. The proposed corrective tax would be comparable to that in the United Kingdom, and would be exceeded only by those in Israel and Poland in a selected group of comparable countries. Australia, Japan,

[13]Successful examples of carbon taxes across the world include the Canadian province of British Columbia, which introduced such a tax in 2008. The carbon tax covers approximately 70 percent of all greenhouse gas emissions of the province, and the rate was increased gradually over time and is now set at $30 per ton of carbon dioxide emitted. An interesting feature is that the tax is meant to be revenue neutral as the proceeds are remitted through tax cuts and credits for low-income households and corporate income tax credits. It is estimated that the province reduced carbon emissions by 10 percent over the first three years of the tax. Along with Finland, Norway, and Sweden, Denmark introduced a carbon tax in the early 1990s. To mitigate the tax burden, other energy taxes were decreased. The tax currently covers about 45 percent of all carbon emissions at a current rate of $31 per ton of carbon dioxide. Industries subject to the European Union emissions trading scheme are generally exempt from the carbon tax. Gradual implementation and differentiation of effective rates between energy uses minimized the impact of tax competitiveness. Primary energy intensity has declined by 26 percent since the introduction of the carbon tax, and carbon dioxide emissions fell by 25 percent during the first decade (World Bank 2014).

and Korea in particular would require lower rates of around $6 per gigajoule due to the lower local pollution externalities caused by sulfur dioxide, nitrogen oxides, and particulates.

An OECD modeling exercise in 2013 found that a modest carbon tax of $1.50 per ton of carbon dioxide emissions would have a very small impact on GDP, especially if the proceeds were used to offset consumption or payroll taxes. While output in carbon- and energy-intensive sectors such as chemicals, construction materials, and steel would contract, other less energy intensive sectors like financial services, food processing, and consumer services would benefit from the relative change in prices. Moreover, employment would also increase as labor is substituted for energy (Parry, Shang, and Wingender 2016). Other models of such policy experiments have reached similar conclusions (World Bank and Development Research Center of the State Council 2013).

A phase-in period where rate increases are announced in advance would allow firms and consumers to adapt and undertake mitigation measures. Revenue recycling—using the proceeds of a carbon tax to reduce other distortionary taxes such as payroll taxes—is also crucial to minimize the impact of higher energy prices on aggregate demand. In the early years of reform, for example, corporate income tax credits could be used to offset the cost of abatement technologies. China should also continue to develop and commercialize cleaner sources of energy such as wind, solar, and hydropower. Ultimately, it is important to maintain the principle of "polluter pays" to ensure the environmental effectiveness of the reform and to achieve the broader goal of rebalancing growth toward less-energy-intensive sectors.

- **Energy and fuel taxes.** Although fuel subsidies have fallen substantially in recent years, the government retains control over several energy markets. State-owned enterprises control most generation, transmission, and distribution of electricity as well as oil refineries. Private electricity generators must sell to the grid at fixed prices, while coal suppliers are required to sell some coal to power generators at below market price; and prices for natural gas are also determined by the government. Liberalization of the sector would promote competition and increase efficiency. Market prices would also better reflect the cost of production and scarcity. In the case of electricity, the government introduced a reform in 2012 explicitly to use household tariffs as a redistributive instrument. As a result, average household electricity prices in China are much lower than in other OECD countries. Despite the distributional benefits of the reform, a preferable option could be to use targeted cash transfers to households and fiscal transfers to provinces.

  China's fuel excise tax remains low relative to world prices. The introduction of a fuel tax in 2009 was partly offset by the removal of other taxes, such that prices remain relatively low compared to world prices. Excise duties on gasoline and other petroleum products could be further increased to cover the externalities associated with greenhouse gas emissions, local pollution, and traffic congestion and accidents. To cover these costs, the effective tax rate on gasoline could increase from 40¢ per liter at present to roughly 55¢ per liter. This would be comparable to other countries' taxes on gasoline and be significantly lower than in Japan (75¢ per liter) and Korea (85¢ per liter). The government could also consider introducing distance- and time-based taxes, which would be far more effective at decreasing congestion since rates could vary by period and place; for example, peak-period pricing for busy roads or cordon tolls around urban centers. Such measures have proved successful in Singapore, London, and Stockholm. Congestion charges would also be preferable to the license-plate rationing now used in some Chinese cities, which can be easily circumvented by owning more than one car or registering a car in a neighboring city.

- **Vehicle taxes.** China's current sales taxes on vehicles are based on engine capacity, with rates varying from 1 percent for vehicles with cylinder capacity below 1 liter, to 40 percent for vehicles with cylinder capacity larger than 4 liters. While engine capacity is a reasonable proxy for the environmental damage caused by cars, a better alternative would be to use a graduated system based on vehicles' emissions. This could take the form of an ad valorem excise tax on vehicle value to meet revenue objectives and a revenue-neutral "feebate" on emission rates to promote environmental objectives. The feebate structure would entail an increasingly large fee or rebate on the purchase price depending on whether a vehicle is more or less fuel efficient than some standard—for example, the average emission rate across all vehicle sales for a given category. The tax rate could be set at a higher value to provide incentives to adopt more-fuel-efficient cars. These parameters could easily be modified to take into account improvements in fuel efficiency of a new car or to increase emission reductions. Vehicle taxes make cars costlier to own and will therefore reduce the overall demand for vehicles. They also provide a good tax handle that has attractive distributional properties since higher-income households typically spend more on vehicles. However, since these taxes do not provide an incentive to reduce the amount of driving, they do relatively less than fuel or distance/place taxes to reduce externalities from emissions, congestion, and accidents.

The environmental tax needs to balance revenue generation with distributional considerations, given the importance of energy prices for low-income households. Increases in energy and fuel prices should be offset for the most vulnerable through assistance programs and improved safety net policies (Parry, Shang, and Wingender 2016). Broad public support must also be secured to ensure sustainable reforms. This requires coordinated and far-reaching communication strategies, improvements in transparency about fiscal costs and the beneficiaries of current policies, and a comprehensive reform plan that includes phased increases in energy prices.

RECURRENT PROPERTY TAXES

Current Situation

Recurrent property taxes are largely absent in China. Real estate tax revenues amount to 1.6 percent of GDP, which is comparable to the OECD average. However, taxes in China are mostly levied on transactions, whereas recurrent taxes take a much larger share of revenue in other countries (see Figure 2.1). Property taxes can raise up to 2 or 3 percent of GDP—although the average across countries is about 1 percent. This depends on exemptions, rate structure, and compliance. Rates usually vary between 0.1 percent and 1 percent of the market value of properties, depending on the type of property (such as commercial versus residential; or special rates applied for agricultural buildings).

Following pilot programs in Chongqing and Shanghai in 2011, a recurrent property tax could be extended to other municipalities and provinces.[14] The tax base should also be extended to ensure that all urban owner-occupied housing—over 85 percent of households in China own their homes—is taxed, with appropriate exemptions for the lowest-valued houses. Over time, the recurrent property tax could replace the numerous transaction-based taxes and fees on land and property levied by local governments. Development of a nationwide registry is underway, but much remains to be done to improve local government capacity for data registration, appraisals, and valuations.

Proposed Reforms

Recurrent property taxes are helpful because they:

- *Do not discourage mutually beneficial transactions because of cash flow constraints.* Macro regressions typically find that recurrent property taxes are among the least distortive to growth (Norregaard 2013). They are also less volatile than most other taxes, and are therefore particularly attractive as a local revenue source. Finally, these taxes are progressive, since high-income households usually tend to also have higher property wealth. Progressivity can be strengthened by the appropriate use of basic allowances.
- *Enhance the autonomy of local government finances.* Local governments in China have almost no control over their own revenue sources. Recurrent property taxes could change that, since they are usually local taxes, often with some restrictions set by the central government, such as national guidelines for property valuation methods, for the types of tax exemptions allowed, and bands for rates. Tax bases are also usually defined nationally to prevent local jurisdictions from competing for marginal footloose invest-

[14]The tax is currently applied to the ownership of a second property. In Shanghai, it applies to newly acquired second properties exceeding 180 square meters for a family of three but is subject to multiple exemptions. For example, the tax is not levied if married children of the owner use a house as their primary residence.

ment. However, tax competition is usually limited due to the relatively low mobility of the base.[15]

- *Are consistent with the benefit tax principle.* A well-designed recurrent property tax can be linked to the quality of local public goods delivery. Local amenities financed by property taxes, such as service delivery, public infrastructure, and environmental outcomes, will be capitalized in the prices of properties. By extension, efficient provision of local services and amenities would be reflected in increased property values, and ultimately in higher tax revenues. This could provide strong incentives for local governments to improve their delivery of services.
- *Contribute—when well designed—to urbanization and help contain real estate risks.* Barnett and Zhang (2014) estimate that fiscally induced pressure drove about one-third of property transactions in large cities in 2012–13, although others estimate the role of taxes to be less significant. Their introduction, however, needs to be timed well and phased in to avoid triggering a slowdown in the real estate market.

Current challenges to implementing a broad-based property tax include the absence of a nationwide registry of real estate, although the Ministry of Land and Resources has recently taken steps to implement registration. As long as proper valuation records remain unavailable, property taxes can be based on the area and location of the property, possibly with corrections for certain characteristics, to approximate value. Many emerging market and developing economies use such area and proxy-based systems. Another difficulty in China is that many properties are government owned and land ownership applies only for fixed periods (typically 70 years). Special attention should also be paid to property taxes on businesses and agriculture, perhaps by setting different rates or exemptions. Transitional arrangements should be carefully considered since the introduction of a recurrent tax in addition to transaction taxes may lead to the perception of "double taxation." The ongoing transition from the business tax to VAT also has important implications for local government revenue.

The central government may decide to set national guidelines for property valuation methods, for the types of tax exemptions allowed, and for bands for rates. Such bands would in principle set a strictly positive bottom threshold. Finally, prices of immovable property vary widely across provinces, so the tax-free basic allowance could be set differently across provinces and cities.

CONCLUSIONS

Tax reforms are an important part of China's efforts to modernize the fiscal framework. Reforms can improve the efficiency of the tax system, and at the same

[15]The so-called new or capital view sees property tax as a tax on capital (including mobile capital) within a local jurisdiction, with the distortions that may imply. See the seminal discussion in Zodrow and Mieszkowski (1986).

time contribute to more inclusive and environment-friendly growth. The country has considerable scope to increase the redistributive role of the tax system. Key steps to achieve this would include shifting away from the heavy reliance on indirect taxes toward direct taxes, transitioning indirect tax toward a well-designed VAT (that is, building on the extension of the VAT to services by replacing the distortive and cascading business tax), strengthening the progressivity of individual income tax, and reducing social security contribution rates, especially for low-income workers.

For direct taxes, a dual income tax for individual income could serve as a model for China. It would be a significant step toward a more integrated income tax by reducing the current 11 categories of taxable income to two broad categories: labor or capital income. Such a dual system would present many advantages from policy and tax administration perspectives. The labor income tax schedule should include progressive tax rates so that it can support redistribution purposes. Taxing all sources of labor income under the same schedule is also regarded as fairer, since individuals with same income are treated the same irrespective of where that income is earned. Sources of capital income would all be taxed at a proportional rate, which should not be too different from the top marginal tax rates applicable to labor income, taking into consideration any burden imposed by corporate income tax. This would strike a good balance between efficiency considerations and equity objectives.

For indirect taxes, the transition to VAT has raised efficiency considerably. Remaining reforms should focus on unifying the multiple VAT rates and improving the refund mechanism to avoid distortions and ease tax administration. At the same time, measures to ensure neutral treatment of property and financial services are important. Introducing a VAT registration threshold could further enhance VAT efficiencies by reducing administrative and compliance costs.

Environmental taxes can be effective for improving energy efficiency and abating pollution. Fiscal instruments can also provide especially strong incentives for power plants to install and operate technology to control emissions.

Ongoing work on the registration of properties and preparatory legislation would contribute to the launch of recurrent property taxes. The introduction of property taxes would be consistent with the benefit principle and facilitate reforms to strengthen local government revenue sources and support urbanization.

Policy sequencing and coordination among agencies are important for tax reforms to be successful. Many of the reforms are intertwined and therefore require careful sequencing to mitigate their impact on fiscal revenue and growth, particularly in light of the misalignment of revenues and spending by central and local governments. For instance, the transition from business tax to VAT would likely reduce tax revenues for local governments, even if the reform is revenue neutral in aggregate. Careful sequencing, however, should not cause delay. Steadfast implementation of reforms is necessary to reach an inclusive and sustainable growth path. Other reforms, such as social security and property tax, would involve several ministries. Policy coordination and the sharing of information among agencies would be key to successful implementation.

REFERENCES

Atkinson, A. B., and J. E. Stiglitz. 1976. "The Design of Tax Structure: Direct versus Indirect Taxation." *Journal of Public Economics* 6 (1976): 55–75.

Barnett, S., and Y. Zhang. 2014. "Fiscal Vulnerabilities and Risks from Local Government Finance in China." Working Paper No. 14/4, International Monetary Fund, Washington.

Brys, B., S. Matthews, R. Herd, and X. Wang. 2013. "Tax Policy and Tax Reform in the People's Republic of China." OECD Taxation Working Paper No. 18, Organisation for Economic Co-operation and Development Publishing, Paris.

Cai, F., Y. Du, and M. Wang. 2011. "Overview of China's Labor Market." Working Paper, Institute of Population and Labor Economics, China Academy of Social Sciences, Beijing.

Cevik, S., and C. Correa-Caro. 2015. "Growing (Un)equal: Fiscal Policy and Income Inequality in China and BRIC+." Working Paper No. 15/68, International Monetary Fund, Washington.

Chen, D., and J. Mintz. 2015. "The 2014 Global Tax Competitiveness Report: A Proposed Business Tax Reform Agenda." University of Calgary, the School of Public Policy, University of Calgary Publication Series 8 (4).

Clements, B., R. de Mooij, S. Gupta, and M. Keen, eds. 2015. *Inequality and Fiscal Policy.* Washington: International Monetary Fund.

Corlett, W. J., and D. C. Hague. 1953. "Complementarity and the Excess Burden of Taxation." *Review of Economic Studies* 21 (1): 21–30.

Crawford, I., M. Keen, and S. Smith. 2010. "Value-Added Tax and Excises." In *Dimensions of Tax Design: The Mirrlees Review*, 275–362. Oxford: Oxford University Press.

de Mooij, R., and M. Keen. 2013. "Fiscal Devaluation and Fiscal Consolidation: The VAT in Troubled Times." In *Fiscal Policy after the Financial Crisis*, edited by Alberto Alesina and Francesco Giavazzi. Chicago: University of Chicago Press.

Diamond, P. A., and J. W. Banks. 2010. "The Base for Direct Taxation." In *Dimensions of Tax Design: The Mirrlees Review*. Oxford: Oxford University Press.

Hinz, R., M. Pallares-Miralles, C. Romero, and E. Whitehouse. 2011. "International Patterns of Pension Provision II: A Worldwide Overview of Facts and Factures of the 2000s." Social Protection Discussion Paper, World Bank, Washington.

International Monetary Fund (IMF). 2010. "A Fair and Substantial Contribution by the Financial Sector—Final Report for the G-20." International Monetary Fund, Washington.

Keen, M., and K. Konrad. 2013. "The Theory of International Tax Competition and Coordination." In *Handbook of Public Economics Vol. 5*, edited by A. Auerbach, R. Chetty, M. Feldstein, and E. Saez. Amsterdam: North Holland.

Lam, W. R., and P. Wingender. 2015. "China: How Can Revenue Reforms Contribute to Inclusive and Sustainable Growth?" Working Paper No. 15/66, International Monetary Fund, Washington.

Mirrlees, J. A. 1971. "An Exploration in the Theory of Optimum Income Taxation." *Review of Economic Studies* 38 (2): 175–208.

Norregaard, J. 2013. "Taxing Immovable Property: Revenue Potential and Implementation Challenges." Working Paper No. 13/129, International Monetary Fund, Washington.

Parry, I., D. Heine, E. Lis, and S. Li. 2014. *Getting Energy Prices Right: From Principles to Practice*. Washington: International Monetary Fund.

Parry, I., B. Shang, and P. Wingender. 2016. "Climate Mitigation Policy in China: Assessing the Options." Working Paper No. 16/148, International Monetary Fund, Washington.

Pigou, A. C. 1920. *The Economics of Welfare*. London: Macmillan.

Piketty, T., and E. Saez. 2013. "Optimal Labor Income Taxation." In *Handbook of Public Economics Vol. 5*, edited by A. Auerbach, R. Chetty, M. Feldstein, and E. Saez. Amsterdam: North Holland.

Ramsey, F. P. 1927. "A Contribution to the Theory of Taxation." *Economic Journal* 37 (145): 47–61.

Saez, E. 2010. "Do Taxpayers Bunch at Kink Points?" *American Economic Journal: Economic Policy* 2 (3): 180–212.

Wang, X., and R. Herd. 2013. "The System of Revenue Sharing and Fiscal Transfers in China." OECD Economics Department Working Paper No. 1030, Organisation for Economic Co-operation and Development, Paris.

World Bank. 2014. *State and Trends of Carbon Pricing 2014*. Washington: World Bank.

———, and Development Research Center of the State Council. 2013. *China 2030: Building a Modern, Harmonious, and Creative Society*. Washington: World Bank. http://documents.worldbank.org/curated/en/2013/03/17494829/china-2030-building-modern-harmonious-creative-society.

Zodrow, G., and P. Mieszkowski. 1986. "Pigou, Tiebout, Property Taxation, and the Underprovision of Local Public Goods." *Journal of Urban Economics* 19 (3): 356–70.

CHAPTER 3

Strengthening Tax Administration

John Brondolo and ZHANG Zhiyong

China's tax administration has improved substantially over the past two decades in the face of major changes in the economy and the tax system (see Chapter 2). This has contributed importantly to a doubling of the tax-to-GDP ratio and the significant reduction in taxpayers' compliance costs since the mid-1990s. As the State Administration of Taxation (SAT) formulates its modernization plan for 2016–20, this chapter examines the results and impacts of previous tax administration reforms, and identifies areas where further reforms are needed to sustain revenue collection and reduce compliance costs over the next five years.

During the early 1990s, China's tax administration was ill-suited to and performed poorly at collecting taxes from an increasingly market-oriented economy. The tax system included some 35 different taxes, many of which accounted for little revenue. A single tax agency collected both national and local taxes, with complex intragovernmental revenue-sharing arrangements. The tax authorities' powers were set out in various statutes and circulars whose legal standing were not clearly established. Most tax administration functions were performed manually and required laborious checking procedures. Tax evasion and taxpayers' compliance costs were very high, and the tax yield had fallen to below 10 percent of GDP.

Since the early 1990s, China has made great progress in creating a modern tax administration. The system now comprises 18 taxes with clear apportionment of revenue between central and local governments. Separate national and local tax authorities have been created to collect central and local government taxes, and the revenue-sharing arrangements have been made more transparent. The tax authorities' powers and taxpayers' rights have been codified in a tax procedures law, and many tax administration procedures have been automated based on a

---

A longer version of the chapter can be found in "Tax Administration Reform in China: Achievements, Challenges, and Reform Priorities" (Brondolo and Zhang 2016). It benefited from insights and support provided by Jun Wang, Michael Keen, Juan Toro, Peter Barrand, Carlos Silvani, Raphael Lam, Alfred Schipke, Jian Fan, Tizhong Liao, Daoshu Wang, Yungen Gao, Wei Wang, Wei Cui, Yukang Wang, Li Liao, and Francisco González-Cos. The authors would like to acknowledge the efforts of many SAT officials, both active and retired, at modernizing China's tax administration over previous decades.

standardized computer system. These changes have helped to reduce tax evasion and compliance costs, and contributed to raising the tax yield to nearly 20 percent of GDP.

Today, China's tax administration finds itself at a new crossroads. The economy is again undergoing significant restructuring, major changes to the tax laws are currently underway, and the relatively easy gains from previous tax administration reforms have been largely reaped. At this juncture, it is useful to ask whether further improvements in tax administration are needed and, if so, what should be the priority areas for reform.

The next section summarizes the background to and impacts of China's tax administration reforms over the past 20 years. The chapter then describes the main features of China's tax administration today and how they have evolved since the early 1990s. It assesses the challenges now facing China's tax system in the following section, and the penultimate section suggests a number of reforms for the SAT to consider in formulating its new five-year modernization strategy. Lessons from SAT's reform experience conclude the chapter.

BACKGROUND

In the late 1970s, China embarked on a bold journey toward a market-oriented economy by opening up trade and investment with the rest of the world and restructuring the domestic economy. Mandatory planning was relaxed, market forces and the non-state sector were allowed to play a greater role in the economy, and the institutions for conducting macroeconomic policy were transformed. These reforms have contributed significantly to the massive structural transformation and rapid economic growth since the early 1980s (IMF 1993).

As the economic reforms unfolded, it became increasingly clear to policymakers that the existing tax system was incompatible with the requirements of an economy that relied increasingly on the market for the allocation of resources and would require a substantial overhaul. Similarly, it was also recognized that tax administration required fundamental changes if it were to effectively secure tax revenue from a new tax system in an increasingly market-oriented economy.

The need to modernize tax administration was made even more urgent by worrisome declines in both the tax-to-GDP ratio and the central government's share of total revenue during the early to mid-1990s. As can be seen in Table 3.1, the tax yield dropped by about 5½ percent of GDP during the period 1990–96, while the central government revenue share declined by nearly 12 percentage points from 1990–93.

The decline in the tax-to-GDP ratio can be traced to three main factors: (1) structural economic factors involving shifts in the different components of GDP, (2) discretionary changes in tax policy, and (3) changes in tax administration effectiveness. Although it is difficult to disentangle their relative importance, a 1997 IMF technical assistance mission found that these factors contributed to

Table 3.1. State Budget Tax Revenue to GDP and Share of Total Revenue 1990–96
(Percent)

	1990	1991	1992	1993	1994	1995	1996
Tax Revenue-to-GDP Ratio	15.1	13.7	12.2	12.0	10.6	9.9	9.7
Central Government Revenue-to-Total Revenue Ratio	33.8	29.8	28.1	22.0	55.7	52.2	49.4

Source: *China Statistical Yearbook* 2014; and IMF staff calculations.
Note: Tax revenue comprises both central and local government taxes. Central government revenue and total revenue include both tax and nontax revenue.

the decline in China's tax yield during the early to mid-1990s.[1] The impact of weak tax administration, which is the main concern of this chapter, was manifested through a growing incidence of tax evasion and the SAT's difficulties in controlling it. Some studies estimated that up to 30 percent of state-owned enterprises, 60 percent of joint ventures, 80 percent of private enterprises, and 100 percent of individual street vendors failed to comply with their tax obligations in the mid-1990s (Yu 1997).[2]

As for central government finances, the decline in its share of revenue during the early 1990s has been attributed mainly to the former intragovernmental revenue-sharing arrangements.[3] However, weak tax administration—in the form of loose central control over local tax offices—was also seen to have contributed to the decline. Prior to 1994, local governments played a major role in financing and directing the operations of the tax offices. As such, local authorities had strong incentive to concentrate revenue collection on local tax bases and shift the tax bases from those that had to be shared with the central government to those over which they had greater control (IMF 1994).

It was in this highly challenging environment of rising noncompliance and declining tax yields that the Chinese authorities launched a major tax administration modernization program in the mid-1990s as an integral part of a broader fiscal and tax reform program. The overriding objective for the tax administration

[1]Structural factors mainly involved: (1) the decreasing share of profits from (relatively highly taxed) state-owned enterprises (SOEs) to (more lightly taxed) non-SOEs; (2) a relative shift in value-added from goods to services, with the former having higher effective tax rates than the latter; and (3) an increase in the trade surplus, which reduced the tax base as exports are excluded (with some exceptions) from the value-added tax (VAT) base. Discretionary changes in tax policy involved: (1) transitional refunds that were provided to domestic enterprises and foreign-funded enterprises (in accordance with guarantees that their indirect tax burdens would not increase) when the new VAT was introduced in 1994, and (2) various tax incentives that were given to enterprises.

[2]Rampant tax evasion and weak tax administration were also widely reported in the Chinese media in the late 1980s and early 1990s, including Xinhua General Overseas News Services (1988).

[3]Prior to the 1994 revenue-sharing reforms, local governments were permitted to keep revenue above a stipulated amount. Under this arrangement, the amounts that local governments were to remit to the central government could be reduced by, for example, investing in local industries, offering tax exemptions, or placing resources in extrabudgetary funds that did not have to be shared with the center (Ahmad 2011).

reforms was to achieve sustainable increases in tax revenue by improving taxpayers' compliance with the tax laws. This objective was to be achieved by replacing the previous form of tax administration with new approaches that were better suited to the rapidly changing economy and tax system.

The modernization program began in 1994 with the splitting of the tax agency into two separate organizations: the National Tax Service (to collect central and most shared taxes) and Local Tax Services (to collect local government taxes and some shared taxes). Once the collection responsibilities for the various taxes were established, the focus of the reforms then shifted to designing and implementing new organizational arrangements, tax administration processes, and information systems.[4] These reforms have continued, at varying intensity, through today.

Since the introduction of the tax administration reforms, both the tax-to-GDP ratio and the central government share of total revenue have increased sharply. As shown in Figure 3.1, the tax-to-GDP ratio, after steadily declining in the early 1990s, increased by nearly 10 percentage points of GDP through the early 2010s, reaching 19.4 percent of GDP in 2013. Similarly, the central government share of revenue, which had fallen to 22 percent of total revenue in 1993 (Table 3.1), more than doubled by 1995 and has averaged about 50 percent of total revenue since then (Figure 3.1).

The steady increase in the tax-to-GDP ratio since the mid-late 1990s resulted from changes in the same three factors that accounted for the decline in the tax yield during the early 1990s: structural economic shifts, tax policy changes, and tax administration factors. While structural shifts in the economy[5] and tax policy changes[6] had important positive impacts, tax administration improvements also played a major role.[7] A 2007 IMF technical assistance mission estimated that the value-added tax (VAT) compliance ratio had increased from about 39 percent of potential VAT revenue in 1997 to 56 percent in 2005 (Figure 3.2).[8]

The tax yield, after steadily increasing for nearly two decades, posted its first decline in 2014, dropping to 18.7 percent of GDP as the economy slowed. Taxpayer compliance can be expected to come under pressure if the economy continues to grow slower than in past years. Maintaining compliance in the face of slower growth is one of the key challenges facing the SAT in the period ahead.

---

[4]These reforms were initially introduced in four pilot cities, then expanded to an additional 14 cities, and ultimately implemented on a national basis by the end of 2003.

[5]Structural factors center on the increasing share of the relatively highly taxed industry and service sectors (including construction and real estate) and the declining share of the lightly taxed agricultural sector (OECD 2013).

[6]Important tax policy changes included the 1994 expansion of the VAT base and the introduction of a new consumption (excise) tax (Lin 2009).

[7]These include reports by OECD (2013), Lin (2009), and World Bank (2003).

[8]The VAT compliance ratio is defined here as the ratio of actual VAT collections to an estimate of potential collections if taxpayers had fully complied with the provisions of the VAT law.

Figure 3.1 State Budget Tax Revenue to GDP and Share of Total Revenues (1990–2014)
(Percent)

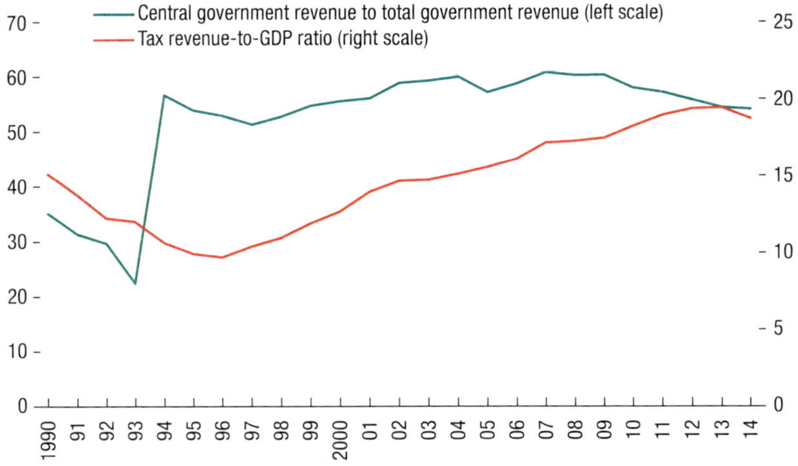

Sources: *China Statistical Yearbook* (various years); and IMF staff calculations.
Note: Tax revenue comprises both central and local government taxes.

Figure 3.2. Value-Added Tax Compliance Ratio
(Percent)

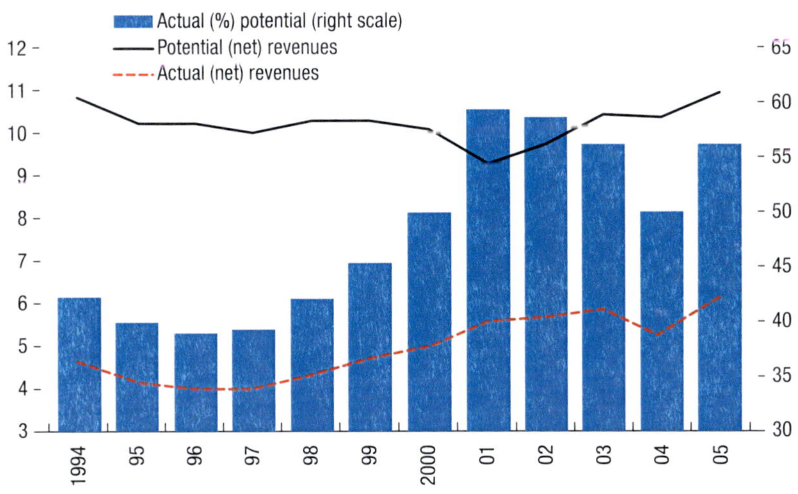

Source: IMF staff calculations.
Note: left scale: VAT actual and potential revenue as percent of GDP; right scale: VAT efficiency ratio in percent.

Table 3.2. Taxpayer Satisfaction Ratings
(Percent)

	2008		2010		2012		2014		2015	
	NTS	LTS	NTS	LTS	NTS	LTS	NTS	LTS	NTS	LTS
Score	76.2	77.7	79.1	79.2	79.8	79.7	82.6	81.5	82.8	81.2

Source: National Bureau of Statistics, State Administration of Taxation.
Note: LTS = local tax services, NTS = National Tax Service.

In addition to boosting tax revenue, there is also evidence that tax administration reform has reduced business compliance costs and improved taxpayers' perceptions about the tax system, particularly in recent years. Regarding the former, the amount of time that medium-sized Chinese companies spend on tax matters has been reduced from 832 hours in 2004 to 261 hours in 2013 (World Bank 2015).[9] Concerning the latter, taxpayer perception surveys conducted by the National Bureau of Statistics since 2008 indicate a steady increase in taxpayer satisfaction with the tax system (Table 3.2).

To the extent that the decrease in time spent on complying with the tax laws and increase in taxpayer satisfaction represent a reduction in compliance costs, it can be inferred that the tax administration reforms have had a positive impact on the business climate. Achieving further compliance cost reductions, as a vehicle for promoting economic growth, is another major challenge for the SAT in the period ahead.

TAX ADMINISTRATION TODAY

To set the stage for assessing the current challenges facing the State Administration of Taxation and for identifying future reform priorities, this section describes key features of tax administration today and how they've evolved over the past two decades.

Policy and Legal Framework

For many years, tax administration in China had been governed by various tax statutes, orders, and regulations whose scope and legal standing were unclear. This situation has been significantly improved by the enactment of the Law on the Administration of Tax Collection (henceforth, the Tax Collection Law) in 1992 and the continuous refinement of the substantive tax laws over the past two decades. These laws and their related regulations provide the policy and legal foundation for China's tax administration today.

[9]By comparison, the world average is 264 hours and the average for Asian and Pacific countries is 229 hours. Some countries have achieved lower times, for example: Australia (105 hours), Canada (131 hours), Denmark (25 hours), Singapore (82 hours), United Kingdom (94 hours), and the United States (175 hours). See World Bank 2015.

The Tax Collection Law establishes the common administrative provisions that apply to all of China's substantive tax laws (on VAT, enterprise income tax, and so on). These include the key rules for each tax administration function (such as registration, filing and payment of taxes, auditing, and so on), SAT's enforcement powers and penalty provisions, taxpayers' rights and obligations, and dispute resolution procedures.

The substantive tax laws provide the administrative authorities that are specific to each of China's 18 taxes. Among these, the Enterprise Income Tax Law is particularly important for tax administration by including both general[10] and specific[11] anti-avoidance provisions. Such provisions are essential for dealing with aggressive tax planning and tax avoidance schemes.

While the Tax Collection Law and the substantive tax laws vest the SAT with powerful tax administration tools, both require updating to deal with emerging challenges to China's tax system. In updating the laws, it is essential to achieve a balance between SAT's enforcement powers and the rights of taxpayers.

Taxpayer Population

China's taxpayer population has undergone significant changes over the past two decades with major implications for tax administration. Most profoundly, the total number of registered taxpayers with business income nearly tripled since 2000 (Table 3.3). To meet the resulting increase in workload, the SAT has introduced major changes to its core tax administration processes and information systems over the past 20 years, as described below.

A second important change has involved transformations in the forms of enterprise ownership (Table 3.4). During 2000–10 the numbers of private enterprises increased tenfold and enterprises from outside the mainland nearly tripled, while the state-owned enterprises (including collectives and cooperatives) declined substantially. With the growth in the private sector, the SAT has had to design new strategies and enhance the skills of its tax officers to ensure the compliance of a large number of private enterprises that respond to market incentives rather than incentives created by an economic plan.

[10]In December 2014, the SAT issued the *Administrative Measures for the General Anti-Avoidance Rules (Trial)*. Under these rules, Chinese tax authorities are authorized to counter transactions deemed to have no commercial purpose other than avoiding tax by re-characterizing the transaction and denying the tax benefits. To avoid its abuse, the tax authorities may not initiate an anti-avoidance investigation until it is approved by the SAT headquarters; headquarters must also approve the final decision of an investigation.

[11]Chapter VI of the Enterprise Income Tax law establishes the arm's length principle for valuing related party transactions, the requirement for taxpayers to report related party transactions to the tax authorities, and the tax authorities' power to adjust a taxpayer's taxable income if the taxpayer fails to comply with the arm's length principle.

Table 3.3. Number of Registered Taxpayers (National Tax System)

	Taxpayers			
	Total	Enterprises	Self-Employed	Other
2000	11,840,000	...	...	...
2005	14,730,000	4,990,000	9,710,000	30,000
2010	19,070,000	7,440,000	11,610,000	20,000
2014	30,760,000	13,740,000	16,950,000	70,000

Source: State Administration of Taxation.
Note: ... = not available.

Table 3.4. Number of Registered Industrial Enterprises
(Annual revenue over RMB5 million)

	2000	2010
Total	**162,855**	**452,872**
Domestic Funded	**134,440**	**378,872**
State-owned enterprises	42,426	8,726
Collectively owned enterprises	37,841	9,166
Cooperative enterprises	10,852	4,481
Private enterprises	22,128	273,259
Other	74,682	80,344
Enterprises with Funds from Hong Kong SAR; Macao, SAR; Taiwan, Province of China	**16,490**	**34,069**
Foreign Funded	**11,955**	**39,976**

Source: National Bureau of Statistics, *China Statistical Yearbook* (2001, 2011).
Note: Data are not presented after 2010 because the 2011 change in the enterprises covered (to those with annual revenue of more than RMB20 million as compared to RMB5 million before 2011) makes comparisons to earlier years misleading.

Organization

China's tax administration consists of two separate tax agencies: (1) a National Tax Service, which collects central government taxes and most taxes shared by central and local governments and (2) Local Tax Services, which collect local government taxes and some shared taxes.

As shown in Annex 3.1, the two tax services are organized into five levels of administration comprising SAT headquarters, provincial, municipal, and county/district offices, and tax stations. Under this setup, SAT headquarters has direct (solid line) authority for overseeing the operations of the National Tax Service as well as appointing and promoting its staff, and funding its budgets. SAT also shared (dotted line) authority with local governments for Local Tax Services. Accordingly, SAT is responsible for monitoring and supporting the Local Tax Services operational activities while local governments are responsible for appointing and promoting staff, and funding their budgets.

The national and local tax services collectively comprise some 750,000 staff in more than 30,000 locations (Table 3.5). A tax administration of this size faces enormous difficulties in designing and consistently applying its operational programs, human resource management policies, computer systems, and other activities. This is made even more difficult by the very small size of SAT headquarters relative to the rest of the organization. Whereas many effective tax agencies

Table 3.5. Number of Organizational Units and Staff by Level of Administration

	Number of Organizational Units		Number of Staff	
SAT Headquarters	1		850	
	National	Local	National	Local
Province-Level	36	35	13,286	13,416
Municipal-Level	353	332	63,580	60,777
Counties and Districts	3,020	2,584	212,049	141,651
Tax Stations	10,151	16,729	101,171	145,812
Total	13,561	19,680	390,086	361,656

Source: State Administration of Taxation (as of December 31, 2014).

commonly assign 3–10 percent of staff to their head office (IMF 2015), SAT headquarters has been allocated only about one-tenth of 1 percent of the organization's staff.

Tax Administration Processes

Prior to the mid-1990s, China had relied on an *administrative assessment* system for assessing, filing, and paying taxes. Under it, tax officers would help SOEs prepare their paper-based tax returns and tax payment forms. Other (non-SOE) taxpayers were required to file their tax returns and supporting documents at the tax office where a tax officer reviewed them in the taxpayer's presence. The inefficiencies of administrative assessment rendered it incompatible with a tax system in an increasingly market-oriented economy, with an increasing workload from a rapidly growing taxpayer population. It was also ineffective at redressing the rampant noncompliance that had contributed significantly to the decline in China's tax-to-GDP ratio during the early 1990s.

To improve compliance and increase administrative efficiency, the SAT replaced the administrative assessment system with *self-assessment*. Under it, taxpayers now prepare their own tax returns and make their own payments without the direct involvement of tax officers, subject to selective audits. To support self-assessment, SAT has continuously streamlined tax filing and payment procedures, enhanced taxpayer services and strengthened its enforcement programs.

The continuous improvements to SAT's core tax administration processes over the past 20 years have contributed importantly to the impressive gains made in taxpayer compliance, tax collection, and reducing business compliance costs as described previously. Achieving further gains in these areas will require enhancing the administrative processes to deal with the new challenges to the tax system.

Human Resources

The SAT has also made strong progress in strengthening its human resources over the past two decades. To enhance the skills of its *existing workforce*, the SAT's tax training academies (in 36 provinces and municipalities) provide induction and technical training to tax officers while its three national tax academies (in Changsha, Dalian, and Yangzhou) provide training to senior officials in selected topics (such as transfer pricing). To enhance the quality of *new staff*, the SAT has built up its cadre of university-trained officers: whereas in 1992 less than 5 percent of staff had university degrees, this proportion had increased to 60 percent in 2014.

While the SAT has succeeded in building an increasingly capable workforce, it has had less success at strengthening other important elements of its human resource management regime. In particular, the SAT's position classification, staff evaluation, and promotion/salary policies have, until very recently, remained largely unchanged and tied to government-wide civil service regulations. Progress in these areas will be crucial to raising the productivity and ethical standing of the SAT workforce in the future. At the same time, SAT's skills enhancement program must provide managers and officers with the requisite skills to implement the agency's key reform priorities and deal with emerging challenges.

Information Systems

The SAT has evolved from a tax agency whose operations were based mainly on low-productivity, manual processes to one that relies increasingly on modern technologies and systems. It has reached this state by having made major investments over many years in its two backbone information systems: (1) the China Tax Administration Information System (CTAIS) and (2) the Golden Tax Project (GTP).

CTAIS is the SAT's core tax administration information system whose nationwide implementation was a major achievement for China's tax administration. The system provides automated support for the core tax administration functions (registration, tax returns and payment processing, taxpayer accounts, and others) for the main central government taxes and shared taxes. It also provides a platform for the tax administration to coordinate its activities with banks (on tax payments) and the national treasury. The system was first developed in 1999 and is now deployed at all tax offices across the country.

GTP is a specialized computer system for detecting and dealing with VAT invoice fraud, which has plagued China's tax administration for many years. It consists of four subsystems: (1) an invoice generation system in which VAT taxpayers use SAT proprietary software and hardware to generate invoices that include a numerical cipher, (2) an invoice certification system that permits taxpayers to claim a VAT input credit only after the SAT has authenticated their purchase invoices by decrypting the ciphers, (3) a cross-checking system that compares sales invoices (submitted by sellers) to purchase invoices (submitted by buyers) and forwards mismatches for investigation, and (4) an investigation system that coordinates follow-up actions on potentially fraudulent invoices (Winn and Zhang 2013).

CTAIS and the Golden Tax Project have provided vital pillars for improving the effectiveness and efficiency of tax administration. The government has recognized their important contributions to increasing revenue performance.[12] The SAT is currently implementing the GTP Phase 3 to replace CTAIS and, in doing so, provide automated support for all taxes (both central and local), include a broader set of tax administration applications (including risk management), and, crucially, tie together the provincial-level databases into a national network of taxpayer information. The successful deployment of this system[13] and further improvements to the VAT system will be crucial to the effective administration of the tax system in the future.

EMERGING CHALLENGES AND OPPORTUNITIES

The SAT faces significant challenges in ensuring the health of the tax system over the next five years. These take two broad forms: (1) external challenges that emanate from the SAT's operating environment and (2) internal challenges from within the SAT itself. There are also a number of opportunities that the SAT could exploit to enhance its operations. Identifying both the challenges and opportunities, as described in this section, is a key first step in setting the SAT's future reform priorities as described in the next section.

External

The SAT is operating in an increasingly complex external environment. Key challenges include slowing economic growth, structural shifts in the economy, and China's continuing integration into the global economy—all of which present heightened risks of lost revenue from noncompliance by taxpayers. Further challenges include the implementation of an ambitious tax reform agenda and the need to promote the business climate by reducing the compliance costs of the tax system.

Slower Economic Growth

China's slowing economy, from double digit to single digit growth under the so-called *new normal*, could have significant implications for tax administration. The economic slowdown can be expected to reduce the rapid growth in tax revenue that had been achieved in previous years. The revenue decline is not a concern in itself to the extent it reflects the normal operation of automatic stabilizers, but would pose a problem for tax administration if it causes a decline in taxpayer compliance. The latter can occur because economic stress creates incentives for distressed taxpayers to use tax evasion as an alternative form of finance for their

[12]Former SAT Commissioner Mr. Renqing Jin reported at a tax conference on information systems in August 2002 that the incidence of fraud-related activities was greatly reduced since the GTP2 system was fully introduced in mid-2001. For example, the detection rate of fraud-related invoices decreased from 8.51 percent in February 2001 to 0.06 percent in mid-2002.

[13]GTP Phase 3 is scheduled to be deployed at all tax offices by the end of 2016.

operations and a means to avoid bankruptcy (Brondolo 2009; CASE 2013).[14] Compliance declines can be expected to differ across industries in line with their relative declines in economic activity. From this perspective, the SAT will need to give special attention to those industries most impacted by the slowdown such as industrial commodities (for example, steel, real estate, and mining).

The economic slowdown will also make it more important than ever to ensure that the tax administration avoids unnecessarily impeding the business climate. Although the SAT has taken many steps to reduce compliance costs over the past several years, Chinese businesses still spend more time dealing with tax matters than taxpayers from comparator countries in the Asia Pacific region and far more time than taxpayers in countries with high-performing tax agencies. A substantial portion of these costs is associated with the administration of the VAT: in 2006, more than 40 percent of the costs incurred by Chinese taxpayers in meeting their tax obligations were attributed to handling VAT special invoices (Xu 2006).

Structural Changes in the Economy

Structural shifts in the economy can also be expected to pose additional challenges for the SAT in the coming five years. Three of the more significant shifts involve the increasing contribution of the services sector, the growing volume of cross-provincial transactions, and a sharp increase in electronic commerce.

Regarding services, this sector is expected to continue to grab a growing share of the economy.[15] This trend will present two particularly significant challenges to tax collection. First, the services sector in China comprises larger numbers of small and unincorporated businesses, as compared to the industry sector (Rosen and Bao 2015), many of which have low rates of tax compliance. Second, the expected growth in the financial services industry and the introduction of new financial products will raise complex tax issues that will require increasing attention to ensure their correct tax treatment.

The increase in cross-provincial transactions presents further challenges to tax administration. Large businesses and high-wealth individuals in China are increasingly carrying out economic activities in multiple provinces. This increase in cross-provincial transactions is in contrast with the SAT's decentralized tax administration—with little exchange of information among the provincial tax

---

[14]Recent experience, in Western countries and China alike, provides evidence that taxpayer compliance tends to worsen in an economic and tight credit conditions. During the global financial crisis, noncompliance with the value-added tax increased in nearly all European Union countries and tended to worsen most where the output contraction was greatest (IMF 2015). In China, a study of close to 190,000 Chinese industrial firms (Cai and Liu 2009) found that corporate income tax evasion is negatively correlated with access to credit.

[15]The State Council's Development Research Center forecasts the service sector share of GDP to increase from its 2011–15 average of 47.6 percent to an average of 51.6 percent during 2016–20, while its share of employment is expected to increase from 42.0 percent to 47.6 percent over the same period (World Bank and Development Research Center of the State Council 2012).

bureaus—and points to the need for a more national approach to administering highly mobile taxpayers.

China's rapid growth in electronic commerce (e-commerce) presents a third, major structural shift in the economy and a growing challenge to tax administration. In 2000 China had yet to develop any significant e-commerce applications and had only 2.1 million Internet users. By the end of 2013, Chinese Internet users reached approximately 600 million and e-commerce growth had topped 70 percent annually from 2009 to 2012. By 2020, China's e-commerce market is forecasted to be larger than those of France, Germany, Japan, United Kingdom, and the United States combined (KPMG 2014).

The growth in e-commerce has been accompanied by the development of new business models, which commonly feature a third-party facilitator who operates an online platform, arranges a sale of a good or service between a producer and consumer of a good or service, and charges a fee.[16] The boom in e-commerce and new business models will confront the SAT with the challenges of identifying online transactions, determining the nature and value of the transactions, and establishing the taxable persons.

Globalization

China has a worldwide income tax system under which its residents—both corporations and individuals—are taxed on income from sources both within China and outside China (with credit for taxes paid on foreign income) and nonresidents are taxed on income only from sources within China. Since the country opened up its economy to trade and investment with the rest of the world in the late 1970s, the Chinese tax system has faced the risk of cross-border tax avoidance and evasion. As mainly a capital-importing country until recent years, the international tax risks have centered on guarding against offshore profit shifting by foreign-funded enterprises that invested in China. These included such risks as transfer pricing, thin capitalization, and indirect transfer of Chinese assets.

With China having now become an increasingly capital-exporting country, the nature of the international tax risks that it faces is changing.[17] While transfer pricing continues to be a central issue, the SAT must now be concerned not only with transfer pricing practices of foreign enterprises in China but also those practices of Chinese-owned subsidiaries in other jurisdictions. Other emerging international risks include cross-border restructuring of Chinese businesses (such as

[16]In China, the new business models include both consumer-to-consumer transactions (such as the Taobao company) and business-to-consumer transactions (such as Alibaba, JD, and Tmall companies). In addition to selling goods, the new business models also deal in services such as "ride-sourcing" where a third-party facilitator arranges for a fee a driver who uses his/her car to transport passengers for a fare (such as Uber and Didi Kuaidi companies). For further information see Consulate General of the Kingdom of the Netherlands in Guangzhou (2015).

[17]China's stock of outbound direct foreign investment increased from 1.1 percent of GDP in 1990 to 6.6 percent of GDP in 2013 (UNCTAD 2015).

acquiring foreign companies and corporate inversions), deferred recognition of income by Chinese companies from their foreign subsidiaries in low-tax jurisdictions, unreported overseas income and assets by Chinese residents,[18] and various aggressive tax planning schemes.[19] The SAT will need to adapt its international compliance programs, in cooperation with other jurisdictions, to deal with these and other similar risks.

New Tax Legislation

The government's tax reform agenda presents additional challenges for the SAT. Over the next five years, major reforms are planned for six taxes: value-added tax, excise tax, resource tax, environment protection tax, property tax, and individual income tax. Such an ambitious reform program will require a major implementation effort by the SAT: taxpayers (especially individuals) will need to be educated in their new obligations, new administrative systems and procedures will need to ensure taxpayers comply with their obligations, and tax officers will require training in applying the new legislation and compliance procedures.

Along with the external challenges, there are also a number of opportunities emanating from the tax system's external environment that the SAT could exploit to strengthen tax administration over the coming years. Most importantly, the Communist Party of China's Central Committee Leadership Group to Comprehensively Deepen Reform has given high-level political support for tax administration reform when it passed on October 13, 2015, the Plan to Deepen Reform of the National and Local Tax Administration System.

Internationally, the growing cooperation among countries in exchanging tax information, both through bilateral and multilateral arrangements, provides the SAT with new opportunities for tackling cross-border tax evasion.

Internal

The increasingly complex environment facing the tax system will put pressures on the SAT's internal administrative capacity. Potential vulnerabilities include the SAT's organizational structure, staff skills, and information systems. The SAT will need to strengthen its capacity in each of these areas to deal with the emerging challenges that it faces.

---

[18]The underreporting can take a wide range of forms from individuals not reporting overseas financial income to Chinese tour operators that fail to report income earned from their overseas tours.

[19]For example, the United States, which also operates a worldwide tax system, has encountered aggressive tax planning schemes that sought to repatriate overseas profits to the United States without causing a U.S. taxable event. This can be done by various schemes including by arranging for the foreign subsidiary of a U.S. company to purchase the stock of its U.S. parent, as part of a triangular reorganization, instead of paying the parent an outright dividend that would be subject to U.S. income tax (IRS 2006).

Organizational Stresses

The SAT's current organizational and staffing arrangements, which have evolved incrementally over the past two decades, have a number of stress points that present risks to the agency's capacity to deal with emerging challenges and implement its modernization strategy. These organizational stresses are manifested in four main areas:

- The small size of SAT headquarters hinders its capacity to design and implement national and international compliance strategies precisely at a time when Chinese taxpayers are increasingly engaging in cross-provincial and overseas taxable activities.
- The very large network of tax offices—while facilitating close support and monitoring of taxpayers—is costly to maintain and presents serious difficulties in managing, ensuring uniform administration, and avoiding collusion.
- The creation of separate national and local tax services—although providing a dedicated organizational focus for collecting national and local taxes, respectively—has had the disadvantages of high budgetary costs for the government (from maintaining two separate agencies) and additional compliance costs for taxpayers (who must deal with two separate agencies in carrying out their tax obligations).
- The SAT's hybrid organizational structure—where staff are organized into units based partly on tax type, partly on type of taxpayer, and partly on tax administration function—has resulted in fragmentation of administrative responsibilities across the organization. This fragmentation is particularly pronounced and harmful in the areas of auditing and large taxpayer administration.

In addressing the above stress points, it is important to recognize that organizational restructuring is always very challenging, particularly for a large tax agency like the SAT. This suggests that priority should be given to implementing those organizational and staffing changes that are most critical to the successful delivery of the SAT's modernization strategy.

Achieving Greater Uniformity in Administration

The effective operation of a national market economy is influenced by the extent to which the tax system is applied in a uniform manner across the country. Notwithstanding the progress that the SAT has achieved over the past two decades in harmonizing its tax administration practices across China, there continue to be differences in the way the tax laws are applied from province to province and city to city.

To some extent, inconsistencies in administration and service delivery are inevitable in a very large country with a decentralized tax agency and weak communications, particularly where the tax agency has a very small headquarters as is presently the case in China. Nevertheless, such inconsistencies can be harmful to the economy by distorting competition across (and within) jurisdictions and industries. They can also raise serious questions in the eyes of taxpayers about the fairness of the tax system if tax laws are applied differently in different locations. With the government seeking to promote the business environment and the rule of law, it is increasingly important for the SAT to achieve greater standardization and consistency in the application of the tax laws.

Critical Skills Gaps

Ultimately, the SAT's capacity to effectively administer the tax system depends on the skills of its managers and staff. While it has steadily strengthened the quality of its workforce over many years, significant skill gaps remain in some important areas, particularly among auditors. Future reform initiatives, such as planned amendments to the Tax Collection Law and other changes in tax legislation, will create further demands for skills enhancement.

In this situation, the SAT needs to identify its key skill gaps and formulate a comprehensive strategy for closing them. Importantly, these efforts need to be directed not only at strengthening the SAT's technical skills but also at improving the capacities of its senior executives and managers. To achieve the best results, the SAT will need to adopt a broad range of skills enhancement approaches and technologies.

Weaknesses in Information Systems

Tax administration is an inherently information-intensive activity where appropriate data and well-designed analytics are critical to the effective administration of the tax system. While the SAT has made great strides in deploying a standardized information system across a large network of tax offices, it has not yet fully realized the potential benefits of information technology. Key weaknesses include the lack of national databases of taxpayer information, the absence of third-party information, and the high compliance costs that some of the SAT's computer systems impose on taxpayers.

In addressing these internal challenges, the SAT could also leverage a number of opportunities to advance tax administration reform. The stability in its leadership—particularly among its commissioners and deputy commissioners—has provided a continuity in reform management that is crucial for implementing medium-term reforms. In addition, various ongoing tax administration reforms—to the SAT's legal framework, administrative processes, and computer systems—provide a strong foundation for future modernization. Crucially, the Chinese leadership has explicitly given its political support to the SAT's modernization strategy as described in the next section.

FUTURE REFORM PRIORITIES

Tax administration reform has an important role to play in supporting the government's economic reform agenda under the 13th Five-Year Plan (2016–20) by mobilizing adequate revenue to pay for high-priority public sector expenditure and helping to promote the business climate. To contribute to these objectives, this section suggests measures that the SAT may consider incorporating into its tax administration modernization strategy for the next five years.

State Administration of Taxation's Modernization Program

The importance of tax administration reform has been recognized at the highest level of the Chinese government. The 13th Five-Year Plan has reinforced the earlier call by the Third Plenum of the 18th Central Committee on the need to strengthen the collection of national and local taxes.[20] The SAT has translated the government's high-level policy goals into a more detailed *Blueprint for Deepening the Reform of Tax Administration*.

The blueprint sets four overarching objectives for tax administration reform: (1) reduce tax collection cost and compliance burdens, (2) increase the efficiency of tax administration, (3) strengthen the awareness of tax compliance, and (4) improve taxpayer satisfaction. These four objectives are underpinned by 31 initiatives that are grouped under six headings.[21] Importantly, this reform agenda has been endorsed by the highest levels of the Chinese government.[22]

By early 2016, the SAT intends to develop a five-year action plan for implementing the blueprint in a step-by-step manner by 2020. In this context, the balance of this section provides guidance on a number of key reform initiatives that the SAT may consider in formulating its action plan.

Amending the Tax Collection Law

The Tax Collection Law (TCL) is crucial to the operation of China's tax system as it sets out the common administrative provisions that apply to all of its substantive tax laws. Updating the TCL, which has had only minor amendments since its enactment in 1992, is a key prerequisite for strengthening tax administration by ensuring the SAT has the legal authorities needed to implement its modernization strategy and deal with emerging challenges.

In amending the TCL, the government should ensure that the revisions achieve an appropriate balance between the powers of the tax authorities and the rights of taxpayers. The former would provide the SAT with the powers needed

[20]See *The Significance of and Guiding Thoughts on Deepening the Reform Comprehensively* as adopted at the Third Plenary Session of the 18th Central Committee of the Communist Party of China on November 12, 2013. Also refer to the *Plan to Deepen the Fiscal Reform* issued by the CPC Politburo on June 30, 2014.

[21]The six headings are (1) streamline the division of responsibilities for tax collection and administration, (2) innovative tax service payment mechanism, (3) transform the tax collection and administration approaches, (4) proactively participate in international cooperation on tax matters, (5) optimization on the tax organizational structure, and (6) establish a joint governance mechanism for tax administration.

[22]The blueprint has been approved by the Central Committee of the Communist Party of China's (CCCPC) Leading Group of Deepening Reform and promulgated by the General Office of the CCCPC and the General Office of the State Council.

to safeguard tax revenue while the latter would help promote the investment environment by providing businesses with greater protections and certainty on the tax treatment of their transactions.

Several amendments are needed to strengthen the SAT's enforcement powers. First, the amendments need to make clear that the TCL is not limited to enterprises, as is currently the case with some key provisions, but also applies broadly to all taxpayers. Second, the law needs to require private sector third parties—including financial institutions and other income payers[23]—to provide the SAT with tax-related information as well as facilitate the SAT's receipt of tax information from other government agencies.[24] Third, the SAT's arrears collection powers need to be enhanced, including by vesting the organization with the power to impose a tax lien on the property of tax debtors, require third parties who owe money to (or hold money on behalf of) a tax debtor to pay some portion of the monies owed (or held) to the SAT in satisfaction of the tax debt, and extend the length of time for eligible tax debtors to pay their arrears installments.

Other amendments are needed to enhance taxpayers' protections. Importantly, the provisions governing the confidentiality of taxpayer information need to be strengthened, taxpayers should be provided with a comprehensive set of procedural protections, and clear guidelines issued on how tax bureaus should apply the law's penalty provisions.[25] The current requirement for taxpayers to pay 100 percent of a disputed tax assessment before they can file an administrative review should be eliminated[26] and replaced by a provision that requires taxpayers to pay only some percentage of the disputed tax liability. In addition, the SAT should have the power to provide taxpayers, upon request, with a binding ruling on how the tax law applies to a particular transaction. Finally, steps need to be taken to ensure that the SAT's administrative review organ has greater independence from the rest of the organization (as described in the next section).

The SAT and Ministry of Finance in November 2014 jointly submitted draft amendments to the TCL to the State Council. During 2015, the SAT coordinated with the Legislative Affairs Office of the State Council in reviewing and addressing comments received from a wide cross section of society, held expert panel discussions, and did further research on improving the TCL. It is expected

[23]The tax laws in some countries vest the tax agency with the authority to require certain persons in highly noncompliant industries to report information to the tax agency on their payments to other persons in the industry. For example, some countries require general contractors in the construction industry to report to the tax agency payments to their subcontractors.

[24]In other countries, the implementation arrangements for exchanging information with other government agencies is commonly set out in a memorandum of understanding between the agencies.

[25]The procedural protections could include, for example, establishing standards and timelines for the tax authorities to issue notices to taxpayers and decide on an administrative review.

[26]Interest should accrue in favor of the tax agency on the percentage of the tax liability not paid by the taxpayer and in favor of the taxpayer on the amount of the tax liability paid to the tax agency, depending on the outcome of the dispute.

that the amendments will be enacted during 2017, which will be crucial for keeping the SAT's modernization program on track.

Aligning the Organizational Modernization Strategy

The successful implementation of the SAT's modernization strategy depends critically on ensuring that its organizational structure is aligned with and supportive of the modernization strategy. In this connection, the SAT would benefit from rationalizing its current organizational structure, strengthening headquarters, consolidating the large network of tax stations, and establishing effective organizational arrangements for administering large businesses and high-wealth individuals.

Over the past 20 years, the SAT's organizational structure has evolved in an ad hoc manner with new departments created to deal with emerging priorities. For example, in 2008 the SAT created a new Taxpayer Services Department and Large Business Department with a view to improving its taxpayer services programs and strengthening the administration of large enterprise groups. A consequence of the organization's ad hoc evolution is that the administrative responsibilities have become increasingly fragmented across the SAT's departments. The formulation of the SAT's modernization strategy provides both an opportunity and a need for the SAT to review its existing organizational arrangements, with a view to achieving greater coherence and efficiency.

As a starting point, the SAT needs to identify the key aims of its modernization strategy and then ensure that they are appropriately reflected in its organizational structure. For example, if the strategy is intended to provide more customized administration to different taxpayer segments—large businesses, medium businesses, small businesses, and high-wealth individuals—then the organizational structure should provide a clear accountability for each key taxpayer segment. Similarly, if the strategy seeks to better protect taxpayers' rights then it would be important to ensure that the SAT's administrative review function is organized in a way that provides it with a high degree of independence from the rest of the SAT.

A second organizational imperative is to clarify the division of responsibilities for the main tax administration functions. On this issue, it is essential to eliminate the current fragmentation of administrative functions that currently exists across the SAT. This is particularly important for the audit function where several departments are authorized to conduct examinations.[27] Similarly, the administration of national and local taxes needs to be better coordinated—for example, by setting up joint tax service halls, co-locating the service counters in the public service centers of local governments, or establishing liaison counters in the tax

[27]Responsibility for the audit function could be allocated as follows: (1) the tax bureaus should examine individuals, small businesses, and medium-sized businesses; (2) the Large Business Department should examine large businesses; and (3) the Inspection Bureaus should investigate serious violations of the tax laws, including those involving fraud and evasion.

service halls of the national and local tax bureaus—to achieve greater efficiencies in administration and reduce compliance burdens for taxpayers.

The extremely small size of the SAT's headquarters relative to its overall staff is a third organizational issue that needs to be addressed. The small headquarters creates a huge impediment to designing, monitoring, and supporting national tax administration programs as well as ensuring their consistent application. While these shortcomings were not a major problem when the economy and tax system were highly provincial-centric, the need for a larger and stronger headquarters has become more important as both have become increasingly national and international in scope. The best solution to this problem would be to gradually increase the number of headquarters staff over time. A second-best approach would be to designate certain municipalities as "centers of excellence" that, under the supervision of SAT headquarters, would be responsible for designing and implementing various national programs.

Along with strengthening headquarters, there is also a need to consolidate the more than 10,000 grassroots' tax stations. While this wide office network provides convenience for taxpayers and allows close monitoring by tax offices, these advantages come at the cost of huge administrative inefficiencies (because the small tax stations are not conducive to specialization), difficulties in ensuring consistent administration, and risks of collusion (due to close contacts between taxpayers and tax officers).[28] With the growing capacity of the SAT's telephone contact centers and its electronic services, substantial efficiencies could be gained without significant losses in convenience and monitoring by consolidating smaller tax stations into larger ones, particularly in urban areas.

An additional organizational issue is the need to strengthen the administration of two critical taxpayer segments: large businesses and high-wealth individuals. Both of these segments account for a large share of tax revenue,[29] have growing volumes of cross-provincial and overseas transactions, and deal with some of the more complex provisions in the tax laws. For these reasons, a strong organizational focus with a national span of control is required to manage their compliance.

For large businesses, the SAT took an important step toward strengthening administration with the creation of the Large Business Department in 2008. Despite this important reform, the department's potential for safeguarding revenue and promoting the business climate has not yet been fully exploited because the department does not have full administrative authority over large businesses but instead shares its authorities with other SAT departments. This situation

---

[28]See IMF 2015 for a description of the disadvantages of too large a network of local tax offices and the potential benefits from streamlined office networks.

[29]The SAT estimates that the largest 45 large enterprise groups account for about 22 percent of the SAT's tax collection while another 300–400 enterprise groups are estimated to account for an additional 20 percent of SAT revenue. In 2012 the top 10 percent of households accounted for about 50 percent of market income and a somewhat lower share of personal income taxes (based on data from the National Bureau of Statistics of China and China Household Finance Survey).

could be improved by expanding the Large Business Department headquarters' authority in overseeing the provincial Large Business Departments.[30] It would also help to vest the department with exclusive responsibility for auditing and issuing tax assessments to large businesses[31] and to increase substantially the number of staff assigned to the department's headquarters, provincial, and municipal departments.

For high-wealth individuals, the SAT has not yet created a special organizational focal point for this important group of taxpayers. Despite their increasingly national and international scope of activities, wealthy individuals are currently administered separately by each local tax office where they receive income. Consequently, the SAT cannot easily monitor their tax activities across provinces and overseas. This weakness could be addressed by creating a specialized high-wealth individuals' unit similar to that of (and, possibly, incorporated within) the Large Business Department.[32] This unit would be responsible for a range of tax administration functions for high-wealth individuals, including taxpayer services, risk assessment, and audit. It would comprise a centralized high-wealth individuals unit at SAT headquarters to oversee, coordinate, and provide technical support to high-wealth individuals units at the provincial or municipal levels.

Extending the SAT's National and International Reach

China's large size, diversity, and intragovernmental revenue-sharing regime has necessarily led to a decentralized system of tax administration. Under this system, taxpayers are administered separately in each province where they earn income, with insufficient coordination across provinces or, in some cases, even within provinces. This decentralized, provincial-centric approach is becoming increasingly incompatible with the growing number of enterprises and individuals with taxable activities that stretch across provincial borders and overseas.

On the domestic front, protecting China's tax bases in the face of increasing cross-provincial transactions will require the adoption of a more national approach to tax administration.[33] Such an approach depends on, among other

[30]An intermediate step may be to arrange for the Large Business Tax Departments in a small number of large municipalities to fall under the direct management of the headquarters' Large Business Tax Department in the same way that some the large enterprise groups in Beijing are administered.

[31]Ideally, the municipal-level Large Business Tax Departments would be designated as a "bureau" in which case they would operate as a separate tax office (with a broad set of administrative authorities for large businesses) instead of one of several "departments" within a municipal tax bureau (with lesser authorities) as is currently the case.

[32]Because high-wealth individuals often have significant ownership stakes in large businesses, some tax agencies place their high-wealth individuals unit within the large business department.

[33]The need for a national approach to tax administration will be further amplified by the authorities' plans to reform the personal income tax by replacing the current schedular system (where different income categories are taxed under separate schedules) with a more comprehensive system (where some income categories—including those earned in different provinces—are aggregated and taxed under a common schedule).

things, three important preconditions: (1) a nationally standardized tax identification number, (2) a centralized database of taxpayer and third party information, and (3) effective organizational arrangements for coordinating the cross-provincial (and overseas) administration of taxpayers.

A nationally standardized taxpayer identification number is crucial to the creation of a national tax administration by tying together individuals' and businesses' tax-related information across locations as well as over time and in relation to other taxpayers. Recognizing this, the SAT is adopting a new identification number for enterprises as part of a whole-of-government reform to business registration. Similar effort will be needed to strengthen the identification system for individual taxpayers.

A second important precondition involves the creation of centralized master-files[34] of taxpayer and third-party information. Since it is not feasible, under current conditions, to immediately create such centralized information depositories for all enterprises and individuals, priority should be given to those taxpayers who are most likely to have cross-provincial and overseas income. Accordingly, the creation of national master-files should begin with large enterprises and high-wealth individuals since these persons tend to carry out more taxable activities in multiple locations than other persons.

A third prerequisite is to establish proper organizational arrangements for coordinating the administration of large enterprises and high-wealth individuals across different locations. As mentioned earlier, coordination could be improved by leveraging the SAT's Large Business Tax Department and by creating a new, high-wealth individuals unit at headquarters and the provincial/municipal levels.

On the international front, China's large and growing volume (and complexity) of international transactions poses substantial risks to tax collection through cross-border base erosion and profit shifting (BEPS) by businesses and individuals. In addressing the international tax risks posed by businesses, a key priority involves implementing the package of 15 measures in the BEPS action plan that has been developed by the OECD and G20 countries (OECD 2015a). This will require introducing changes to China's domestic legislation and the SAT's administrative practices as well as tax treaty provisions. In making these changes, the SAT will give particular attention to the following BEPS measures:

- Improve the transfer pricing rules—which govern the valuation of transactions within a multinational enterprise group—to better align the apportionment of profits across the entities in the group with the economic activities that generate the profits. This will require revisions to the SAT's *Implementation Measures of Special Tax Adjustments (Circular No. 2).*

[34]A taxpayer "master-file" refers to a database of tax-related accounts information for each taxpayer (type of taxes that they are liable to pay, frequency of filing and payment, amounts of tax paid and owed, assessment of additional tax, interest, penalties, and so on).

- Introduce a country-by-country reporting regime that will require China-based parents of large multinational enterprise groups to file with the SAT an annual report containing tax-related information for each jurisdiction in which the groups do business and for the SAT to share this information with other tax agencies. Implementing this regime will require revising Circular No. 2 (referred to above) and signing the Country-by-Country Multilateral Competent Authority Agreement.
- Incorporate anti-abuse provisions into China's tax treaties with other countries. These will include adopting a new definition of permanent establishment (PE)—the existence of which entitles a country to tax the profits of a foreign enterprise—to prevent the artificial avoidance of PE status, for example, by replacing distributors with commissionaire arrangements. The SAT intends to introduce these changes through both bilateral renegotiations of China's tax treaties and the adoption of a new multilateral instrument.
- Improve the operation of the mutual agreement procedure (MAP), which is a mechanism that tax agencies use to resolve tax treaty-related disputes (typically involving double taxation) between taxpayers and tax agencies. The SAT will strengthen its capacity in this area by allocating additional resources—including personnel, funding, and training—to its MAP function.

In addition to above international issues, the SAT will also need to pay greater attention to the tax risks associated with the increasing overseas investments by Chinese enterprises, including those involving income shifting to foreign subsidiaries in low-tax jurisdictions, improper deferral of Chinese tax by claiming that income generated by their foreign subsidiaries is not subject to current taxation in China under China's rules on controlled foreign corporations, improper claiming of foreign tax credits, and avoidance of Chinese tax by repatriating cash from controlled foreign corporations without recognizing dividend income. Controlling these risks will require changes in China's tax legislation and strengthening the SAT's international compliance programs.

In mitigating international tax risks posed by individuals, a crucial task will be to implement the multilateral and bilateral exchange of information agreements that China has entered into with other jurisdictions.[35] These agreements require, among other things, foreign financial institutions to report to the SAT information and assets held by Chinese taxpayers (and Chinese financial institutions to report the same information on foreign taxpayers to foreign tax agencies). Putting these agreements into operation will require, among other things, translating their

[35]China signed the Multi-lateral Convention on Mutual Administrative Assistance in Tax Matters on August 23, 2013, and on December 16, 2015, ratified the Multi-lateral Competent Authority Agreement on automatic exchange of information. China also entered into an agreement in substance to the bilateral exchange information with the United States in relation to the United States Foreign Tax Account Compliance Act on June 26, 2014.

reporting and due diligence requirements into domestic law, creating the administrative and information technology infrastructure needed to collect and exchange information, and establishment of confidentiality safeguards on the use of the information.

Expanding the Use of Compliance Risk Management

Over the next five years, China's tax system will face a range of new and complex compliance risks. Some risks, such as those discussed in this chapter, have already been identified; other risks not presently known may arise in the future. To safeguard revenue in an environment fraught with many complex risks, the SAT needs to fully develop a compliance risk management approach to tax administration.

In essence, compliance risk management provides a systematic approach to identifying and ranking the major tax compliance risks, developing a comprehensive set of treatments for mitigating the risks, and establishing a set of indicators to assess the treatments' impact on the risks identified. Leading tax agencies typically develop compliance management strategies at three levels:

- Tax level, by identifying the most material compliance risks facing each major tax (irrespective of market segment or industry)
- Segment level, by identifying the major compliance risks that are prevalent to relatively homogenous groups of taxpayers (such as large, medium-sized, and small businesses, and high-wealth individuals) and, in some cases, for important industries within those segments
- Taxpayer level, by evaluating the risk posture of individual enterprises and persons.

In recent years, the SAT has taken important first steps toward developing a risk management approach to tax administration. Beginning with the large taxpayer segment, the SAT has piloted the development of compliance management strategies at the taxpayer level.[36] This assigns each taxpayer into one of three risk categories—high, medium, and low—and then applies different treatments depending on their risk level. Building on this, the SAT issued the *SAT Opinion Concerning the Strengthening of Tax Risk Management Work* in September 2014. This is intended to standardize tax risk management nationally by establishing uniform approaches for risk identification, rating and ranking risks, risk treatments, and evaluation and feedback.

In the period ahead, it will be important for the SAT to extend its risk management approach, beyond assessing the risks of individual taxpayers, to identifying and dealing with major compliance risks at the tax level and taxpayer segment level. In doing so, a separate compliance management strategy should be developed for each major tax (such as individual income, enterprise income,

[36]In addition to large businesses, the SAT is piloting the development of risk management strategies for other taxpayer segments in Jiangsu and Henan provinces.

value-added) and major taxpayer segments within each tax (such as large taxpayers, high-wealth individuals, and small businesses). As an example, Annex 3.2 provides a high-level illustration of a compliance management strategy for a taxpayer segment (in this case, medium-sized businesses) that the IMF assisted in developing for another country's tax agency.

To ensure appropriate headquarters direction and oversight, it would be useful to assign a senior headquarters official with the responsibility for designing and overseeing the implementation of each compliance management strategy.[37] To facilitate coordination among the provincial tax bureaus, the SAT could establish a national compliance management steering committee, chaired by headquarters and including the tax heads of selected provinces, to approve the compliance strategies and coordinate cross-provincial activities (such as cross-provincial audits). To avoid conflicts and duplication of work, it would also be important for all departments to adopt a common risk management framework, which should be applied in a coordinated manner to cover all of the SAT's compliance improvement activities (such as taxpayer services, audit, arrears collection, proposed legislative changes, and so on).

Enhancing Core Tax Administration Processes

The SAT's core tax administration processes—including those involving registration, taxpayer services, audit, arrears collection, and dispute resolution—need to be enhanced to deal with emerging tax compliance risks and to exploit the new legal authorities that the SAT is expected to be granted under the planned amendments to the Tax Collection Law. It is also important to ensure that the administrative processes—and, hence, the tax laws—are applied in a more uniform matter across China than is currently the case so as to achieve a level playing field among taxpayers and to avoid distorting economic activities.

To this end, the SAT intends to upgrade its core tax administration processes in two stages by first standardizing the processes around the SAT's current best practices and then by introducing a new set of innovative practices. The first stage was completed with the nationwide implementation of the National Tax Administration Standards (version 1.0) on May 1, 2015.[38] The second stage will be guided by the National Tax Administration Standards (version 2.0), which is to be introduced over the next several years beginning with pilots at the national level in Jiangsu and local level in Henan provinces. In designing the new practices, the SAT could consider some of the suggestions that follow.

[37]For example, for each major compliance risk, the Australian Taxation Office assigns a senior executive as the "risk owner" with overall responsibility for overseeing the management of a particular risk and another senior official as its "risk manager" with responsibility for the risk's day-to-day management in terms of coordinating the rating of the risk, developing the risk mitigation strategy, formulating operational plans for implementing the risk mitigation strategy, and monitoring the strategy's impact on bringing the risk under control.

[38]These standards unified the processes for 612 tax administration matters under 11 major categories, 152 subcategories, and 1,087 forms and certificates.

Registration

To reduce business compliance costs and facilitate exchange of information among government agencies, the government is adopting a whole-of-government approach to enterprise registration. Under it, four government agencies—the SAT, National Bureau of Statistics, Administration for Industry and Commerce, and the Quality and Technology Supervision Bureau—will adopt a single business identifier and a one-stop registration process based on the new 18-digit Uniform Social Credit Code. The new business identifier is to be issued by the Administration of Industry and Commerce. Most agencies are expected to adopt this new identifier by 2017.

Although the Administration of Industry and Commerce will be the custodian of the business identification numbers, the SAT has a very strong interest in maintaining the integrity of the identifiers given their importance in tax administration. To this end, appropriate governance arrangements need to be put in place to ensure that the SAT has a role in deciding on critical issues concerning the design, operation, and ongoing maintenance of the national identification numbering system. One possibility would be to create an interagency steering committee that would be responsible for reviewing and approving the system's strategic direction, its key operational features, and infrastructure decisions. The SAT should have membership on and an important role in this steering committee.

For individuals, the SAT has not yet incorporated into its reform plans improvements in the registration process and identification numbers for self-employed and other natural persons. With the expected reform of the personal income tax and property tax as well as the tax information exchange initiatives that China is contemplating with other tax jurisdictions, it is imperative to strengthen the taxpayer identification system for individuals. This will require arrangements for introducing a nationally standardized identifier for self-employed persons (including individual industrial and commercial households), identifying and eliminating duplicate identification numbers for natural persons, and developing a centralized taxpayer register for individuals. These arrangements could usefully begin with high-wealth individuals—due to their extensive cross-provincial and international dealings—and gradually expanded to additional categories of individual taxpayers.

Taxpayer Services

Consistent with the government's objective of reducing taxpayers' compliance costs and promoting the business climate, the SAT has launched its "Spring Breeze Project." This initiative has been designed to streamline frontline tax administration procedures, delegate decision-making authority to lower levels in the organization, and improve services for taxpayers—all with a view toward making it easier, faster, and cheaper for taxpayers to fulfill their tax obligations. In implementing the project, further gains in service delivery could be achieved by the following:

- Benchmarking the SAT service offerings against those of leading tax agencies. Here, leading tax agencies have achieved substantial benefits by expanding the types of queries that can be handled by the telephone contact centers, making greater use of email and text messaging in taxpayer service delivery, introducing online applications (such as electronic registration, request to pay a tax debt in installments), and creating individualized taxpayer portals that allow businesses and individuals to have access to and self-manage their personal tax information and history.[39]
- Migrating taxpayer assistance from relatively costly and burdensome in-person visits at tax offices to (less costly and more convenient) use of call centers and websites. This would require enhancing the range of online and phone services provided by the SAT as described above. Adopting a more centralized approach to service delivery would allow the SAT to achieve potentially large gains in administrative efficiency by reducing the large number of small tax offices whose main function is to provide basic services to taxpayers.
- Preparing taxpayers for the anticipated changes to the business, individual income, and property taxes. The latter two reforms could add to the tax rolls large numbers of new taxpayers many of whom have little previous experience in paying taxes. A dedicated taxpayer services program will be needed to help these new taxpayers to understand and fulfill their new tax obligations.

Filing and Payment

The SAT has made good progress in reducing the time and effort in complying with the tax laws. Nevertheless, Chinese businesses still spend more time on tax matters than those in some regional competitor countries and far more time than in leading tax agencies. To promote the investment climate, additional measures are needed to further reduce these costs.

One important area for reducing compliance costs involves the VAT. The VAT is estimated to account for about 40 percent of business tax compliance costs. The high costs occur because the VAT administration in China requires more documentation, more reporting, more steps in the process, and more involvement of tax officers than in most other countries.

A number of actions could be taken to reduce these high compliance costs. A large amount of paperwork could be eliminated by simplifying the VAT return and its data requirements.[40] Further cost reductions could be achieved by better aligning the SAT's rules with commercial practices on the timing for crediting

---

[39]Refer to OECD 2010 for relevant benchmarks.

[40]For example, Chinese taxpayers may need to file up to two VAT returns (the main return and export refund return) and more than 10 appendices with up to 800 data fields every month—which imposes far greater compliance costs than most other VAT countries, including China's regional competitors. See Ernst and Young (n.d.) for a further description of the complexities of China's VAT and opportunities for reducing compliance costs.

VAT paid on inputs.[41] Perhaps the biggest gains could be made through technological improvements to the VAT computer system. In these and other areas, the SAT would benefit from consulting and co-designing the reforms with key external stakeholders, including industry associations, tax professional bodies, and software vendors.

A second promising area for compliance cost reduction is to further simplify the taxation of very small (micro) businesses. While the personal income tax law currently includes a simplified lump-sum payment regime for small businesses, many of its cost-reducing benefits have been eroded by requiring each small business to prepare an annual statement that the tax authorities use to determine the value of the lump-sum payments. This requirement adds substantially to the compliance costs of small businesses (that must prepare the annual statements) and the tax authorities (that must process large numbers of statements in setting the lump-sum assessment). These costs far outweigh the trivial amount of tax revenue that these small businesses pay—both individually and collectively—and thereby undermine the very purpose of a simplified regime.

To reduce the costs of the lump-sum regime, all micro-businesses could be subject to the same lump-sum payment regardless of their actual amount of sales or industry. This arrangement would eliminate the need for these businesses to file an annual statement and tax authorities to process the statements. Eligibility for the regime would be limited to very small businesses with sales below some very low threshold. Under this regime, the lump-sum payment(s) could be linked to and made a requirement for the issuance of an annual business license. While applying the same lump-sum tax to all micro taxpayers, as proposed here, would result in some inequities, this cost would be the price for greatly simplifying the system and, thereby, reducing its compliance and administrative costs.

As important as it is to reduce existing compliance costs, it is equally important to avoid increasing the cost of compliance from new reforms. This would be particularly important in reforming the personal income tax. Here, the SAT should seek to preserve, to the extent possible, the existing features of the personal income tax that help to minimize compliance costs for taxpayers and administrative costs for the SAT. These include maximizing the withholding of tax at source, minimizing the number of persons who are required to file tax returns, limiting deductions to those that can be easily incorporated into the withholding regime, and avoiding the introduction of expenditure-based tax allowances (such as allowances based on the amount of mortgage payments, educational expenditure, and charitable contributions).

[41]Under current arrangements, a taxpayer is not able to claim an input VAT credit unless it has actually received the VAT paper invoice and has had the invoice formally verified by the tax authorities. Hence, an unverified input VAT invoice cannot be credited on a taxpayer's VAT tax return even though it has most likely been booked in the taxpayer's accounting system. This disconnect in timing between a taxpayer's accounting system and the SAT's VAT system results in large variances that require businesses to undertake substantial manual interventions to adjust (Ernst and Young n.d.).

Audit

To date, the SAT has relied heavily on cross-matching tax invoices between sellers and purchasers as the main vehicle for identifying and dealing with non-compliance. While invoice cross-matching appears to have helped bring under control the previous rampant incidence of fraudulent VAT invoices, it has been far less successful at mitigating other forms of underreporting that have plagued the VAT.[42] Nor will the cross-matching of VAT invoices, by itself, mitigate underreporting of tax due for other taxes such as the corporate and personal income tax.

Reducing tax underreporting and safeguarding revenue will require the SAT to considerably strengthen its audit program beyond cross-checking invoices. Priority areas for enhancing audit capacity should include the following:

- **Making greater use of analytical methods.** The growing amount of data that is becoming available to the SAT—and the additional amounts of third-party information that may become available with the planned amendments to the Tax Collection Law—provides a rich repository of information for developing analytical methods to detect emerging compliance risks and the taxpayers who pose such risks.
- **Improving basic audit methods.** This will require auditors to be trained in and provided tools to examine the entire operations of a business, identify material issues and inconsistencies in the taxpayer's accounts, and probe until these issues are resolved. As a starting point, the SAT should develop a nationally standardized audit manual setting out the methods for auditing each of the main tax types.
- **Adopting limited-scope audits.** The SAT's audit program currently relies on comprehensive audits covering multiple taxes, tax periods, and tax issues. Broader audit coverage could be achieved by making greater use of limited-scope audits covering one (or a few) taxes and tax issues.
- **Developing industry specialization.** Like in other countries, revenue risks in China vary across industries due to differences in their contributions to tax revenue, relevant provisions in the tax laws, and compliance patterns. For this reason, the SAT's audit program needs greater industry specialization, including by developing industry-specific audit technique guides and methods.

[42]Examples include failing to charge VAT on final sales to consumers, failing to submit VAT tax returns and pay VAT despite issuing VAT invoices, improperly classifying a taxable transaction as exempt, improperly charging VAT at a lower rate, sham invoices for transactions that have not taken place (including sham invoices issued by bankrupt companies in collusion with taxpayers claiming credit on the basis of these invoices), incorrectly deducting VAT input tax from exempt sales, and structuring transactions to gain a tax advantage in a way that was not intended in the law (aggressive tax planning).

- **Introducing coordinated audits for large enterprises and high-wealth individuals.** Given their complex and increasingly national (and international) scope of operations, the SAT will need to adopt a coordinated, cross-provincial approach to auditing these two taxpayer segments. It will also require the SAT to strengthen its international compliance programs in relation to outbound investment by Chinese residents.

Arrears Collection

International experience has demonstrated that tax arrears tend to increase, sometimes sharply, in countries that experience a significant slowdown in economic growth. In such situations, tax agencies need sufficiently strong powers, on the one hand, to recover tax arrears and, on the other hand, provide those viable businesses with good compliance histories appropriate breathing space to pay their tax debts. With China's rapid economic growth slowing, it will be important to strengthen the SAT's arrears collection powers and the administrative procedures for applying these powers.

In this context, the planned amendments to the TCL are crucial. These are expected to vest the SAT with the authority to allow taxpayers to pay their tax arrears over an extended period of time and to impose a tax lien on a tax debtor's real property. In addition, the TCL should authorize the SAT to issue a default assessment against those taxpayers who fail to file a tax return. Key issues in each of these areas include the following:

- **Installment arrangements.** The draft amendments to the TCL would extend the period taxpayers could pay tax arrears from three monthly installments (under the current law) to 12 monthly installments. Implementing this new provision would require the SAT to (1) develop administrative policy on the terms and conditions for granting an installment arrangement and design the administrative guidance for applying the policy, (2) prescribe the type of information that a taxpayer must provide to the SAT to support a request for an installment arrangement, (3) train collection officers in evaluating requests for an installment arrangement,[43] and (4) set the level of management approval required to accept an installment request.
- **Tax liens.** A lien is a legal encumbrance on an asset owned by a tax debtor that allows for the recovery of monies if the asset is disposed of. The lien is also a necessary legal step before an asset can be seized and sold to satisfy a debt. Implementing this provision would require the SAT to (1) develop administrative policy and guidance on when and how a tax lien may be imposed (and removed), including whether the lien may be imposed on an administrative basis or must first require certification of the debt by a court;

[43]The evaluation should include an *ability to pay analysis,* which is a detailed assessment of the taxpayer's current and future capacity to pay or borrow funds based in part on the financial statement prepared by the taxpayer.

(2) determine the types of property that may be subject to the lien; (3) train collection officers in identifying and locating properties on which the lien may be imposed, and the procedures for imposing (and removing) the lien; (4) determine the notification procedures and forms for imposing a lien; and (5) decide the level of management approval required before a lien may be imposed.

- **Default assessments.** When a taxpayer fails to file a tax return, many tax agencies are authorized to use any reasonable method for determining the amount of tax owed by the taxpayer. In doing so, some tax agencies are allowed to use a previous period's tax liability (plus an uplift factor) to establish the tax liability for the current tax period. Such a default assessment has the advantage of more quickly establishing the tax liability and thereby accelerating its collection than by auditing the taxpayer. Moreover, the issuance of a default assessment does not prevent the tax agency from eventually auditing a delinquent taxpayer if it is believed that the actual tax liability could exceed the default assessment.

Dispute Resolution

A well-designed system for minimizing disputes between taxpayers and the tax authorities, and for resolving disputes when they arise, is an essential element of an effective tax administration. Such a system can also help promote the business climate by reducing taxpayers' compliance costs in their dealings with the tax agency. To this end, a number of measures could be considered for improving the SAT's dispute resolution system:

- As a first step, the SAT could reduce the potential for tax disputes by converting more of its informal guidance into formal regulations and providing greater detail in the regulations. Traditionally, the SAT has been lower-than-average issuer of formal regulations compared to other ministries and agencies (Cui forthcoming). By publishing more regulations—following public consultation—with greater detail the SAT could provide both taxpayers and tax officers with a clearer and more reliable basis for applying the tax laws, thereby promoting the rule of law and reducing the scope for disputes.
- The draft amendments to the Tax Collection Law provide for the establishment of a private advance ruling regime. Such a regime allows taxpayers to request from the SAT a written ruling on how the tax laws apply to a particular fact pattern described by the taxpayer. Experience in other administrations—and feedback from stakeholders within China—indicate that such a service would be very popular by providing taxpayers with greater certainty on the application of the tax laws prior to making an important investment decision. Implementing this provision will require the SAT to design administrative guidelines and procedures governing its application.

- No matter how clearly the tax regulations are publicized and how widely advance rulings are made available, disputes on the correct application of tax laws are inevitable. Therefore, ensuring the community's confidence in the fairness of the tax system requires, among other things, an administrative review mechanism that is perceived to be fair and independent. This could be facilitated by creating within the SAT a network of administrative review units that report vertically to a higher-level administrative review unit instead of to the head of a higher-level tax bureau as is the existing arrangement.[44] Although the current statutory framework for administrative reviews, which applies to all ministries, may limit the opportunities for reform in this area, the SAT may have scope to pilot in a few locations a quasi-independent review organ along the lines described here.

Strengthening Human Resources and Information Technology

Human Resources

Earlier human resource management reforms equipped tax officers with the skills required to deal with the most pressing challenges to the tax system in previous periods. Addressing the emerging challenges to the tax system will require further human resource management reforms. To this end, the SAT needs to formulate a comprehensive human resources management strategy to right-size the workforce, enhance staff skills, and improve the incentives for staff to achieve high levels of productivity and ethical behavior.

Right-sizing the workforce entails ensuring sufficient numbers of staff are allocated to the different levels of the organization and across administrative functions. One priority in this area should be to increase the size of the headquarters' staff. With only 850 officials, headquarters is far too small to effectively carry out its functions—including designing national policies and programs, monitoring the operations of the tax offices, and providing guidance to the tax offices—in an organization comprising some 750,000 tax officers spread across 36 provincial-level tax bureaus.

Another right-sizing priority is to ensure sufficient numbers of tax officers are allocated to each tax administration function. Here, the SAT could usefully benchmark its staff allocation against the norms in other tax jurisdictions. In this connection, OECD tax agencies allocate, on average, 36 percent of their staff to verification activities (including audit), 27 percent to account management (including taxpayer services), 11 percent to tax arrears collection, 9 percent to other tax operations, and 17 percent to support and other activities (including 3 percent to human resources

[44]Administrative reviews are currently heard by an administrative review organ at one level within the SAT organization above that where the dispute has arisen, Although this arrangement provides some degree of independence, it still creates a perception of bias in favor of the tax authorities since the administrative review organ reports to the head of a (higher-level) tax bureau who has an interest in achieving a collection target and thereby in sustaining lower-level decisions, particularly in those cases involving substantial amounts of tax revenue.

management).[45] Notwithstanding some of China's unique features, the SAT's staff allocation would not be expected to diverge too sharply from international averages. Where it does, the SAT should carefully analyze the factors accounting for the divergence to determine whether they are justified or require correction.

Concerning staff skills, the SAT needs a strategy for identifying and prioritizing those areas for skills and knowledge enhancement. Such a strategy should begin with an evaluation of current skills levels against future requirements and then provide a plan for filling identified gaps. This approach is needed not only to enhance the capacity of SAT staff at dealing with current challenges, but also to prepare staff for implementing key reforms in the SAT's modernization strategy.

In implementing its skills enhancement program, SAT headquarters should play a greater role in establishing the training priorities and standardizing course curricula, for which in the past the provincial training academies have been given wide discretion. In delivering training, the SAT could usefully exploit modern training technologies—including e-learning—to extend training opportunities to more staff.

In addition to right-sizing and enhancing the skills of its workforce, the SAT's human resource management reforms also need to strengthen its performance management policies. Here, the SAT's recent Digital HR initiative holds great promise. Under this pilot project, organizational units and individual staff members are now evaluated on the basis of a broader set of performance measures than just the revenue target. To create incentives for staff to achieve greater productivity and more integrity, the new performance evaluation system needs to be linked more closely to remuneration increases and promotions, and the pilot project should be implemented throughout the SAT.

Information Technology

The SAT has made impressive progress over the last 20 years in developing a standardized information system (China Tax Administration Information System) to support core tax administration functions and a specialized system (Golden Tax Project Phases 1 and 2) to control VAT invoice fraud. Further improvements will need to be made to the SAT's information systems—including to its data stores, analytical tools, and technologies—in order to safeguard revenue and reduce compliance costs.

Although the China Tax Administration Information System has been deployed at all provincial and municipal levels, these subnational computer networks have not yet been tied together at the national level to create centralized databases of tax information. Consequently, the SAT cannot easily compile the type of national data that is crucial for evaluating the performance of its operational programs and field offices, conducting data mining and risk analysis, and tracking taxpayers' activities across provinces and with related entities. To address these shortcomings, it will be essential for the SAT to create a national data center (or centers) of tax-related information as envisaged in the Golden Tax

[45]See OECD 2015b.

Project 3 that is to replace the China Tax Administration Information System, as described earlier.

In creating a national data center, the SAT will need to make decisions on a wide range of technological and non-technological issues. These include the number of data centers and their geographic and organizational placement, the types of hardware and software to acquire, the types of information to be collected, and the applications for processing the information and using it to detect noncompliance. Two prerequisites for data centers are the existence of a national taxpayer identification numbering system and robust legal authorities for the SAT to collect third-party information, both of which were described earlier.

Other information technology challenges concern the SAT's specialized system for VAT administration. This system has been designed to certify and cross-match invoices between purchasers and sellers to detect fraudulent invoices. Although the SAT views the VAT system as having contributed significantly to the increases in VAT collections, it should also be recognized that the system imposes very high compliance costs on taxpayers. In addition to simplifying the information reporting requirements of the VAT return itself, two technological improvements could help reduce the VAT's compliance costs.

First, the VAT system software should be designed to automatically extract the VAT information required by the SAT from companies' internal accounting systems. As it stands now, businesses spend substantial time and resources in printing invoices, manually extracting information from their internal systems, and transmitting/receiving transactions-level data with the SAT. The costs associated with these tasks could be eliminated or, at least, greatly reduced by better aligning the SAT's computer systems to the accounting systems used by businesses. This points to the importance of the SAT working in closer cooperation with other stakeholders—including tax professionals' bodies, industry associations, and software vendors—in developing new versions of the VAT software.

Second, steps should be taken to facilitate the introduction of electronic invoicing (e-invoicing). International experience has shown that e-invoicing has the potential not only to substantially reduce businesses' compliance costs with the tax system, but also to expedite commercial transactions and increase business competitiveness (Toro 2007). At this time, the SAT is at an early stage in deploying an e-invoicing system. To move this initiative forward, the authorities will need to establish a legal mechanism for authenticating electronic invoices (that is, an electronic signature) as well as establish a robust technological platform to operate the system. Such a platform will require major investments in software development and hardware, including high-speed Internet connection, wide-area communication networks with high transmission capacity, and robust applications and database servers. As in the case of the VAT system software, the SAT could achieve many benefits by developing the e-invoicing system in close cooperation with external stakeholders in the tax system.

Building a Modern Performance Measurement System

Traditionally, the SAT has relied on the annual tax collection target as a key measure for evaluating the performance of its tax offices. This measure has had the advantages of the close link to the government's key fiscal objectives (mobilizing tax revenue) and its relative ease of measurement.

Despite its advantages, over-reliance on the collection target for measuring performance can have significant (negative) unintended consequences by creating perverse incentives for tax officers to take inappropriate actions to achieve their target.[46] Not only does this risk undermining taxpayers' confidence in the fairness and integrity of the tax system, but it can also have a negative impact on the economy by interfering with the operation of automatic stabilizers. That is, when the economy slows down and, as a consequence, tax receipts fall behind the collection target, tax officers will tend to intensify their actions to achieve the target. Such actions could put further pressure on businesses and worsen an economic downturn.

For this reason, the SAT should adopt a more balanced set of measures than the tax collection target for evaluating the performance of its tax offices. These measures could include targets for (1) tax administration results (with quantitative and quality measures for each tax administration function), (2) taxpayer satisfaction (typically measured by independent surveys), and (3) tax officer engagement (also commonly measured by a survey). The targets can be set at the organizational level (provinces, municipalities, districts, and so on) and then cascaded down to managers and tax officers as part of their individual performance evaluation.

Given its long history and well-entrenched use, the tax collection target is likely to remain a key performance measure for the SAT. To lessen its disadvantages, it would be important to supplement the collection target with a broader set of measures as described above. This would be facilitated by the nationwide deployment of the Golden Tax Project 3 computer system—which will give the SAT the capacity to compile national data on key tax administration operations—and the national implementation of the Digital HR pilot project as described earlier in this section.

CONCLUSIONS

China's tax administration has reached an important juncture. Over the past 20 years, the SAT has successfully transformed its operations to administer a new tax system in an increasingly market-oriented economy. As China embarks on its 13th Five-Year Plan, the SAT once again needs to adapt itself to deal with a new and challenging environment.

[46]For example, by encouraging auditors to issue inflated audit assessments when tax collections are falling behind the target or encouraging taxpayers to incur tax arrears in current periods (which can be paid in subsequent periods) when collections are exceeding targets.

The SAT's capacity to mobilize tax revenue is facing growing challenges. The slowdown and structural changes in the economy are reducing the growth of China's tax bases and creating incentives (and new opportunities) for tax avoidance and evasion. Further revenue pressure can be expected as Chinese businesses and individuals increase their overseas investments, creating additional scope for noncompliance.

In addition to safeguarding revenue, the slowing economy makes it more important than ever for the SAT to help promote the business climate by reducing business compliance costs. It also heightens the importance of creating a more even playing field across sectors and locations through more uniform tax administration.

While addressing the mounting challenges to the existing tax system, at the same time the SAT will need to implement the government's ambitious tax reform agenda. This will require a major effort to train tax officers and educate taxpayers in applying the changes to the tax laws.

The above-mentioned challenges create a new and complex environment for tax administration much like the situation that confronted the SAT in the early 1990s. To effectively address these challenges, the SAT will need to implement a comprehensive modernization strategy just as it did 20 years ago. Key reforms priorities could include the following:

- The Tax Collection Law should be amended to expand the SAT's enforcement authorities and enhance taxpayers' protections. Enforcement authorities should expand the SAT's ability to access tax-related information from third parties and to recover tax arrears. Taxpayer protections should be enhanced by strengthening the confidentiality of taxpayer information, providing greater procedural protections to taxpayers, introducing an advance rulings regime, and eliminating the current requirement for taxpayers to pay 100 percent of a tax assessment before filing an administrative review.
- The SAT's organizational structure should be aligned with and supportive of its modernization strategy. This would entail increasing the size of headquarters, eliminating the current fragmentation of administrative responsibilities across different departments, consolidating the large network of grassroots tax offices, strengthening the organizational arrangements for large taxpayers and high-wealth individuals, and creating a more independent administrative review organ within the SAT.
- Comprehensive compliance risk management strategies should be developed—for each major tax, each taxpayer segment, and individual taxpayers—to identify, rank, and mitigate the main risks to the tax system. These should give priority to mitigating the compliance risks associated with large businesses and high-wealth individuals, the growth of the services sector (including electronic commerce), international tax issues, and increasing tax arrears that could result from the slowing economy.
- Core tax administration processes need to be strengthened and standardized. The SAT's audit and arrears collection programs require strengthening

while the information reporting requirements for the value-added tax and the tax assessment procedures for micro businesses should be simplified. In addition, a system needs to be established for monitoring tax offices' adherence to the new national standards for the core administrative processes.

- The SAT's computer systems need to be both strengthened and made easier for taxpayers to use. Priority areas for strengthening include creating nationally centralized databases of taxpayer information (beginning with large enterprise groups and high-wealth individuals) and exchanging data with third parties. Simplifying ease of use should focus on reducing business compliance costs of the value-added tax computer system.
- In the human resources area, key priorities should be to substantially increase the number of staff assigned to headquarters, ensure that appropriate numbers of staff are allocated to each tax administration function, align the SAT's training programs with the requirements of its modernization strategy, and introduce human resource management policies that create incentives for staff to achieve higher productivity and greater integrity.

The initiatives suggested above represent an ambitious reform agenda that needs to be carefully managed. In doing so, the SAT can draw upon the lessons it has learned in reform management over the past two decades. These confirm the following good practices:

- Strong and stable leadership is crucial to medium-term institution building. The stability in the SAT's leadership has facilitated business continuity, coherence of direction, and effective reform management. These advantages need to be preserved.
- In designing new tax legislation, due consideration needs to be given to the SAT's administrative capacity and taxpayers' compliance abilities. The planned amendments to the personal income tax, for example, should minimize the number of taxpayers required to file tax returns, maximize the withholding of tax at source, and limit deductions to those that can be easily incorporated into the withholding regime.
- Implementing major tax administration reforms requires sustained efforts over a prolonged period. Such efforts are best guided by a medium-term strategic plan that clearly sets out the reforms' goals and objectives, key initiatives, broad timetable, and measures of success.
- Piloting major reforms prior to their national implementation has been an integral part of the SAT's reform management. This approach has provided the SAT with many benefits—including minimizing risk, developing consensus, and providing opportunities for learning-by-doing—and should be continued.
- The SAT has benefited substantially from technical cooperation with other tax agencies and international institutions. While international practices can provide useful reference points for reform, they need to be adjusted to the local conditions in China and implemented with these conditions in mind.

Annex 3.1. Organizational Chart of China's Tax Administration

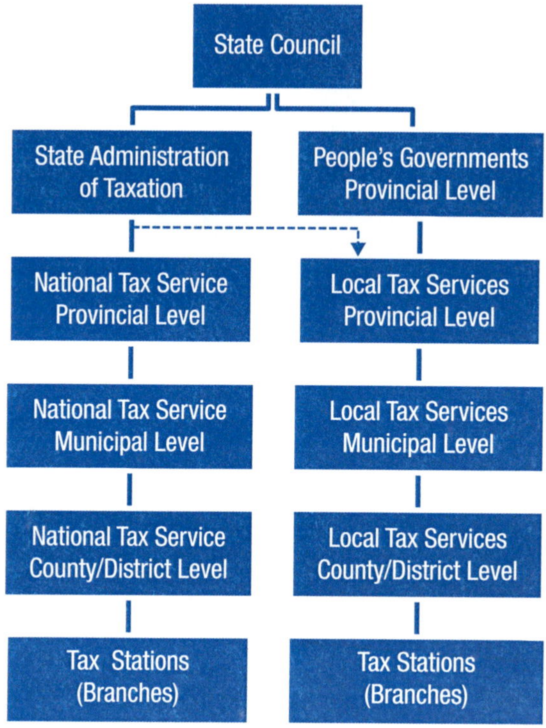

Source: State Administration of Taxation 2014.

Annex 3.2. Illustrative Compliance Management Strategy for Small Businesses

1. Strategy Overview To support business development and encourage voluntary compliance, small businesses will be provided better access to professional services and bookkeeping tools. Strategies for this segment are guided by risk profiling and rely on strengthening intelligence. Risk treatments are designed to be preventative, low cost, and project based.

2. Segment Profile

2.1 Definition Businesses with sales below the value-added tax registration threshold, excluding those eligible for the patent or benchmark regime.

2.2 Amount/type of tax revenue:

Tax Type	Revenue (billions)
PIT	27.52
CIT	5.24
VAT	7.43
ROY	0.12
EXC	0.014
WHT	5.73
Other	7.12
Total	53.17

Revenue from this segment represents about 1.9 percent of total tax collections

2.3 Number/type of taxpayers: Mostly sole traders, limited liability companies and partnerships. About 50,000 legal entities; nearly 150,000 sole traders, with varying levels of business/financial skills.

2.4 Number/type of tax returns: Small businesses have multiple tax obligations, and entities are required to file quarterly. Most do not require audit certification.

2.5 Key industries: Wholesale and retail, construction, manufacturing, and professional services.

3. Priority Risks (high, medium, low)

3.1 Registration risk: Medium
Some are unregistered; others are not registered for all taxes.

3.2 Filing risk: Medium
Small businesses are prone to drop out of the system due to complexity or cash flow problems. Some drop out because of competition from unregistered businesses.

3.3 Underreporting risk: Medium
Both deliberate and inadvertent underreporting occurs. Low business acumen results in errors and the informal economy sees deliberate omissions.

3.4 Payment risk: Medium
Cash flow pressures are prevalent and payment default is common. Almost 80% of arrears cases are small, representing only about 5% of debt by value.

4. Risk Treatments

4.1 Measures for facilitating compliance
Simplified registration, filing, and payment processes to reduce errors
New business assistance program (right-from-the-start approach)
Easily accessible tax administration advice tailored to the needs of small businesses and delivered through multiple channels
Improved accessibility to professional advice in partnership with small and medium enterprise incubators
Free electronic and paper-based bookkeeping tools
Early intervention calls, visits, and letters to prevent errors from occurring
Closer working relationships with State Registration Department

4.2 Measures for dealing with noncompliance
Comprehensive audits for highest risk cases
Hidden economy campaign
Limited-scope risk-based audits
Use of small business benchmarks for prevention and detection
Income verification program
Outbound telephone calls for small arrears cases
Voluntary disclosure initiative with concessional penalty imposition

4.3 Measures for simplifying tax policy design Small businesses will be taxed under a simplified regime (based on turnover or cash flow) with simple tax returns and no requirement to submit financial statements.

5. Compliance Indicators

Registration:	% increase in registration
	% reduction in lost registrants
Filing:	% increase in on-time filing
Reporting:	% increase in audit strike rates
	% of audit acts sustained on dispute
Payment:	% reduction in arrears
	% increase in collections of audit acts

6. Workflows

Number of:
- Assistance products
- Voluntary disclosures
- Registration checks
- Outbound calls
- Pre-filing letters

Number of:
- Advisory visits
- Limited-scope audits
- Comprehensive audits
- Debt collection actions

7. Capacity Development

Information Systems, Data Management, and Analytics
Fully implement self-assessment and optimize e-tax.
Streamline registration, filing, and payment processes.
Ensure risk management supports compliance strategy (rather than driving them).

Staff Development
General and functional management, technical, industry specialization, service, and communication skills training

Administrative Tools and Procedures
Develop channel management strategy, optimize call center and web services.
Design a new business program.
Build alliances with the tax profession and other agencies servicing small businesses.

Management and Organization
Integrate compliance strategies into operational plans.
Appoint a senior headquarters official to oversee development of small business compliance strategy.

Source: IMF technical assistance report.
Note: CIT = corporate income tax; EXC = excise tax; PIT = personal income tax; ROY = rest of the year; VAT = value-added tax; WHT = withholding tax.

REFERENCES

Ahmad, Ehtisham. 2011. "Should China Revisit the 1994 Fiscal Reforms?" Working Paper 52, LSE Asia Research Centre, London.

Brondolo, John. 2009. "Collecting Taxes during an Economic Crisis: Challenges and Policy Options." Staff Position Note SPN/09/17, International Monetary Fund, Washington.

Brondolo, John, and Zhiyong Zhang. 2016. "Tax Administration Reform in China: Achievements, Challenges, and Reform Priorities." Working Paper WP/16/68, International Monetary, Fund, Washington.

Cai, Hongbin, and Qiao Liu. 2009. "Competition and Corporate Tax Avoidance, Evidence from Chinese Industrial Firms." *The Economic Journal* 537: 764–95.

Center for Social and Economic Research (CASE) and CPB Netherlands Bureau for Economic Policy Analysis. 2013. "Study to Quantify and Analyze the VAT Gap in the EU-27 Member States Final Report for the European Commission." CASE, Warsaw, Poland. http://ec.europa.eu/taxation_customs/common/publications/studies/index_en.htm.

Consulate General of the Kingdom of the Netherlands in Guangzhou. 2015. *China Cross-Border E-Commerce, Opportunities for Dutch Companies*. Beijing: Consulate General.

Cui, Wei. Forthcoming. "When Does the Chinese Executive Branch Make Law?" Paper submitted to both the Canadian Law and Economics Association Annual Meeting at the University of Toronto on September 23, 2016, and the Society for Empirical Legal Studies Annual Conference in Durham, North Carolina, on November 18 or 19, 2016.

Ernst and Young. n.d. "A Look Inside China's VAT System." London.

Internal Revenue Service (of the United States) (IRS). 2006. "Treatment under Section 367(b) of Property Used to Purchase Parent Stock in Certain Triangular Regulations." Internal Revenue Bulletin 2006-41, Notice 2006-85, October 10, Washington.

International Monetary Fund (IMF). 1993. "China at the Threshold of a Market Economy." Occasional Paper 107, Washington.

———. 1994. "Economic Reform in China: A New Phase." Occasional Paper 114, Washington.

———. 2015. "Current Challenges in Revenue Mobilization: Improving Tax Compliance." Staff Report, Washington. http://www.imf.org/external/pp/longres.aspx?id=4944.

KPMG. 2014. "E-Commerce in China: Driving a New Consumer Culture." *China 360*, January. http://www.kpmg.com/CN/en/IssuesAndInsights/ArticlesPublications/Newsletters/China-360/Documents/China-360-Issue15-201401-E-commerce-in-China.pdf.

Lin, Shuanglin. 2009. "The Rise and Fall of China's Government Revenue." East Asia Institute Working Paper No. 150, National University of Singapore, Singapore.

National Bureau of Statistics of China. Various years. *China Statistical Yearbook*.

Organisation for Economic Co-operation and Development (OECD). 2010. "Survey of Trends and Developments in the Use of Electronic Services for Taxpayer Service." Centre for Tax Policy and Administration, Paris.

———. 2013. "Tax Policy and Tax Reform in the People's Republic of China." OECD Taxation Working Paper No. 18, Paris.

———. 2015a. *OECD/G20 Base Erosion and Profit Shifting Project: Final Report*. Paris.

———. 2015b. *Tax Administration 2015: Comparative Information on OECD and Other Advanced and Emerging Economies*. Paris.

Rosen, Daniel, and Beibei Bao. 2015. *Broken Abacus? A More Accurate Gauge of China's Economy*. Center for Strategic and International Studies, September 2015. Lanham, Maryland: Rowan & Littlefield.

State Administration of Taxation (SAT). 2014. "State Administration of Taxation Annual Report 2014." State Administration of Taxation, Beijing, China.

Toro, Juan. 2007. "Electronic Invoicing in Latin America—Opportunities for the IDB to Support its Consolidation." Study commissioned by the Inter-American Development Bank, Washington, DC.

United Nations Conference on Trade and Development (UNCTAD). 2015. *World Investment Report 2015, Reforming International Investment Governance*. New York: UNCTAD.

Winn, Jane, and Angela Zhang. 2013. "China's Golden Tax Project: A Technological Strategy for Reducing VAT Fraud." *Peking University Journal of Legal Studies* 4: 1–33.
World Bank. 1990. *China: Revenue Mobilization and Tax Policy*. Washington.
———. 2003. "Implementation Completion Report on a Loan/Credit/Grant in the Amount of US$50 Million to the People's Republic of China for a Fiscal Technical Assistance Project." Report No. 25892, June 6, Washington.
———. 2015. "The Global Picture. The Changing Face of Tax Compliance in 189 Economies Worldwide." In *Paying Taxes 2015*. Washington.
——— and Development Research Center of the State Council. 2012. *China 2030: Building a Modern, Harmonious, and Creative Society*. Washington.
Xinhua General Overseas News Services. 1988. "Tax Evasion Is Huge, at Times Violent Problem in China."
Xu, Shanda. 2006. "Construction of Phase III of Golden Tax Project Needs to Achieve Five Breakthroughs." Speech during the meeting of the National Tax System Information Construction, July 26.
Yu, Dingcheng. 1997. "Jingji Zhuo, Shuishou Zhu Kong." Yiagzhou Daxue Shuiwu Xueyan Xuebao, cited in Shuanglin Lin, "The Rise and Fall of China's Government Revenue," East Asia Institute Working Paper No. 180, June 3, 2009.

CHAPTER 4

A Medium-Term Expenditure Framework for More Effective Fiscal Policy

HOLGER VAN EDEN, DAVID GENTRY, AND SANJEEV GUPTA

China has made modernizing its fiscal framework a key reform priority. This comes at a critical time as the country continues to move toward a more market-based allocation of resources and a greater role for the private sector. A modernized fiscal framework will allow the government to more effectively manage the economic cycle and signal that fiscal policies are sustainable, that expenditure policies over the medium term are focused on strategic and equitable development, and that resources are spent effectively and efficiently.

A key part of the fiscal reforms will be to move forward in implementing a medium-term expenditure framework, or MTEF. This objective was already reflected in the conclusions of the Third Plenum of the 18th Party Congress in late 2013. An MTEF will require a significant strengthening of technical and institutional capacity of the Ministry of Finance, the National Development and Reform Commission (NDRC)—China's planning ministry—and the spending ministries and agencies. It will also require a greater emphasis by policymakers, including those at the highest level, such as at the State Council and in the National People's Congress (NPC), on deciding and managing public finances with a more medium-term perspective on the financial impact and outcomes of government policies. A pilot MTEF document has already been produced, covering 2015–17, which will evolve and be refined over the coming years, if international experience is any guide.

At present, the strategic direction of government policies is set through the five-year plan (the 13th Five-Year Plan was approved by the National People's Congress in March 2016), while spending is determined for only the coming year in the annual budget. These tools are no longer adequate for managing the economic transformation and structural reforms aimed at rebalancing the economy away from investment- and credit-led growth, expanding social safety nets, reforming intergovernmental fiscal relations, and coping with an aging population.

At present, a gap exists between the strategic direction of the five-year plan and allocation through the annual budget. The five-year plan is aspirational and focused on capital expenditure projects, but not always subject to realistic resource constraints. The annual budget is largely incremental, less attuned to changing policy priorities, and focused on recurrent expenditure and transfers. Moreover, it only covers central government spending. Neither instrument is sufficient to ensure the fiscal discipline, the strategic allocation of resources, and the improvement of spending efficiency needed for sustainable and stable development of the public sector as a whole.

Three issues, specific to China, call for introducing an MTEF. First, overall fiscal expenditure, deficits, and public debt levels that should concern policymakers are considerably larger than those in the central government budget (the State Budget). This is because China's public expenditure is heavily devolved to lower levels of government that greatly depend on transfers from the central government. Some 65 percent of overall government expenditure takes place through local government (Figure 4.1, panel 1), while over 70 percent of central government expenditure consists of intergovernmental transfers. Public investment is even more heavily skewed toward local government (see Chapter 6 on local government debt and fiscal risks).

At the same time, China does not have a fiscal framework that covers all government expenditure at all levels. This has limited the ability of policymakers to ensure overall fiscal discipline and mitigate fiscal risks. Even though central government deficits have remained in the range of 2–3 percent of GDP, those of "augmented" general government—a concept that incorporates the off-budget fiscal activity of China's local government financing vehicles—have been between 7 and 10 percent of GDP over the past few years (Figure 4.1, panel 2). Similarly, official general government expenditure and debt are still below other Asian emerging market economies, but exceed their average if the augmented definition is used (see Figure 4.1, panels 3 and 4). An MTEF will help manage the fiscal policy stance of the general government as a whole, and should include any remaining off-budget fiscal activity.[1]

Second, social spending pressures are likely to increase in the coming years as the population rapidly ages. This implies that ensuring the effectiveness and efficiency of expenditure will increase in importance, so that room can be created for needed spending on pensions and health care (see Chapter 5 on social security and Clements and others 2015). The MTEF will let spending departments and lower government levels plan and execute their expenditure programs more efficiently.

[1]The IMF, in its analysis of Chinese general government finances, has used the terms "augmented" deficit and "augmented" debt to indicate the sum of formal general government borrowing (which includes borrowing by central government, pilot borrowing by local government before 2015, and formal local government borrowing since 2015) and borrowing through local government financing vehicles, which can be considered off-budget/informal local government borrowing because local government directs this borrowing and is liable for it. A full discussion of the "augmented" concept can be found in Appendix III of the China 2014 Article IV Consultation Staff Report (IMF 2014).

Figure 4.1. China—Fiscal Trends of Central, Local, and General Government
(Percent)

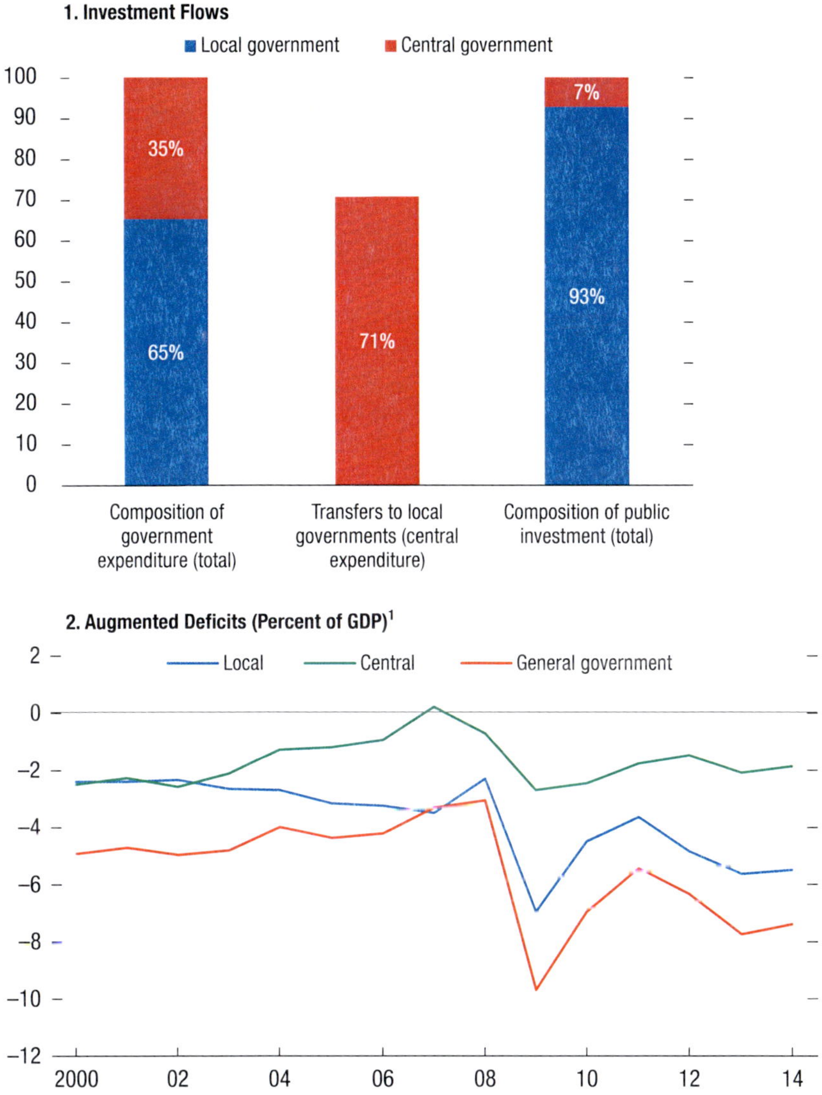

Sources: National Bureau of Statistics of China; IMF *World Economic Outlook*; and IMF staff estimates.
[1] See footnote 1 in the main text for the definition of "augmented."

Figure 4.1. China—Fiscal Trends of Central, Local, and General Government *(continued)*

3. Augmented General Government Expenditure[1]
(Percent of GDP)

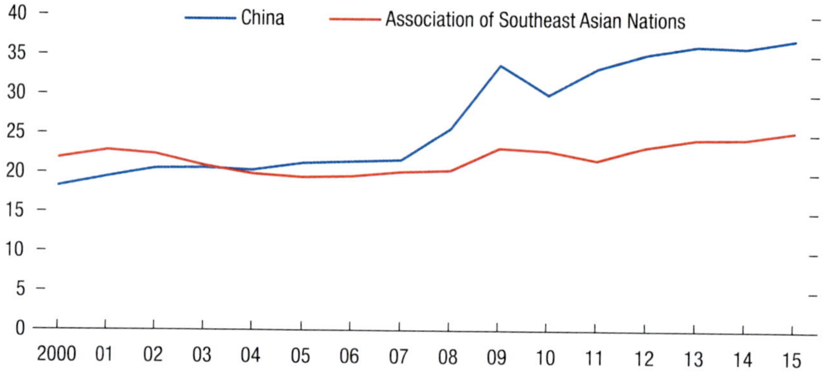

4. Augmented General Government Debt[1]
(Percent of GDP)

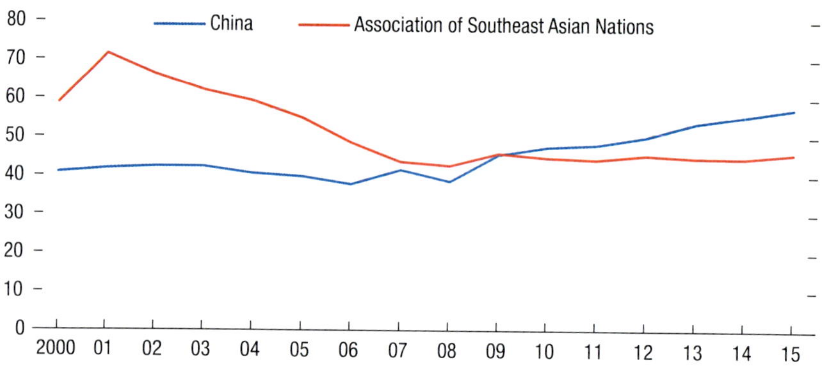

Sources: National Bureau of Statistics of China; IMF *World Economic Outlook*; and IMF staff estimates.
[1] See footnote 1 in the main text for the definition of "augmented."

Third, an MTEF will help improve spending discipline both in ministries and departments and at provincial and lower government levels. Imposing hard budget constraints on spending has sometimes been problematic, especially at the local government level. The MTEF will promote development of more realistic and targeted expenditure policies. It will support local governments in adjusting their policies to resource envelopes rather than, as in the past, relying on informal borrowing arrangements. The introduction of formal local government borrowing and a halt to informal borrowing over the next few years will harden budget constraints on local governments. An MTEF at the central government level will signal the level of transfers to be expected and require local governments to cope

Figure 4.2. Medium-Term Expenditure Frameworks Globally, 2008

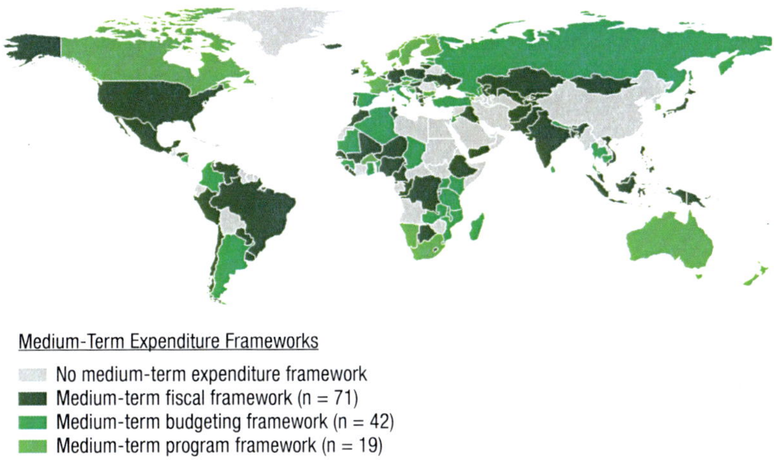

Source: World Bank 2012.

with their budget constraints more decisively. Development of MTEFs at the provincial level, currently underway, will further help lower-level local governments deal with their fiscal constraints.

This chapter starts with a discussion of the international experience with MTEFs and the main issues to consider in their development. The major improvements achieved in China's budget planning process in recent years are discussed, as well as the limitations of the current annual budget process. The various types of MTEFs are then defined in more detail, and their use by other countries is explained, as are the main building blocks of the MTEF process and the typical stages in its development. A number of important design choices that Group of Twenty (G20) countries have chosen to incorporate in their MTEFs are reviewed. The chapter subsequently takes a look at who in government is best placed to prepare the constituent parts of an MTEF, and how to sequence the overall MTEF introduction. These issues are linked to the possible implications for China. The chapter concludes with a number of recommendations.

BACKGROUND

China is not alone in reorienting fiscal and budgetary policies toward the medium term. The MTEF trend is international; already by the end of 2008, some 132 countries were in the process of introducing some form of medium-term fiscal framework (Figure 4.2). The three types of MTEF identified in the figure are discussed later in this chapter.

While use of the MTEF is widespread, both Japan and the United States, due to a variety of domestic issues, have been unable to implement the instrument beyond its most basic form, that is, the medium-term fiscal or budgetary outlook. These two countries project expenditures over the medium term, either in aggregate (fiscal outlook) or as detailed lines of expenditure categories (budgetary outlook). But such outlooks, useful as they may be, do not qualify as a "framework" because no (political) decisions are made on policy measures to reconcile the expected revenue envelope with the targeted fiscal stance. Outlooks give information on trends of expenditure, but are unreliable as forecasts. This dichotomy between outlooks and frameworks highlights that MTEFs are not a straightforward reform. In fact, MTEFs have been designed differently in different countries, often focused on the policy and institutional priorities that the annual budget process could not address.[2]

International experience suggests China will need to analyze what aspects of the present budgeting system are unsatisfactory, including perhaps some of the issues described above, and to make this a driving factor in the MTEF design process. China will need to develop its own brand of MTEF in the coming years. Among the essential building blocks are (1) setting medium-term fiscal policy targets, covering both local and central governments, consistent with fiscal sustainability and stability; (2) adopting top-down medium-term macroeconomic and fiscal forecasting; (3) developing a bottom-up "baseline" expenditure forecasting methodology; and (4) developing a strategic decision-making phase in the budget process to decide on the use of the "fiscal space" (or lack of it) available to the government. These building blocks are explained in detail later in this chapter.

These are, however, only the main ticket items of the reform process. In addition, MTEF design should consider the following:

- macro-fiscal forecasting capacity
- the part of the government or public sector to be covered by the MTEF
- anchoring the framework to a possible fiscal rule
- the time horizon of the framework
- whether the MTEF should be "fixed" or "rolling"
- the time schedule of MTEF preparation within the budget cycle
- the way and the format in which the MTEF is used for State Council and National People's Congress decision making
- the rollover of the framework from one year to the next
- the linkage of the MTEF to the five-year plan and to the annual budget
- the division of institutional responsibilities for MTEF preparation (both within the Ministry of Finance and with other players, such as the NDRC)
- the sequencing of the introduction of the instrument

[2]Experiences of a diverse set of countries that have implemented MTEFs are described in Harris and others 2013, Schiavo-Campo 2012, Doe 2008, Holmes and Evans 2003, and Oxford Policy Management 2000.

How the MTEF is used for decision making is especially important. Aside from the many technical requirements, the Chinese authorities need to introduce the reform in a way that policymakers will actually use to decide on fiscal and budgetary policies over the medium term. In many developing and emerging market economies MTEFs have remained a technocratic, outlook-focused exercise, delinked from the budget process and with no real effect on political decision making—an outcome that China will want to avoid.

THE BUDGET PROCESS—GREAT IMPROVEMENTS IN RECENT YEARS

China has made great strides in reforming budget management in recent decades. Until the early 2000s, the annual budget was based on a functional classification, which was helpful in understanding the spending purpose of resources. In practice, however, it left too much uncertainty about the budget entity that would actually spend the resources. For example, education expenditure could be spent by various sectors/ministries: to support agricultural development, to train military specialists, or to strengthen educational programs of the Ministry of Education and Sciences. The introduction of departmental budgets assigned resources to individual departments and greatly improved transparency and the predictability of resource allocation.

Introducing elements of program budgeting strengthened this further. The departmental budgets were split into "basic expenditure," classified mostly along economic lines, and "projects," which are a mix of expenditure programs and capital investment projects. Given the split between basic and project expenditure, the programmatic classification in China does not yet cover all departmental expenditure. This means that programs do not contain all overhead or salary expenditures, still leaving the budget as an imperfect tool for deciding allocations.

The Ministry of Finance faces capacity constraints in assessing the realism of budget requests from departments, which reinforces the tendency to increase budget lines incrementally during the preparation of the annual budget, or to use standard costs that are not a good representation of actual costs given the diversity of costs in China. Despite these shortcomings, the introduction of program budgeting is a major step in better aligning expenditures with policy objectives, and has strengthened the policy focus of budget allocations.

From the Ministry of Finance's point of view, establishing departmental budgets has hardened their budget constraints. Under the functional budget system, the precise allocation for departments was often decided through in-year negotiations between the ministry and departments. The adoption of departmental budgets has also helped develop performance accountability: what level of resources would be used for achieving which results. In recent years, China has added a basic performance monitoring framework to the departmental budgets.

Other improvements to the budget process in the 2000s included wider coverage of the State Budget through the joint presentation and approval of its various components: the State Budget comprises the General Funds Budget (which covers expenditures and revenues of central government departments), the Government-Managed Funds Budget (which comprises the extrabudgetary funds), the State-Owned Enterprise Fund Budget, and the Social Security Fund Budget. Within the General Budget, the current and capital budget are now presented jointly, although China, in many ways, still has a dual budget process, with the Ministry of Finance responsible for recurrent and small capital expenditures and the NDRC responsible for the major capital projects.

While program budgeting and integration of current and capital expenditure planning can be improved, the most pressing obstacle to modern fiscal and budget management is the annual nature of the budget framework. The main limitations of the annual budget in China are the following:

- The coverage and time horizon of the annual budget limits application of fiscal discipline and the identification of fiscal risks in the wider government sector. As discussed, the coverage of the State Budget has improved and now includes all of the central government. However, an MTEF could be based on a fiscal framework that covers all of general government (including subnational government) and identifies risks three to four years into the future. This would provide a better understanding of the fiscal stance of government as a whole, the possible adjustment needed from the central government to accommodate the fiscal position of local government, or to negotiate a sharing of the fiscal space among layers of government (see Box 4.1).
- It is difficult to take into account shifts in expenditure trends within the central government looking only at an annual budget. Such shifts can make fiscal discipline and sustainability over the medium term problematic, even for the central government. Trends in expenditure programs are often not stable. Especially in the social sector, programs may start slowly, but then increase rapidly. This leaves policymakers with little time to react. This has been the experience of many advanced economies as they developed the welfare state in the 1960s and 1970s. A number of emerging market economies in southeast Asia are already starting to experience pressures on recurrent expenditure induced by demographics, new social spending programs, and decreasing growth rates.[3] Figure 4.1, panel 3, shows the considerable increase in the size of government in Association of Southeast Asian Nations countries over the past 10 years (over 5.5 percent of GDP). An MTEF would provide an early warning to policymakers to make necessary policy changes in a gradual manner.

[3]According to a United Nations projection, both east and southeast Asia are experiencing a rapid deceleration of fertility, with their shares of the 65+ age cohort set to quadruple and triple, respectively, by 2050.

Box 4.1. What Is Fiscal Space?

Fiscal space refers to the room for new policy initiatives, or—if fiscal space is negative—the need for spending cuts or additional revenue, given the government's fiscal targets.[1] In a medium-term expenditure framework, fiscal space is estimated over the medium term and can be calculated as the difference between the macro revenue estimates plus the deficit target, minus the baseline of expenditure. The baseline of expenditure is estimated as the total expenditure on all government policies and activities *assuming no change in policies relative to the present budget*. Of course, in some cases, the government will want to make reallocations between sectors or spending units or to reduce the budget of one or more spending units to create more fiscal space for new proposals of other units.

Figure 4.1.1. The Concept of Fiscal Space

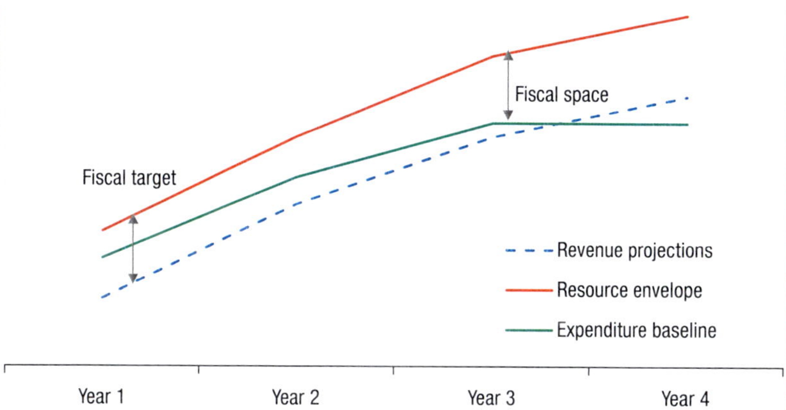

Source: IMF staff.

[1]For example, see Heller 2005; and Schick 2009.

- Implementing countercyclical fiscal policy over the economic cycle is challenging if it is merely based on an annual budget. It is difficult to judge the cyclical and structural components of economic growth in an annual context. A medium-term budget should allow policymakers to better plan and execute stimulus and consolidation strategies by identifying fiscal space and possible policy measures over a medium-term horizon.[4]
- Annual budgets are not well suited for providing strategic direction to expenditure. In annual budgeting, attempts at strategic decision making are

[4]For additional explanation on how fiscal rules can serve countercyclical fiscal policy, see IMF 2016.

basically repeated every year, maximizing the opposition to change by stakeholders. In principle, China's five-year plan should give strategic direction to program expenditure. However, the plan does not translate directly into sectoral expenditure allocations given its public investment focus. Further, the five-year plan is not based on the latest macroeconomic forecasts, but rather on macroeconomic targets. Thus it lacks the prioritization under realistic resource constraints that defines the budgeting process.

- As discussed, annual budgets do not provide budget managers in departments and at lower levels of government enough planning certainty. This often means that programs may not be prepared and executed well. Together with variability in funding this can lead to stop-go expenditure policies and an associated decrease of expenditure efficiency. Especially for local governments and for public investment, such uncertainties can have a considerable negative impact on expenditure effectiveness and efficiency.

HOW DOES AN MTEF WORK?

China is not the only country to experience the limitations of annual budgeting. The MTEF was developed in the late 1970s and early 1980s in countries such as Australia, the Netherlands, and New Zealand. Larger Organisation for Economic Co-operation and Development countries followed. The United Kingdom introduced its MTEF in the late 1980s. For European countries in the euro area, an MTEF became a requirement with the establishment of the single currency.

An MTEF can be defined as an institutional mechanism for setting multiyear objectives for fiscal policy and budget expenditure and ensuring that these are respected in budget formulation, approval, and execution. Three categories of MTEF are commonly defined in the literature, aligned with their stage of development: (1) the medium-term fiscal framework (MTFF), (2) the medium-term budget framework (MTBF), (3) and the medium-term program framework (MTPF). MTEFs encompass all three of these categories, although the literature is not always fully consistent on this point, and sometimes equates MTEFs just with MTBFs or MTPFs. This chapter follows the World Bank (2012) in usage of the term, which is that an MTEF encompasses all three categories. Figure 4.3 shows that MTBFs and MTPFs are quite common in advanced economies, but are still quite rare in Asia.

The MTFF is focused on fiscal aggregates and seeks to reconcile fiscal policy objectives (usually for the overall fiscal deficit) with aggregate expenditure and revenue estimates over the medium term. Policy measures presented are high level; for example, new tax rates, salary increases of civil servants, or introduction of significant legislation. These measures are reconciled to equate the resource envelope and fiscal targets with the top-down expenditure estimates over the time horizon of the MTFF. This is usually the first stage of MTEF development.

In the second stage, the MTBF goes through the same process but details expenditure at the level of the annual budget. This requires the reconciliation

Figure 4.3. Types of Medium-Term Expenditure Frameworks
(Number of economies)

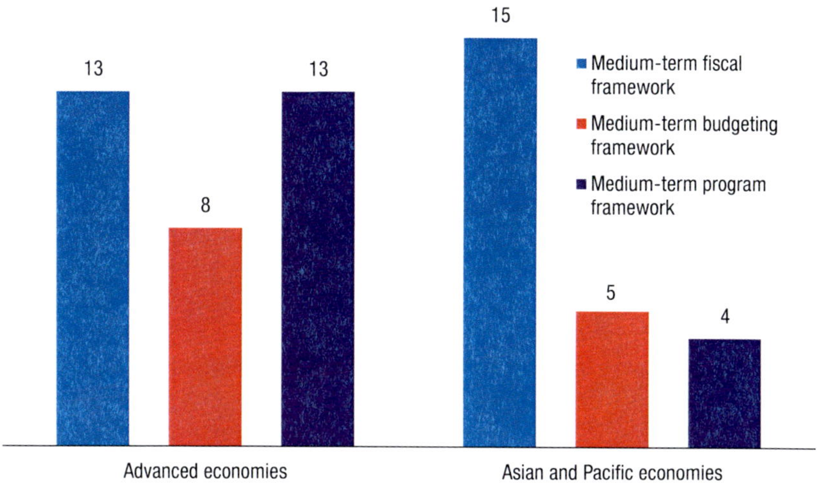

Source: World Bank 2012.

process to identify basically all expenditure and revenue measures at the same level of detail as in the annual budget. The MTBF requires preparation of annual budgets over the time horizon used, in practice, usually three to four years.

The MTPF encompasses both an MTFF and an MTBF but adds two features. First, the MTPF presents annual and out-year budgets in a programmatic format; second, these programs are linked to medium-term output and outcome targets. For example, Australia includes statements of objectives, deliverables, and key performance indicators for all major spending programs covering the full period of its MTEF. An MTPF is obviously a much more labor-intensive exercise than an MTFF. In addition, an MTPF requires a level of advanced decision making that many countries may not be ready for.

Coinciding with these three stages of development are the three main purposes for which MTEFs are usually introduced: (1) to enhance aggregate fiscal discipline, (2) to improve strategic allocation, and (3) to strengthen the effectiveness and efficiency of expenditures. To clarify what an MTEF implies, it is useful to separate the process of preparing an MTEF into four components:

- First comes the *setting of fiscal policy objectives* over the medium term. Fiscal policy sets targets for deficit, debt, or other fiscal aggregates based on objectives for sustainability and macroeconomic stability. In contrast with the annual budget, MTEFs are always driven by fiscal policy. In countries with only annual budgets, especially those that are prepared incrementally from year to year, budgets often drive fiscal policy, not the other way around, which can easily derail public finances. Very important in setting medium-term fiscal objectives is the realization that the impact of government on the economy is driven by general government, not just the central government. If the MTFF part of the MTEF covers only budgetary central government, and local government is a substantial part of overall government, fiscal policy will not reflect the actual influence of government on the macro economy.

In any case, an MTEF document should always contain a statement of fiscal strategy. This statement would clarify the fiscal objectives of government, such as fiscal sustainability, stabilization of the macro economy, size and economic composition of the public sector (that is, the balance of recurrent and capital spending), and possibly issues of intergenerational equity. The statement would then clarify how these high-level objectives are to be achieved (debt reduction, expenditure control, revenue mobilization, and so on). Specific targets for the main fiscal aggregates would be specified over the medium term. These can be qualitative and/or quantitative. If the government has translated its fiscal policy objectives into a numerical rule or rules, as many advanced and emerging market economies have done, the implications would be specified here.

- The second component in the development of the MTEF is *top-down forecasting*. An MTEF is based on a medium-term macroeconomic framework. This consists of a set of forecasts of key macroeconomic parameters, GDP growth, and the GDP deflator being the most important. The forecast should reflect a genuine forecast for the economy, not an aspirational target. Basing an MTEF on the latter usually leads to overestimation of the resource envelope, and the MTEF would not have the desired impact on fiscal discipline, and key budgetary decisions would still be postponed until they appear in the annual budget. It is the aspirational nature of strategic planning instruments, including their macroeconomic underpinnings, that has prompted many countries to introduce an MTEF.

  Once medium-term macroeconomic forecasts have been developed, the next step is to forecast revenue and expenditure at an aggregate level, again over the medium term. Given the fiscal targets and the revenue and expenditure forecasts, the aggregate fiscal space for new policy measures can now be calculated (Box 4.1). As discussed, planned cutbacks and revenue measures can increase fiscal space over the medium term even further to make space for additional expenditure priorities.
- The third step of the MTEF, developing the expenditure baseline, applies primarily to MTBFs and MTPFs. The baseline consists of the bottom-up projection of expenditures at the level of detail of the budget under the assumption of no policy change. The expenditure estimates are no longer calculated based on macroeconomic equations, but on aggregating all departmental budgets and line items in those budgets, with the assumption that no new policy is approved. In MTBFs and MTPFs, fiscal space is then calculated based on the difference between revenue forecasts and the baseline plus the fiscal deficit target (as borrowing increases fiscal space). This is

a much more detailed and accurate estimation of fiscal space than in the MTFF, which uses a top-down forecast of ongoing expenditures.

While the bottom-up forecasting under unchanged policies sounds straightforward, in practice it is not. Good baseline estimates require that the annual budget be costed accurately and that the implication of existing policies for expenditures can be forecast in the out-years with some confidence. In practice, that is no easy task, especially the latter. Some budget lines may be forecastable for the out-years of the MTEF based on simple formulas, or established limits, but expenditure programs will usually evolve with their cost base. Social expenditure programs, for example, will often depend on the state of the economy or on demographic factors. Estimates of capital investment will require the expenditure pattern for existing projects, but also for projects to be initiated in the out-years. Developing baseline estimates will require numerous assumptions to be made on costing the forward years, and detailed instruction must be provided to line ministries, to be assured that the underpinnings of the baseline are similar across line ministries.

Often ministries of finance make simplifications in that process that lead to inaccurate baseline estimates. For example, in many developing and emerging market economies, the baseline is calculated by multiplying the annual budget by the GDP deflator (constant program effort) or nominal GDP growth (constant program effort relative to the size of the economy). Both simplifications are often far from what actually transpires. In many cases, the macroeconomic forecast of aggregate expenditures is a better estimate of the baseline than one based on a crudely developed bottom-up baseline methodology. In practice, good baselines cannot be developed by the Ministry of Finance alone, as it is unlikely to have a full insight into the cost drivers of line ministry budgets. Input from line ministries, and perhaps also the planning ministry if it has spending responsibilities, becomes essential. For this reason, the transition from MTFF to MTBF requires full involvement of spending departments in the MTEF reform.

Once a sound baseline for existing policy is established, the resultant budget estimates should be projected through the agreed economic parameters. When deciding the appropriate parameters for inflation, a number of countries apply a charge on the baseline, referred to as an efficiency dividend. This can offer significant microeconomic benefits and strengthen overall fiscal discipline, as described in Box 4.2.

- The fourth step of the MTEF process is the *decision-making phase*. This comprises the development of a package of policy measures, estimated over the medium term on the expenditure and revenues side, that allows usage of available fiscal space or, put differently, that balances expenditure and revenue estimates to achieve fiscal targets. This reconciliation phase requires the costing of new policy measures over the medium term or of the expansion or reduction of existing policies. This can be even harder than estimating the baseline, as little experience has been gained yet with the new policies being

Box 4.2. Efficiency Dividend

A number of countries, such as Australia and Sweden, have introduced a charge against the baseline forecast for most agencies. This charge—often called an efficiency or productivity dividend—has become an integral component of some budget estimation methodologies.

Such dividends aim to do the following:

- Provide managers specifically and agencies generally with the incentive to continually seek new or more efficient means of undertaking ongoing government business.
- Allow government to redirect a portion of efficiency gains to higher-priority activities, be they tax reductions or other expenditure priorities.
- Increase the predictability of funding through providing a baseline that is affordable.
- Show clearly that, like the rest of the economy, the public sector can generate efficiencies resulting from improvements in management and administrative practices.

The arithmetic of applying an efficiency dividend is most compelling. The compounding of the savings over time means that, after five years, a 1.5 percent dividend annually will reduce running costs by 7.3 percent in real terms, or as much as 9.3 percent assuming annual inflation of 5 percent.

considered. The policy package would contain the estimates for the new policies of the coming budget. In the most advanced MTEFs, policy reforms to be initiated in later years would also be added to the package of policy measures. It is, in any case, quite common to leave a planning reserve for new policy initiatives in the out-years. Doing so leaves larger uncertainty over expenditure and revenue policies, but in dynamic economies it provides room for the introduction of new government policies without cutbacks in existing programs.

A major challenge of the fourth step is how to stage the MTEF for political decision making, as part of the overall budget process. Countries that have successfully integrated their MTEF into the budget process have usually done so by deciding on the main elements of the MTEF a number of months ahead of decision making on the annual budget. In this prebudget or strategic budgeting phase, decisions are made on the fiscal targets over the medium term, main elements of new policy and their costing, and expenditure ceilings for the annual budget and in some countries for the outer years of the MTEF as well.

As elsewhere, for an effective decision-making phase based on a new MTEF, strong collaboration among ministries in China will be critical, especially between the Ministry of Finance and the NDRC. Also, to ensure that fiscal targets are met over the medium term, approval by the State Council and the National People's Congress of a package of policy measures covering the entire period will be needed. Implementing an MTEF can in the initial years be quite taxing. Line ministries will often retain their traditional focus on the coming budget year, and the quality of the out-year costing could then be a concern. For this reason, countries usually start with an MTFF, which requires neither a bottom-up expenditure baseline nor costing of all budget lines. An MTFF requires agreement on fiscal targets over the medium term and the main elements of a package of measures that will make fiscal targets achievable.

A crucial part of the MTEF is how the instrument is rolled over from one year to another. If used for decision making over the medium term, then the first out-year of the present MTEF should become the budget year of the new MTEF. MTEFs are adjusted for changes to the macroeconomic forecasts and new costing of the baseline. However, such adjustments should be clearly traceable from one year to the next, with the effect of linking the MTEF in one year with the MTEF in the next.

What often happens, however, especially in developing economies, is that MTEFs are not connected and not properly rolled over from year to year, that is, the MTEF exercise is basically redone every year. This can have multiple causes. Most common is that too little effort is made negotiating out-year budget lines between the Ministry of Finance and line ministries (which in the case of China would also involve the NDRC), because policy priorities change or the macro forecasts had large errors. Under these circumstances, redoing the MTEF makes sense, but then the country does not really have an expenditure framework for the medium term. Instead it could be viewed as having a medium-term outlook, either at the fiscal or the budget level. Such fiscal or budget outlooks have their uses, but line ministries soon lose interest in their preparation as it does not lead to meaningful decision making over the medium term. Figure 4.4 presents the typical development path of an MTEF.

WHAT ARE THE MTEF DESIGN CHOICES FOR CHINA?

MTEFs differ from country to country. Nonetheless, some requirements are common to any MTEF, and others can be chosen based on the priorities for improving fiscal and budget management. Below, some of the issues that the Chinese authorities may want to address are discussed.

Macro-Fiscal Forecasting Capacity

For a successful MTEF, China's macro modeling and forecasting capacity needs to be strengthened. The macro framework for the five-year plan is prepared by the NDRC. This framework, however, is aspirational in character. It consists of targets not forecasts. For keeping an MTEF up to date, countries usually update the macro framework twice a year. At present, the macro framework for the five-year plan is updated only once in its whole term. Macro forecasts are prepared annually for budget preparation purposes. The time horizon of the macro forecast would need to be at least equal to that of the MTEF. Who should undertake this task in the Chinese context is one of the institutional issues discussed later in this chapter.

The Ministry of Finance prepares the medium-term fiscal outlook presented in the five-year plan. For the MTEF, it will need to be done on the basis of

Figure 4.4. Typical Stages in Developing Medium-Term Budget Planning Instruments

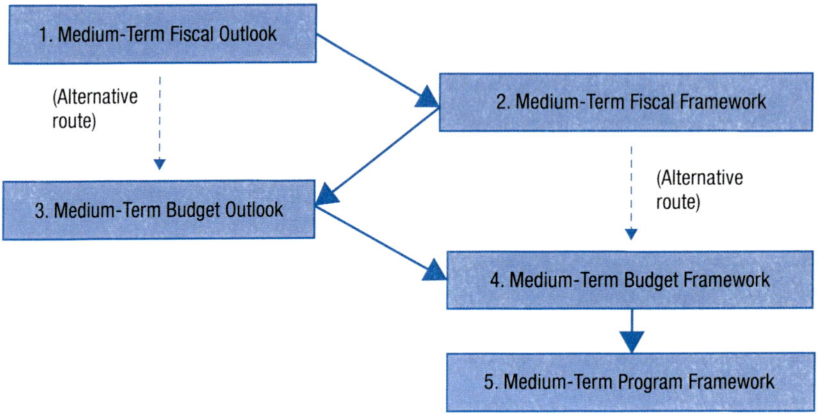

Source: IMF staff.

regularly updated macro forecasts. The accuracy of the fiscal forecast will need to improve, as the MTEF will be used as a tool for medium-term decision making. Large forecast errors will undermine the credibility of the framework and diminish the interest in its use. Weak forecasting capacity is the main reason countries get stuck in the fiscal or budgetary outlook phase of MTEF development.

MTEF Coverage

In principle, an MTEF functions best as an instrument of fiscal policy and discipline if it covers as large a part of the public sector as possible. Only then are limits on spending shared by all. But there are practical limitations to this principle. The central government can in practice have no authority over local government spending. Also, the inclusion of extrabudgetary funds can be problematic as they often provide for mandatory expenditure programs that cannot be curtailed. International experience has shown that the possibility of noninclusion of expenditure in the framework will provide incentives to spending departments to set up extrabudgetary channels or offload spending responsibilities to the subnational government. There is extensive literature on how planning mechanisms such as the MTEF create an incentive to engage in off-budget expenditure, creative accounting, fiscal escape routes, and so on.[5] Private financing guaranteed by the state and public-private partnerships are examples of often-used escape routes for government spending.

[5]For examples, see Koen and van den Noord 2005 and Irwin 2012.

One way to obviate such inadvertent use would be to have the medium-term fiscal framework cover all of general government. Now that the authorities have "opened the front door" of (formal) local government finance and "closed the back door" of (informal) borrowing (through local government financing vehicles), the central government can set the fiscal target for general government and divide the borrowing quota between central and local government. This means that the resource envelope for central government is based on its expected revenues plus a deficit target that implies sustainability for the entire government.

However, when expanding the MTEF to the detail required in an MTBF or MTPF, the government would be well advised to limit the MTEF to the coverage of the State Budget. It is these detailed expenditures that are under its control and worth planning for within a medium-term framework.

Anchoring the Framework to a Fiscal Rule

This discussion is linked to the issue of coverage. Any MTEF will have a set of fiscal targets over the medium term; otherwise the resource constraint is not a hard one and no expenditure ceilings are set by the framework (which means the framework is not a framework, but an outlook). However, a fiscal rule implies that fiscal targets over the medium term are set not based on judgment and discretion, but by a formal or informal rule, which can be either nonnumerical or numerical.

The Ministry of Finance has in the past used an informal numerical fiscal rule that general government should not have a deficit higher than 3 percent of GDP (in practice the rule applied to the central government, as until 2014 local governments were not allowed to borrow). The National People's Congress formally approved the rule in 2015 as part of the annual budget, but this decision could be amended from year to year. A general discussion about the cost and benefits of fiscal rules is beyond the scope of this chapter, as is the question of whether China should adopt a fiscal rule enshrined in law, what type of rule is best, or what limit it should have.[6] It is a positive step, however, that the authorities have clarified that a fiscal rule governing general government should guide fiscal policy and MTEF formulation.

Whatever the basis for fiscal policy, fiscal policy objectives will translate into expenditure ceilings over the medium term. An important design element of an MTEF is how such medium-term ceilings will be applied to government expenditure. Some OECD countries for example have excluded mandatory expenditures such as social security and interest payments, given that these expenditures cannot be changed without entitlement reform or are difficult to forecast over the medium term. Most countries have taken some intermediate position, excluding some but not all mandatory expenditure. The reason is that excluding too much expenditure from the ceiling determination will require much larger adjustments

[6]For a general discussion on fiscal rules, see IMF 2009.

to discretionary expenditure. Including mandatory expenditure to some extent will force entitlement reform if it really becomes necessary.[7]

Time Horizon of the Framework

This practical aspect of MTEF design is usually guided by several factors. First, the volatility of the economy can make forecasting four to five years out difficult. Some countries keep their framework limited to three years (or even two years in a very few cases). Second, the political priorities of government can change considerably. Third, the term of government can be used to set the duration of the MTEF. This implies that the government policy agenda is represented by the MTEF in the first year of the administration.

Finally, in China, the alignment of the MTEF with the five-year plan would have benefits. To have the five-year plan fully costed and prioritized against the available resource ceiling could strengthen the link between plan and medium-term budget. Further discussion on this topic is necessary, but given the limits to macro forecasting and of costing of out-year policy measures, China may want to consider a time horizon of only three years. This would help increase the credibility of the MTEF. It would also point out that strategic planning documents, such as the five-year plan, have a different aim than the budget. Linking the two directly would probably have only limited benefits and may actually make the preparation of both more difficult.

Fixed or Rolling MTEF

This also alludes to the time horizon, but in a different way. Under a fixed system, the framework would be established for the term of the administration or of the duration, for example, of the five-year plan. Every year the MTEF would become a year shorter. The out-years that are not part of the MTEF would have the character of a fiscal or budgetary outlook.

The rolling MTEF, on the other hand, would gain a new year, every year, so the length of the MTEF would always be the same. Rolling frameworks are internationally the most common. They have the benefit of not leaving large uncertainty between planning periods.

Embedding the MTEF in the Budget Process

As noted above, the MTEF and the budget should be closely integrated. One of the main reasons MTEFs fail to have an effect is because the ministries of finance treat them as two separate documents, sometimes prepared by two different teams within the ministry. For an advanced MTEF, an MTBF, or an MTPF, the budget should represent the first year of the period covered by the MTEF. The MTFF presents the fiscal targets, outlook, and agreed main policy measures for the medium term, and for the annual budget.

---

[7]See Robinson 2016.

MTEFs are usually prepared at least once, but often twice, per year. If once a year, the MTEF is prepared and approved together with the budget. In many advanced economies, the MTEF is prepared twice a year. The first time allows for a strategic phase in the budget process. Assuming a budget calendar that follows the calendar year, this phase usually takes place around March–April and allows for the main strategic allocation decisions to be made before the detailed budget is prepared.[8] In the strategic phase, the overall deficit and expenditure ceiling is set to reflect the fiscal policy stance. In the case of an advanced MTEF, expenditure ceilings per ministry are set both for the budget year and for the out-years of the MTEF. If no ceilings are set for the out-years, no decisions can be made on allocations in the out-years, and the MTBF or MTPF reverts to a medium-term budgetary outlook.

A Real or a Nominal MTEF

This, again, is a design element in which countries have made different choices. Most countries define the MTEF in nominal terms, using estimates for price inflation and other cost drivers to estimate the baseline and new expenditure that can be implemented within the resource envelope. This has the benefit of expenditure ceilings being set in nominal amounts. Price shocks are then not compensated automatically by the framework.

A number of countries define the MTEF in real terms. This makes it much easier to see whether expenditure programs are scheduled to increase in real terms, stay constant, or decrease. However, the implication of an MTEF in real terms is that every year an inflation adjustment is automatically made to expenditures. In countries with substantial inflation rates, say higher than 3–4 percent, setting the framework in nominal amounts decreases the risk of public finances getting out of control by the automatic accommodation of inflation shocks.

The design choices discussed here have to some extent already been taken by the Ministry of Finance in its pilot MTEF prepared for internal use in 2014. The choices made include a time horizon of three years (2015–17), updating of the MTEF on a rolling basis, presentation in nominal terms, a focus on a framework for fiscal aggregates, and an outlook on detailed program expenditures. The latter part includes central government expenditures, including, importantly, all transfers to subnational governments. The MTEF also includes all anticipated policy decisions in the forward years.

This is an ambitious start, which reflects the authorities' strong commitment to a multiyear approach to budgeting. Given the rapid introduction of the MTEF pilot, it is likely that some aspects of the design need to be further developed. Other countries have typically gone through a period, often lasting a number of

[8]Given that China's fiscal year is from April through March, the strategic phase of budget preparation, that is the discussion by the State Council of the first MTEF in the annual cycle, would be around June–July of the prebudget year. A second, updated version would be included in the budget documentation in March.

years, of adjusting the MTEF design in order to obtain maximum benefit. Therefore, it is to be expected that the nature and performance of the MTEF in China will evolve over the coming years.

WHO SHOULD BE RESPONSIBLE FOR DEVELOPMENT OF THE MTEF?

The above discussion assumes that that developing the MTEF is the work of the Ministry of Finance. In most countries around the world, ministries of finance are responsible for fiscal policy and for the budget, so it is only logical that they would have the lead in developing medium-term fiscal and budgetary frameworks. As in other countries with planning ministries, however, we believe that in the Chinese context the NDRC would also need to play an important role. Line ministries also have their role to play in the MTEF once it moves beyond the MTFF phase.

The MTEF is a document intended to fill the gap between the national plan, the five-year plan in China, and the annual budget. For many countries, the MTEF was developed in situations where the national plan had been discarded and ministries of planning had been disbanded (or merged into the Ministry of Finance). The lack of multiyear planning was in many OECD countries one of the reasons for developing the MTEF. In most emerging market and developing economies, planning ministries still play a crucial role in providing strategic direction to government policies and in reviewing, selecting, and monitoring capital investment projects. In China, the NDRC has this role, and the five-year plan is a prestigious and influential document. For this reason, it will be important to ensure that the MTEF and five-year plan are consistent in the first year of the five-year plan, and in the year of the five-year plan update. However, on the use of the requisite macro framework, the MTEF should not compromise. It should be based on realistic macro forecasts, not on aspirational targets.

What concrete roles should the Ministry of Finance, the NDRC, and line ministries carry out with respect to the MTEF? The following could be considered:

- **Macro forecasting.** Although it is advisable that the Ministry of Finance develop its own macro-forecasting capacity, the lead institution in preparing the macro framework could be the NDRC. The NDRC currently prepares the framework for the five-year plan and the annual projections for the budget. It could be tasked with making the medium-term forecasts for the macro economy. Assignment of this responsibility to another part of government is not uncommon in many countries. The Ministry of Finance should develop macro-forecasting capacity in parallel, to be able to discuss the feasibility of the NDRC's projections. Most macro frameworks prepared for MTEFs are dubbed "*cautious, but realistic.*" It has been argued repeatedly here that forecasts should not be aspirational, but it is equally important not to be too cautious as this will lead to systematic underestimation of revenue, and supplementary budgets would be required during budget execution every year. This disrupts the budget process and to some extent negates the multiyear planning of expenditures.

- **Investment programming.** China has a large public investment program, and it is essential that a central institution play a supervisory and coordinating role. The NDRC would seem best placed to develop a costed and prioritized multiyear pipeline of projects that would be integrated into the MTEF. The Ministry of Finance would set the overall ceilings for investment expenditure over the medium term, just as it does for the annual budget now, and the NDRC would review and select, with input of the Ministry of Finance on costing, the projects aligned with the five-year plan, and with the highest benefit to the Chinese economy. The MTEF would also require coordination between the Ministry of Finance and the NDRC on the integration of recurrent and capital budgets, that is, allocating funds to the recurrent budget to ensure full productivity of past and current capital outlays. The MTEF is specifically used by countries to better allocate maintenance and operational expenditure for capital assets. In many countries, such integration is lacking, harming the efficiency of public investment.
- **Setting multiyear fiscal policy.** Developing the fiscal policy statement, including multiyear targets for the main fiscal aggregates, is mainly a task for the Ministry of Finance. Usually, finance ministries set up separate fiscal policy offices, either inside their budget office or parallel to them. This choice usually comes down to the existing focus of the budget office. If the focus is very detailed and engaged in the budget preparation of many first-level spending units, it usually makes sense to develop a separate fiscal policy office. If the budget office has already delegated much of the detailed budget preparation to line ministries, and has taken a more strategic role in preparation of the budget, a fiscal policy unit can be integrated into the budget office. Many ministries of finance in Asia have chosen to set up separate fiscal policy offices (Indonesia, Malaysia, Thailand). Establishing separate units for fiscal and budgetary policy carries coordination risks in that the MTEF and budget may not be well integrated.
- **Fiscal forecasting.** The Ministry of Finance will also need to make top-down multiyear estimates of fiscal aggregates on the basis of the NDRC's macro forecasts. Good forecasting requires in-depth understanding of existing tax policy and revenue administration and an understanding of major expenditure programs, especially the mechanics of expenditure sensitivity to the business cycle (that is, the automatic stabilizing properties of various programs such as social welfare and unemployment insurance schemes) and benefit programs (such as pensions) whose funding is determined by the number of eligible individuals. Internationally, revenue forecasting is often done by a separate unit within the Ministry of Finance, which interacts closely with tax policy and administration entities.

- **Baseline estimates of expenditure programs.** Once the MTEF moves beyond the MTFF stage, the baseline of expenditure should be prepared by the budget office, the Budget Department in the Chinese context, but in cooperation with line ministries and agencies. Often the initial estimates are made, or should be made, by the line ministries, given their much deeper understanding of the cost structure of their programs. Accurately estimating program expenditure for the annual budget is quite taxing by itself. Baseline estimates of expenditure programs over the medium term can have the additional difficulty of being influenced by exogenous variables, as discussed earlier. For this reason, introducing baseline estimates for decision making is often only done after extensive piloting in cooperation with selected line ministries.
- **Reconciliation of resource envelope, baselines, and new policy measures.** Development of new spending and revenue packages is clearly a responsibility of the Ministry of Finance—specifically, its budget office. Just as with the annual budget, inputs from policy departments within the Ministry of Finance, the NDRC, and line ministries will be extremely important. Costing of annual and medium-term expenditure cutbacks on existing programs, of new taxation initiatives, and the introduction of new program expenditures will be for the Ministry of Finance to estimate and present to the State Council.

SEQUENCING THE INTRODUCTION OF THE MTEF TO MAKE IT A SUCCESS

Many MTEFs globally have not lived up to expectations. In some countries, the basic public financial infrastructure for MTEFs is lacking. The list of prerequisites for successful MTEFs includes a credible annual budget, effective fiscal reporting and cash management, and reliable budget execution. Capacity in macro forecasting, planning and budgeting, and sectoral policy analysis can be added to this list.

Two more considerations can either make or break an MTEF. First, the commitment of the policymakers to using the instrument. In the Chinese context, without support from the NDRC and State Council for the new budget management tool, effective implementation will be difficult. Second, the MTEF document needs to be clear and provide insight into the fiscal and budgetary objectives, strategy, and concrete policy measures of government over the medium term. For initial support not to dwindle, benefits from using the instrument should be evident. Benefits such as more effective fiscal policy, enhanced budget predictability and discipline, better insight into expenditure trends, and improved strategic direction will all depend on the clarity, accuracy, and dependability of the exposition in the MTEF document.

For these reasons, sequencing of MTEF reform is important. Too many countries attempt to produce an MTBF or even an MTPF too quickly. It would seem more appropriate for China to start with an MTFF. This would not require the support of the line ministries. It would allow fiscal policy to be placed in a medium-term perspective, and set fiscal policy of general government at a sustainable level and attuned to the business cycle. It would focus on bringing the augmented deficit under control. That should be a policy priority of government. The reconciliation process of bringing fiscal space into equilibrium with new policy measures would be based on major expenditure programs and tax measures only. This means that the technical requirements would lie mainly in the sphere of fiscal policy, macro and fiscal forecasting, and costing of major policy proposals.

The introduction of an MTFF could coincide with presentation of a budgetary outlook, a forecast of expenditure at the level of detail presented in the budget based on expenditure planning foreseen by the Ministry of Finance. The MTFF plus budget outlook would need only limited support of line ministries. The extension of the MTFF to a full MTBF or even an MTPF, while tempting for its promise of improved expenditure planning, allocation, and predictability, would need to wait until extensive piloting and development efforts have been done by the Ministry of Finance and line ministries. It should be noted that countries such as Australia did not disclose their MTEF and related projections in the early years of its MTEF development for fear of political repercussions. Only when sufficient confidence has been achieved in developing a baseline methodology for bottom-up expenditure forecasting, in costing new policy proposals at a detailed level, and in being able to connect this year's MTEF to the previous year's and the following year's should that next step in the reform process be attempted.

CONCLUSIONS

China has recognized a need to strengthen its budget planning instruments by setting itself the goal of developing a medium-term expenditure framework. The 2014 revised budget law that came into force in early 2015 is a landmark achievement that directs this reform and will set China's fiscal and budgetary management on a much sounder footing.

At present, the budget is still determined on an annual basis, which is not well aligned with the aspirations of medium-term expenditure planning and aggregate fiscal management. The strategic direction of government policies needs to be couched within realistic expenditure constraints, which are not always provided through the five-year plan. Despite significant progress in modernizing the annual budget process, the authorities quite rightly intend to take the next step in budget process reform. This step will help ensure fiscal discipline and identify fiscal risks at an earlier stage. At the same time, it will facilitate countercyclical fiscal policy and help plan government expenditure programs more effectively and efficiently.

In the coming years, China will need to develop its own MTEF. Among the essential capacity-building prerequisites are formulating medium-term fiscal policy targets that are based on sustainability and stability objectives, strengthening top-down macroeconomic and fiscal forecasting, establishing a bottom-up expenditure baseline, and developing a strategic decision-making phase in the budget process on the use of fiscal space over the medium term.

Importantly, preparation of the MTEF will require setting fiscal policy objectives over the medium term for the whole of general government. As the surge in public investment has shown over the past decade, it is important to be able to direct, but also to control, the impact of fiscal policy of both central and local government on the economy. The MTEF will also need to be based on a sound medium-term macroeconomic framework, reflecting the real economic outlook rather than economic targets.

The MTEF will present policy measures over the medium term to allocate available fiscal space to achieve its fiscal targets. Rolling over the MTEF from year to year is crucial, adjusting for changes in macroeconomic forecasting and new costing. The time horizon of the MTEF could start with three-year time horizons to gain traction.

Finally, it is essential to incorporate the MTEF into the budget process and into political decision making to reap its full benefits. International experience suggests that without political support, the MTEF could remain a largely technocratic exercise, and will not get serious consideration from spending departments.

Moving toward an MTEF is a substantial, multiyear reform. It will require collaboration across ministries. International experience suggests that while finance ministries are key for its development and operation, other line ministries, such as the NDRC in China, will also play important roles.

Sequencing of the reform process is important. China could start with a limited MTEF, an MTFF, that places fiscal policy in a medium-term perspective, particularly bringing off-budget local government spending in check. A medium-term budget outlook could present details on expected expenditures as foreseen by the Ministry of Finance. China could then gradually fill in other components of the MTEF to move toward a full medium-term budget framework over the medium term. Success in establishing the MTEF will provide a very necessary bridge for policymakers over the current gap between the national strategic five-year plans and the annual budget process.

REFERENCES

Clements, B., K. Dybczak, V. Gaspar, S. Gupta, and M. Soto. 2015. "The Fiscal Consequences of Shrinking Populations." Staff Discussion Note 15/21, International Monetary Fund, Washington.

Doe, L. 2008. "The 2008 World Bank/CABRI/OECD Survey of Budgeting Practices and Procedures in Africa and Asia." *IMF PFM Blog*. October 24, 2008. http://blog-pfm.imf.org/pfmblog/2008/10/the-2008-world.html.

Harris, J., R. Hughes, G. Ljungman, and C. Sateriale. 2013. "Medium-Term Budget Frameworks in Advanced Economies: Objectives, Design, and Performance." Chapter 4 in *Public Financial Management and Its Emerging Architecture*. Washington: International Monetary Fund.

Heller, P. 2005. "Understanding Fiscal Space." Policy Discussion Paper 05/4, International Monetary Fund, Washington.

Holmes, M., and A. Evans. 2003. *A Review of Experience in Implementing Medium Term Expenditure Frameworks in a PRSP Context: A Synthesis of Eight Country Studies*. London: Overseas Development Institute.

International Monetary Fund (IMF). 2009. "Fiscal Rules—Anchoring Expectations for Sustainable Public Finances." Staff Paper, International Monetary Fund, Washington.

———. 2014. *China Article IV Consultation Staff Report*. Washington.

———. 2016. "Flexible Fiscal Rules and Countercyclical Fiscal Policy." Working Paper No. 16/8, International Monetary Fund, Washington.

Irwin, T. 2012. "Accounting Devices and Fiscal Illusions." Staff Discussion Note 12/02, International Monetary Fund, Washington.

Koen, V., and P. van den Noord. 2005. "Fiscal Gimmickry in Europe: One-Off Measures and Creative Accounting." OECD Economics Department Working Paper 417, Organisation for Economic Co-operation and Development, Paris.

Oxford Policy Management. 2000. "Medium-Term Expenditure Frameworks—Panacea or Dangerous Distraction?" *Oxford Policy Management Review*, Paper 2, May 2000.

Robinson, M. 2016. "The Coverage of Aggregate Expenditure Ceilings." *OECD Journal on Budgeting* 15 (1): 125–45.

Schiavo-Campo, S. 2012. "Of Mountains and Molehills: The Medium-Term Expenditure Framework. Sustainability and Efficiency in Managing Public Expenditure." Paper presented at the Conference on Sustainability and Efficiency in Managing Public Expenditures 24–25 July 2012, Seoul.

Schick, A. 2009. "Budgeting for Fiscal Space." *OECD Journal on Budgeting* 2009/2. Paris.

World Bank. 2012. *Beyond the Annual Budget: Global Experience with Medium-Term Expenditure Frameworks*. Washington: World Bank.

CHAPTER 5

Social Security Reform for Sustainability and Equity

MAURICIO SOTO AND SANJEEV GUPTA

China's population is aging rapidly. The old-age dependency ratio (the population ages 65 and older as a share of the population 15–64) is projected to increase from 13 percent in 2015 to 47 percent in 2050.[1] This is a relatively fast increase compared to the rest of the world, where the old-age dependency ratio is expected to only double over this period. By 2050, China's old-age dependency ratio will be at about the level projected for the developed economies.

Population aging will lead to pension spending pressures, with such spending projected to increase 6.2 percentage points to 10.1 percent of GDP over 2015–50. Already today, benefits exceed contributions (excluding central government subsidies) in some provinces. These pressures are likely to get accentuated in the long term, unless major policy changes are implemented. Over 2015–50, the actuarial imbalance (present discounted value of benefits minus contributions) of the Chinese pension system is estimated at nearly 125 percent of 2015 GDP. Today, pension coverage is nearly universal, but not necessarily adequate—about 60 percent of the elderly receive annual average pensions that are about RMB1,000 (or 2½ percent of GDP per capita). Under these parameters, reforms would be needed to maintain fiscal sustainability and address adequacy.

Recent reforms have focused on fostering gradual integration across pension schemes. However, the pension system remains fragmented and imposes impediments on labor mobility, with separate schemes depending on the type of worker and location. Management of pension systems remains at the provincial level, and rules vary slightly across provinces and schemes. Furthermore, the social contribution rates are relatively high and regressive. In the medium term, reforms could help provide adequate incentives to contribute to the system and to allow portability of benefits across regions and schemes.

Sound and equitable pension reforms could also contribute to the rebalancing of the economy toward domestic consumption. By ensuring sustainability

The authors would like to thank Professor ZHENG Bingwen, Director of the Social Security Center at the Chinese Academy of Social Sciences, for insightful comments and recommendations on this chapter. The authors are also grateful for valuable suggestions from Csaba Feher and Philippe Wingender, and for the input and support from editors.

[1]This chapter uses demographic projections from the United Nations (2015).

through gradual and transparent parametric reforms, retirement incomes would be more predictable, partly reducing the need for precautionary saving (Chamon, Liu, and Prasad 2013). Furthermore, by enhancing the adequacy of benefits for rural and urban residents, social security could help to redistribute income to older, lower-income households, which have higher propensity to consume (Yang, Zhang, and Zhou 2012).

This chapter reviews the pension system, followed by an examination of its demographic context and challenges in China. It considers ways to contain potentially higher pension costs, followed by conclusions.

PENSION SYSTEM LANDSCAPE

China's segmented pension system has separate old-age insurance schemes for (1) salaried workers in the private and state-owned enterprise sectors (Pensions for Urban Workers and Staff), (2) employees in the government and public-affiliated entities (Pensions for Civil Service and Public Sector Units), and (3) the rest of nonsalaried workers (Pensions for Urban and Rural Residents) (Table 5.1). The pension system is fragmented both across schemes (enterprise workers and urban and rural residents) and geographically (although the central government provides guidelines and financing, the schemes are administered at the local, provincial, or prefecture levels).

- *Pensions for Urban Workers and Staff* function on a pay-as-you-go basis, with some partial prefunding (reflecting years with combined contributions from workers, employers, and the state). Under the schemes, pensions are contributory, but the central government is responsible for covering any deficits. About 25 percent of the population ages 15–59 contributes to these schemes. At retirement, benefits are the sum of a traditional defined benefit formula plus a defined contribution portion, which in practice functions as a notional defined contribution pension (benefits depending on contributions and a notional return). Over 83 million people (40 percent of people ages 60 and older) receive benefits from the enterprise pension system (covering salaried workers). Average annual benefits are nearly 50 percent of GDP per capita. Individuals participating in the enterprise system often receive supplementary separation benefits financed by the enterprises. In 2014 total expenditure in this system was estimated at about 3 percent of GDP.
- *Pensions for Civil Service and Public Unit Workers* provide old-age insurance for workers in the government (civil service) and public service units, including schools and hospitals. Participants in this plan have traditionally not paid contributions, and pensions are fully funded by the budget. This scheme covers about 4 percent of the population ages 15–59. At retirement, after 35 years of service, pensions depend on a formula that provides 85 percent of the wage at retirement.[2] Pensioners from this scheme are 6½ percent

[2]Before 2006, after 35 years of service, civil servants were entitled to a combination of 100 percent of the portion of the salary corresponding to the base and seniority and 82 percent of the post and position pay (Leckie 2009).

Table 5.1. Summary of China's Pension System

	Pension for Urban Workers and Staff	Pensions for Civil Service and Public Service Units	Pensions for Urban and Rural Residents
Coverage	Salaried workers in the enterprise sector	Civil service and public service workers	Urban and rural residents 16 years and older not covered by pensions for urban workers
Funding	Pay as you go, partially funded	Pay as you go	Base pension: pay-as-you-go, contributory component; funded
Contribution (% of wages)	8% worker and 20% employer	Noncontributory, pensions funded from budget	Workers choose contribution category from RMB100–500 (rural) and RMB100–1,000 (urban); government contribution of at least RMB30
Benefit Formula	Defined benefit formula for the employer contribution (notional) defined contribution account for the worker; contribution	Defined benefit formula	Flat base pension plus annuity from funded defined contribution account
Pensionable Age	Age 60 (men) 55 (women)	Age 60 (men) 55 (women)	Age 60 (men and women)
Contributions in 2014			
Billion RMB	1,873	0.0	70
Percent of GDP	2.9	0.0	0.1
Contributors in 2014			
Thousand	241,174	39,182	354,335
Percent of pop. 15–59	25.9	4.2	38.1
Expenditure in 2014			
Billion RMB	1,980	382	159
Percent of GDP	3.1	0.6	0.3
Beneficiaries in 2014			
Thousand	83,201	13,517	151,127
Percent of pop. 60 and older	39.8	6.5	72.2
Average Annual Benefit in 2014			
Thousand RMB	23.8	28.2	1.1
Percent of GDP per capita	51.5	61.1	2.3

Sources: Ministry of Finance of the People's Republic of China 2015; and IMF staff calculations.

of the population ages 60 and older with average benefits near 61 percent of GDP per capita. In 2014 expenditure in this system was about 0.6 percent of GDP. Since 2013 reforms have aimed to establish a fairer and more sustainable pension system for the public sector, including setting the principles for a contributory scheme in 2015 (Li 2015).

- *Pensions for Urban and Rural Residents* combine a flat, pay-as-you-go "basic" pension (financed solely by the state) with an individual account component (intended to be fully financed by contributions and government subsidies). About 40 percent of the workforce contributes to this scheme. Individuals can choose their level of annual contributions in RMB100 increments, RMB100–500 for rural residents and RMB100–1,000 for urban residents. The government matches these contributions by at least RMB30 per year. The basic pension requires individuals to contribute for a minimum of 15 years to receive benefits. Over the past 5 years, the system expanded rapidly through special transition rules to provide basic pensions to the current elderly who never contributed.[3] Today, about 150 million elderly (over 70 percent of the population ages 60 and older) receive basic pensions. Average benefits are modest, as noted, representing about 2½ percent of GDP per capita. This explains the relatively low expenditure (estimated at 0.3 percent of GDP in 2014).

Important reforms have been implemented over the past 20 years, largely aimed at ensuring long-term sustainability in Pensions for Urban Workers and Staff, increasing the traditionally low coverage of the system (in 1995, only about 20 percent of the elderly received pensions) and better integrating the different schemes. The 1997 and 2005 reforms changed the architecture and expected generosity of the Pensions for Urban Workers and Staff.[4] Prior to 1997, workers with 35 years of contributions were generally eligible for pensions that replaced up to 80 percent of the average wage in the province from which they retired. The old formula was replaced by three components:

- The first intended to be a smaller version of the previous pensions, with benefits calculated as 0.5 percent of the base wage for each year of contribution. This component provides a degree of redistribution in the system (Li 2014).
- The second is estimated as 0.5 percent of the individual's career-average wage for each year of contributions.
- The third component was an individual account funded with 8 percent of wages, where the benefits depended on the accumulation of the account and interest (generally the one-year bank rate) converted to a monthly pension at retirement dividing the balance by an annuity factor of 139.

This change in architecture reduced the generosity of the pension system: at retirement after 35 years of contribution, a worker who earns the average

[3]Other countries have expanded their pension systems rapidly. For example, Korea introduced the national pension in 1988, which became universal for all labor force participants by 1999 (Kim 2014).

[4]State Council 1997, 2005.

provincial wage would receive a pension slightly under 60 percent of the average provincial wage.[5] The reform set a transition path where the new rules applied fully for all individuals entering the labor force after 1997 ("*Xinren*"), but benefits granted under the old formula remained unchanged for those who claimed pensions before the law ("*Laoren*"). For those in the middle ("*Zhongren*"), the benefits combine the old and new systems, depending on the years of contributions in the old system. Today, *Laoren* are less than 15 percent of the total number of pensioners, and the rest are *Zhongren*. Current benefits for new entrants are very similar to those for *Laoren*, since those retiring in 2016 have nearly 20 years under the new system. This reform largely explains the fall in replacement rates in 1997–2015, over which the average expenditure per pensioner declined from over 70 percent of the urban wage in 1995–99 to under 50 percent in 2007, remaining stable after that (Figure 5.1).

The deployment of Pensions for Urban and Rural Residents after 2010 achieved universal pension coverage of the elderly. The number of pensioners as a share of the population 60 and older increased steadily in the 1990s and 2000s, then rapidly climbed to over 100 percent in 2010–12 (Figure 5.2).[6] The steady increase largely reflects a gradual increase in the contributors to Pensions for Urban Workers and Staff, which roughly tracks the increase in urban employment in the labor force (Figure 5.3). The rapid climb since 2009 is due to the introduction of the Pensions for Urban and Rural Residents, which went from covering less than 1 percent of the elderly in 2009 to over 75 percent in 2013.

Recent reforms have focused on fostering better integration across pension schemes. For example, the State Council announced measures to integrate the Pensions for Civil Service and Public Service Units effective October 2015 (Yu 2015).[7] Although the details of the implementation are still being refined—including grandfathering parameters for those with significant years of service under the previous regime—the objective of the reform is to gradually equalize pensions for government workers to those in the private and enterprise sector. Further measures to adjust the contribution rates across systems are under consideration.[8] Under the new scheme, both the government as an employer and public employees will make mandatory contributions to social security

[5]For workers earning the provincial average wage through their career, the first and second component provide 35 percent (0.5 × 35 × provincial wage, 0.5 × 35 × career wage). Assuming returns are equal to wage growth, an 8 percent contribution would generate a balance of 2.8 times the average wage after 35 years, which divided by 139 and multiplied by 12 months produces a pension of 24.17 percent of the wage. For this hypothetical worker, the Urban Workers and Staff pension would replace 59.2 percent of preretirement earnings (35 percent + 24.17 percent).

[6]This share is higher than 100 percent because some pensioners (mostly women, who can retire at 55 years of age) are younger than age 60.

[7]Includes employees in ministries and public entities.

[8]In parallel to social security reform, the basic wage of government employees was raised by 60–110 percent, with a higher increase at entry levels, also effective October 2014. This was the first wage increase since 2006. A grade-point system was introduced to allow for a pay rise without a change in rank. The basic wage usually accounts for about half of compensation.

Figure 5.1. Urban Workers and Staff Expenditure per Pensioner, 1995–2013
(Percent of average urban wage)

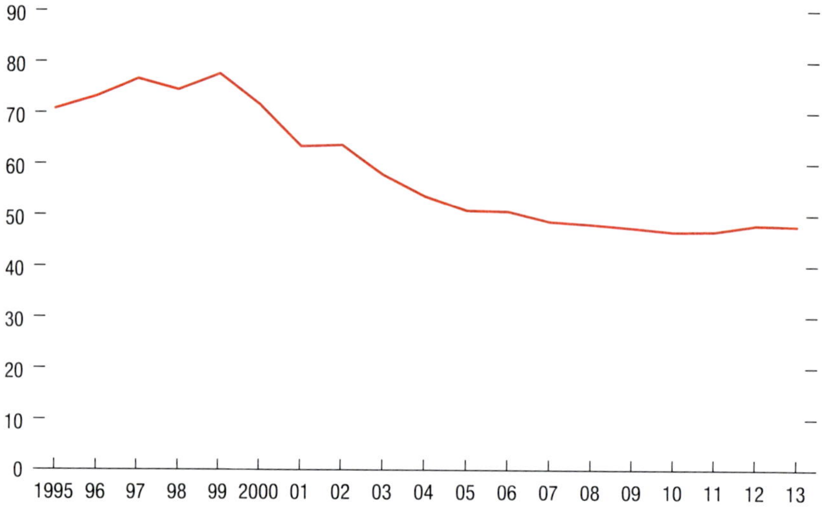

Sources: National Bureau of Statistics 2014; and IMF staff calculations.

Figure 5.2. Pensioners by Pension Scheme
(Percent of population ages 60 and older)

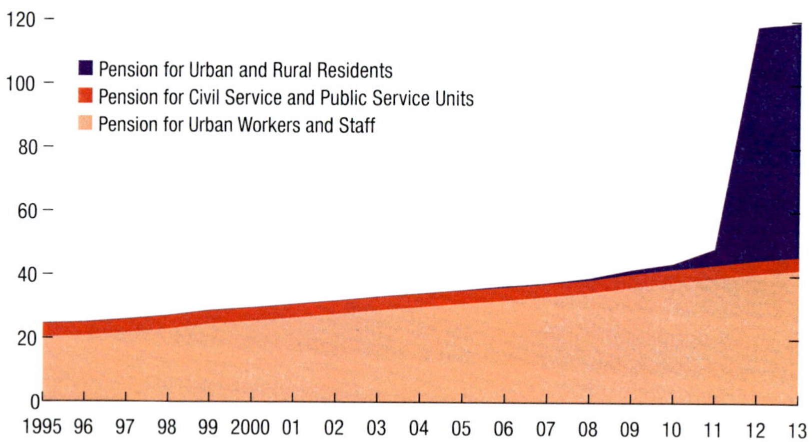

Sources: National Bureau of Statistics 2014; United Nations 2015; and IMF staff calculations.

Figure 5.3. Contributors to Urban Workers and Staff Pensions and Urban Employment

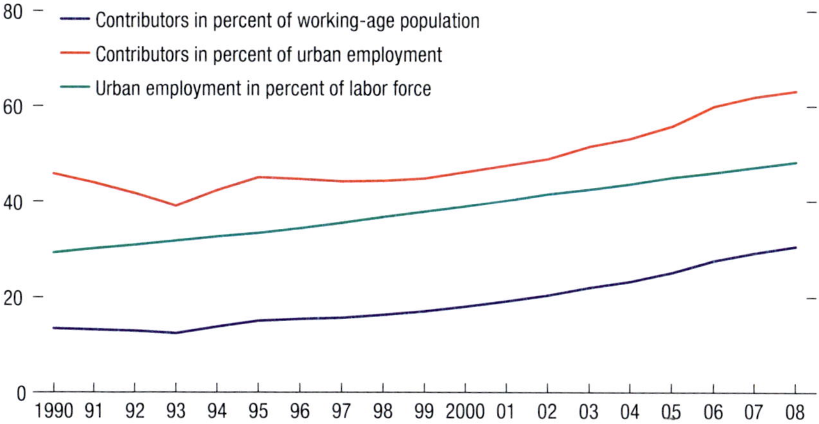

Sources: National Bureau of Statistics 2014; United Nations 2015; and IMF staff calculations.

(20 percent and 8 percent, respectively) and voluntarily to severance pay (8 percent and 4 percent). Employees' benefit accruals increase with more years of contribution. While public employees account for a small fraction of the workforce, the public employee scheme often is a benchmark for benefit payouts and portability in other systems, given state influence in the economy.

INTERNATIONAL PERSPECTIVES

Current public pension expenditure does not seem high relative to international comparators, but as noted earlier substantial aging pressures are expected.[9] At 4 percent of GDP in public pension expenditure, China seems at about the emerging market economy average (Figure 5.4) but well below the Organisation for Economic Co-operation and Development (OECD) average. With an old-age dependency ratio of 13 percent, the current age profile is also similar to the emerging market economy average. However, looking forward, China's aging challenge seems more acute than comparators—the old-age dependency ratio increases much more rapidly than in other emerging market economies. China's old-age dependency ratio will approach 25 percent (today's average in the

[9]Taking a longer time horizon, Clements and others (2015a) show that substantial fiscal pressures related to aging are expected in the more and less developed economies, including from public retirement income programs.

Figure 5.4. Benchmarking the Chinese Pension System

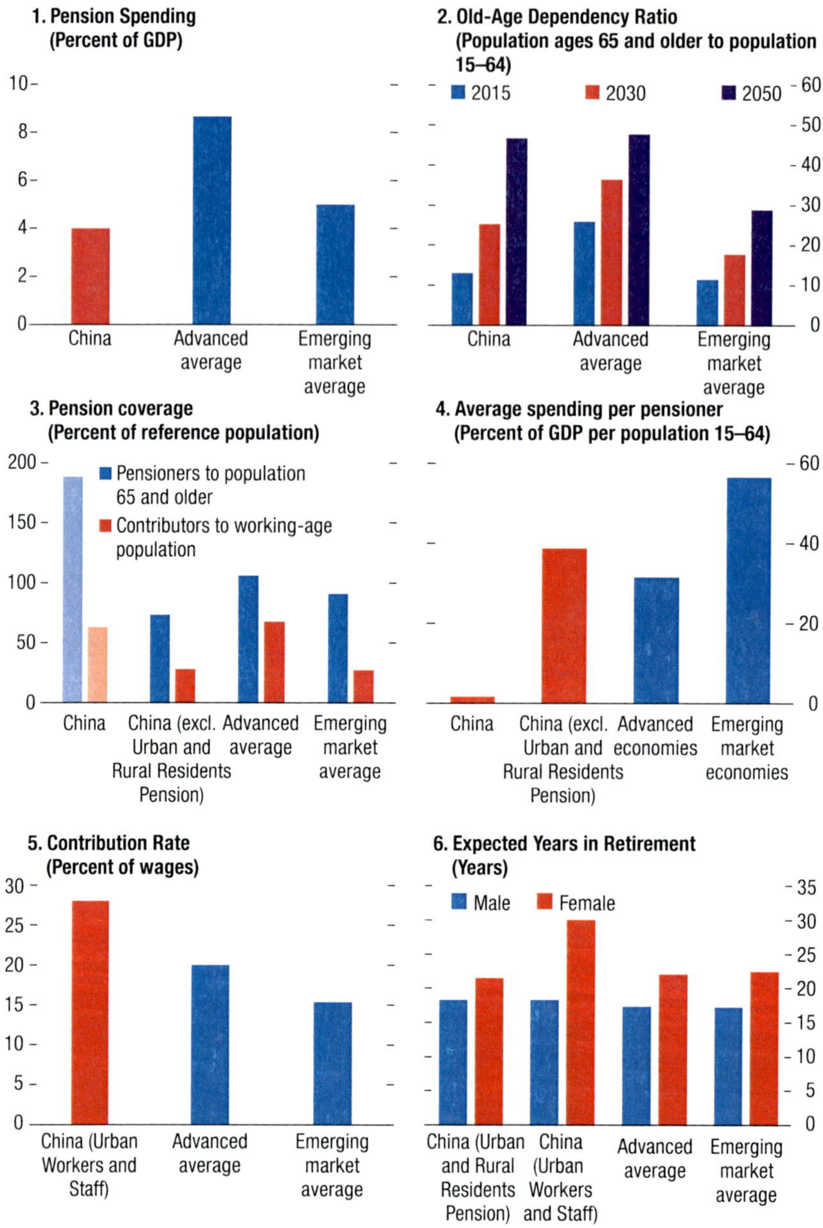

Sources: National Bureau of Statistics 2014; United Nations 2015; and IMF staff calculations.

advanced economies) by 2030 and 47 percent (about the current level in Japan) by 2050.

China recently achieved universal pension coverage by providing relatively low benefits to pensioners through Pensions for Urban and Rural Residents. Coverage rates for both pensioners (190 percent of the population ages 65 and older) and contributors (63 percent of the population ages 15–64) is substantially higher than comparators in advanced and emerging market economies, with the difference largely due to the recent expansion of the Pensions for Urban and Rural Residents.[10] Excluding this scheme, pensioner coverage (74 percent) and contributor coverage (27 percent) are at about the average in emerging market economies.

Benefits seem low, reflecting relatively modest benefits from Pensions for Urban and Rural Residents, which explains why China offers universal coverage at relatively low expenditure. Excluding Pensions for Urban and Rural Residents, benefit generosity is between the averages for advanced and emerging market economies, providing average pensions that are slightly above 40 percent of GDP per population ages 15–64.

Two key parameters of pension systems in China seem out of line with comparators. The contribution rate of the Pensions for Urban Workers and Staff (at 28 percent of wages on average) is well above the averages for advanced (20 percent of wages) and emerging market economies (15 percent of wages) and appears very regressive due to a high minimum threshold. This fact implies limited room to improve the sustainability of the system with additional revenue—increases in contribution rates could push the share of contributors in the working population lower. In addition, retirement ages are relatively low even after taking into account different life expectancy across countries. In particular, for Urban Workers and Staff and the Civil Service and Public Service Units, life expectancy at the retirement age is one year higher for men and 3½ years higher for women than in advanced and emerging market economies.

BASELINE PROJECTIONS AND MEASURES OF SUSTAINABILITY

Public pension expenditure is projected to increase rapidly in 2015–50. Assuming unchanged benefit generosity and coverage of the different pension schemes, public pension expenditure is projected to increase, largely owing to aging, from 4.0 percent of GDP in 2015 to 10.1 percent of GDP in 2050 (Table 5.2). Most of this increase (4.8 percentage points) is due to Pensions for

---

[10]Pensioner coverage is substantially higher than 100 percent in China because individuals receive pensions as early as age 55 for women and 60 for men. In the advanced economies, the average is 107 percent.

Table 5.2. Baseline Projections for Urban Workers and Staff and Urban and Rural Residents Pensions

	Expenditure and Revenue (Percent of GDP)			2015–50	
	2015	2030	2050	Change	Present Discounted Value (Percent of 2015 GDP)
UWS					
Contributions	2.7	2.7	2.7	0.0	82
Expenditure	3.1	5.2	7.9	4.8	165
Balance	–0.4	-2.5	-5.2	–4.8	-83
Civil Service and Public Service Units					
Contributions	0.0	0.0	0.0	0.0	0.0
Expenditure	0.6	1.0	1.5	0.9	32
Balance	–0.60	-1.0	-1.5	–0.9	-32
URR					
Contributions	0.1	0.1	0.1	0.0	3.1
Expenditure	0.3	0.4	0.7	0.4	13.8
Balance	–0.2	–0.3	–0.6	–0.4	-11
Total					
Contributions	2.8	2.8	2.8	0.0	85
Expenditure	4.0	6.6	10.1	6.2	210
Balance	–1.2	-3.8	-7.3	-6.2	–125

Source: IMF staff calculations.
Note: The baseline projections do not take into account the recent reform to integrate Civil Service and Public Service Units into the UWS scheme. The present discounted value calculation assumes a discount rate of 1 percentage point above the real growth rate of GDP. URR = Urban and Rural Residents; UWS = Urban Workers and Staff.

Urban Workers and Staff, largely reflecting their bigger part in current spending.[11]

Absent reforms, these increases suggest a substantial fiscal deterioration that threatens the sustainability of the pension system. The share of contributors in the labor force is assumed to be constant, and thus pension contributions to GDP remain roughly constant over time.[12] This implies that the pension balance

[11]Pension expenditure to GDP (PE/GDP) is the product of four main factors: benefit ratio (average pension to GDP per worker), pensioner coverage (number of pensioners to the population 65 and older), the inverse of the labor force participation rate (workers to population ages 15–64), and aging, represented by the old-age dependency ratio (population ages 65 and older to population 15–64):

$$\frac{PE}{GDP} = \frac{\frac{PE}{pensioners}}{\frac{GDP}{workers}} \times \frac{pensioners}{pop65+} \times \frac{pop15-64}{workers} \times \frac{pop65+}{pop15-64}.$$

The projections in this chapter use the latest data from the United Nations (2015) for the demographic trends. For labor force participation, the chapter uses International Labour Organization projections up to 2020 and assumes these remain constant after that. For the pension parameters, the main assumption is that both the benefit ratio and the pensioner coverage remain constant.

[12]The projections are moderately sensitive to this assumption. For every 10 percentage point increase in the share of contributors in the labor force, the present discounted value of the balance would improve by 14 percentage points of 2015 GDP.

(contributions minus expenditure) is projected to worsen from –1.2 percent of GDP in 2015 to –7.3 percent of GDP in 2050. In present discounted value, the sum of the pension deficits over 2015–50 is nearly 125 percent of 2015 GDP—83 percent in the Urban Workers and Staff scheme, 32 percent in the Civil Service and Public Service Units scheme, and 11 percent in the scheme for Urban and Rural Residents. Roughly, if reforms are not implemented and pension deficits are financed by borrowing, public debt will increase by 125 percentage points over the next 35 years.[13]

OPTIONS FOR REFORM

Parametric Reforms to Enhance Pension Sustainability

There are no easy options to address the large pension imbalance—estimated at nearly 125 percent of 2015 GDP in present value terms. But a combination of a few options—for example, increasing retirement ages, modifying pension indexation, reviewing benefit formulas, and making the Civil Service and Public Service Units scheme contributory—could help address the bulk of the pension imbalance over the long term. These options can have a substantial fiscal impact—altogether, under reasonable assumptions, they could reduce the pension imbalance from 125 percent to 31 percent of GDP (Table 5.3). Of course, these should be implemented gradually and evaluated carefully to ensure that the system remains not only fiscally sustainable, but also equitable and inclusive.[14] Of these options, increasing retirement ages seems particularly attractive, as it can partly address sustainability concerns gradually without reducing replacement rates. Increasing retirement ages would also promote labor force participation at older ages, with a positive impact on growth.[15] However, an increase in retirement ages alone will not be sufficient to ensure sustainability and inclusiveness of the social security system and would need to be accompanied by other reforms.

- *Increasing retirement ages.* One possibility is to aim to gradually raise statutory ages for men and women to age 67 by 2050 for all schemes.[16] This increase would reduce pension expenditure by nearly 4 percentage points of GDP in

[13]Other researchers find similar estimates. Li and Zhang (2013) find the average of estimates by Chinese and international organizations for the "unfunded pension liability" of the Urban and Rural Residents Scheme at RMB3.5 trillion in 2010 (86 percent of 2010 GDP). Ma, Zhang, and Li (2012) estimate the actuarial imbalance of the Pensions for Urban Workers and Staff over 2013–50 at 83 percent of 2011 GDP (Zuo 2013).

[14]Using an overlapping generations model calibrated for China, Song and others (2015) show that a gradual approach to ensure sustainability is superior in terms of welfare relative to sudden adjustments. Their analysis compares a pure pay-as-you-go (where benefits are adjusted automatically but gradually to offset the impact of aging) with sudden adjustments to regain sustainability (both through sharp parametric reform or a shift through full funding where the government issues bonds to compensate for past contributions).

[15]Pension reforms can have an important impact on labor supply. He, Ning, and Zhu (2015) find that pension reforms explain 38 percent of the increase in labor supply in China since 1995.

[16]The Third Plenum blueprint aims to "study and implement a policy to progressively raise the retirement age" (Central Committee 2013).

Table 5.3. Parametric Reform Options to Improve Sustainability

	2015	2030	2050	Present Discounted Value (Percent of 2015 GDP)
Baseline (Percent of GDP)				
Pension Contributions	2.8	2.8	2.8	85
Pension Expenditures	4.0	6.6	10.1	210
Balance	−1.2	−3.8	−7.3	−125
After Parametric Reforms to Improve Sustainability (Percent of GDP)				
Pension Contributions	2.8	2.9	2.9	88
Pension Expenditures	4.0	3.5	4.7	119
Balance	−1.2	−0.6	−1.7	−31
Impact of Parametric Reforms to Improve Sustainability (Percentage points of GDP)				
1. Increase Retirement Age to 67 by 2050[1]				
Urban Workers and Staff	0.0	−1.7	−3.2	−49
Civil Service and Public Service Units	0.0	−0.3	−0.6	−9
Urban and Rural Residents	0.0	−0.1	−0.2	−3
Total	0.0	−2.1	−4.1	−61
2. Index Pensions Fully to Prices[1]				
Urban Workers and Staff	0.0	−0.9	−1.4	−27
Civil Service and Public Service Units	0.0	−0.2	−0.3	−5
Urban and Rural Residents	0.0	−0.2	−0.2	−4
Total	0.0	−1.3	−1.9	−36
3. Reduce Benefits by 5 Percent (excluding Urban and Rural Residents)[1]				
Urban Workers and Staff	0.0	−0.3	−0.4	−8
Civil Service and Public Service Units	0.0	−0.1	−0.1	−2
Total	0.0	−0.3	−0.5	−9
4. Contributions to Civil Service and Public Service[2]				
Civil Service and Public Service	0.0	0.1	0.1	3

Source: IMF staff calculations.

Note: The present discounted value calculation assumes a discount rate of 1 percentage point above the real growth rate of GDP.

[1]Positive = increase in spending.

[2]Positive = increase in revenue.

2050 and cut the present discount value of the pension imbalance by 61 percentage points of GDP. A milder schedule of reforms (such as a more gradual and lower statutory retirement age at 65) will be less effective in addressing the sustainability of the pension system.[17] After 2050, it seems appropriate to link the statutory age of retirement to life expectancy, which implies an approximate increase of one year and three months per decade under current United Nations projections.[18] Increases in retirement ages should be accompanied by

[17]Increases in retirement ages are underway in most OECD countries, with a clear trend to equalize retirement ages for men and women (OECD 2013). In the long term, at least 14 of 32 countries will have retirement ages between 67 and 69 (OECD 2012).

[18]There are different ways to link pensions to life expectancy, including through benefits (Finland, Germany), qualifying conditions (Denmark, France), and retirement ages (Denmark, Greece, Italy) (OECD 2011). Other countries have introduced automatic adjustments to link the indexation to the sustainability of the pension system (Canada, Spain) (OECD 2015).

adequate provisions for the poor, whose life expectancy tends to be shorter than that of the general population. These include strengthening labor market regulations to ensure equal opportunities for older workers, retraining programs, and the availability of disability pensions and social assistance for the most vulnerable (Clements and others 2015b).

- *Modifying pension indexation.* The current system is roughly indexed to a mix of wages and prices.[19] Moving toward full price indexing, under which benefits are indexed to consumer prices once received for the first time, would reduce pension expenditure by 1.9 percentage points of GDP in 2050 and reduce the present discount value of the imbalance by 36 percentage points of GDP.
- *Reviewing the benefit formula.* For example, changing the accrual rate from 1 percent per year of contributions to 0.95 percent in the scheme for Urban Workers and Staff and reducing benefits by 5 percent in the Civil Service and Public Service Units schemes would reduce pension expenditure by 0.5 percentage point in 2050 and reduce the present discount value of the imbalance by 9 percentage points of GDP.[20]
- *Making the Civil Service and Public Service Units scheme contributory.* This action is part of the ongoing reform. Since the Civil Service and Public Service Units scheme covers government employees, contributions of the government as an employer (20 percent of wages) do not have an impact on overall fiscal sustainability—contributions of government as an employer are both fiscal expenditure (part of the wage bill) and revenue (social contributions), which offset each other. This offsetting explains why, once completed, this option would have only a modest impact on sustainability, reflecting the employee contribution of 8 percent of wages.

Reforms to Increase Adequacy and Boost Incentives to Contribute

In addition to improving fiscal sustainability, pension reforms can enhance efficient functioning of the pension system, including boosting adequacy, facilitating labor market flexibility, and allowing for greater portability across regions.[21] However, these options might exacerbate the funding imbalance of the pension system, widening the present discounted value of pension deficits by about 67 percentage points of 2015 GDP (Table 5.4).

[19]For Pensions for Urban Workers and Staff, this is because the portion of the pension that depends on the provincial average is fully indexed to regional wage growth while the portion that depends on the career-average wage is nominally fixed. In 2016 pensions were increased by 6.5 percent.

[20]Countries typically reduce benefits in indirect ways, for example by reducing the reference salary used for pensionable earnings. These cuts can be across the board (Austria, Finland, Germany, Italy) or protecting those with low pensions (France, Portugal, Sweden) (D'Addio 2014).

[21]Complementary measures might also be helpful in enhancing the functioning of the pension system and increasing equity, including strengthening administrative capacity and labor reforms to promote formality and ensure employment opportunities for older workers (Clements, Feher, and Gupta 2015).

Table 5.4. Other Reform Options to Improve Equity and Labor Markets

	2015	2030	2050	Present Discounted Value (Percent of 2015 GDP)
Impact of Reforms to Enhance Equity and Labor Incentives (Percentage points of GDP)				
1. Increase Base Benefit for Urban and Rural Residents[1]				
Urban and Rural Residents	0.0	2.0	3.3	58
2. Gradually Reduce Contribution Rate[2]				
Urban Workers and Staff from 28 to 24 percent	0.0	–0.4	–0.4	–9

Source: IMF staff calculations.
[1]Positive = increase in spending.
[2]Positive = increase in revenue.

- *Raising Urban and Rural Resident Benefits.* Current base benefits for pensioners covered by the Urban and Rural Residents scheme are only 2.5 percent of per capita GDP. This level is well below comparable noncontributory social pension programs in the world, which on average provide benefits of about 15 percent of GDP per capita.[22] As such, it raises concerns about the adequacy of benefits. One option for reform is to gradually increase these benefits to at least 10 percent of GDP per capita. At the current retirement age of 60 years, this would increase expenditure by 3.4 percentage points of GDP in 2050 and widen the pension imbalance by 65 percentage points of 2015 GDP, all of which would need to be financed by the state as these are noncontributory welfare benefits.[23] To offset part of this imbalance, it would be necessary to increase retirement ages in this scheme.
- *Reducing contribution rates.* At 28 percent of wages, contribution rates remain relatively high and very regressive due to a high minimum threshold (Figure 5.5).[24] To the extent that these are perceived as a tax, these levels raise concern about labor market flexibility and introduce incentives for informal work. One option could be to gradually reduce contributions in the scheme for Urban Workers and Staff from 28 to 24 percent of wages. In addition, the minimum contribution threshold could be revised. This would be consistent with the Third Plenum blueprint, which states the need to reduce social contributions "appropriately and in a timely manner" (Central Committee 2013).[25] Such reduction would reduce revenue by

[22]HelpAge International. Social Pensions Database. http://www.pension-watch.net/about-social-pensions/about-social-pensions/social-pensions-database.

[23]If accompanied by increasing the retirement age to 67 by 2050, boosting the base pension would increase the imbalance by 50 percent of 2015 GDP.

[24]Contributions can be a higher share of earnings for low-income workers—under current rules employee contributions are based on imputed earnings, which covers about 30 percent of the urban workforce (Lam and Wingender 2015).

[25]Consistent with this pronouncement, unemployment insurance contribution rates were reduced from 3 to 2 percent of wages in 2015.

Figure 5.5. Average Tax Wedge, by Income Level
(Percent of gross income)

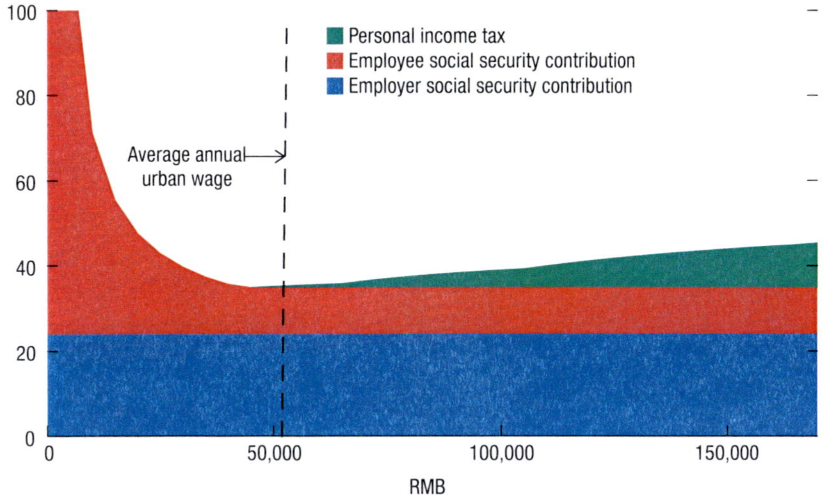

Sources: CEIC; IBFD; and IMF staff calculations.

about 0.4 percentage point of GDP every year and would widen the pension imbalance by 9 percentage points of 2015 GDP.

- *Allowing for better portability*. Today, systems are administered at the local provincial and prefecture level and, at least in theory, Urban Workers and Staff pension rights can be transferred across provinces. In practice, this remains cumbersome—for example, depending on the province, it is not clear whether the years of contribution (a key parameter when transferring pension rights) start at zero when a worker moves to a new province. In the medium term, this could be addressed by a fully integrated pension system pooled at the national level. In the short term, one solution is to introduce a centralized registration database, including earning and contribution histories for all pension participants.[26]

Reforms to Finance Legacy Cost from the General Budget

This is often recommended by researchers as a part of a comprehensive package of reform (Dorfman and others 2013; Dunaway and Arora 2007; Lee 2010). It seems to be attractive in that it could help pension finances in an instrumental way, since a large part of the pension imbalance is related to the pension promises

---

[26] One potential way to promote integration is by centralizing payments. For example, in 2012 Denmark introduced a centralized institution to manage payments of different social security benefits (OECD 2014).

Figure 5.6. Present Discounted Value of Pension Expenditure 2015–50, Current and Future Accruals
(Percent of 2015 GDP)

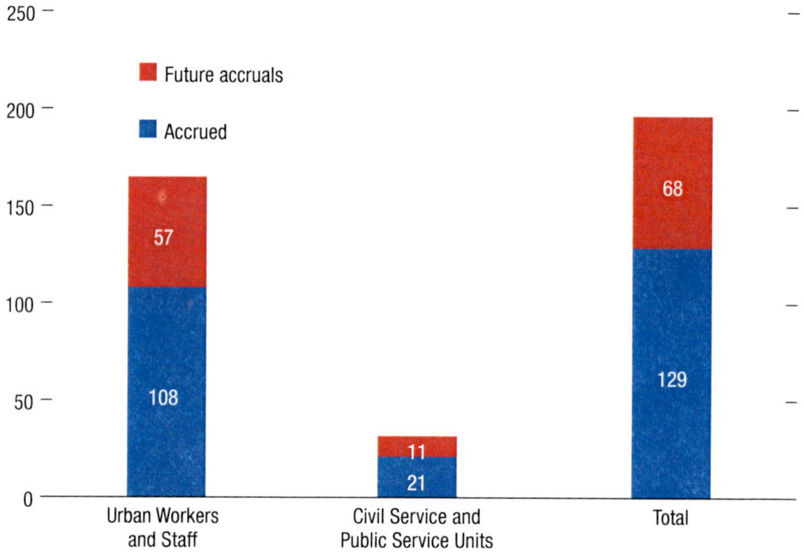

Sources: National Bureau of Statistics 2014; and IMF staff calculations.

made to date. However, the potential size of the legacy cost is large—combined accrued liabilities from the schemes for Urban Workers and Staff and Civil Service and Public Service Units add up to 129 percent of 2015 GDP (Figure 5.6). To finance such costs, one would need additional annual revenue of 4.6 percent of GDP over 2015–50—an amount that would require substantial tax reforms and would likely displace other priority expenditure.

Of course, such a proposal should not be taken in isolation, but rather combined with the reforms above. With parametric reforms, it is possible to reduce the imbalance to a more manageable, but still challenging, amount—31 percent of 2015 GDP (equivalent to an annual flow of 1.1 percent of GDP in 2015–50). If, in addition to this, reforms to increase the adequacy of Urban and Rural Residents as well as those to reduce contribution rates are to be financed by general revenue, then this would require an additional 67 percent of 2015 GDP from general revenue (equivalent to an annual flow of 3.3 percent of GDP in 2015–50).

In sum, the pension system has a large imbalance, which would likely need a combination of parametric reforms and some level of general revenue financing. But the size of the former is likely to be large, requiring a careful analysis between the balance of revenue and expenditure consolidation measures (Lam and Wingender 2015) and parametric reforms.

CONCLUSIONS

The Chinese population is aging rapidly, with important implications for the sustainability of the public pension system. Based on demographic projections from the United Nations, an increase in public pension expenditure of 6.2 percentage points of GDP in 2015–50 is projected, assuming the main parameters of the system—benefit generosity and coverage—remain unchanged. In present discounted value, the imbalance of the pension system over this period is 125 percent of 2015 GDP.

Beyond fiscal pressures, the pension system remains fragmented and imposes impediments for labor mobility. Separate pension systems exist for workers of private and state-owned enterprises, rural and urban residents, and civil service and public service units. Pension systems are managed at the provincial level, and differences remain in terms of contributions, eligibility, and benefit rules across provinces and schemes.

Transition to a sound and equitable pension system will be critical to domestic rebalancing of the economy. Social security reforms have the potential to boost consumption and address inequality, and can reduce the need for household precautionary savings, mitigate labor market distortions, and make growth more inclusive.

While some measures are in progress, comprehensive reform can go a long way in addressing these challenges. Among the available options to strengthen the finances of the pension system, raising retirement ages seems the most attractive. Statutory ages of retirement remain lower than in international comparators, particularly for women. Raising the retirement ages for men and women gradually to age 67 would reduce the imbalance of the pension system by close to half. But that alone will not ensure sustainability; other reforms can include indexing benefits to prices and modifying benefit formulas slightly. Yet it seems that some degree of budget support might be required, at least to finance the distributive components of the system and to finance measures to raise the adequacy of Rural and Urban Resident Pensions and lower contribution rates.

Fostering greater integration of the system remains an important challenge, particularly in light of the continued transformation toward a more urban and skill-intensive labor market (Meng 2012; Lam, Liu, and Schipke 2015). One feasible option to facilitate this transition is to develop an integrated database of career earnings and contributions for scheme participants, as well as setting up clear and homogenous rules for transfers across provinces and schemes. This would go a long way toward developing a true, integrated, national social insurance system.

REFERENCES

Central Committee of the Communist Party of China (Central Committee). 2013. "Decision on Some Major Issues Concerning Comprehensively Deepening the Reform." Adopted at the Third Plenary Session of the 18th Central Committee of the Communist Party of China on November 12. http://www.china.org.cn/chinese/2014-01/17/content_31226494.htm.

Chamon, Maros, Kai Liu, and Eswar Prasad. 2013. "Income Uncertainty and Household Saving in China." *Journal of Development Economics* 105 (2013): 164–177.

Clements, Benedict, Kamil Dybczak, Vitor Gaspar, Sanjeev Gupta, and Mauricio Soto. 2015a. "The Fiscal Consequences of Shrinking Populations." IMF Staff Discussion Note 15/21, International Monetary Fund, Washington.

Clements, Benedict, Ruud de Mooij, Sanjeev Gupta, and Michael Keen. 2015b. *Inequality and Fiscal Policy.* Washington: International Monetary Fund.

Clements, Benedict, Csaba Feher, and Sanjeev Gupta. 2015. "Equity Considerations in the Design of Public Pension Systems." In *Inequality and Fiscal Policy,* edited by B. Clements, R. de Mooij, S. Gupta, and M. Keen. Washington: International Monetary Fund.

D'Addio, Anna Cristina. 2014. "Pension Reforms and Risks: Challenges for Pension Systems in Advanced European Economies." In *Sustainable and Equitable Pensions: Challenges and Experiences,* edited by B. Clements, F. Eich, and S. Gupta, Washington: International Monetary Fund.

Dorfman, Mark C., Robert Holzmann, Philip O'Keefe, Dewen Wang, Yvonne Sin, and Richard Hinz. 2013. *China's Pension System: A Vision.* Washington: World Bank.

Dunaway, Setegen, and Vivek Arora. 2007. "Pension Reform in China: The Need for a New Approach." IMF Working Paper 07/109, International Monetary Fund, Washington.

He, Hui, Lei Ning, and Dongming Zhu. 2015. "Rapid Aging and Pension Reform: The Case of China." Working Paper, Unpublished.

Kim, Seong Sook. 2014. "Providing Adequate Old-Age Pensions in the Republic of Korea." In *Sustainable and Equitable Pensions: Challenges and Experiences,* edited by B. Clements, F. Eich, and S. Gupta. Washington: International Monetary Fund.

Lam, W. Raphael, Xiaoguang Liu, and Alfred Schipke. 2015. "China's Labor Market in the 'New Normal.'" IMF Working Paper 15/151, International Monetary Fund, Washington.

Lam, W. Raphael, and Philippe Wingender. 2015. "China: How Can Revenue Reforms Contribute to Inclusive and Sustainable Growth?" IMF Working Paper WP15/66, International Monetary Fund, Washington.

Leckie, Stuart H. 2009. "Civil Service and Military Pensions in China." Paper presented in the workshop on Civil Service and Military Pension Arrangements in Selected Countries in Asia-Pacific, Institute of Economic Research, Hitotsubashi University, Tokyo.

Lee, Hung Yu. 2010. "Pension Reforms in the People's Republic of China." In *Enhancing Social Protection in Asia and the Pacific: The Proceedings of the Regional Workshop,* edited by S. W. Handayani. Manila: Asian Development Bank.

Li, Yan, and Xiaojing Zhang. 2013. "China's Sovereign Balance Sheet Risks and Implications for Financial Stability." In *China's Road to Greater Financial Stability: Some Policy Perspectives,* edited by U. Das, J. Fiechter, and T. Sun. Washington: International Monetary Fund.

Li, Yuanfang. 2015. "Pension Reform in China's Public Sector: Motivation, Process and Impact." Presented at Seminar on Assessing the Impact of Structural Reforms, Paris, June 1, 2015.

Li, Zhen. 2014. "The Basic Old-Age Insurance of China: Challenges and Countermeasures." Unpublished.

Ma, Jun, Xiaomeng Zhang, and Zhiguo Li. 2012. *A Study of China's National Balance Sheet.* Beijing: Social Sciences Academic Press.

Meng, Xin. 2012. "Labor Market Outcomes and Reforms in China." *Journal of Economic Perspectives* 26 (4): 75–102.

Ministry of Finance of the People's Republic of China. 2015. "National Social Insurance Fund Budget." http://sbs.mof.gov.cn/zhengwuxinxi/gongzuodongtai/201505/t20150508_1229044.html.

National Bureau of Statistics. 2014. *China Statistical Yearbook 2014.* Beijing: China Statistics Press.

Organisation for Economic Co-operation and Development (OECD). 2011. *Pensions at a Glance. Retirement Income Systems in OECD and G20 Countries.* Paris: OECD Publishing.

———. 2012. *OECD Pensions Outlook 2012.* Paris: OECD Publishing.
———. 2013. *Pensions at a Glance 2013 OECD and G20 Indicators.* Paris: OECD Publishing.
———. 2014. *OECD Pensions Outlook 2014.* Paris: OECD Publishing.
———. 2015. *Pensions at a Glance 2013 OECD and G20 Indicators.* Paris: OECD Publishing.
Song, Zheng, Kjetil Storesletten, Yikai Wang, and Fabrizio Zilibotti. 2015. "Sharing High Growth across Generations: Pensions and Demographic Transition in China." *American Economic Journal: Macroeconomics* 7 (2): 1–39.
State Council, People's Republic of China. 1997. "Document No. 26: The Unified Basic Old Age Insurance System." Beijing.
State Council, People's Republic of China. 2005. "Document No. 38: Decision on the Urban Enterprise Pension System." Beijing.
United Nations. 2015. *World Population Prospects: The 2015 Revision.* New York: United Nations.
Yang, Dennis Tao, Junsen Zhang, and Shaojie Zhou. 2012. "Why Are Saving Rates So High in China?" In *Capitalizing China,* edited by J. P. H. Fan and R. Morck. Chicago: Chicago University Press.
Yu, Zhou. 2015. "Reform of Pension System Worries Public Sector Workers." *Global Times.* January 18. http://www.globaltimes.cn/content/902576.shtml.
Zuo, Xuejin. 2013. "Reforming Pensions to Ensure Equitable and Adequate Retirement Incomes in China." In *Sustainable and Equitable Pensions: Challenges and Experiences,* edited by B. Clements, F. Eich, and S. Gupta. Washington: International Monetary Fund.

CHAPTER 6

Local Government Finances and Fiscal Risks

W. RAPHAEL LAM, WEI JIANING, AND HOLGER VAN EDEN

Local governments play a critical role in executing fiscal policies in China. Aside from providing basic public services, they undertook sizable public investment that has contributed to remarkable growth. Much of the large-scale fiscal stimulus since the global financial crisis was carried out through local governments. Along with public infrastructure investment, local governments have also contributed to the real estate boom through land development. In addition, research has attributed competition among prefectural local governments as a significant factor in China's growth success (Song, Storesletten, and Zilibotti 2011).

Yet although local governments have played a key role in growth, their revenue base is small relative to their spending obligations. Local government tax revenue accounted for nearly half of total government revenue, while spending obligations were roughly two-thirds of the total (Wang and Herd 2013). Even accounting for transfers from central government, they still faced a structural shortfall. Until the revised budget law was effective, local governments, with the exception of a few pilot programs, were formally prohibited from borrowing. They therefore had strong incentives to circumvent financing constraints by obtaining revenue from land sales and setting up financing vehicles to borrow from banks and capital markets and to undertake build-and-transfer arrangements.

Recognizing the buildup of risk in local government finance, the authorities revised the budget law with effect from the beginning of 2015. Reform measures in the budget law focused on containing risk from local government finance, developing the bond market for local governments, and addressing intergovernmental relations. The government also introduced a debt-swap program to facilitate the transition by converting financing-vehicle debt to local government bonds.

We are thankful for comments from the Development Research Council of the State Council, experts from the Ministry of Finance, the People's Bank of China and the Chinese Academy of Social Sciences, Philippe Wingender, CUI Lu (Ministry of Finance), TANG Tao (People's Bank of China), ZHAO Weixin (Renmin University of China), and YI Cheran (University of Science and Technology Beijing). Sung Jung provided excellent research assistance.

While the budget law and related directives could strengthen local government finances, key hurdles remain, and success will rest on decisive implementation. For example, circumvention to borrow in ways prohibited in the budget law continues, as the Ministry of Finance notes. Local government bond markets remain underdeveloped despite growing in size. As a result, policy priorities will be to further strengthen local government finances by reining in possible circumvention, developing greater liquidity and credit discipline in the bond market, formulating a resolution framework for potential financial distress of local government, monitoring emerging risks from public-private partnerships, and aligning intergovernmental revenue and spending.

This chapter reviews the structural features of local government finances, noting the misalignment of revenue that is falling short of spending obligations at local levels. An outline of the current reform measures, including the revision to the budget law, to strengthen local government finances follows. Although the budget law and related directives will contribute to sounder finances for local governments, key hurdles remain in implementation and in fully resolving structural misalignment. Policy options to strengthen local government finances given existing reform initiatives are discussed, followed by conclusions.

STRUCTURAL FEATURES OF LOCAL GOVERNMENT FINANCES

Local governments in China play a critical role in executing fiscal policies. Four broad subnational government levels exist (provincial, prefectural, county, township), with an informal village government below the township level. Each government level reports to the level above it, similar to the arrangement of the People's Congress at each subnational level. Provincial government consists of 36 provinces, autonomous regions, and provincial-level municipalities. Over 3,000 prefectural and county-level governments undertake most public services and investment. Prefectures and counties are often densely populated, ranging from 150,000 to 2 million residents.

Local governments receive transfers from an upper level, while providing for those at lower levels. County governments typically have the highest spending obligations (in relative terms) and are therefore the most dependent on transfers.

Local government financial positions vary significantly across regions. In general, metropolitan areas have stronger fiscal positions than inner regions (Figure 6.1 and Brys and others 2013), with indirect taxes comprising more of their revenue (Annex 6.1 and Annex Tables 6.1.1 and 6.1.2). Tax revenue accounts for 18 percent of GDP in large provincial-level municipalities on average, compared with about 12 percent of GDP in other provinces. On a consolidated basis, including lower-level government, provinces are generally in deficits.

Figure 6.1. Local Government Revenue and Tax Sharing System

1. Sources of Provincial-Level Government Revenues
(Percent of 2014 provincial GDP averaged across provinces and municipalities)

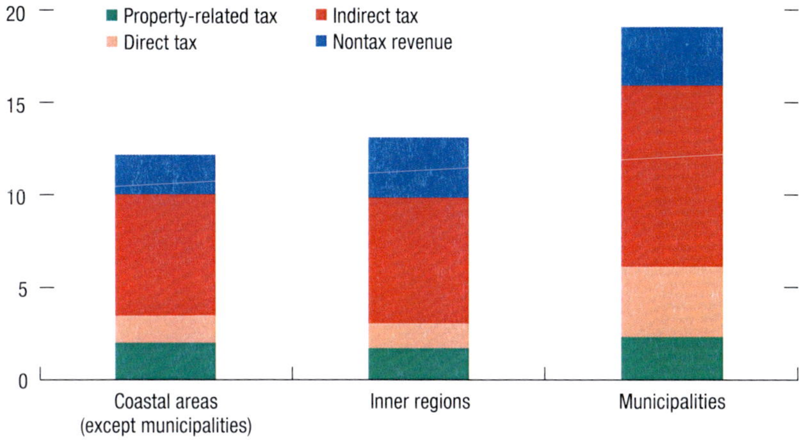

Sources: CEIC; and IMF staff calculations.

2. Government Tax and Nontax Revenue across Provinces
(Percent of 2014 local government GDP)

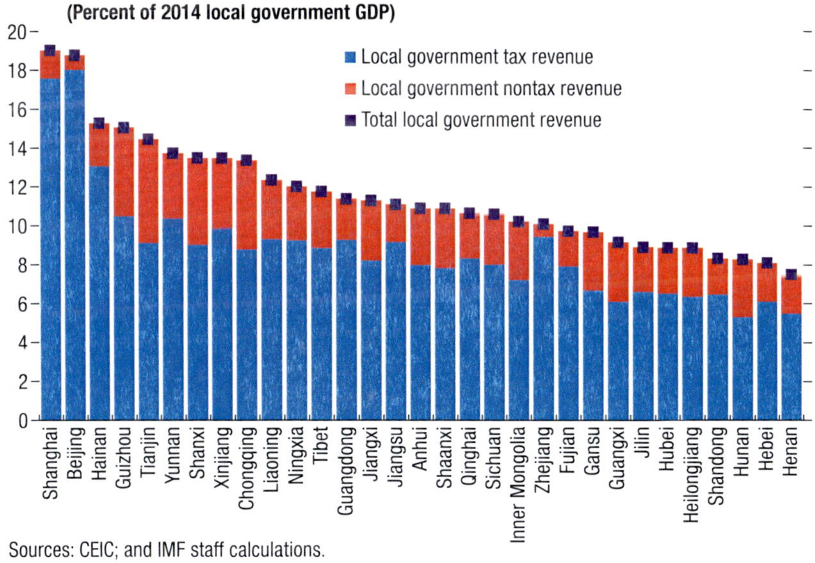

Sources: CEIC; and IMF staff calculations.

Figure 6.1. Local Government Revenue and Tax Sharing System *(continued)*

3. Fiscal Budget Balance[1]
(After transfers from central government; percent of 2014 provincial GDP)

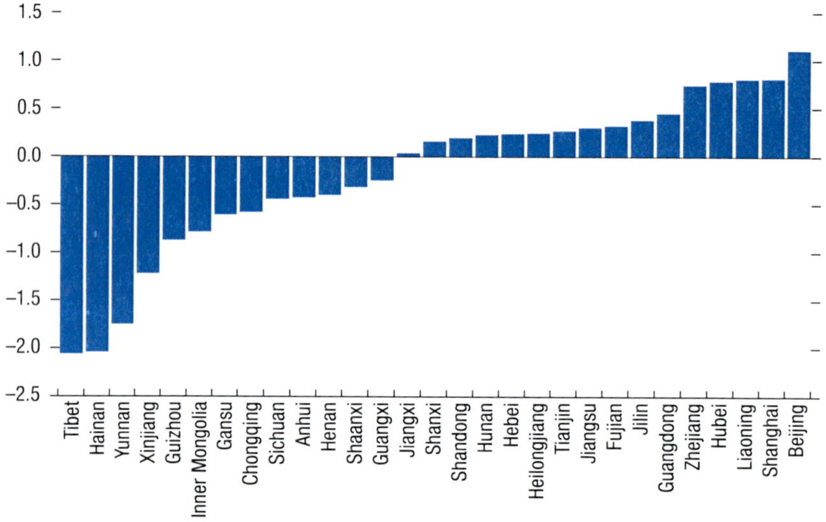

Sources: CEIC; and IMF staff estimates.
[1] Excludes Xinjiang and Qinghai.

4. General Government Revenue
(Percent of 2015 total revenue)

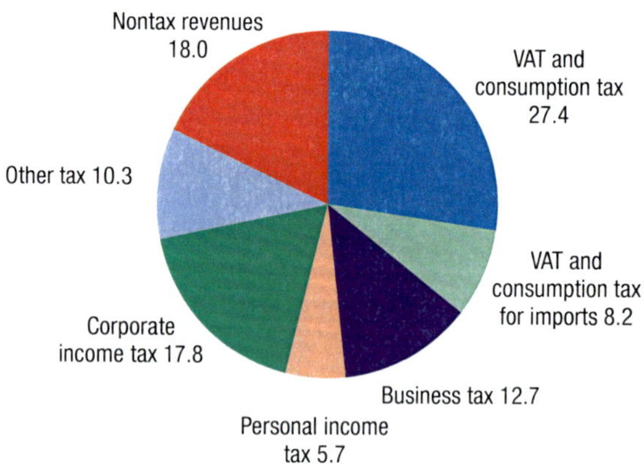

Sources: CEIC; and IMF staff calculations.
Note: VAT = value-added tax.

Figure 6.1. Local Government Revenue and Tax Sharing System *(continued)*

5. Fiscal Relation on Revenue Sharing
(Percent of 2014 total government revenue)

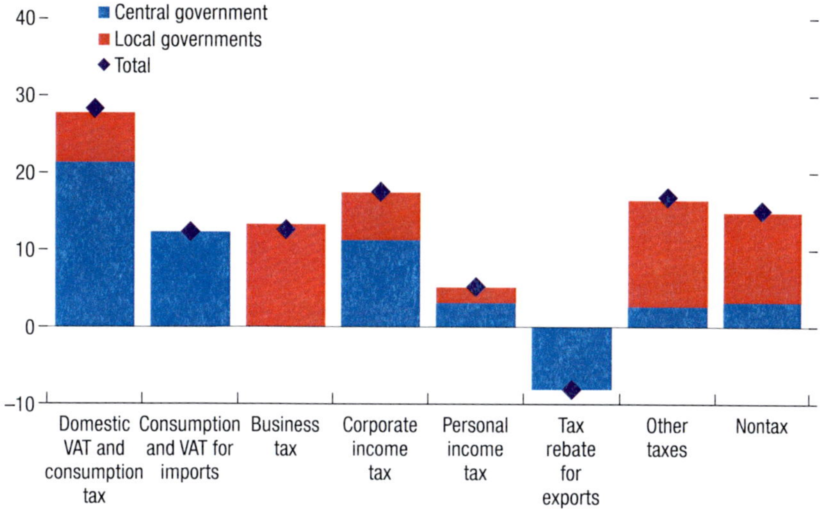

Sources: CEIC; and IMF staff calculations.
Note: VAT = value-added tax.

6. Fiscal Position across Subnational Governments
(Percent of 2014 GDP)

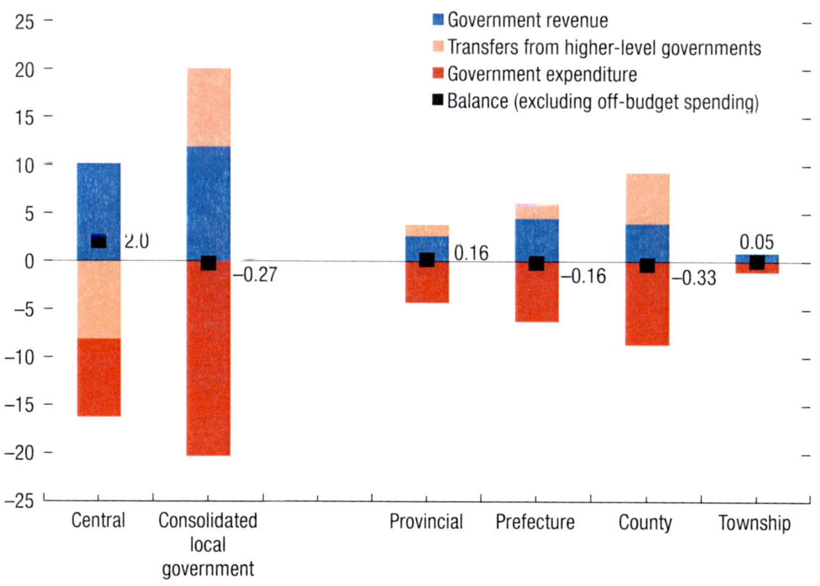

Sources: CEIC; and IMF staff estimates.

Local governments face structural challenges in their finances. First, their spending obligations often far outstrip their revenues.[1] Although the central government provides transfers amounting to more than two-thirds of local government revenue, the transfers do not fully cover the misalignment. Second, each level of local government was required to maintain a balanced budget and was prohibited from borrowing (except in a few pilot cases) prior to the adoption of the revised budget law in 2015 (see below). As a result of these two constraints, local governments have relied on other means of financing, such as land-sale revenue, and have circumvented those constraints by establishing quasi-fiscal local government financing vehicles (LGFVs) to borrow from banks (against their land collateral) or to undertake other financing for infrastructure projects.

Local government financing vehicles (LGFVs) are distinct entities owned by local governments, typically established for public infrastructure. In fact, the increase in infrastructure spending after the global financial crisis was mostly financed off budget through borrowing by LGFVs. They are legally registered as corporations and have public sector objectives, in contrast with state-owned enterprises, which tend to run on a mostly commercial basis (Appendix III of IMF 2014). In many cases, local governments shared the LGFVs' responsibilities to service debt and provide guarantees on their debt.

Financing through LGFVs has contributed to growing fiscal risks. Along with the reliance on land-sale revenue, off-budget LGFV borrowing has grown substantially in recent years. Expanding the definition of government to include LGFV activities, the "augmented" fiscal deficit of general government was about 10 percent of GDP in recent years (Annex 6.2 and Figure 6.2). The flip side of the rapid increase in off-budget spending has been the rise of "augmented" local government debt to RMB28 trillion, or 41.7 percent of GDP as of end-2015, of which more than two-thirds was explicit government debt (IMF 2016; Lam and Wingender 2015). Based on these augmented balances, fiscal space has been considerably more limited than headline data suggest. The large augmented fiscal deficits raise questions about local governments' ability to continue financing the current level of spending and service their debts (Barnett and Zhang 2014), including the following:

- Aggregate debt has masked wide disparities across regions. Debt ratios in some provinces have reached over 100 percent of annual fiscal revenue and over 60 percent of provincial GDP. The debt burden is often higher for provinces that rely more on off-budget LGFV financing (Figure 6.2).

[1]Tax revenue broadly consists of three types: (1) central taxes exclusively to finance central government spending, which mostly include taxes related to foreign trade such as duties, trade-related value-added tax, luxury taxes, and export rebates; (2) local government taxes under the control of local governments, such as property-related taxes and business operation taxes; and (3) taxes shared between the central and local governments, including personal and corporate income taxes and the value-added tax (excluding the trade-related component).

Figure 6.2. Local Government Finances

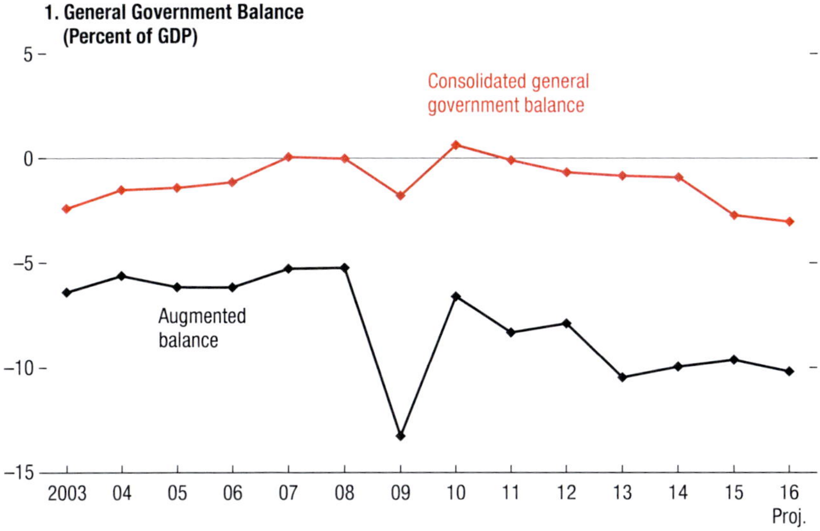

Sources: CEIC; and IMF staff estimates.

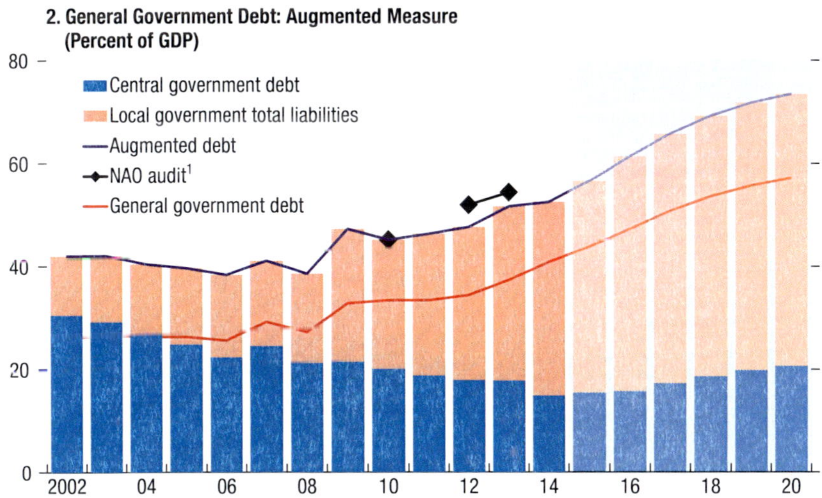

Sources: National Audit Office (NAO); and IMF staff estimates.
[1] Includes explicit government debt, government-guaranteed debt, and the liability that the government may incur obligations.

Figure 6.2. Local Government Finances *(continued)*

3. Expansion of Local Government Financing Vehicles (Percent of provincial GDP)

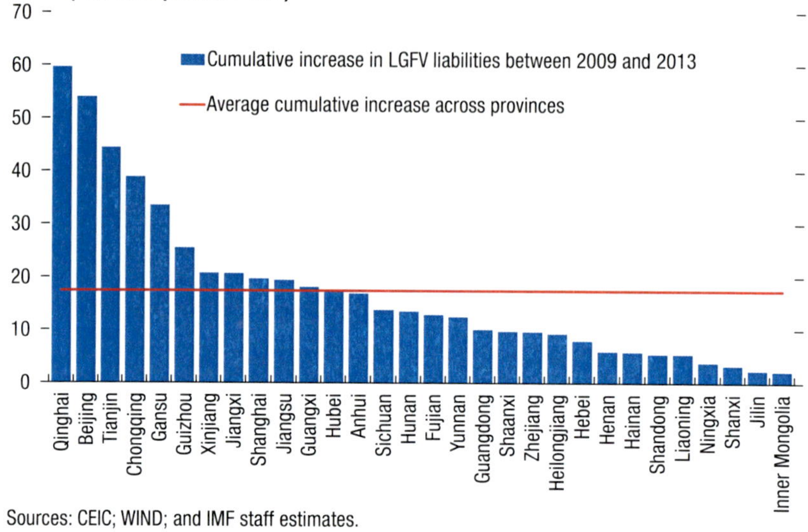

Sources: CEIC; WIND; and IMF staff estimates.
Note: LGFV = local government financing vehicle.

4. Local Government Explicit Debt and Other Obligations[1, 2] (Percent of 2014 provincial GDP)

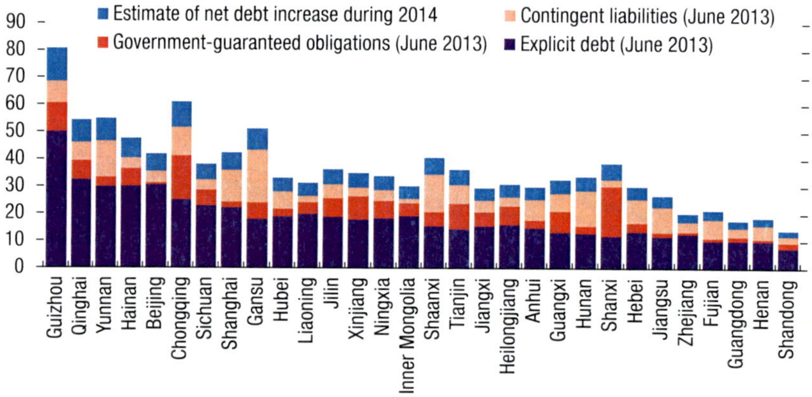

Sources: National Audit Office (NAO); provincial audit offices; and IMF staff estimates.
[1] The NAO published debt figures as of end-June 2013, which included explicit debt and all government-guaranteed debt and contingent liabilities. This figure shows the ratio of the debt figures to the 2014 GDP.
[2] 2014 figures estimated based on a rise of 18–20 percent in provincial debt using preliminary release of debt figures in Hainan Province.

- Vulnerabilities are closely linked with the financial sector and real estate markets because of the reliance on land-sale revenue and large bank exposures (about RMB4 trillion or 5 percent of GDP between 2010 and 2014).[2]

RECENT MEASURES TO STRENGTHEN LOCAL GOVERNMENT FINANCES

The government recognized the growing risks emanating from local government finances and the web of vulnerabilities linked to other sectors. It has committed to reforms to address structural misalignment of local government finances and took multiple measures in recent years, including the following:

- *National audit.* A comprehensive national audit in 2013 sought to identify local government borrowing across provinces. The audit found that most debt was through bank loans and build-and-transfer arrangements via financing vehicles. The audit provided a strong basis for subsequent policy design to resolve fiscal risks.
- *Pilot program on bond issuance.* The Ministry of Finance initiated a pilot program in 2010, which allowed the central government to issue debt on behalf of local governments. The pilot program later also authorized selected provinces to sell bonds directly subject to a quota during 2011–14.[3] Prior to the revised budget law in 2015, the local government bond market remained small, with an outstanding balance of 6.2 percent of GDP in 2014. The local government bond market has expanded as bond financing is the only option permitted under the revised budget law for local governments.
- *Revisions to the budget law.* The revised budget law, effective from 2015, aimed to strengthen the transparency and accountability of the budget framework and local government finances (Annex 6.3).
    - The budget law, along with the State Council's directive (2015 No. 43), aimed to replace unregulated LGFV borrowing with regulated public-private partnerships (PPPs) and provincial bond financing nationwide (known as the strategy of "opening the front door while closing the back door"). All other forms of local government borrowing or guarantees are prohibited.
    - In terms of debt monitoring, the central government has set aggregate limits on bond issuance and used a set of indicators, such as debt to GDP

[2]The aggregate gross land sale revenue was sizable at about 7 percent of GDP (net land sale revenue was 2½–3 percent of GDP after accounting for expenses related to city construction, land development, and compensation for relocation). In some provinces, as much as one-fifth of tax revenue (excluding land sales) comes from real estate.

[3]Interest on local government bonds is exempt from taxes and can be traded in both interbank and securities exchange markets. The interbank market is the dominant platform (trading in the China Futures and Exchange Trading System) and accounts for over 90 percent of bond turnover. The exchange markets trade bonds through public auctions at the Shanghai and Shenzhen stock exchanges.

and debt service to fiscal revenue, to monitor fiscal risk in an early warning system. Local government bond issuance also required credit ratings and disclosures of local budgets, as well as legislative approval at the provincial level or of the National People's Congress.

- The law also envisaged greater use of general transfers to better align local government revenue and spending.

Interim steps were taken to smooth the implementation of the new budget law. First, ongoing local government infrastructure projects were allowed to borrow in the original ways in 2015. Second, the government promoted greater use of PPPs to leverage private participation in infrastructure projects. Third, the debt-swap program was introduced to replace maturing local government debt (identified in the national audit) with bonds, beginning in 2015, over a horizon of three to five years (Figure 6.3).

The debt-swap program has also contributed to the expansion of the local government bond market, which has steadily increased to about 8.7 percent of GDP by June 2016. At the same time, the debt-swap program has restructured local government debt by extending the maturity from one to three years to an average of five to seven years and reducing the interest burden for local government by about 400 basis points.[4] Spreads over sovereign bonds were tight at about 30–50 basis points for public auctions and 40–70 basis points for targeted placements, which did not fully reflect underlying credit risks. As banks were the key investors in these bonds, they faced a lower interest margin and extended the maturity of claims, thereby widening balance sheet mismatch. In return, banks gained the certainty that local government would honor such obligations, instead of an implicit guarantee on claims against LGFVs. Banks' capital buffers would improve because the risk weight of capital would drop from 100 percent on LGFV loans to 20 percent on local government bonds. The net impact varies across banks and depends on their exposure to local governments.

However, key hurdles remain in the implementation of the budget law, including the following:

- *Possible circumvention.* The budget law does not fully resolve the problems of moral hazard in local government financing. As the authorities maintain an ambitious growth target, local governments will have an incentive to support growth through alternative financing. They may seek to circumvent the rules, for example, to obtain financing through service contracts, or continue to provide guarantees in ways that are prohibited.[5] In that context, LGFV bond issuance began to pick up again in April 2015 after the temporary decline in 2014. Monitoring of local government debt against regula-

---

[4]Bonds issued so far have been plain vanilla with bullet maturities of 3, 5, 7, and 10 years, at fixed rates, offering regular coupon payments, and in domestic currency.

[5]*People's Daily,* May 27, 2016, "Debt-Swap Program Will Not Crowd Out Private Capital," republished on the Ministry of Finance website (in Chinese). www.mof.gov.cn/zhengwuxinxi/caizhengxinwen/201605/t20160527_2040795.htm.

Figure 6.3. Local Government Bond Markets

1. Local Government Bond Issuance (Billions of RMB)

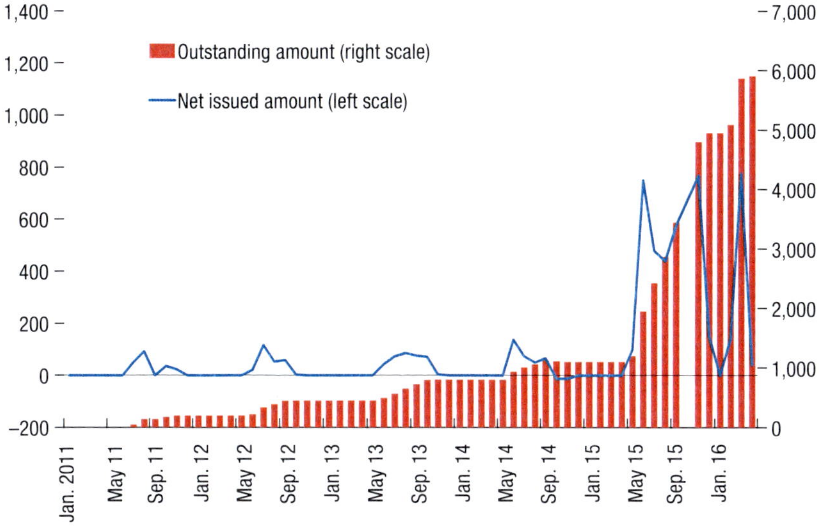

Sources: WIND; and IMF staff estimates.

2. Local Government Financing Vehicles Bond Issuance (Billions of RMB)

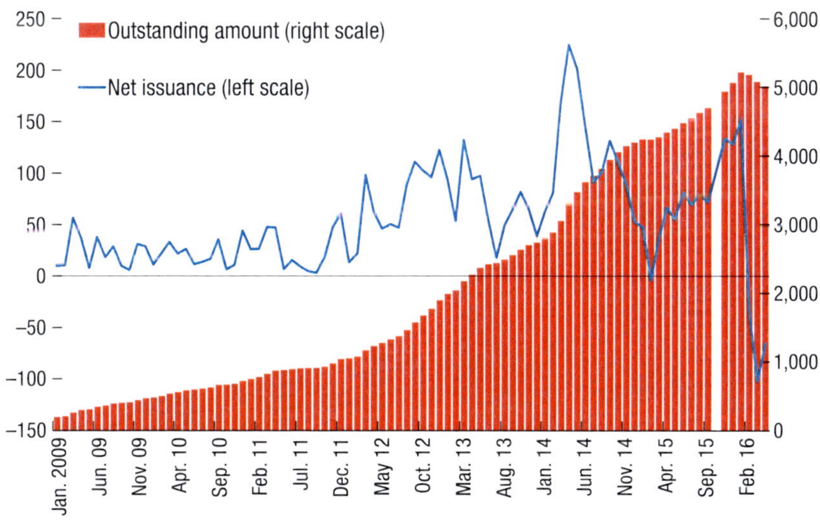

Sources: WIND; and IMF staff estimates.
Note: The data cover bonds issued by urban investment companies.

Figure 6.3. Local Government Bond Markets *(continued)*

3. Uses of Local Government Debt
(Percent of local government debt in Jiangsu Province)

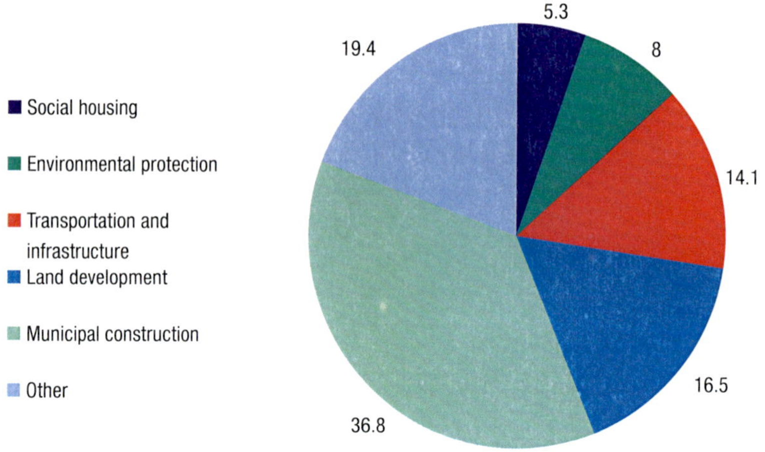

Source: Local government, Jiangsu Province.

4. Bond Yield across Augmented Fiscal Sectors
(Percent; maturity of three-year bond)

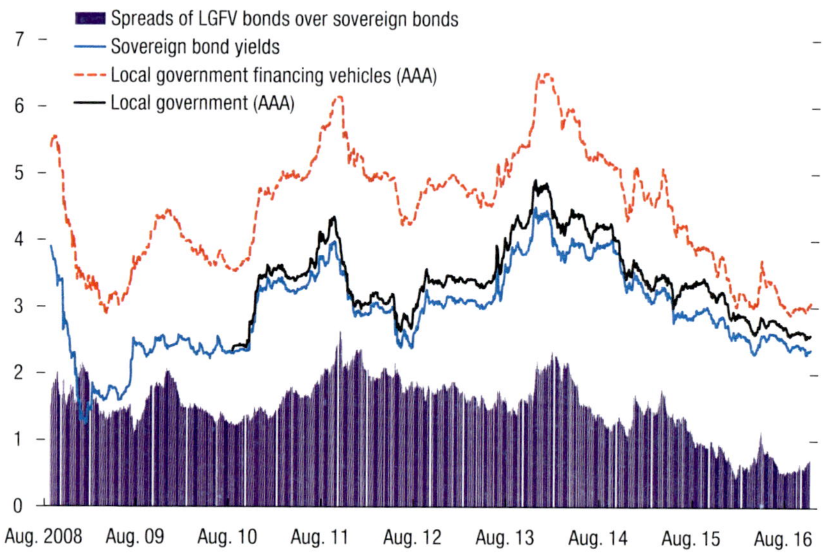

Source: WIND.
Note: LGFV = local government financing vehicle.

tory limits and financial benchmarks is challenging given the availability and frequency of data release.

- *Impediments in the local government bond market.* The bond market remains illiquid despite growing rapidly. Quotas for bond issuance across provinces are not rule based, nor are they aligned with multiyear planning. At the moment, the regulations on bond markets are fragmented: the overall ceiling of issuance is set by the Ministry of Finance and the National People's Congress, while the securities regulator regulates bonds in open exchanges, and the banking regulator monitors banks' bond holdings.
- *Lack of a resolution framework in debt management.* The budget law specifies an early warning system in monitoring local government debt, but does not account for resolution in case local government faces distress or repayment difficulties. This creates uncertainty and possibly reduces investors' willingness to hold those bonds.
- *Emerging risks from PPPs.* The execution rate of PPPs remains low, at about 20 percent of total commitments, partly because of high administrative costs and limited private capital participation. More important, misuse of PPPs may become more prevalent as a source of contingent liabilities unless they are subject to adequate governance and transparency.
- *Structural misalignment remains.* Although the budget law envisages greater use of fiscal transfers, it does not fully resolve the structural misalignment of greater spending obligations than revenue at local levels.

POLICIES TO STRENGTHEN SUSTAINABLE LOCAL GOVERNMENT FINANCES

Decisive implementation of the budget law, along with further reforms, would need to address remaining hurdles outlined above, including:

- *Enhancing financial oversight and disclosures to limit circumvention.* To avoid possible circumvention, timely and credible disclosure and audits of local government finances are necessary to assess debt-related financial and fiscal risks.[6] The disclosure and audit could also strengthen market discipline by investors and rating agencies and be combined with multiyear budget planning (see Chapter 4). Moreover, the Ministry of Finance can also develop financial disclosure guidelines to ensure consistency across local govern-

[6]The Ministry of Finance uses a debt-to-GDP ratio of 60 percent and debt-to-revenue ratio of 100 percent as thresholds for monitoring the risk. Additional indicators can include (1) debt-service-to-free-revenue ratios that capture free revenue not otherwise dedicated to specific uses or committed by contract for repayment; (2) debt service to current primary balance, which assesses the risks before interest payments; and (3) current-surplus (deficit)-to-revenue ratio, local-wage-to-current-expenditure ratio, and local-tax and fees-to-revenue ratios.

ments while transitioning to the accrual-based accounting system. A formal rule-based approach to borrow would simplify and make transparent the credit allocation process, and improve predictability of financial flows to local government. Over the medium term, when a sound, rule-based framework is established for regulating local government borrowing, lower-level governments, such as prefectures and cities, could be allowed to borrow independently.

- *Developing a sound bond market with greater liquidity and credit discipline.* Promoting the sound development of the bond market is critical as it will increasingly be an important source of financing. Several measures could facilitate the development of the bond market. Specifically:
    - *Broaden the investor base.* A wider investor base, particularly long-term investors such as insurance companies and pension funds, would help accommodate the increasing size of bond issuance. Opening the bond market to foreign qualified investors can also enrich price discovery, expand liquidity, and strengthen the financial reporting to be more in line with international best practices.
    - *Better differentiate credit risks.* Differentiation of credit risks through market discipline will require stronger rating standards. For example, the rating agency should disclose the methodology, including the weights assigned to various factors. The cap on bond coupons—spreads over sovereign bond yields—should be gradually phased out.
    - *Strengthen regulation and supervision.* An efficient bond market has the salient feature of offering fair and equitable treatment between investors and issuers. Ensuring policy coordination and information sharing among regulators are key aspects for the adequate supervision of local government bond markets.
- *Formulating a resolution framework.* The government has recently announced contingency measures to resolve potential financial distress of local governments. Overall, the framework contains elements to (1) define the role and responsibilities of various stakeholders, (2) specify the threshold that would trigger enhanced oversight, and (3) identify steps to resolve financial risk. Decisive enforcement can place local government finance on a sounder footing.

In case of restructuring local government debt, international experience suggests a transparent and impartial administrative or judicial mechanism (World Bank 2013a, 2013b). Enhanced oversight could involve progressive loss of local budget autonomy if a local government is unable to address financial risks (Wei 2014). Typically it involves a sequence of establishing restructuring plans depending on the corrective actions and the specified time frame (van Eden and others 2015).[7] For example, Norway and North

[7]For instance, the adjustment of fiscal positions to meet debt services may take a few years. The plan could include annual benchmarks to measures progress.

Table 6.1. International Examples of Enhanced Oversight Mechanisms

Norway (Since reforms in 2001)	North Carolina (Since 1931)
• Register for Control of Approval of Financial Obligations (ROBEK)	• Local Government Commission reviews, approves, and sells all bonds issued by cities, counties, and special districts.
• Systematic periodic monitoring	• Systematic, periodic monitoring
• Indicator: Budget balance = current revenue – current expenditure – debt service (interest and principal)	• Indicator: Fund balance, or the difference between assets and liabilities, as percent of operating expenditure (minimum 8 percent to borrow)
• If negative must correct in two years, or if fails to follow plan, local government is listed in ROBEK. Borrowing by local government listed in ROBEK must be approved by the central government.	• First put on watch list; if continues, central government can take over control of local finances
• Stronger adjustment took place in 10 years after ROBEK. Well-performing local government is rewarded with fewer controls (including on borrowing). Additional disciplinary effect from increased public awareness of deficits.	• Since 1942, no North Carolina city, county, or special district has failed to meet a bond obligation. The local government commission has had to take over financial control of only three cities and one water and sewer district.

Source: IMF staff.

Carolina in the United States have a framework to resolve fiscal distress (Table 6.1).

For China, the framework can contain measures to raise intergovernmental transfers and/or to prohibit further bond issuance and allocate losses to creditors, while ensuring minimum moral hazard and disruptions to public services. The framework would apply to subprovincial-level governments. The provinces would execute monitoring and oversight. Local governments that experience repayment difficulties but do not pose systemic risks could be subject to conditionality during the debt restructuring. The revised budget law prohibits any bail-out of the provinces.

- *Monitoring emerging PPP risks.* Close monitoring can prevent the misuse of PPPs, build-to-transfer arrangements, and other innovative financing vehicle activity. Any use of PPPs as "side doors" for off budget financing should be prohibited. Stronger guidelines in specifying the distinct role of public and private capital may help reduce barriers and uncertainty, which in turn will attract private participation. Any contingent liabilities for local governments arising from PPPs should be fully assessed against fiscal risks.
- *Aligning structural mismatch of intergovernmental revenue and spending.* Anchoring local government finances on a sound footing calls for better alignment of fiscal relations between central and local governments. While international experience does not point to a uniform blueprint, theoretically the shortfall can be narrowed by increasing transfers or taking on a greater share of spending from the central government and/or granting more tax authority to local governments (Annex 6.4). In a majority of countries, misalignment has been resolved in part by raising the local government tax base. Reforms to strengthen the portability of

pension, health care, and education benefits, as well as tax reforms to improve local government revenue, will take time to mature and correct for the misalignment.

- *Complementary policies to avoid sharp fiscal tightening.* Advancing reforms to strengthen local government finances might bring unintended fiscal tightening. As a result, the adjustment would likely require a comprehensive multiyear plan and consistent macroeconomic policies. An orderly and gradual tightening of off-budget spending will put local government finance on a sounder footing (IMF 2014), while the on-budget spending on proconsumption measures can help mitigate the growth slowdown. Monetary conditions might also need to stay accommodative to facilitate restructuring of local government bonds.

CONCLUSIONS

Local governments have been a key driver of investment-led growth, but have faced a structural shortfall of revenue relative to their large spending obligations. This has created incentives to obtain financing through land sales and to set up financing vehicles to borrow from banks and capital markets. Limited oversight has given rise to the rapid buildup of vulnerabilities in local government finances.

Recognizing these issues, authorities have embarked on measures to strengthen local government finances, including the implementation of a revised budget law and other related directives. The goals are to (1) contain excessive risks emanating from local government borrowing, (2) develop the local government bond markets for sustainable financing, and (3) overcome misalignment in intergovernmental finances. However, key hurdles remain in the implementation. This includes possible circumvention by local governments to continue off-budget borrowing and an underdeveloped bond market. At the same time, structural misalignment of local government revenue and spending remains.

The success of reforms is by no means guaranteed and rests on implementation. Further steps are needed to fully establish a sustainable regulatory framework, including enhancing oversight and disclosure, developing the bond market with greater credit discipline and liquidity, establishing a resolution framework for potential financial distress on local government debt, and closer monitoring of emerging risks from PPPs. Putting local government finances on a sound footing also calls for the alignment of intergovernmental fiscal relations.

ANNEX 6.1. TAX SHARING AND DISTRIBUTION OF FISCAL REVENUE

Annex Table 6.1.1. Tax Sharing Arrangement between Central and Subnational Governments

As of 2014	General Government	Central Government	Local Government	Percent of Total Tax Revenues and Social Security Contributions	Legal Sharing Rate	
	Billions of RMB					
Tax Revenue	11,918	6,004	5,914	80.4		
Central Taxes						
Consumption	891	891	. . .	6.0	100	0
Consumption and VAT of imported product	1,443	1,443	. . .	9.7	100	0
Tariffs	284	284	. . .	1.9	100	0
Refund of tax for export	−1,136	−1,136	. . .	−7.7	100	0
Cargo	5	5	. . .	0.0	100	0
Vehicle purchase	289	289	. . .	1.9	100	0
Shared Taxes[1]						
Value added[2]	3,086	2,110	975	20.8	75	25
Enterprise income	2,464	1,581	883	16.6	60	40
Individual income	738	443	295	5.0	60	40
Stamp	154	65	89	1.0	97	3
Subnational Taxes						
Operation	1,778	7	1,771	12.0	1	99
Resource	108	. . .	104	0.7	0	100
City maintenance and construction	364	18	346	2.5	0	100
House	185	. . .	185	1.2	0	100
Use of urban land	199	. . .	199	1.3	0	100
Value added of land	391	. . .	391	2.6	0	100
Vehicle	54	. . .	54	0.4	0	100
Occupancy of cultivated land	206	. . .	206	1.4	0	100
Contract	400	. . .	400	2.7	0	100
Tobacco	14	. . .	14	0.1	0	100
Other	0	. . .	0	0.0	0	100
Social Security Contributions[3]	2,910		2,910	19.6	0	100
All Taxes and Social Security Contributions[4]	14,828	6,004	8,824	100	40	60
Nontax Revenues						
Operating expense in administration dept.	521	37	484	. . .	. . .	. . .
Penalty income	172	9	163	. . .	. . .	. . .
Special project income	371	41	330	. . .	. . .	. . .
Other income	301	139	162	. . .	. . .	. . .
Total Government Revenues (including social security contributions)	16,193	6,228	9,965	. . .	38	62

Sources: CEIC; and IMF staff estimates.

[1] Following the completion of value-added tax reform, the tax sharing arrangement is temporarily split equally between the central and local governments.

[2] Value-added tax (VAT) sharing is temporarily changed to 50:50 after the full extension of VAT to all services in May 2016.

[3] Estimates based on social security contributions ratio to GDP.

[4] The sharing of tax revenues, if excluding social security contributions, will be about 50.4 percent and 49.6 percent, respectively, for the central government and local governments.

Annex Table 6.1.2. Distribution of Fiscal Revenues in Subnational Governments[1]

	General Government	Central Government	Local Government	Subnational Governments[1]				Revenue of Subnational Government in Percent of GDP
	Billions of RMB			Provincial	Prefecture	County	Township	
	As of 2014			Percent of Total Subnational Gov. Tax Revenue				
Tax Revenues								
Value-added tax	3,086	2,110	975	19.6	32.0	31.9	16.6	1.5
Business tax/operations	1,778	7	1,771	29.2	30.5	29.1	11.3	2.8
Urban maintenance and development tax	364	18	346	6.4	44.5	36.1	13	0.5
Corporate income tax	2,464	1,581	883	37.8	31.1	23	8.1	1.4
Personal income tax	738	443	295	34.6	31.2	25.1	9	0.5
Property tax	776		776	8	37.9	39.7	14.5	1.2
Resource tax	108		104	19.4	16.7	37	26.9	0.2
Other	828	65	764	6.3	32.2	40.7	20.7	1.2
Total of subnational government tax revenues			5,914	23.3	32.9	31.1	12.7	9.3
Percent of GDP			*9.3*	*2.2*	*3.1*	*2.9*	*1.2*	
Nontax Revenues		As of 2014		Percent of Subnational Government Nontax Revenue[1]				
Operating expense in administration dept.	521	37	484	35.6	31.1	28.9	4.4	0.8
Penalty income	172	9	163	36.4	31.8	27.3	4.5	0.3
Special project income	371	41	330	16.7	33.3	50.0	0.0	0.5
Other income	301	139	162	41.2	29.4	23.5	5.9	0.3
Nontax revenues for subnational government			1,674	35.6	31.1	28.9	4.4	2.6
Memorandum Item:				Percent of 2014 National GDP[3]				
Land sales receipts[2]		40	3,422	1.4	2.0	1.8	0.2	5.4

Sources: CEIC; and Wang and Herd 2013.

[1] Distribution across subnational governments based on local fiscal statistical yearbook for 2009.

[2] For local governments, the receipts consist of compensation from "newly constructed land use" fund; compensation from the "transfer of usage rights for government-owned land" fund; revenues from government-owned land fund and cultivation fund of agricultural land.

[3] The distribution across subcentral governments is based on the relative share in 2009.

ANNEX 6.2. AUGMENTED DEBT AND DEFICITS WITH A BROADER DEFINITION OF GOVERNMENT

A significant amount of activity that is fiscal in nature, such as a majority of local government infrastructure spending, is not included in China's general government data. Since the financial crisis in 2008–09, such off-budget infrastructure spending has become an important countercyclical tool. To better assess the contribution of fiscal policy to stabilizing output and the concomitant rise in indebtedness, the augmented fiscal data are constructed by expanding the perimeter of government to include off-budget infrastructure spending. The broader concept includes government-guaranteed debt and debt for which the government has rescue responsibility if borrowing entities cannot repay.

Under the broader concept, the augmented fiscal debt rose to 56 percent of GDP in 2015, because the augmented fiscal deficit (about 10 percent of GDP per year) has been much higher than the headline fiscal deficit (Table 6.2.1).

Because of data gaps, the augmented fiscal data estimates rely partly on assumptions, and thus need to be read with caution and can serve only as a complement, not a substitute, to the standard fiscal definitions. Estimating the augmented fiscal data involves numerous assumptions, and the uncertainty around the estimates suggests some caution in interpreting the results.

Nonetheless, it is clear that China has considerably less fiscal space than indicated by conventional general government data. Additional sources of vulnerability include possible contingent liabilities related to the financial sector, state-owned enterprises, and actuarial shortfalls in the pension system. However, a comprehensive assessment would also need to account for the government's holding of financial and nonfinancial assets, such as the China Investment Corporation, national pension fund, and the equity stake in state-owned enterprises.

ANNEX 6.3. KEY FEATURES OF THE REVISED BUDGET LAW

The revised budget law has been a significant step and provided a legal basis for fiscal reforms. The implementation since 2015 was a step toward modernizing the fiscal framework by 2020. The amendments aimed to strengthen the oversight of local government finance and enhance the effectiveness of fiscal management (Table 6.3.1).

Full Coverage to Achieve a Consolidated Budget

The budget law required the adoption of a multiyear budget framework, which specifies the conditions on how to manage annual deficits and surpluses. The multiyear budgeting would allow the government to better manage fiscal policy across economic cycles. Any deficits in local governments would be subject to approval from the National People's Congress. The government would also take a consolidated approach incorporating all existing government funds into the budget. Fiscal budget and outturn would be published within 20 days of approval by the People's Congress.

Annex Table 6.2.1. China: General Government Fiscal Data

	Billions of RMB	2011	2012	2013	2014	2015	2016
							Projections
	Fiscal Balance						
	Authorities' Definition						
(1)	Revenue[1]	10,537	12,020	13,036	14,137	16,032	15,892
(2)	Expenditure[2]	11,387	12,820	14,276	15,497	17,647	18,072
(2a)	Headline expenditure	10,925	12,595	14,021	15,179	17,577	
(2b)	Contribution to budget stabilization funds	289	25	116	82	70.4	70.0
(2c)	Other adjustments	173	200	138	237		
(3)	Fiscal Balance (authorities) (1)–(2)	–850	–800	–1,240	–1,360	–1,615	–2,180
	Percent of GDP[3]	–1.7	–1.5	–2.1	–2.1	–2.3	–2.9
	IMF Staff Estimates						
(4)	Revenue	13,081	15,016	16,538	18,158	19,949	20,735
(4a)	Authorities' definition of revenue	10,537	12,020	13,036	14,137	16,032	15,892
(4b)	(+) Social security contributions	2,576	3,141	3,452	3,919	4,466	4,714
(4c)	(+) Transfers from state-administered SOE fund	118	150	165	202	256	269
(4d)	(–) Withdrawal from stabilization funds	150	295	115	100	806	140
(5)	Expenditure	14,234	16,838	18,651	20,463	22,995	24,282
(5a)	Authorities' definition of expenditure	11,387	12,820	14,276	15,497	17,647	18,072
	Of which: interest payment	238	264	306	359	404	589
(5b)	(+) Social security expenses	1,888	2,393	2,862	3,367	3,936	4,355
(5c)	(+) Transfers to state-administered SOE fund	116	140	151	200	208	226
(5d)	(+) Adjustment for local government spending	200	250	0	0	0	0
(5f)	(+) Local government spending financed by net land sale proceeds[4]	1,105	1,459	1,617	1,717	1,175	1,300
(5i)	(–) Contribution to stabilization funds	289	25	116	82	70	70
(5j)	(–) Other adjustment[2]	173	200	138	237	–100	–400
	General Government Net Borrowing/Lending (4)–(5)+(5f)	–47	–363	–497	–587	–1,871	–2,247
	(percent of GDP)	–0.1	–0.7	–0.8	–0.9	–2.7	–3.0
(6)	Fiscal balance (IMF staff estimate) (4)–(5)	–1,153	–1,822	–2,113	–2,305	–3,046	–3,547
	(percent of GDP)	–2.4	–3.4	–3.5	–3.6	–4.4	–4.7

(continued)

Annex Table 6.2.1. China: General Government Fiscal Data *(continued)*

	Billions of RMB	2011	2012	2013	2014	2015	2016
							Projections
	Estimates of Augmented Balances						
(6)	Overall fiscal balance	−1,153	−1,822	−2,113	−2,305	−3,046	−3,547
(6a)	(−) Estimate of additional local government infrastructure spending financed by debt	2,847	2,395	4,061	4,072	3,571	4,020
(7)	Augmented Balance	−3,999	−4,217	−6,175	−6,377	−6,617	−7,567
	(percent of GDP)	−8.2	−7.8	−10.3	−9.8	−9.5	−10.1
	of which: interest payment on LGFV borrowing	*758*	*975*	*1,161*	*1,423*	*1,557*	*1,582*
(5f)	(+) Net land sale proceeds[4]	1,105	1,459	1,617	1,717	1,175	1,320
(8)	Augmented Net Lending/Borrowing	−2,894	−2,757	−4,558	−4,659	−5,443	−6,247
	(percent of GDP)	−6.0	−5.1	−7.6	−7.2	−7.8	−8.3
	General Government Debt						
(12)	Central government debt	7,204	7,757	8,675	9,566	10,660	11,657
	Percent of GDP	18.6	17.7	17.6	14.8	15.3	15.6
(13)	Local government debt[6]	13,249	15,894	19,955	24,045	28,217	33,397
	Percent of GDP	27.3	29.4	33.4	37.1	40.5	44.6
	Of which:						
(13a)	Bank loans to LGFVs	9,510	9,370	10,311	13,188		
(13b)	LGFV corporate bond issuance	1,092	1,997	2,744	4,198		
(13c)	Trust loans	743	1,118	1,369	1,732		
(13d)	Local government bonds (excluding debt swap)	200	450	800	1,100	1,700	2,880
	Debt Swap	0	0	0	0	3,200	8,200
(13e)	Other (new funding sources since 2010)	1,705	2,959	4,731	3,827		
	(Imputed) explicit debt				15,400	18,226	21,899
	(Imputed) contingent debt		1,346		8,645	9,991	11,498
	Implied fraction of contingent debt that will turn into local government debt				10.00%	10.00%	10.00%
					7,780.9	8,991.9	10,348.3
(12)+(13)	Augmented Debt	22,273	25,470	30,450	33,611	38,877	45,053
	In percent of GDP	45.8	47.1	51.0	51.8	55.8	60.1

(continued)

Annex Table 6.2.1. China: General Government Fiscal Data *(continued)*

Billions of RMB	2011	2012	2013	2014	2015	2016
						Projections
General Government Debt (IMF staff estimate)[7]	16,081	18,405	22,045	25,830	29,885	34,705
Percent of GDP	33.1	34.0	36.9	39.8	42.9	46.3
General government debt (including only explicit government debt, assuming no off-budget borrowing from 2015)[8]	7,404	8,207	9,475	24,966	26,660	28,837
Percent of GDP	15.2	15.2	15.9	38.5	38.3	38.5

Sources: CEIC; China Ministry of Finance; National Audit Office; and IMF staff estimates and projections.

Note: SOE = state-owned enterprise.

[1] Includes central and local governments' withdrawal from budget stabilization funds.

[2] Includes adjustments for local government balance carried forward, redemption of local government bonds, and government bonds issued under government-managed funds.

[3] GDP in this table refers to expenditure-side nominal GDP.

[4] Net land sale proceeds refer to the portion used to finance current and infrastructure spending, which is estimated by subtracting the acquisition cost, compensation to farmers, and land development from the gross land sale proceeds.

[5] The overall net lending/borrowing includes net land sale proceeds as a decrease in nonfinancial assets recorded above the line.

[6] Includes local government bonds and other market financing through the use of local government financing vehicles (LGFVs).

[7] IMF staff estimates are based on the explicit debt and fractions (less than 19 percent according to the National Audit Office estimate) of the government-guaranteed debt and liabilities that the government may incur.

[8] Estimates of debt levels before 2015 include central government debt and explicit local government debt (identified by the Ministry of Finance and National People's Council in September 2015). The large increase in general government debt in 2014 reflects the authorities' recognition of the off-budget local government debt borrowed previously. The estimation of debt levels after 2015 assumes zero off-budget borrowing from 2015 to 2021.

Annex Table 6.3.1. The 2015 Fiscal Budget under the New Budget Law

	Measures under the Revised Budget Law
(1)	**Improve oversight of local government finances** Allow provincial governments to issue bonds, but subject to conditions and preapproval, and require all debt to be disclosed on the budget. Local governments are prohibited from other financing sources, including their financing vehicles; implement an early warning system and risk assessment of local government debt (Document 43).
(2)	**Introduce a multiyear budgeting framework covering all government funds** Adopt a consolidated approach incorporating all existing government funds into the budget. Adopt a rolling three-year budgeting framework. Move toward budgeting through a spending rather than a deficit target to avoid procyclicality of fiscal stance. Require both central and local governments to publish their budgets and outturns within 20 days of approval by the People's Congress.
(3)	**Strengthen fiscal transfers between central and local governments** Tighten and reduce the use of earmarked transfers. Move toward a general fiscal transfer that aims to provide basic public services.

Source: Ministry of Finance.

Local Government Financing

The government adopted the strategy to "open the front door and close the back door" in local government financing. The budget law allowed local governments to issue bonds and reflect this on the budget, but the amount, usage, and issuance would require prior approval by the National People's Congress through the State Council. Under the law, other means of local government financing were prohibited, including guarantees. A transitional period was granted for 2015 to avoid unintended tightening of fiscal positions. Moreover, the law envisaged an early warning system and risk assessment of local government debt.

Fiscal Transfers

The budget law tightened the use of earmarked transfers, which were common but created rent-seeking activity by local governments. The law would move toward a general fiscal transfer that covered basic public services, with periodic evaluations.

ANNEX 6.4. INTERNATIONAL EXPERIENCE[8]

Intergovernmental Relations

Anchoring local government finances on a sound footing calls for better alignment of fiscal relations between central and local governments. Across Organisation for Economic Co-operation and Development economies, tax autonomy of local governments varies significantly (Annex Figure 6.4.1). On one hand, in countries

[8]Prepared by Philippe Wingender.

Annex Figure 6.4.1. Tax Revenue on Income, Profit, and Capital Gains across Countries

(Percent of tax revenues by tax autonomy indicators)

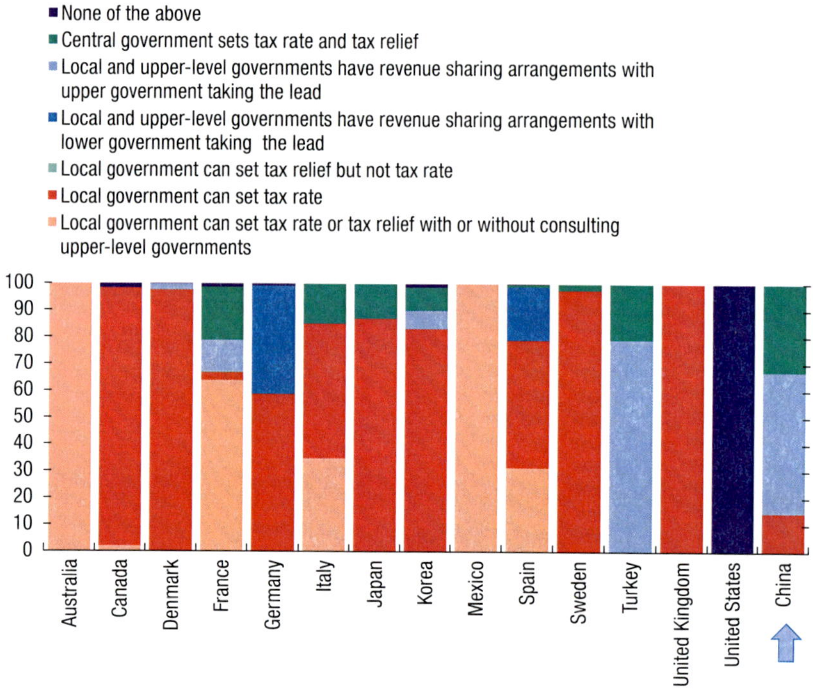

Sources: Organisation for Economic Co-operation and Development; and IMF staff estimates.

like Australia and Mexico, for example, local governments have full authority to set the tax rate or introduce tax cuts without consulting upper-level governments. On the other, upper-level government, such as in China and France, retains almost complete authority in setting tax rates and has a tax sharing arrangement with lower-level governments.

Other countries usually have explicit fiscal rules, clear tax authority, or sharing arrangements across different levels of government. Local governments are often allowed to borrow if backed by the central government, while others rely more on market discipline. Sole reliance on market discipline is rare, except for a few cases, such as the United States. Aligning the intergovernmental relationship is difficult in any country and takes a long time (Annex Figure 6.4.2).

Managing Local Government Debt

Ex Ante Measures

These include fiscal targets for aggregates such as the deficit, debt level, revenue, and spending. Balanced-budget rules for subnational governments, for

Annex Figure 6.4.2. Institutional Arrangements for Local Governments

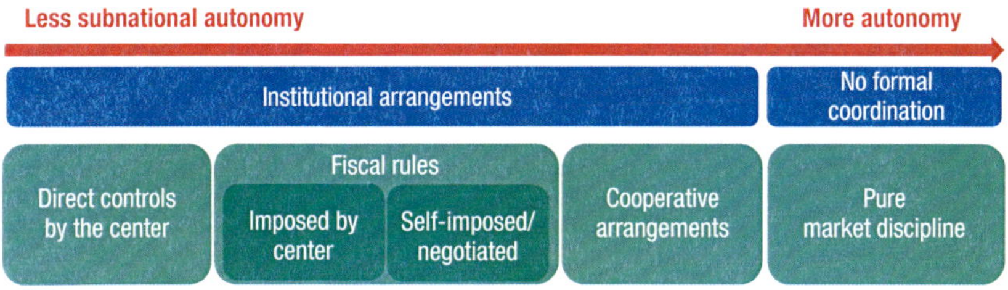

Source: IMF staff.

example, have gained in popularity, especially in large federal countries. These measures can be an important tool for fiscal policy management, but setting targets at the proper level requires careful consideration. For example, there are important trade-offs when setting debt limits for local governments. If thresholds are set too low, the lack of borrowing can limit investment and affect growth prospects. On the other hand, when targets are set too high, excessive local government borrowing can lead to macroeconomic and financial instability. In addition to targets, some central governments also use direct controls to ensure that subnational governments' fiscal management is in line with national principles. Examples include the centralization of all government borrowing with subsequent on-lending to subnational entities. Direct control measures can also take more benign forms such as having to request permission or having to justify borrowing from private markets. While direct control measures are not as widespread as fiscal targets, governments tend to rely on them more in times of fiscal strain.

Another set of ex ante tools consists of procedure-based systems that ensure transparency and consistency of local government policies and accountability of managers. Examples include guidelines for reporting and publishing of fiscal accounts and the use of multiyear budgeting to improve fiscal policy coordination and response to shocks and alternative scenarios. Independent auditing of subnational financial accounts is also an important component used in many countries. Several countries, such as Mexico, require subnational governments to subscribe to a credit rating system in order to access financial markets.

Ex Post Measures

In addition to ex ante measures, central governments also need ex post measures to deal with subnational government insolvency. Simply relying on market forces can be insufficient if the risks are not priced efficiently due to implicit guarantees. There are three key elements to a financial distress or insolvency framework for local governments: (1) definition of a trigger for the procedure, (2) provisions to resolve local government debts collectively and to negotiate debt restructuring, and (3) plans for fiscal adjustment to bring expenditure in line with revenue. Ex post measures must also ensure that insolvent subnational governments remain able to deliver essential public services during a debt restructuring procedure. They should also enable subnational governments to eventually regain some level of creditworthiness. An insolvency mechanism must also protect creditor rights to reduce borrowing costs and encourage financial market development.

Country Experience

Brazil. Despite having had fiscal targets on the total debt stock and new borrowing of subnational governments—expressed as percentages of revenue—Brazil experienced three subnational debt crises in the 1980s and 1990s. The last episode occurred in 1997, with a federal restructuring of states' debt equivalent to 11.5 percent of GDP. Unlike previous attempts at reducing moral hazard and hardening budget constraints, the central government's restructuring program this time was conditioned on states' fiscal and structural reforms. The Fiscal Responsibility Law, which was adopted in 2000, now imposes constraints on the overall level of spending and on budget balances of all subnational governments. It also restrains systemically large categories of spending such as wage expenditure. The central government sets overall limits on the debt level of subnational governments—determined in percent of current revenue net of transfers—and is also in charge of monitoring compliance and enforcing sanctions for local officials and governments. The law also established harmonized rules for budget planning and reporting. Crucially, the reform was effective at increasing transparency and clarifying the costs associated with default, thereby improving the credibility of hard budget constraints on subnational governments.

India. In response to rising debt levels among states, India embarked on a fiscal reform program in the early 2000s. The goal was to control the growth of current expenditures (such as wages and pension) and reform the taxation system (such as moving from a turnover tax to a value-added tax. Importantly, central government on-lending to states was also replaced by market-based financing. Oversight of states' fiscal policy now relies on a combination of imposed and coordinated fiscal rules as well as direct control measures by the central government. For example, the Indian constitution prohibits states from borrowing abroad. Other measures include the provision under which states with a debt-service ratio in excess of 20 percent are classified as having debt stress, triggering the central government's close monitoring of additional borrowing by the state. Coordinated fiscal rules among states' own legislation are now all based on the national Fiscal Responsibility Law, which recommends fiscal deficits below 3 percent of gross state domestic product. Most state laws also require governments to present a medium-term fiscal plan along with the annual budget. Several laws also have led to improvements in disclosure of fiscal risks such as contingent liabilities as well as reporting of any significant changes in accounting policies.

France. Unlike Brazil and India, France is a unitary state with a long tradition of centralization. However, two recent waves of decentralization have given more powers to local governments, and, since 2003, local governments have increased financial autonomy. The management framework of subnational governments' borrowing includes the use of fiscal targets such as a limit on annual debt service, including interest paid on guaranteed loans, of 50 percent of operating revenue. Direct control measures include a prohibition on borrowing for uses other than capital investment and the fact that debt payments are a compulsory expenditure item that must be fully budgeted. In addition, no single borrower may receive a guarantee in excess of 5 percent of operating revenue; and total guarantees cannot exceed 50 percent of the debt of the entity receiving the guarantee. The central government has retained a strong supervisory role of local government finances. Ex post measures include the stipulation that local governments cannot go bankrupt and public assets cannot be pledged as collateral. Moreover, if a subnational government becomes insolvent, the central government will enforce fiscal adjustment and facilitate debt negotiations with creditors. Importantly, the central government does not provide any guarantees for local government borrowing, though small exceptional assistance is available to ensure continued service delivery. Local governments can also be placed under central control if they fail to meet the mandated fiscal targets.

REFERENCES

Barnett, S., and Y. Zhang. 2014. "Fiscal Vulnerabilities and Risks from Local Government Finance in China." Working Paper No.14/4, International Monetary Fund, Washington.

Brys, B., S. Matthews, R. Herd, and X. Wang. 2013. "Tax Policy and Tax Reform in the People's Republic of China." OECD Taxation Working Paper No. 18, Organisation for Economic Co-operation and Development Publishing, Paris.

International Monetary Fund (IMF). 2014. "China: 2014 Article IV Staff Report." Country Report No. 14/235, International Monetary Fund, Washington.

———. 2016. "China: 2016 Article IV Staff Report." Country Report No. 16/17, International Monetary Fund, Washington.

Lam, W. R., and P. Wingender. 2015. "China: How Can Revenue Reforms Contribute to Inclusive and Sustainable Growth?" Working Paper No.15/66, International Monetary Fund, Washington.

Song, Z., K. Storesletten, and F. Zilibotti. 2011. "Growing Like China." *American Economic Review.* 101 (1): 196–233.

van Eden H., F. Conway, J. Medeiros de Morais, D. O'Connell, and T. Youngberry. 2015. "Strengthening Local Government Borrowing Reform." IMF Technical Assistance Report. Unpublished.

Wang, X., and R. Herd. 2013. "The System of Revenue Sharing and Fiscal Transfers in China." OECD Economics Department Working Paper No. 1030, Organisation for Economic Co-operation and Development, Paris.

Wei, J. N. 2014. *Local Government Debt: Resolving Risks and New Forms of Municipal Financing.* Beijing: China Machine Press.

World Bank. 2013a. *China 2030: Building a Modern, Harmonious, and Creative Society.* Washington, World Bank.

———. 2013b. *Until Debt Do Us Part: Subnational Debt, Insolvency, and Markets.* Washington, World Bank.

CHAPTER 7

Interest Rate Transmission in a New Monetary Policy Framework

MA JUN

China's 13th Five-Year Plan highlighted the need for transition to a market-based monetary policy framework. The transition will involve changing the intermediate target of monetary policy from measures of money supply (such as M2) to a policy interest rate.

All central banks in developed economies and in many emerging market economies have completed this transition in the past few decades. In most countries, the transition from monetary targeting to interest rate targeting was driven largely by three factors:

- The correlation between the quantitative target—such as money supply—and economic growth and inflation has weakened, making it more difficult to achieve prescribed economic goals and price stability through controlling the money supply.
- Money demand has become less stable and predictable in light of financial innovation. Targeting the money supply alone may generate unintended volatility in market-driven interest rates.
- The monetary policy transmission mechanism from the policy rate to market interest rates (such as bond yields and deposit and lending rates) and the real economy has become more effective.

As China moves toward an interest-rate-based monetary policy framework, gaps remain. The country has largely met the first two conditions (as mentioned above) for the transition to targeting interest rates, but the influence of policy rates on market rates remains questionable. It is unclear to what extent a change in the policy rate would affect bond yields and deposit and lending rates (which eventually affect the real economy).

The author is Chief Economist of the Research Bureau of the People's Bank of China (PBC). The opinions expressed in this chapter are those of the author and do not necessarily represent those of the PBC or the IMF. The contents of this chapter are based on the Chinese language book by Ma and Ji (2016).

Better understanding of the transmission mechanism, particularly on its channels and effectiveness, is critical for three reasons:

- If empirical research concludes that interest rate transmission is completely ineffective, China should not advance hastily toward the new framework to guide the economy.
- If the transmission is effective, but this is not well documented by empirical studies, policymakers may be reluctant to push the reform. As a result, the outdated and less-effective framework might stay in place for too long.
- If the transmission mechanism is somewhat imperfect but uncertainty surrounds the degree of influence or the underlying factors for gaps, policymakers may not be able to carry out well-targeted reform to improve the transmission mechanism.

This chapter summarizes the research findings on China's monetary policy transmission mechanism based on Ma and Ji 2016, drawing on major theoretical and empirical studies to summarize the need for a new intermediate target for monetary policy. Results from static and dynamic general equilibrium models are used to analyze the transmission mechanism in a perfect regime without friction, which serves as a benchmark for the discussion of the current regime and the factors that limit the effectiveness of transmission. Empirical results on the effectiveness of interest rate transmission in China relative to other countries are included. The chapter also discusses soft budget constraints for local government financing vehicles (LGFVs) and state-owned enterprises (SOEs) and their impact on interest rate transmission. It demonstrates the need for an interest rate corridor to reduce volatility in rates, which will help monetary transmission, looks at other factors that inhibit interest rate transmission, and provides specific policy recommendations.

THE NECESSITY OF CHANGING THE INTERMEDIATE TARGET

Central banks have a core mandate to achieve their final goals (such as price, employment, and output) through their monetary policy tools. To reach the final goals, a central bank aims to achieve an intermediate target, which is either a money supply indicator or an interest rate, with reasonable precision through application of policy instruments (such as open market operations or a reserve requirement ratio). The intermediate target should be closely related to the final goals.

International experience suggests that over the past few decades most central banks have abandoned money supply measures as the intermediate target and shifted to using an interest rate. The transition is largely due to a significant weakening of the relationship between money supply and the real economy (Table 7.1). Friedman and Kuttner (1992) found that, based on a vector autoregression model, the correlation between money supply and nominal income

Table 7.1. Intermediate Target of Monetary Policy Shifting to Policy Rates around the World

Economy	Posttransition Intermediate Target	Timing of Anchoring Monetary Policy Using Interest Rate
United States	Federal funds rate	1980s
Germany	Refinance rate	1980s
Japan	Overnight borrowing rate	1980s
Korea	Overnight interest rate	1990s
India	Repo rate	1990s
Taiwan Province of China	Discount rate	1990s
Australia	Overnight interest rate	1980s
Canada	Overnight interest rate	1980s

Source: Authors.

and prices in the United States began to weaken significantly in the 1980s. Through a Granger causality test and variance decomposition analysis, Bernanke and Blinder (1992) noted that the federal funds rate had more forecasting power on real variables in the economy than M1 and M2, which contributed to the shift to the federal funds rate as an intermediate target in the United States. In 1975, Canada launched "monetary gradualism" to contain inflation risks by targeting M1 range. Since inflation remained high even as Canada was able to achieve its M1 target for a few years, this illustrates the weakening relationship between money supply and economic variables. A former governor of the Bank of Canada remarked that "we did not abandon money supply; it abandoned us."

What has caused the weakening of the correlation between money supply and real economy indicators? Most research has demonstrated that all countries experienced instability in money demand during the transition from a monetary policy framework. Many factors may cause shocks to money demand. They include financial innovation; technological advances; and changes in expectation, monetary deepening, and opening of the capital account. Financial innovation, for example, accelerates the intermediation of liquidity to new financial instruments (some are included in money supply statistics while others are not), which adds volatility to the money supply. Technological advances improve the efficiency of payments and therefore may reduce money demand, while the monetization of the economy tends to increase it (Yi 2004). In addition, the volume of demand for local currencies by nonresidents is difficult to estimate in an open capital account.

Research also suggests that fixing money supply as an intermediate target would bring excessive interest volatility. Walsh (2010) established a general equilibrium model that includes the New Keynesian Phillips curve with a forward-looking IS curve and a money demand function. The model shows that as money demand is unstable, the targeting of specific money supply growth would generate volatility in market interest rates, which in turn would generate excessive volatility in the real economy. Our empirical study based on data from 12 countries that have made the transition from monetary targeting

Figure 7.1. Volatility of Interest Rate and Money Supply Growth in the Transition from a Monetary Policy Framework to Interest Rate Targets

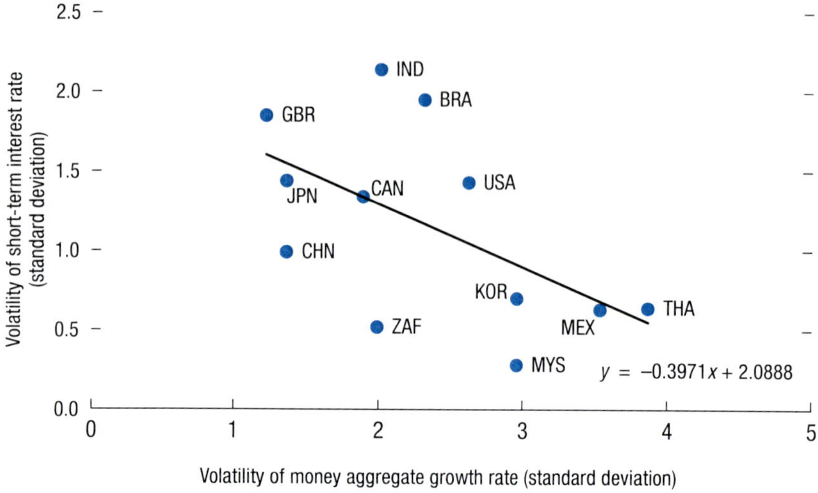

Source: Authors' estimates.
Note: BRA = Brazil; CAN = Canada; CHN = China; GBR = United Kingdom; IND = India; JPN = Japan; KOR = Korea; MEX = Mexico; MYS = Malaysia; THA = Thailand; USA = United States; ZAF = South Africa.

to interest rate targeting shows that the more stable a country's money supply growth, the higher the volatility of short-term interest rates (Figure 7.1). Excessive volatility in interest rates would make it more difficult for private lenders and borrowers to predict profits and costs, and therefore dampen incentives for investment and consumption. Market participants might also hoard liquidity to avoid risks.

China's data also show a significant weakening of the correlation between the intermediate target of the M2 growth rate and the real economy. Fixing M2 growth at a particular rate can no longer ensure that economic goals are achieved. Instead, it often leads to excessive interest rate volatility. Specifically, monetary targeting causes the following:

- ***Significant weakening of the correlation between quantitative goals and real economy indicators.*** Our calculation shows that the correlation between the M2 growth rate and the lagged nominal GDP growth rate was 0.43 during 1990–2006, and declined to 0.29 during 2007–15 (Figure 7.2). Similarly, the correlation between M2 growth and lagged growth in consumer prices was 0.75 between 1990 and 2006 and dropped to 0.06 during 2007–15. The weakening of the correlation illustrates the challenges of using M2 as the intermediate target for monetary policy. Bai and others (2016) employ a series of structural vector autoregressive

Figure 7.2. Weakening Correlation between M2 Growth and the Real Economy
(Correlation coefficient between 0 and 1)

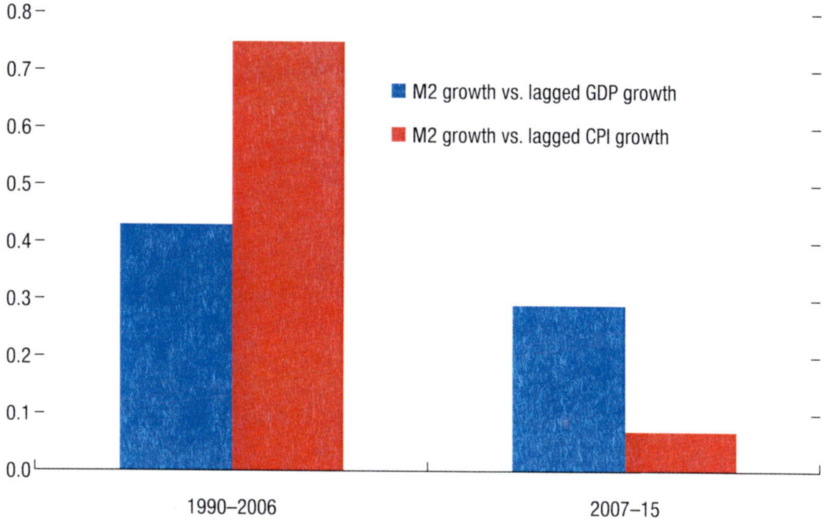

Sources: WIND; and authors' estimation.
Note: CPI = consumer price index.

(SVAR) models with variables such as M2 growth, short-term interest rates (seven-day repo rate), inflation rates (consumer price index [CPI] year-over-year growth rate and producer price index year-over-year growth rate), and output (industrial value added) growth. Their findings also indicate that the transmission efficiency of China's monetary policy has experienced a structural change since 2011.[1]

- *Monetary targeting also causes excessive volatility in market rates.* Analysis of China's short-term interest rate volatility over the past 15 years (after controlling for the trend of the seven-day repo rate using HP filters) shows that the standard deviation of short-term interest rates has risen almost threefold since 2006 from 0.24 to 0.90. The coefficient of variation (standard deviation divided by average interest rate) shows that the overnight interest rate volatility is several times higher in China than in the Europe, Japan, Korea, and the United States. We believe that the fundamental cause of higher interest volatility in China in recent years has been that money

[1]Bai and others (2016) further decompose the CPI growth rates by upstream and downstream industries and add more macro variables, such as global oil price and real effective exchange rate to the SVAR models, with well-designed identification ordering. They show that the weakening transmission efficiency of monetary policy is robust among different model settings.

demand has become increasingly unstable but money supply growth has not been flexible enough to accommodate the demand shocks.

Money demand in China has faced structural changes since 2008 (Liao and Tapsoba 2014). The R^2 in a regression of money demand function was 0.51 between 1990 and 2006, and declined to 0.38 during 2007–15.[2] It is evident that money demand function in China has become unstable.

The above two conditions—declining correlation between M2 and the real economy and rising interest rate volatility—suggest that the transition to a monetary policy framework centered on a policy rate is inevitable. The third condition for a successful transition is a proper interest rate transmission mechanism. If the policy rate does not transmit effectively to other market rates, including bond yields and lending and deposit rates, the move to the new framework will not effectively allow policymakers to achieve the end goals of monetary policy.

At present, there is no consensus on whether the third condition has been met. The answer to this question will form the basis for determining whether China is ready to transition to a new monetary policy framework. Accordingly, subsequent sections analyze the theoretical framework of interest rate transmission in China in both static and dynamic models, followed by empirical analysis. Specific bottlenecks are also identified that inhibit interest rate transmission in China, and reform options are analyzed.

INTEREST RATE TRANSMISSION UNDER A PERFECT REGIME

Although there is broad consensus that China's interest transmission faces significant bottlenecks, few studies have examined the question using the systemic framework featured in the next sections, which summarize the findings of our analysis of China's interest rate transmission mechanism based on static and dynamic general equilibrium models.

First, the mechanics of interest rate transmission under an ideal regime are analyzed, that is, one without quantitative controls and other institutional restrictions. A static model and a dynamic stochastic general equilibrium (DSGE) model consisting of agents, including the central bank, commercial banks, enterprises, and investors, is developed (Ma and Wang 2014; Ma, Wang, and Li 2015; Ma and others 2015). These models describe the mechanics of how the policy rate is transmitted to market interest rates, including bond yields and lending and deposit rates, and calculate the transmission

[2]Research has shown that the demand for money is stable only when the money stock, income, and the opportunity cost of money remain at a long-term cointegrating relationship. When the demand for money is stable, it can be estimated based on aggregate income (or aggregate output) and the short-term interest rate. In the regression of $m_t = \alpha_t + \beta_t y_t + \gamma_t r_t + \varepsilon_t$, the larger the R^2, the more predictable and stable the demand for money.

efficiency through calibration of the dynamic model. Considered first is the case without institutional restrictions such as a cap on the loan-to-deposit ratio, quantitative restrictions on loans, interest rate controls, or access restrictions on bond markets.

The analysis shows that without institutional restrictions, policy rate transmission to market rates is effective. That is, a change in the policy rate leads to a change in other market rates in the same direction, with the degree of response depending on the preference and cost coefficients of market participants. Moreover, the transmission of the policy rate to bond yields is mainly through arbitrage in the bond market, while the transmission to deposit and lending rates is mainly achieved through portfolio rebalancing of banks and investors.

- **Bond yields.** From a bank's perspective, when the policy rate rises (for example, due to contractionary open market operations), a liquidity shortage in the banking system would lead to a decline in funds available for banks to invest in bonds, which drives up bond yields. In a developed financial market, where ample and effective instruments for arbitrage exist, the transmission will be rapid, leading to an arbitrage between bonds of different maturities (shorting long bonds when the policy rate rises). The arbitrage allows changes in the policy (short-term) rate to be quickly transmitted to yields on bonds of medium- and long-term tenure.
- **Lending rates.** When the short-term policy rate rises, bond yields will rise (as above). Banks will then allocate more assets to bonds, reducing funds available for lending. The decline in funds for lending in the whole banking system will, in turn, drive up lending rates.
- **Deposit rates.** When the policy rate rises, it drives up bond yields. Residents will increase their investment in bonds and reduce savings (held in bank deposits). The decline in savings will incentivize banks to raise rates to keep deposits.

INSTITUTIONAL CONSTRAINTS ON INTEREST RATE TRANSMISSION

Various institutional restrictions in China have constrained the interest rate transmission mechanism. The legacy restrictions from quantitative and price control regimes inevitably weaken the efficiency of policy rate transmission. The theoretical model developed by Ma and Wang (2014) shows that a plethora of factors—such as the loan-to-deposit ratio, quantitative loan limits, the relatively high required reserve requirement, soft budget constraints on some borrowers, and regulatory arbitrage by shadow banking—have all helped weaken interest rate transmission.

Empirical results from our DSGE model described in Ma and others 2015 also illustrate that institutional restrictions have blocked transmission of the policy rate to market interest rates (Table 7.2). The smooth transmission that would

Table 7.2. Impact of Different Institutional Constraints on Interest Rate Transmission

Institutional Constraint	Policy Rate Transmission	Impact on Transmission (Relative to the benchmark model) Lending Rates	Deposit Rates	Bond Rates
Deposit Reserve Ratio	Effective	Weakened	Weakened	Weakened
Loan-to-Deposit Ratio	May fail	Weakened	Uncertain	Strengthened
Quantitative Limit on Loans	May fail	Weakened	Weakened	Weakened
Bond Issue Quota	Effective	Strengthened	Strengthened	Strengthened
Bond Transaction Cost	Effective	Strengthened	Weakened	Strengthened
Soft Budget Constraint	Effective	Weakened	Weakened	Weakened
Lack of Market Liquidity	Effective	Weakened	Weakened	Strengthened
Shadow Banking	Effective	Weakened	Weakened	Weakened

Source: Author's theoretical models.

exist in a perfect market is possible because agents such as banks and households can freely reallocate assets to achieve their profit or utility maximization goals. In reallocating the assets (among bonds, bank loans, deposits), they affect market prices (interest rates). Institutional constraints or disguised taxation on bank operations (such as a high deposit reserve requirement) increase the cost, or "friction," for asset and liability rebalancing (that is, they restrict the flexibility of reallocation of assets and liabilities) or directly limit asset allocation (quantitative limits on the loan-to-deposit ratio and caps on loans are examples). These restrictions eventually block the efficient transmission of policy rates to deposit and lending rates. Five specific conclusions are made for China:

- **The deposit reserve requirement has been excessively high**. In the past, due to the current and capital account "twin surpluses" in China's international balance of payments, the PBC, the central bank, had to raise the reserve requirement to keep overall liquidity under control. However, our models show that raising the reserve requirement would weaken the transmission from policy rate to bond yields and bank deposit and lending rates. For instance, our DSGE model shows that, compared with the 10 percent reserve requirement regime, a reserve requirement of 20 percent of bank deposits would result in about an 8 percent loss in the efficiency of the interest rate transmission. Our empirical study using data of listed companies also indicates that a high reserve requirement significantly weakens the transmission from short-term market rates to bank lending rates.
- **Binding caps on the loan-to-deposit ratio weaken the transmission**. Our theoretical model suggests that the cap on the loan-to-deposit ratio will weaken the transmission from the policy rate to lending rates. Empirical results from our DSGE model also show that the more binding the cap on the loan-to-deposit ratio, the weaker the transmission of the policy rate to lending rates. At the extreme, the transmission mechanism could completely fail. Our empirical study of data from listed companies does suggest that

the cap on the loan-to-deposit ratio has weakened in a statistically significant way the transmission of the policy rate to market interest rates.

- **Quantitative loan limits squeeze the transmission.** Our theoretical model shows that when quantitative limits on loans are binding for all banks, a change in policy rate will have no impact on lending rates; as such, a change in the policy rate cannot be transmitted to lending rates at all. When a quantitative limit on loans is applied to selected banks only, the transmission from the policy rate to lending rates still exists but is weaker. At the same time, the transmission from the policy rate to deposit rates and bond yields would also weaken. This conclusion is supported by our empirical test based on the DSGE model.
- **Soft budget constraints on enterprises skew lending rates.** Due to implicit guarantees, some LGFVs and SOEs face soft budget constraints. The theoretical and empirical models show that enterprises under soft budget constraints have access to loans at lower interest rates and tend to borrow more than they would if such constraints did not exist. It is also demonstrated that as a result of soft budget constraints, the transmission of the policy rate to market interest rates would be less effective than in an economy where all firms faced hard budget constraints.
- **Shadow banking also weakens the transmission.** Some shadow banking activities in China (such as trust loans) are driven by regulatory arbitrage—such as evading quantitative limits on capital requirements, reserve requirements, and caps on loan-to-deposit ratios. It is demonstrated that although shadow banking may increase overall financing in the economy, it also tends to weaken the transmission of the policy rate to the real economy through banks and the bond market.

In addition, studies on how bond issuance quotas, high transaction costs, and liquidity shortages may affect interest rate transmission have been conducted. Our basic conclusion is that all these situations would, to a varying degree, lower the efficiency of interest rate transmission.

Measuring the Effectiveness of Interest Rate Transmission

Our empirical analyses found that interest rate transmission is generally less efficient in China than in developed economies and some emerging market economies. Several methodologies are used to estimate the impact of a change in the short-term interest rate (policy rate) on bond yields and on bank lending rates. Our conclusion is that although changes in China's short-term interest rates do affect bond yields and lending rates, their influence is weaker than in developed economies and some developing economies. At the same time, the transmission through the bond market is stronger than through the banking system.

Transmission through the Bond Market

Our analysis shows that transmission of short-term rates to bond yields is less effective in China than in other countries. A beta analysis to compare the

Table 7.3. Sensitivity of Treasury Bond Yields to Short-Term Interest Rates

	Impact of Short-Term Interest Rates on Bonds of Different Maturities (Beta)			
SHIBOR	**6 Months**	**2 Years**	**5 Years**	**10 Years**
7-Day Repo Rate	0.65	0.55	0.30	0.16
United States	0.55	0.49	0.32	0.19
Korea	0.83	0.64	0.46	0.26
United Kingdom	0.73	0.64	0.61	0.47
India	0.82	0.72	0.69	0.45
SHIBOR	0.75	0.40	0.43	0.36

Source: Author's estimates.
Note: SHIBOR = Shanghai Interbank Offered Rate.

transmission of short-term interest rates with Treasury bond yields in China and four other countries—India, Korea, the United Kingdom, and the United States—found that changes in China's short-term interest rates do have a noticeable impact on bond yields of different maturities. The sensitivity (beta) varies across bonds of different maturities. In particular, the transmission effect of short-term interest rates on bond yields tends to be weaker for longer maturities. It is also found that, relative to India, Korea, the United Kingdom, and the United States, changes in short-term interest rates in China have a smaller impact on medium- and long-term Treasury bond yields. In particular, the average sensitivity of Treasury bond yields to short-term interest rate changes is about 30 percent smaller in China than in other countries (Table 7.3).

Similarly, results also stand using SVAR.[3] The SVAR model is used to estimate and identify the impact of monetary policy shocks on yield curves in China and the United States. To single out the impact of short-term rates on bond yields, variables such as the output gap, money supply, and consumer price inflation are controlled for in the model. In addition, the predictive power (the ability to transmit information through expected channels) of the yield curve is analyzed. Specifically:

- The impulse response of a short-term interest rate shock on the Chinese Treasury bond yield is statistically significant. But such a response is weaker than in the United States. This conclusion is consistent with the cross-country beta analysis.
- During 2010–15, the impulse response of China's bond yields to short-term interest rate shocks improved somewhat. This may indicate that bond market transmission has benefited from rising liquidity and the development of derivatives products.
- China's Treasury bond yields are somewhat predictive of GDP growth, consumer price inflation, and interest rates. This implies that the yield curve can, to some degree, enhance policy rate transmission through the expectation channel.

[3]See more details about the SVAR model in Annex 7.1.

Table 7.4. Impulse Response of Treasury Bond Yields to Short-Term Interest Rates: A United States–China Comparison

(Percent, 2002–15)

	China		United States	
Maturity	**Current Response**	**Maximum Response**	**Current Response**	**Maximum Response**
1 Year	28	68	50	76
3 Year	15	47	30	62
5 Year	8	31	17	50
7 Year	6	15	4	44
10 Year	−5	−27	−12	38
20 Year	−6	−29	−18	19

Source: Author's estimates.

Table 7.5. Impulse Response of Treasury Bond Yields to Short-Term Interest Rate: United States–China Comparison

(Percent, 2010–15)

	China		United States	
Maturity	**Current Response**	**Maximum Response**	**Current Response**	**Maximum Response**
1 Year	39	65	48	74
3 Year	26	49	32	61
5 Year	14	41	19	59
7 Year	6	37	8	49
10 Year	3	28	5	40
20 Year	2	15	4	22

Source: Author's estimates.

In sum, China's short-term interest rate shocks do transmit to bond yields, though with weaker effects than in the United States (as shown in Tables 7.4 and 7.5). Based on data from the past five years, when comparing the maximum response of all maturities, the average bond-yield sensitivity to a change in the short-term interest rate in China is about 77 percent that in the United States.

Many factors have contributed to the weaker transmission in China's bond market than in bond markets in other countries. It is believed that the difference can be explained by the Treasury bond maturity structure, inadequate liquidity in segments of the bond market, underdevelopment of the derivatives market, and restrictions on market access for certain financial institutions. These factors have weakened or distorted interest rate transmission.

Transmission through the Banking System

It is found that interest rate transmission through the banking system is much less efficient in China than in the United States. Using several models, the transmission of market interest rates to bank lending rates is measured. The correlation between China's short-term market interest rate and the prime lending rate is between 0.4 and 0.5. A regression analysis using data on listed banks shows that the elasticity of lending rates to short-term market rates is between 0.60 and 0.67, if the impact of central bank benchmark rates is not controlled for. The elasticity falls to 0.16–0.17 after controlling for changes in benchmark rates. These two estimates can be seen as the upper and lower bounds of the effectiveness of short-term rate transmission to lending rates. In the United States, the effectiveness of policy rate transmission to bank lending rates is about 0.8, according to Gambacorta, Illes, and Lombardi (2014). This implies that the effectiveness of short-term rate transmission to bank lending rates in China is 20–80 percent that in the United States, with a mean value of about 50 percent. In other words, China's interest rate transmission through the banking system is probably about half that in the United States.

Several factors explain the weakness in market rate transmission to lending rates in China. First, in the past few years China's short-term interest rates have been fairly volatile, leaving banks unwilling to use market rates as the basis for pricing loans. Second, commercial banks have been equally reluctant to use Treasury yields as the benchmark for deposit interest or for pricing loans. Third, interest rate hedging instruments are not yet fully developed, and banks have not been permitted to enter the bond futures market. Fourth, securitization, which could establish a link between market rates and lending rates, is still nascent. Fifth, our empirical study, using data from 16 banks, shows that several policy and institutional factors have significantly weakened the market rate transmission to lending rates. These factors include the cap on the loan-to-deposit ratio, the high reserve requirement, and soft budget constraints mentioned earlier.

The Effect of Soft Budget Constraints

Soft budget constraints are widely perceived as limiting the effectiveness of interest rate transmission. Since LGFVs and SOEs are less sensitive to changes in interest rates as borrowers, monetary policy employing the interest rate as an intermediate target struggles to achieve the objective of macroeconomic stability. Soft budget constraints are reflected in two ways:

- The financing cost does not necessarily reflect changes in liquidity conditions and risks (since changes in the policy rate and credit risk do not effectively alter the financing costs for firms under soft budget constraints).
- Financing behavior is insensitive to interest rates (since changes in interest rates do not necessarily affect the amount that firms under soft budget constraints can borrow). At the same time, excessive borrowing by firms with soft budget constraints crowds out private sector entities in the loan and bond markets.

Empirical analyses were conducted to assess the extent to which soft budget constraints affect interest rate transmission. In doing so, the sensitivity of LGFV bonds and the aggregate bond market issuance to changes in interest rates was estimated in a sample of 3,820 LGFV bonds sold between January 1997 and September 2014. The model included variables such as the coupon rate and size of bonds issued, the financial performance of the issuer, credit rating, macroeconomic conditions, market interest rates, and fiscal conditions in the region where the issuing LGFV was located. The model was used to test the sensitivity of LGFV bond sales and funding costs to changes in market interest rates, using that of non-LGFV bonds as a benchmark. Several key findings were made:

- The pricing of LGFV bonds has become increasingly sensitive to changes in short-term market rates. Our model shows that for every 1 percentage point rise or fall in the interbank seven-day repo rate, the coupon rates of LGFV bonds move 0.34 percentage point in the same direction. Moreover, in recent years, the LGFV coupon rates reflect more significantly the financial health (or credit risks) of the issuers. The credit rating of LGFV bonds has also exercised some market discipline on the LGFV bond issuance. The higher the rating of a bond and its issuer, the lower the coupon rate.
- The size of LGFV bond issuance has become sensitive to the real risk-free rate. However, rising risk premiums have not yet effectively influenced the volume of LGFV financing.
- Amendments to the budget law in September 2014 to separate LGFV debt from that of local governments should contribute to weakening the expectation of implicit guarantees on LGFV debt.[4] Reforms guided by the revised Budget Law will exercise a more rigid budget constraint on local governments and their financing platforms. As the budget constraints are being hardened, LGFV borrowing should become increasingly market based and more sensitive to changes in interest rates. This will contribute to improvement in the interest rate transmission mechanism.

Stabilizing Short-Term Rates through an Interest Rate Corridor

Market acceptance of a policy rate is an important step toward building the new monetary policy framework. Only when the market recognizes the policy rate as the guiding monetary policy signal will financial institutions and the bond market price deposits, loans, and bonds according to how it changes. It is believed that stabilizing the short-term interest rate is a condition for the formation of the policy rate. For this purpose, it is suggested that the People's Bank of China establish an interest rate corridor.

Operational experience from many countries suggests that an interest rate corridor can effectively reduce short-term interest rate volatility (see Niu and others 2015). When liquidity is in short supply, the interest rate corridor can stem excessive demand for liquidity caused by "panic borrowing" by financial institutions on the interbank market. In times of unpredictable liquidity shocks, the interest rate corridor acts as an automatic stabilizer.

Moreover, an interest rate corridor can reduce the cost of operating monetary policy. A highly credible interest rate corridor reduces the need for commercial banks and other financial institutions to hoard funds. As a result, it reduces the size and frequency of PBC interventions in the open market and limits the chance

[4]Under the revised Budget Law, the Ministry of Finance and local People's Congress have direct "quantitative control" over local government debt limits, while LGFVs no longer receive implicit government guarantees. The reform also intends to improve the transparency of local government budgets and strengthen the supervision of LGFV financing through the local People's Congress, and by making balance sheets of local governments public.

that the policy rate will reach the top of the interest rate corridor. The optimal range of the interest rate corridor depends on the central bank's aversion to volatility in interest rates, the cost of the liquidity facility and open market operations, and the size of external shocks.

It is now necessary for China to establish an interest rate corridor. Difficulty in stabilizing interest rates has occurred primarily because of many unpredictable shocks to money demand. Shocks have resulted from financial innovation, capital account liberalization, fiscal operations, firms selling shares to the public, and seasonal factors. Interest rate volatility is measured by the coefficient of variation (average daily interest rate standard deviation divided by average interest rate) of overnight rates. Between 2012 and June 2015 the coefficient of variation for the Shanghai Interbank Offered Rate (SHIBOR) was 1.7 times that of the dollar rate volatility in the London Interbank Offered Rate (LIBOR), 1.9 times the overnight rate volatility in Korea, 3 times the overnight rate volatility in Japan, and 4.4 times the overnight rate volatility in India.

Adopting an interest rate corridor would help stabilize commercial banks' expectations, avoid sudden spikes in interest rates that would exacerbate liquidity hoarding, and eventually help stabilize interest rates. Unless volatility in short-term interest rates is reduced significantly, commercial banks will not be willing to adopt them as the basis for pricing loans and deposits, which is the basis for interest rate transmission

The creation of an interest rate corridor requires a set of corresponding reforms. For example, the M2 growth rate as an intermediate target of monetary policy needs to lose its central role in the decisions of top policymakers in the move toward interest rate stability. A more liberal system of qualified collateral for the standby loan facility needs to be introduced, alongside improvement in its transparency. A better framework for analyzing the linkages between interest rates, money supply, and real economic indicators will be essential to improving liquidity management and operation of the interest rate corridor. Interagency coordination and information sharing should also be strengthened so that liquidity forecasting can be improved and to reduce interest rate volatility caused by "unpredictable" demand.

Other Factors Affecting Transmission

The foregoing analyses focused on the determinants of interest rate transmission as directly related to monetary policy operations. These include, among others, the reliance on an M2 growth target, the use of quantitative instruments (such as the cap on the loan-to-deposit rate, quantitative limits on loans, and high reserve requirements for banks), the lack of market acceptance for short-term rates and bond yields to serve as the basis for pricing financial products, the underdevelopment of interest rate derivative products, and restrictions on access to the bond market. However, a few other factors have also deterred the transmission of short-term market rates to funding costs for corporates.

The following problems reduce funding availability and push up borrowing costs for small enterprises, technology firms, and green firms, even if liquidity is abundant in the interbank market and short-term rates are very low. In other words, they also serve as "blockages" to the efficient functioning of interest rate transmission.

- **Maturity mismatch due to excessive reliance on bank financing.** In China, more than 60 percent of social financing comes from bank lending. However, since the average maturity on Chinese banks' liabilities is only six months, banks are unable or unwilling to provide sufficient long-term loans for fear of taking too much risk. This means that even if the PBC has injected sufficient liquidity into the system, it may not result in a substantial increase in long-term financing—and therefore long-term interest rates may not fall as much as expected. One solution is to develop the corporate bond market, which will enable more companies to raise long-term funds directly from the market.
- **Mismatch of risk preferences between capital providers and fundraisers.** Again, most funds available are from banks, which have a strong preference for low-risk projects. However, the majority of new companies pose significantly higher risks than banks are willing to accept. If regulators force banks to extend more loans to risky companies such as small enterprises, higher nonperforming loans in the banking system may result. This mismatch of risk preferences between lenders and borrowers has also contributed to the funding difficulties of these firms. The main solution to this problem is to develop a healthy equity market, by avoiding regulatory disruptions to public share sales and providing support to various forms of private equity financing (including angel investors, venture capitalists, and private equity funds).
- **Regulatory restrictions on small banks.** Village banks in rural China sometimes offer much lower lending rates to small and micro firms than microlenders in the same locations (field-based evidence suggests by as much as 9 percentage points). This is because village banks are allowed to take very low-cost deposits (at an annual rate of 4–5 percent) but microlenders are not. Microlenders can use only their own funds (capital) or borrow from third parties at an annual rate of 12–13 percent. So why not authorize more village banks so as to reduce the funding costs of small firms? The answer is that regulations require all village banks to have an established bank as a "main sponsor." Even though many investors are interested in launching new village banks, they are unable to find sponsors. Most large banks are not interested in holding the shares of these minibanks because this would increase their reputational risk on a return that would be of negligible size. Therefore, while the intention of this regulation is to prevent financial risks, it also impedes the development of village banks and their potential to play an important role in reducing borrowing costs for firms.
- **Lack of specialized guarantee facilities.** Specialized guarantee agencies or programs can substantially reduce the risk premiums and funding costs of firms. For example, in 2005, the U.S. Congress authorized a guarantee program operated by the U.S. Department of Energy to support loans to

new energy projects. Since initially the "experts" believed 10 percent of these loans would likely default, the government allocated budgetary funds to cover the expected losses. However, by putting in place an operation involving the best venture capital investors and technology professionals, the final loss rate was only 2.28 percent. With a very small amount of public funds, the government successfully mobilized about 50 times the amount of private funds and thereby accelerated the development of this strategic industry. In China, partial guarantees for loans to support energy-saving projects under the International Finance Corporation's China Utility-Based Energy Efficiency Finance program proved equally successful thanks to professional management. Between 2006 and 2015 the program supported 170 projects, and the average default rate was less than 1 percent. China has already established many guarantee companies, but many of them lack specialization and professional managers. Some guarantee companies cover all sectors and invest in many different regions, although their risk management capacity is weaker than that of banks. Some guarantee companies started by local governments are run by former government officials who do not have professional experience, and their incentive structures make it difficult to attract professional talent. The key to future success is to develop specialized guarantee agencies across a few sectors and regions and to ensure that they operate in accordance with market-based approaches.

- **Underdevelopment of credit information system.** Asymmetric information has been another cause of funding difficulties for many small firms. In the absence of financial data, credit histories of borrowers, and other due-diligence information, banks will generally not provide loans. When they do, the loans tend to be very costly and carry very stringent collateral and guarantee requirements. World Bank studies suggest that establishment of a credit information system can substantially improve the availability of funds to small firms. In China, the credit information system has evolved over 20 years to play a positive role in corporate financing. However, the system still faces several problems, including the lack of integration of data in the hands of different government agencies, the dominance of government ownership, and limited application of big data technologies. Development of a more effective credit information system should involve the integration of corporate credit data with information from industrial and commerce bureaus, tax administrations, public security bureaus, environmental agencies, and customs. It should introduce market competition from privately owned credit bureaus, apply various big data and data-mining technologies, and include transaction data to help quantify the likelihood that borrowers will default.

POLICY RECOMMENDATIONS

Transitioning to a new monetary policy framework that uses interest rates as the intermediate target will require an effective transmission mechanism.

Improving the mechanism through reforms is thus essential over the next few years. The following reforms will help improve the transmission mechanism:

1. **Changing the point target of M2 growth to monitoring an M2 growth range.** Market rates are determined jointly by money demand and supply. With financial innovations and opening up of the capital account, money demand will become increasingly unstable. Targeting a specific M2 growth rate may artificially create excessive volatility in short-term interest rates. Banks will therefore be reluctant to use market rates to price loans and deposits, making it difficult to form a policy rate and an effective interest rate transmission mechanism.

   When the money demand function is not stable, improving the flexibility of money supply is important. This means that it is needed to allow M2 growth to deviate from the preset M2 growth target.[5] It is suggested that the current M2 growth target be changed from a point (12 percent for example) to a range (such as 9–15 percent) for monitoring purposes. This change would have three effects: (1) Changing the target of M2 growth rate from a point to a range will demonstrate a greater tolerance for M2 volatility and a greater emphasis on interest rate stability. This will create an accommodating condition for the establishment of the interest rate corridor. (2) The change from "target" to the term "M2 growth rate for monitoring" means there will no longer be an absolute ceiling and floor. (3) A shift (with a transition period of the next few years) from a target point to a monitoring range will signal the gradual approach adopted by the central bank in moving toward the new monetary policy framework, as opposed to a sudden abandonment of the M2 target.

   Once the M2 monitoring range and the interest rate corridor are in place, the resulting improvement in market confidence in short-term-rate stability will lay the foundation for the transition to a new monetary policy framework that uses the interest rate as the intermediate target. The role of the M2 growth rate or range will further diminish over the longer term.

2. **Establishing an interest rate corridor in phases to limit market rate volatility and foster the market acceptance of the policy rate.** It is necessary to create an interest rate corridor to lower interest rate volatility and establish conditions to guide the formation of the policy rate. In China's context, the process may take several years. A possible road map will consist of several steps: (1) creating a de facto interest rate corridor around an implicit policy rate without necessarily announcing it (as M2 will likely remain the official intermediate target for a while) and (2) gradually narrowing the de facto interest rate corridor. In the process, the declining interest rate volatility will guide markets to develop expectations that a certain short-term interest rate will become the policy rate in the future. Banks will then become more inclined to

[5]The reason is that demand for money faces random shocks and thus causes interest rate volatility when money supply growth is fixed. To lower interest rate volatility, volatility in money supply growth must be allowed to rise.

price their products based on this interest rate and other market rates. The prime lending rates will also increasingly reflect the movements of this policy rate. (3) When these elements are in place, the central bank can formally announce the elimination of the benchmark deposit and lending rates, and the new policy framework will be anchored to the short-term policy rate instead of the M2 growth rate. The central bank can then establish an official, or explicit, interest rate corridor, with the interest rate for the standby loan facility as the ceiling and the interest rate for excess reserves as the floor. Within the official corridor, a narrower de facto interest rate corridor can be maintained through frequent open market operations, supported by a proper collateral system for accessing the central bank's liquidity provisions.

3. **Reducing or removing legacy policy constraints on interest rate transmission.** Reforms can focus on the following areas:
    - *Removing the cap on the loan-to-deposit ratio.* Consensus has been reached to abolish the cap on the loan-to-deposit ratio. In August 2015 the Standing Committee of the National People's Congress amended the Commercial Banking Law and changed the cap on the loan-to-deposit ratio to a monitoring indicator.
    - *Removing the quantitative limits on bank loans.* In the future, the macroprudential management framework should no longer focus on setting quantitative loan limits for individual banks; instead it should focus on providing incentives for prudent bank behaviors with respect to capital adequacy, liquidity, and asset quality. In January 2016 the introduction of the Macro-Prudential Assessment Framework by the People's Bank of China had already taken a step in that direction.
    - *A gradual reduction of the legal reserve requirement.* Due to the change in China's balance-of-payments situation, foreign exchange reserve accumulation is no longer the source of monetary expansion. To ensure adequate liquidity in the financial system, the PBC will need to gradually lower the legal reserve requirement to improve the money multiplier while expanding the monetary base through the use relending facilities and open market operations. When choosing between expanding the monetary base and increasing the money multiplier (through cuts in the reserve requirement), considerations will need to take into account that a cut in the reserve requirement could help interest rate transmission and lower banks' operating costs, as well as corporate sector financing costs. At the same time, avoiding an excessively high reserve requirement can help improve Chinese banks' international competitiveness.
4. **Speeding up reforms that harden budget constraints for local governments, LGFVs, and SOEs.** Fiscal reforms to reclassify local government debt and improve its disclosure will tighten local government off-budget constraints. Efforts to establish a municipal bond market through the debt-swap program, better credit rating, and mandatory disclosures will also reduce their off-bud-

get borrowing. Under the reformed system, local governments and LGFVs will be more self-disciplined in borrowing, thereby reducing the need for quantitative limits on borrowing imposed by the central bank or bank regulator. At the same time, increasing the sensitivity of SOEs' borrowing to interest rate changes through more forceful SOE reforms will be essential.

5. **Improving the functioning of the bond market.** The bond market can be improved in several ways. First, the government can improve the maturity structure of sovereign bond issuance to help strengthen monetary policy transmission. Compared with Australia, the United Kingdom, the United States, and other countries, issuance of Chinese Treasury bonds with maturities below two years and above 10 years is not frequent enough. In particular, the issuance frequency of Treasury bonds with maturity less than two years is only one-tenth of that in the United States. Second, banks should be allowed to trade Treasury bond futures, and efforts should be made to further develop interest rate swaps and inflation-linked bonds. Third, market access restrictions should be eased or removed to allow more foreign investors to participate in the domestic bond markets. Efforts should include increasing the QFII and RQFII quota,[6] streamlining the review and approval procedures for quota management, and removing market access controls on the domestic interbank market. Fourth, the market must be allowed to play a greater role in banks' pricing of financial products. Banks will increasingly price their loans and deposits as well as other financial products based on market rates. This would require strengthening the market-based pricing mechanism through the elimination of quantitative restrictions and more effective pricing of credit risks.
6. **Complementary reforms include the following:** Further develop the corporate bond market to provide new funding sources for mid- and long-term projects to ease the maturity mismatch facing banks and corporates. Speed up the development of equity financing channels and avoid government disruption to the initial public offering function of the stock market. Relax market access restrictions on banks serving SMEs. Incubate guarantee companies with sector specialties to reduce unnecessary risk premiums. Develop the credit information system by integrating data managed by different ministries and encourage market competition.

CONCLUSIONS

China is moving toward a new monetary policy framework with interest rates as its intermediate target. However, a critical condition for the successful transition to the new framework is effective transmission from the policy rate to market rates, including deposit and lending rates as well as bond yields. Our research found that multiple factors, such as the cap on the loan-to-deposit ratio,

[6]Qualified foreign institutional investor and renminbi qualified foreign institutional investor.

quantitative loan limits, the deposit interest rate ceiling, the high reserve requirement, soft budget constraints on some borrowers, excessive volatility of short-term rates, and the lack of derivative instruments, may weaken the interest rate transmission mechanism. Numerical simulations based on our DSGE model further indicate that the cap on the loan-to-deposit ratio, quantitative loan limits, and the deposit interest rate ceiling dampen the transmission efficiency the most compared with other financial friction and distortions.

Improving interest rate transmission through reforms is essential over the next few years. Establishing an interest rate corridor could reduce interest rate volatility and improve the market acceptance of the policy rate, while encouraging banks to price loans based on market rates. Other reforms that could help strengthen interest rate transmission include shifting from an M2 growth target to an indicative range, removing quantitative loan limits, lowering the reserve requirement ratio, hardening budget constraints for LGFVs and SOEs, developing the interest rate derivatives market, and reducing access restrictions on the bond market.

ANNEX 7.1. SVAR MODEL SPECIFICATION

Based on Bernanke and Mihov (1995), a simple SVAR model is constructed to empirically identify the monetary policy stance in China, as demonstrated below:

$$A_0 Z_t = A_1 Z_{t-1} + A_2 Z_{t-2} + \cdots + A_q Z_{t-q} + e_t.$$

A subtle difference in the vector, X_{2t}, between China and the United States is allowed. Specifically, for China,

$$Z_t = \begin{bmatrix} X_{1t} \\ S_t \\ X_{2t} \end{bmatrix}, X_{1t} = \begin{bmatrix} Gap_t \\ CPI_t \end{bmatrix}, S_t = [R_t], X_{2t} = \begin{bmatrix} M2_t \\ R7_t \\ YearX_t \end{bmatrix};$$

while for the United States,

$$Z_t = \begin{bmatrix} X_{1t} \\ S_t \\ X_{2t} \end{bmatrix}, X_{1t} = \begin{bmatrix} Gap_t \\ CPI_t \end{bmatrix}, S_t = [R_t], X_{2t} = [YearX_t],$$

where GAP_t denotes the output gap, and CPI_t denotes CPI year-over-year growth rate. $Year\,X_t$ is the bond yields with different maturities, and R_t expresses the central bank benchmark rate. As measures of quantity-based and price-based monetary policies in China, $M2_t$ and $R7_t$ denote the M2 year-over-year growth rate and interbank interest rate, respectively, to capture its transitional monetary policy framework.

Two separate subsamples from January 2002 to June 2015 are selected to estimate the impulse responses to benchmark interest rate shocks before and after the global financial crisis. The identification strategy simply follows the lower triangular matrix, as defined below:

$$A_0 = \begin{bmatrix} a_{11} & 0 & 0 & 0 & 0 & 0 \\ a_{12} & a_{22} & 0 & 0 & 0 & 0 \\ a_{31} & a_{32} & a_{33} & 0 & 0 & 0 \\ a_{41} & a_{42} & a_{43} & a_{44} & 0 & 0 \\ a_{51} & a_{52} & a_{53} & a_{54} & a_{55} & 0 \\ a_{61} & a_{62} & a_{63} & a_{64} & a_{65} & a_{66} \end{bmatrix} \text{ and } A_0 = \begin{bmatrix} a_{11} & 0 & 0 & 0 \\ a_{21} & a_{22} & 0 & 0 \\ a_{31} & a_{32} & a_{33} & 0 \\ a_{41} & a_{42} & a_{43} & a_{44} \end{bmatrix}$$

for China and the United States, respectively.

To measure the mentioned variables above, inflation rates are introduced (monthly smoothed CPI year-over-year growth rate for China and core CPI year-over-year growth rate for the United States), as well as central bank benchmark rates (the one-year deposit rate for China, and the federal funds rate for the United States), an interbank interest rate for China (seven-day repo rate), money supply for China (M2 year-over-year growth rate), and bond yields for China and the United States with different maturities (one year, two year, five year, seven year, 10 year, 20 year). Data for the China output gap are based on estimates of the macroeconometric model developed by the macroeconomic forecasting team of the PBC Research Bureau and are smoothed monthly, while those for the United States are from reports of Oxford Economics.

The estimation results of our SVAR model are consistent with those from the beta analysis.

REFERENCES

Bai, C. E., S. Lin, K. Shi, and Z. Song. 2016. "Monetary and Exchange Rate Policies under Chinese Dual-Economy." Manuscript.

Bernanke, B. S., and A. S. Blinder. 1992. "The Federal Funds Rate and the Channels of Monetary Transmission." *American Economic Review* 82 (4): 901–21.

Bernanke, B. S., and I. Mihov. 1995. "Measuring Monetary Policy." NBER Working Paper No. 5145, National Bureau of Economic Research, Cambridge, MA.

Friedman, B. M., and K. N. Kuttner. 1992. "Money, Income, Prices, and Interest Rates." *American Economic Review* 82 (3): 472–92.

Gambacorta, L., A. Illes, and M. Lombardi. 2014. "Has the Transmission of Policy Rates to Lending Rates Been Impaired by the Global Financial Crisis?" BIS Working Paper No. 477, Bank for International Settlements, Basel.

Liao, W., and S. J.-A. Tapsoba. 2014. "China's Monetary Policy and Interest Rate Liberalization: Lessons from International Experiences." Working Paper No. 14/75, International Monetary Fund, Washington.

Ma, J., and H. L. Wang. 2014. "Theoretical Models for Policy Rate Transmission Mechanism." People's Bank of China Working Paper No. 2014/1, Beijing.

Ma, J., K. Shi, H. L. Wang, and L. S. Wang. 2015. "A Study of Interest Rate Transmission Dynamics." In *Transmission Mechanism of the New Monetary Policy Framework*, edited by J. Ma and M. Ji. Beijing: China Finance 40 Forum.

Ma, J., L. Wang, and J. Q. Li. 2015. "Interest Rate Transmission Mechanism under Institutional Constraints: A Static Analysis." In *Transmission Mechanism of the New Monetary Policy Framework*, edited by J. Ma and M. Ji. Beijing: China Finance 40 Forum.

Ma, J., and M. Z. Ji. 2016. *Interest Rate Transmission under the New Monetary Policy Framework* (Chinese edition). Beijing: China Financial Publishing House.

Niu, M. H., L. N. Zhang, X. Zhang, X. T. Song, and J. Ma. 2015. "Interest Rate Corridor, Interest Rate Stability, and Adjustment Cost." In *Transmission Mechanism of the New Monetary Policy Framework*, edited by J. Ma and M. Ji. Beijing: China Finance 40 Forum.

Walsh, C. E. 2010. *Monetary Theory and Policy.* Cambridge, Massachusetts: MIT Press.

Yi, G. 2004. *China Monetary Reform Process.* Beijing: Commercial Press.

CHAPTER 8

Capital Account Opening and Capital Flow Management

KARL HABERMEIER, ANNAMARIA KOKENYNE IVANICS, SALIM M. DARBAR, CHIKAKO BABA, ZHU LING, AND VIKTORIYA ZOTOVA

China is the world's leading trading nation. Yet, remarkably, it is much less well integrated with the global financial system, and the country's extensive controls on international capital flows are an important brake on its international financial integration. Will this situation remain mostly unchanged in the next decade, or will we see accelerated capital flow liberalization?[1]

The Chinese government has repeatedly stated its intention to achieve convertibility of the renminbi under the capital account.[2] However, it has not published an official timetable or road map to achieve this. The intention to liberalize capital flows is consistent with the IMF's institutional view, which highlights that "[c]ountries with extensive and long-standing measures to limit capital flows are likely to benefit from further liberalization in an orderly manner. There is, however, no presumption that full liberalization is an appropriate goal for all countries at all times" (IMF 2012a).

The authorities appear to have adopted a strategy of "managed convertibility." The challenge is to flesh out the main elements of such a strategy. This chapter contributes to the discussion by attempting to shed light on the following questions: What is the current degree of capital account convertibility, and how effective are capital controls? Is there a case for China to continue to pursue capital flow liberalization? Why are pressures growing for China to quicken the pace? How can China manage the potential risks of liberalization, in particular those associated with capital outflows?

This chapter argues that China has made significant progress in removing capital controls, but that capital movements are still much more tightly controlled than in most advanced economies. The effectiveness of controls differs significantly across types of transactions, however, and there is evidence of growing

[1]Capital flow and capital account liberalization are used interchangeably to describe the removal of controls on inward and outward flows on the financial account.

[2]Suggestions for the 13th Five-Year Plan for National Economic and Social Development (dated October 29, 2015) state that "China will realize the renminbi's convertibility under capital accounts in an orderly way."

circumvention. While the pace of capital flow liberalization should be fine-tuned to fit the prevailing macroeconomic environment and the health of the financial system, in the medium term China needs to adjust its approach to managing capital flows to make it more consistent with its very large cross-border trade flows and increasingly large cross-border financial flows. In the new regime, it would probably be desirable to transition from quantitative restrictions and quotas to price-based measures such as taxes and levies, from residency-based administrative controls to currency-based regulation and supervision, and from ex ante approval to ex post reporting and surveillance, as controls are gradually relaxed.[3]

HALF OPEN OR HALF CLOSED? CAPITAL ACCOUNT CONVERTIBILITY TODAY

China's Capital Controls

China has made considerable progress over the years in liberalizing capital flows (Box 8.1), but it still has one of the world's highest levels of de jure capital account restrictiveness.[4] Figure 8.1 plots the de jure measure of capital account restrictiveness against GDP per capita for 186 countries in 2015. This measure is based on the IMF's *Annual Report on Exchange Arrangements and Exchange Restrictions* (AREAER).[5] The AREAER divides capital account transactions into 56 categories: China reports on 53 of them, and 43 are reported to have some degree of control, hence the de jure measure is 43/53, or about 0.8.

The State Administration of Foreign Exchange (SAFE) classifies capital account restrictiveness differently. According to its classification, as of February 2015 only five out of 40 categories of transactions are *unconvertible*, 18 are *partially convertible*, seven are *generally convertible*, and 10 are *convertible*.[6] A category that is considered *convertible* can still be subject to controls, albeit not exchange controls. For example, even though nonresidents face no currency exchange restrictions when they purchase domestic real estate, the purchases are allowed only on the basis of need and for the buyer's own use.

---

[3]The authors are grateful to SAFE for helpful comments provided on this chapter.

[4]De jure measures of capital controls are based on the laws and regulations governing capital controls.

[5]Various indices measure the degree of capital account openness, and each has its own imperfections. Most indices of de jure controls on capital accounts, including the one used in this chapter, draw on the IMF's AREAER as a primary source of information on rules and regulations related to capital transactions. Many indices indicate extensive controls for China, although minor variations across indices reflect differences in the coverage of underlying transactions and subjective judgments (see IMF 2010 for a comparison of these indices).

[6]In SAFE's classification, *unconvertible* refers to those items forbidden by legislation or de facto practice, *partially convertible* refers to the situation where some subitems are permitted and others are not, *generally convertible* refers to those items permitted after registration or report, and *convertible* refers to those items without exchange restrictions (SAFE presentation, February 2015).

Box 8.1. A Brief History of China's Capital Flow Liberalization

China was a closed economy before DENG Xiaoping's economic reforms in 1978. Since then, it has become a major destination for foreign direct investment (FDI). As it became more integrated with the rest of the world, China declared current account convertibility and accepted the obligations of Article VIII of the IMF Articles of Agreement in 1996.

Despite current account convertibility and steps to liberalize inward FDI, China's capital account remained inconvertible. Most cross-border financial transactions were either heavily restricted or strictly prohibited, and restrictions on capital outflows were tightened in response to the Asian financial crisis in 1997–98.

China began to ease capital controls after joining the World Trade Organization (WTO) in 2001 to meet its commitments on financial sector liberalization as part of its WTO obligations. Foreign-funded banks, including their subsidiaries in China, have been accorded national treatment. As a first major step in portfolio investment liberalization, China introduced the Qualified Foreign Institutional Investor scheme in 2002, which gives selected foreign investors limited access to the domestic financial market.

After the shift in policy from discouraging outflows to a balanced opening of the capital account, the Qualified Domestic Institutional Investor system was launched in 2007. Since then, conditions for outward direct investments were significantly relaxed, and those for individual capital transfers were slightly eased. Given a strong reserve position and appreciation pressures, the surrender requirement of foreign exchange revenue from current transactions was eliminated, leading to fewer foreign exchange conversions from such transactions into yuan, the renminbi's currency unit. The program for outward investments was also extended to qualified retail investors under the Qualified Domestic Individual Investors scheme to allow for outward portfolio investment in the Shanghai Free Trade Zone and will be gradually expanded.

China also tested its liberalization policy before implementing it in designated areas, by selected companies, or in free trade zones. For example, a pilot program was started in Shanghai in 2013 and expanded to other cities. The Shanghai and Hong Kong Stock-Connect Program has encouraged increased capital flows through equities between the mainland and Hong Kong SAR.

While direct investment is among the least controlled categories of flows and SAFE considers it to be *convertible*, it remains subject to various impediments. Outward direct investment is largely liberalized (except for sensitive countries, regions, and industries), but significant restrictions remain on inward direct investment.[7] That said, administrative procedures have been simplified.

Overseas lending by domestic commercial banks is virtually unrestricted, while residents need approval from SAFE to borrow abroad, which seems somewhat at odds with the usual approach, which is generally to liberalize inflows

[7]A minimum offshore asset requirement of $100 million is imposed on foreign investors, who also must be financially sound and have good credit and mature management experience to invest in China. Strategic inward direct investments are subject to a three-year holding period, during which acquired shares cannot be traded or transferred. The repatriation of funds from liquidation of direct investment requires SAFE registration (except for investment and repatriation in renminbi), while the repatriation of profits requires only verification by the bank conducting the transfer.

Figure 8.1. Income Level and De Jure Financial Account Restrictiveness
(GDP per capita in logarithm [x-axis] and de jure index [y-axis], 2015 or latest available)

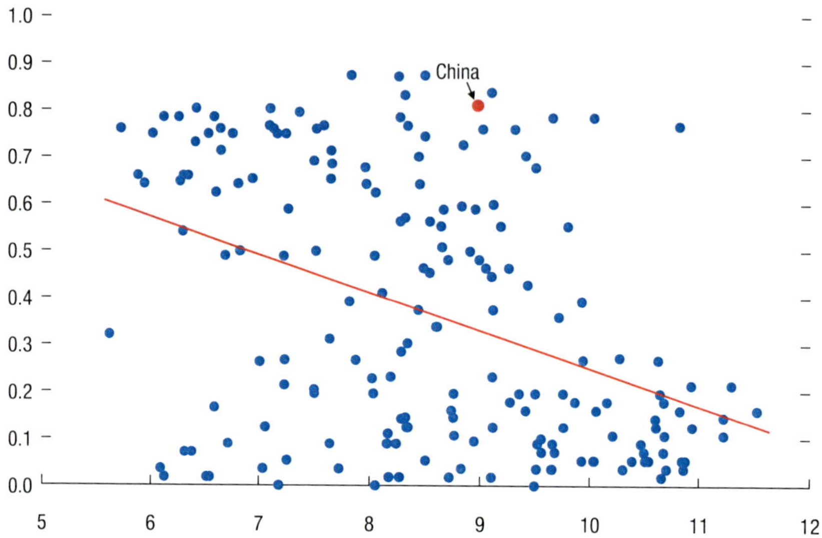

Sources: World Bank, *World Development Indicators*; IMF Annual Report on Exchange Arrangements and Exchange Restrictions database; and IMF staff calculations.
Note: 186 IMF member countries, including their territories where data are available.

before outflows. Overseas lending by domestic financial institutions has expanded faster than domestic loans in recent years, and nearly 90 percent of the overseas loans are denominated in foreign currencies (Figure 8.2).

The total value of overseas loans at the end of the third quarter of 2015 topped 4 percent of China's annual GDP. These overseas loans appear to develop in tandem with outward foreign direct investment (FDI), suggesting that the loans finance the overseas projects of Chinese state-owned enterprises (SOEs).[8] To the extent these loans represent directed lending, they potentially increase financial sector vulnerabilities.

At the other end of the spectrum, both inward and outward portfolio investments are more tightly controlled. Portfolio outflows are more restricted than inflows, and none of the related categories are *convertible* by the SAFE classification. The regulators' strategy so far has been to allow portfolio inflows before outflows, to limit the size of flows using quotas and qualified investor systems, and to liberalize transactions conducted in renminbi to a greater extent than those in foreign currencies (see Box 8.2 and Table 8.1). For instance, while domestic

[8]SOEs dominate China's outward FDI. For example, private firms accounted for only 9.5 percent of China's outward FDI in 2012 (Alon and others 2014).

Figure 8.2. Overseas Loans by Domestic Financial Institutions

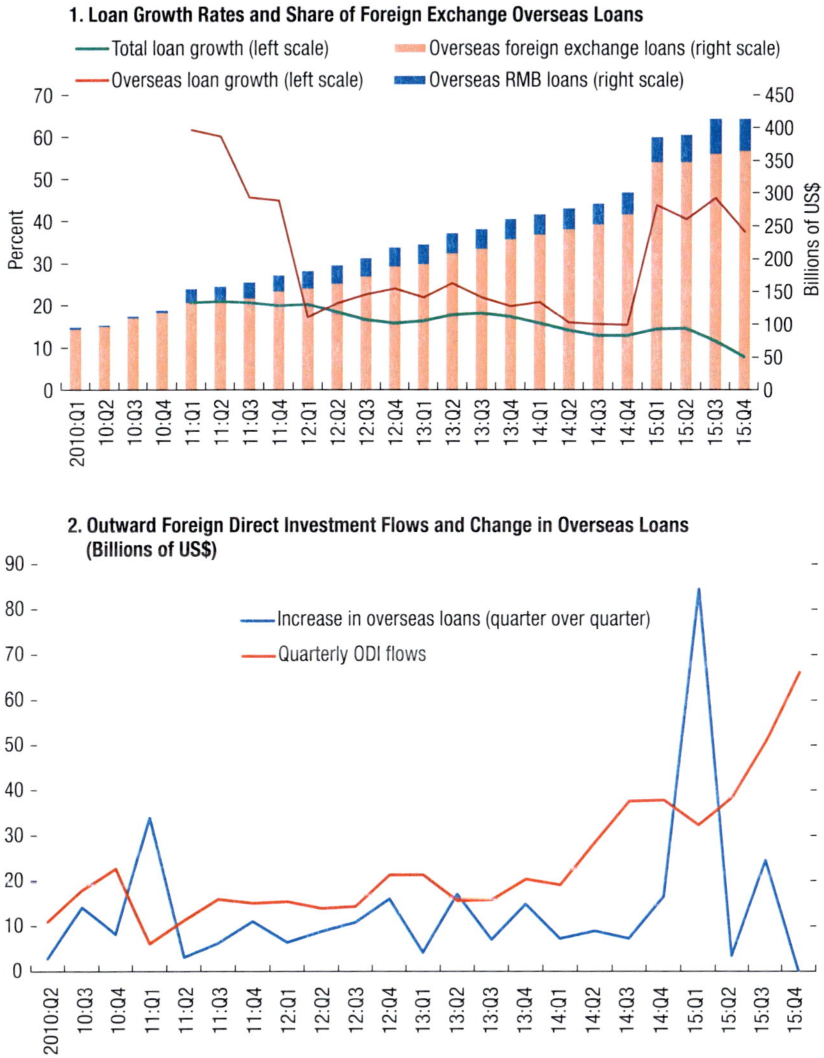

Sources: State Administration of Foreign Exchange; People's Bank of China (Sources and Uses of Credit Funds of Financial Institutions); and IMF staff calculations.
Note: Domestic financial institutions in the figure include the People's Bank of China, depository financial institutions, and nondepository financial institutions. ODI = outward foreign direct investment.

Box 8.2. Liberalization Schemes on Cross-Border Portfolio Investment

The Qualified Foreign Institutional Investor (QFII) system allows qualified foreign institutional investors, including banks and nonbank financial institutions (with the exception of hedge funds), limited access to the Chinese financial markets.

The China Securities Regulatory Commission assesses the qualifications of applications. Each qualified investor is subject to a quota, which is approved by the State Administration of Foreign Exchange (SAFE). The quota is capped at $5 billion per investor except for sovereign funds, central banks, and governments. The cap on aggregate quotas is set at $150 billion. The quota cannot be transferred or traded. Within the quota limit, investors can invest only in a subset of domestic financial products such as shares, fixed-income instruments, and stock index futures approved by the commission. Each investor may buy no more than 10 percent of the total shares of any listed company, and the aggregate purchase of all QFII investors combined may not exceed 30 percent of the shares of any listed company. Investors face a minimum investment requirement of $20 million, and most investments are subject to a one-year holding period. After this period, the repatriation of principal and profits is limited: investors can repatriate at most 20 percent of the onshore Chinese assets they held at the end of the previous year. Open-end China funds are subject to less-stringent requirements. Since February 2016 a wider range of foreign investors can invest in the Chinese Interbank Bond Market without quotas.

Like the QFII, the Renminbi Qualified Financial Institutional Investor (RQFII) system allows qualified foreign institutional investors to invest in the domestic financial market. RQFII investors and QFII investors differ in three major ways. First, RQFII investors must use the renminbi to invest in Chinese financial markets, while QFII investors may use other currencies as well. The second difference is the holding period: open-end China funds are not subject to any holding period, while the rest are subject to a one-year holding period similar to QFII investors. The third difference is that no official cap is placed on RQFII quotas, while QFII quotas are subject to official caps. The total allocated quota for RQFII investments reached RMB1,210 billion in May 2016.

The Qualified Domestic Institutional Investor (QDII) system allows qualified domestic institutional investors, including banks and nonbank financial institutions such as securities firms and insurance companies, to invest in overseas financial markets. To be qualified, an investor needs approval from its relevant industry regulator. Each qualified investor is subject to a SAFE-approved quota. There is no official cap on aggregate or individual quotas. If an investor fails to use its quota within two years of approval, SAFE may reduce it. The quota cannot be transferred or traded. Qualified banks may not invest in commodity derivatives, hedge funds, or securities with credit ratings below BBB. Each investor may hold no more than 10 percent of a foreign company's voting shares. And the aggregate of the QDII quota is small (US$90 billion), about 1 percent of China's 2014 GDP. The program on Qualified Domestic Individual Investor (QDII2) allows qualified individual retail investors in the Shanghai Free Trade Zone to invest in overseas financial markets.

The Shanghai–Hong Kong Stock Connect gives Chinese retail investors access to the Hong Kong SAR stock market and Hong Kong SAR investors access to Chinese stock markets. There is a minimum investment requirement of 0.5 million yuan for Chinese investors, but not for Hong Kong SAR investors. Unlike other pilot schemes, investors do not need to be approved as qualified investors, nor are they subject to individual quotas. However, daily limits and an aggregate quota are imposed on gross flows. The daily limit on southbound flows (from Shanghai to the Hong Kong SAR stock market) was reached for the first time on April 8, 2015. Nonetheless, the limit had not been reached again as of October 31, 2015. In December 2015 the mutual recognition of funds was launched, allowing investors in the mainland and Hong Kong SAR to invest in qualified cross-border mutual funds.

Table 8.1. Summary of China's Schemes to Ease Controls on Portfolio Investments, September 2015

Scheme	Target Flows	Start Year	Quota Limit	Total Quotas Allotted (Billion)	Cap on Individual Quota	Cap on Total Quotas	Minimum Investment Required	Currency
QDII	Portfolio outflow	2006	Yes	$90	No	No	No	Any
QFII	Portfolio inflow	2002	Yes	$79	$1 billion	$150 billion	$2 million	Any
RQFII	Portfolio inflow	2011	Yes	RMB412	No	No	No	RMB
SHKSC *Southbound*[2]	Equity outflow	2014	No[1]	. . .	No	RMB250 billion[1]	RMB0.5 million	RMB
SHKSC *Northbound*	Equity inflow	2014	No[1]	. . .	No	RMB300 billion[1]	No	RMB
MRF	Portfolio inflow/ outflow	2015	. . .	. . .	50% of the fund's total assets	No	No	Any

Sources: People's Bank of China publications; and State Administration of Foreign Exchange.

Note: . . . = not available; MRF = mutual recognition of funds; QDII = Qualified Domestic Institutional Investor; QFII = Qualified Foreign Institutional Investor; RMB = renminbi; RQFII = Renminbi Qualified Foreign Institutional Investor; SHKSC = Shanghai Hong Kong Stock Exchange Connect.

[1] Though SHKSC investors are not subject to individual quota limits, they are subject to a daily limit and an aggregate quota on total flows. Net southbound flows are capped at RMB10.5 billion per day and RMB250 billion in aggregate, and net northbound flows are capped at RMB15 billion per day and RMB300 billion in aggregate.

[2] Southbound refers to investment flows from Shanghai (mainland) to Hong Kong SAR and northbound refers to investment flows from Hong Kong SAR to Shanghai.

companies can list and issue bonds abroad, foreign companies cannot be listed on Chinese stock markets, nor are they allowed to issue bonds denominated in foreign currencies in China.[9] With respect to capital flows in renminbi, the Renminbi Qualified Financial Institutional Investor (RQFII) system has no cap on aggregate quotas, while the Qualified Foreign Institutional Investor (QFII) system does, and resident nonfinancial entities may also keep yuan funds received abroad on offshore accounts without any limitation. Despite the gradual increase in aggregate quotas, the total portfolio investment quota for nonresidents reached only 3 percent of Chinese stock market capitalization[10] and 17 percent of the total trading volume on the China interbank bond market in September 2015. Recent liberalization steps allowing wider access to the interbank bond market and equity markets may increase foreign participation.

Renminbi Internationalization

Capital flow liberalization in China and renminbi internationalization are deeply intertwined. Since the global financial crisis, the authorities have pursued

[9]Yuan-denominated bond issuance by foreign companies was allowed from September 2014.

[10]For example, foreign holdings of U.S. corporate equities were about 20 percent as of end-September 2015.

renminbi internationalization as a key policy (see Chapter 9 on renminbi internationalization). A major challenge in managing this process is to delineate the relationship between renminbi internationalization and capital flow liberalization (He 2014). Even if a currency is convertible (that is, both the current and financial account are liberalized), it may not necessarily be widely used internationally. For example, the currencies of Australia, Canada, and New Zealand are not widely used even though they are fully convertible. On the other hand, the international use of a currency does not require a fully open capital account, at least in the initial stage, although some capital account openness is necessary (He and McCauley 2010). To ensure adequate liquidity in the offshore markets, the renminbi supply would need to increase further. Given the current account surplus in China, one way to inject more yuan into global financial markets would be to liberalize capital flows. Indeed, renminbi liquidity in the global financial system crucially depends on the willingness of non-Chinese residents to borrow in yuan (He and McCauley 2012). Ultimately, full internationalization of the renminbi will be a function of its scale, stability, and liquidity (Eichengreen 2013).[11]

The relationship between renminbi internationalization and capital flow liberalization is complex. Capital flow liberalization would, in principle, support greater internationalization. It would also tend to eventually reduce the spread between onshore and offshore exchange rates (in Hong Kong SAR, for example). However, it is possible that the influence of liberalization on the spread is not straightforward in the short term.

Conversely, internationalization can complicate liberalization, because it creates more opportunities for the circumvention of capital controls. The safe liberalization of capital flows requires that remaining controls are effective. The use of the renminbi in cross-border transactions provides carry trade and arbitrage opportunities to both residents and nonresidents through trade channels (Yu 2014; Zhang 2015). Internationalization will thus also have an effect on spreads between offshore and onshore rates: the larger the offshore renminbi market becomes, the easier it will be to structure transactions for arbitraging any material deviations between the two exchange rates. Consequently, each liberalization step needs to be considered in light of how the international use of the renminbi will affect capital flows.

The removal of controls thus needs to be pursued on two tracks whose paces must remain consistent. Capital flow liberalization needs to progress by lifting controls on cross-border transactions in foreign exchange but also in yuan, which raises the question of whether liberalization on one track can progress faster than liberalization on the other. Inconsistency between the pace of renminbi liberalization and foreign exchange could lead to adverse outcomes. For example, if renminbi liberalization progresses faster, it may undermine controls on transactions

[11]The IMF has agreed to add the renminbi to the special drawing rights basket starting October 1, 2016. Although its inclusion in the basket is not likely to have an immediate impact, in the medium to long term it is expected to make the renminbi more international. Importantly, central banks are likely to include the currency in their reserve assets.

in foreign exchange. Conversely, if controls are removed faster on foreign exchange transactions, resulting in increased access of nonresidents to the onshore foreign exchange market and investment opportunities, it may adversely affect the spread between onshore and offshore exchange rates.

Are Controls Still Binding?

A wide range of views has been expressed about the effectiveness of China's capital controls. It has been argued that controls are not binding or are losing their effectiveness because they have become easier to circumvent under current account convertibility, ongoing renminbi internationalization, and capital flow liberalization. The opposite view holds that the low share of portfolio inflows in China—compared with emerging markets with open capital accounts—is a result of strict capital controls on portfolio flows (IMF 2011a). China is, indeed, among the least financially open countries in its income range (Figure 8.3), based on one important measure of financial integration.[12] It is also much less open than advanced economies, and Figure 8.4 shows that it ranks with India as the least open among the BRICS (Brazil, Russia, India, China, and South Africa).[13] Data on foreign portfolio investment into China show that investment in the domestic debt market is much lower than in advanced economies with liberalized capital accounts (Table 8.2).

Assessing the effectiveness of China's capital controls is also difficult owing to their complexity and recent changes. The regulatory framework includes many layers and types of controls, combined with qualitative and quantitative limitations. Moreover, controls such as approval requirements or tight monitoring of investments are not fully transparent, and their effect is hard to assess. In recent years, China has simplified its regulations. It reduced the number of regulations by more than 60 percent from 700 in 2009, lowered the number of transactions that require administrative approval by 44 percent, and shifted the focus of new regulations to mitigating risks in the financial sector. The full effect of these changes will become apparent only in the next few years.

Capital flow data show developments in line with progress in capital flow liberalization. The volume of capital inflows to China has grown rapidly since the early 2000s, while it became volatile after the global financial crisis (Figure 8.5). In 2014 the volume of capital inflows was about 4 percent of GDP. Although flows are traditionally tilted toward FDI inflows, in line with the design of capital controls, recently that has been changing with a steady increase in portfolio inflows and generally more volatile debt flows. As a result of the asymmetric liberalization, outflows lagged behind inflows, and picked up only in the mid-2000s

---

[12]The sum of external liabilities and assets (excluding official reserves) in percent of GDP.

[13]External liabilities and assets are measured as a stock that depends on historical flows, and therefore may not be a good reflection of the existing capital controls. Moreover, the level of financial integration not only is determined by the degree of capital controls, but depends on other factors, such as trade openness, GDP per capita, and stock market capitalization (Lane and Milesi-Ferretti 2003).

Figure 8.3. Income Level and De Facto Financial Integration
(GDP per capita in logarithm [x-axis] and de facto financial integration [y-axis], as of 2014 or latest available)

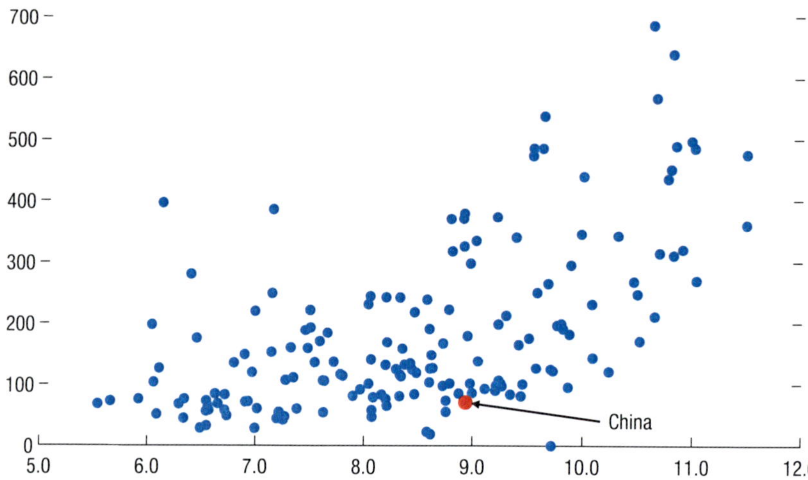

Sources: World Bank, *World Development Indicators*; updated and extended version of the Lane and Milesi-Ferretti (2007) data sets; and IMF staff calculations.
Note: De facto financial integration is measured by the sum of external assets (excluding official foreign exchange reserves) and liabilities in percent of GDP. Countries with a ratio exceeding 700 are not shown in the chart.

(Figure 8.5). FDI and portfolio outflows represent less than 1 percent of GDP, and outward portfolio investments are small while FDI outflows accelerated in 2015. The remaining outflows are large and volatile. Prominent components contributing to their growth in the past five years are trade credit and advances, loans by banks, and the nonbank sector's investments in currency and deposits. In part, these outflows consist of increases in residents' foreign currency deposits after the annual ceiling was eased in 2007. Non-FDI capital flows tend to fluctuate because enterprises adjust their profit repatriation with exchange rate expectations (Bayoumi and Ohnsorge 2013).

More generally, trends in capital flows also depend on factors other than capital flow liberalization, such as macroeconomic conditions and incentives. For example, a change in macroeconomic conditions, such as expectations of economic slowdown, may trigger capital outflows through channels that had been liberalized before, but macroeconomic conditions did not create incentives for outflows through such channels until recently. It is therefore difficult to gauge the effectiveness of capital controls using only the volume of flows.

At the same time, leakage is apparent. On the inflow side, rapid growth of inward remittances and weak current investment income transfers by foreign companies are evidence of circumvention through current account transactions when expectations for exchange rate appreciation are strong (Ma and McCauley

Figure 8.4. China: De Facto Financial Integration, 1990–2014
(Percent of GDP)

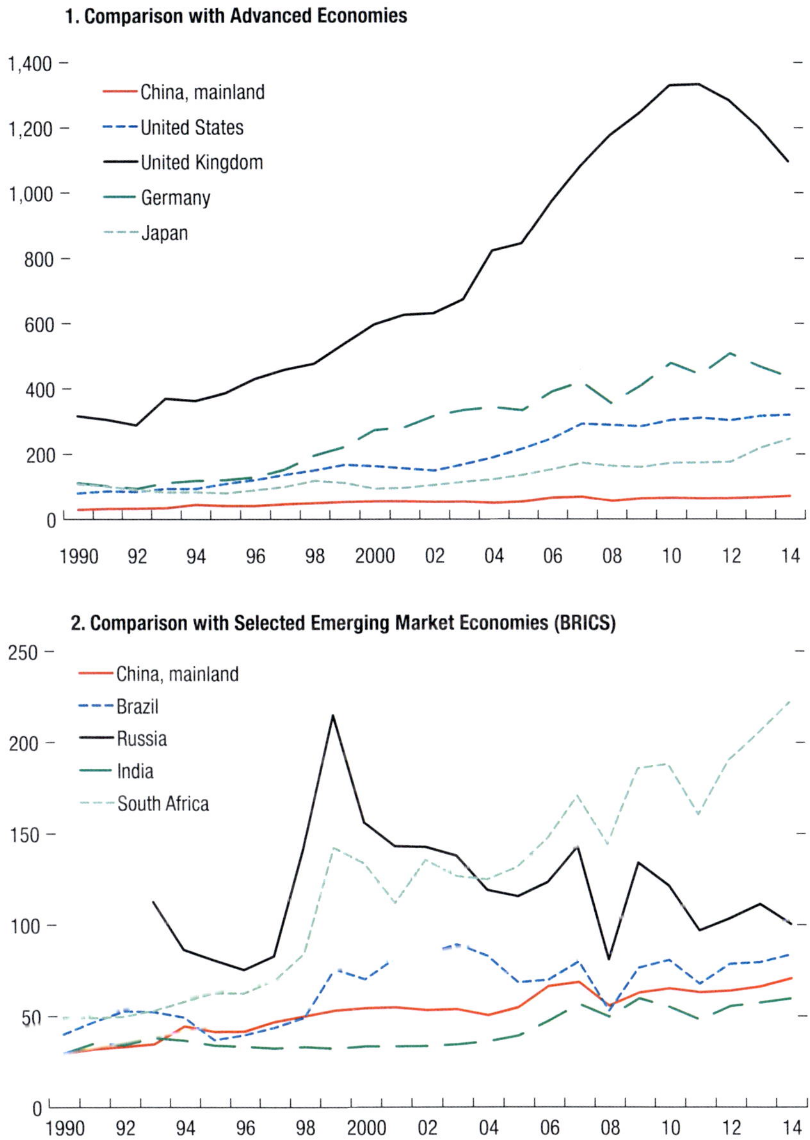

Source: Updated and extended version of the Lane and Milesi-Ferretti (2007) data set.
Note: De facto financial integration is measured by the sum of external assets (excluding official foreign exchange reserves) and liabilities in percent of GDP. BRICS = Brazil, Russia, India, China, and South Africa.

Table 8.2. Portfolio Investments in Selected Economies, December 2015[1]
(Percent of GDP)

	Short-Term Debt	Long-Term Debt	Equity	Total
Australia	6.0	45.3	25.0	74.6
Austria	2.4	80.6	11.6	95.2
Belgium	10.5	69.1	45.3	126.5
Canada	5.5	44.1	29.3	78.9
Chile	0.7	16.2	7.1	24.0
China	1.0	1.5	4.9	7.1
Czech Republic	3.7	14.3	2.5	21.2
Denmark	5.9	58.1	56.5	121.2
Estonia	0.0	4.7	4.0	8.8
Finland	4.1	72.9	41.5	119.6
France	8.2	72.0	40.0	120.6
Germany	5.4	50.8	27.4	83.5
Greece	0.1	17.1	6.3	23.5
Hungary	0.1	30.7	7.0	38.0
Iceland	0.6	38.5	5.7	46.2
Ireland	14.8	158.1	429.7	607.7
Israel	0.2	9.6	27.6	37.2
Italy	2.7	55.0	13.9	71.5
Japan	6.1	9.2	30.5	44.9
Korea, Republic of	1.8	10.4	20.6	31.0
Luxembourg	52.9	1,064.6	3,755.5	4,908.5
Mexico	1.2	18.4	8.0	28.1
Netherlands	10.3	170.7	70.4	251.4
New Zealand	1.6	22.6	10.4	36.2
Norway	3.5	50.4	18.5	73.8
Poland	0.0	20.3	5.6	26.2
Portugal	2.5	47.0	13.2	62.8
Slovak Republic	0.2	29.9	0.6	30.8
Slovenia	0.1	50.3	1.8	49.8
Spain	4.1	55.9	21.9	82.2
Sweden	11.1	65.1	47.7	124.3
Switzerland	1.8	12.6	121.0	135.6
Turkey	0.5	11.8	4.8	17.2
United Kingdom	6.2	47.5	61.7	117.6
United States	3.3	31.9	21.6	56.8
OECD	4.4	40.6	35.4	80.6
OECD excluding Ireland, Luxembourg, and Netherlands	4.2	36.4	27.5	68.1

Sources: Coordinated Portfolio Investment Survey; IMF, International Financial Statistics database; and IMF staff calculations.
Note: OECD = Organisation for Economic Co-operation and Development.
[1] The Coordinated Portfolio Investment Survey (CPIS) provides data on economies' cross-border holdings of portfolio investment securities. This table shows the aggregate investments from 82 economies (that participated in the CPIS) in the countries listed in the rows as of end-2015. The countries shown in the rows belong to the OECD, plus China. Total may not equal the sum because of rounding or data being unavailable or not disclosed to preserve confidentiality.

Figure 8.5. China: Capital Inflows and Outflows, 1990–2015
(Percent of GDP)

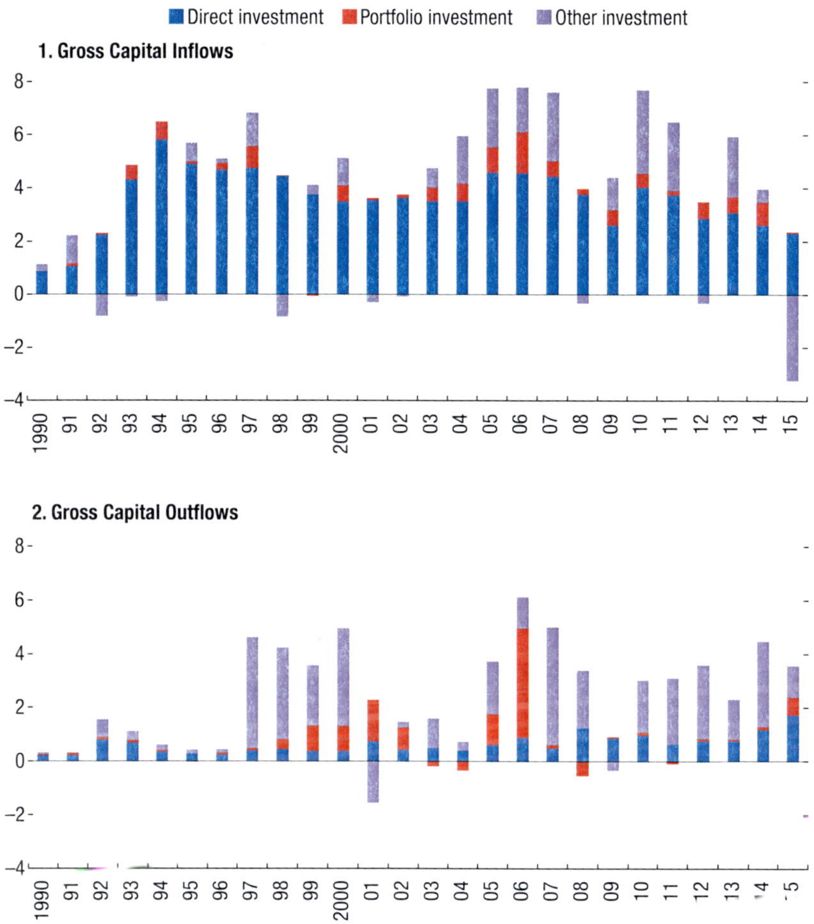

Source: IMF, International Financial Statistics database.
Note: Gross inflows are defined as the sum of inward foreign direct investment, portfolio liabilities, and other investment liabilities in the balance of payment statistics. Gross outflows are defined as the sum of outward foreign direct investment, portfolio assets, and other investment assets.

2008). In addition, swings in net flows of errors and omissions in the balance of payments can be interpreted as unrecorded capital inflows to China (Prasad and Wei 2007). Similarly, leakage leading to outflows takes place through false invoicing of trade payments and delays in repatriations.[14] A study estimated that between 2000 and 2005, average annual trade mis-invoicing flows were $48 billion (2.2 percent of 2005 GDP) on a net basis, and $236 billion (10.6 percent of 2005 GDP) as an absolute sum of under- and overrecording (Beja 2008). And since about 2009, net errors and omissions in China's balance of payments have turned negative, potentially indicating increasing net capital outflows (Figure 8.6).

More recently, from 2015, increased capital outflows have been reported against the backdrop of weakening market confidence in China's growth. Some interpret these episodes as evidence that capital controls are not binding. Data show that, in 2015, gross outflows continued at a steady pace ($389 billion, or 3.6 percent of GDP) while inflows fell, mostly because of declines in external loans and nonresidents' deposits (by $352 billion or 3.2 percent of GDP), which was cushioned by inward FDI (see Figure 8.5). As a result, official foreign exchange reserve holdings dropped by $514 billion, or 4.9 percent of GDP, between December 2014 and December 2015.[15] In part, this drop can also be attributed to Chinese residents converting their domestic currency deposits into foreign currency deposits.[16]

Evidence using price data shows that arbitrage between onshore and offshore renminbi markets has been imperfect, supporting the notion that certain capital controls in China are still effective. Because of the difficulties in measuring variations in the openness of the rather complex capital control system, researchers often measure the effectiveness of market arbitrage in exchange rates or interest rates to gauge how strict capital controls actually are. Studies show that significant spreads between onshore and offshore interest rates and deviations from covered interest parity exist (Ma and McCauley 2008), and that the renminbi-covered interest differential is not shrinking (Cheung and Herrala 2014).

Likewise, for exchange rates, the spread expanded significantly during times of market pressure, indicating market segmentation (Figure 8.7). A recent study confirms the persistent deviations between onshore and offshore renminbi

[14]According to an article by the vice president of the People's Bank of China and the president of SAFE (Yi 2015), regulators found 1,776 Chinese companies that exported goods but reported no export revenue in 2014, amounting to 6 percent of total exports.

[15]In an attempt to curtail outflows, in September 2015 China announced that from October 15, 2015, banks would have to hold an unremunerated reserve requirement of 20 percent on all their forward sales of foreign exchange and similar derivative transactions. The reserve requirement would have to be met in U.S. dollars and be frozen for a year.

[16]In a press conference on October 22, 2015, the deputy administrator of SAFE indicated that Chinese residents bought foreign exchange to increase foreign exchange deposits or repay domestic foreign exchange loans.

Figure 8.6. China: Net Errors and Omissions, 1997–2015

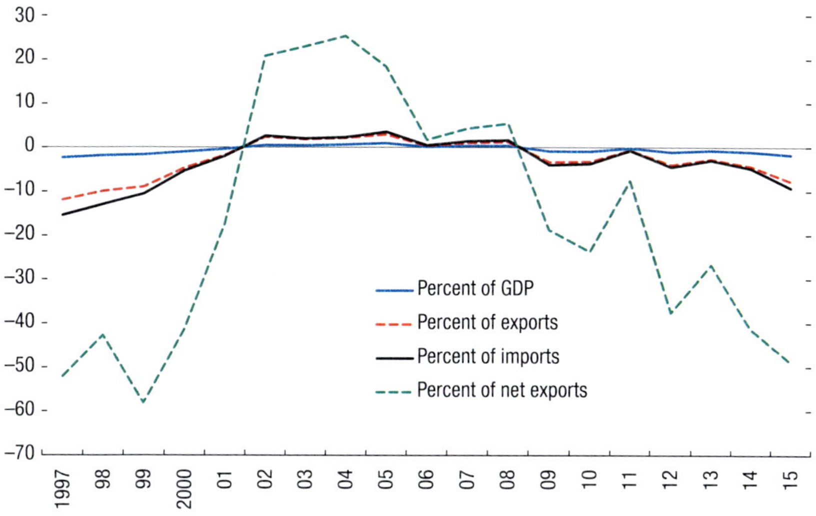

Source: IMF, World Economic Outlook database.

exchange rates. It also shows that the volatility of the deviations is reduced by policy measures liberalizing cross-border renminbi outflows, while less of an effect was found from measures allowing renminbi funds to flow back onshore (Funke and others 2015). Although there is evidence that links between onshore and offshore yuan forward rates have strengthened recently (Maziad and Kang 2012), the lack of full integration is still attributed to capital controls (Craig and others 2013). Nonetheless, because capital flow liberalization is ongoing, the effectiveness of controls and their effect on the spread may change over time.

Overall, studies have shown that remaining controls on capital transactions in China continue to have an effect, but not uniformly across different types of transactions, and that there is evidence of circumvention. Recent spillovers from turbulence in the Chinese stock market and pressure on the yuan following the change in exchange rate policy in August 2015 indicate that financial integration may be deeper than previously thought. Further analysis is needed, however.

THE CASE FOR AND AGAINST FURTHER LIBERALIZATION

In recent years, there has been a heated debate in China about the pros and cons of further opening up the capital account, the relationship between capital

Figure 8.7. China Onshore and Offshore Exchange Rates, 2010–16

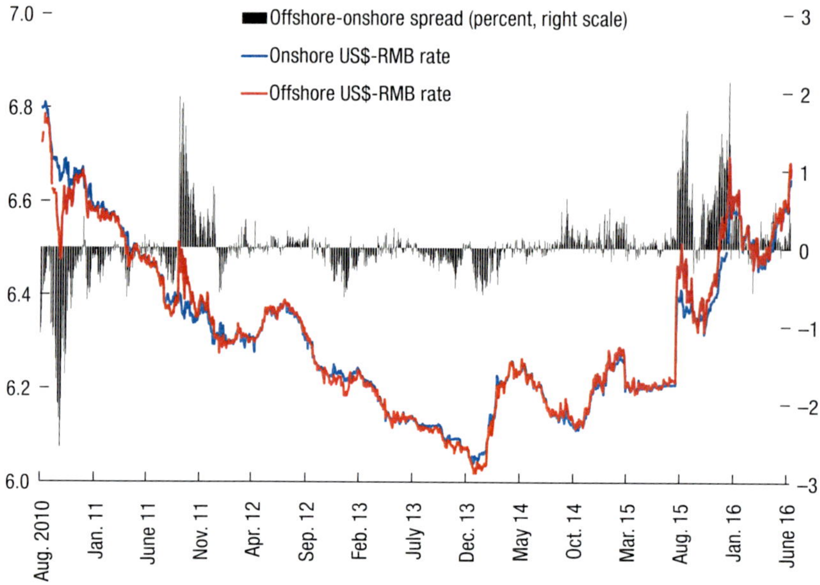

Source: Bloomberg L.P.
Note: Daily midday spot exchange rates for yuan per dollar for August 2010 through June 2016. The spread is calculated in percent of the onshore exchange rate.

flow liberalization and capital flow management, and the sequencing of financial sector reforms with capital flow liberalization.[17]

Proponents of liberalization argue that existing capital controls are becoming less binding, and that large and volatile short-term inflows are increasingly destabilizing the domestic financial system and rendering monetary policy ineffective. They see an urgent need for the private sector to diversify the country, credit, currency, and market risks of their portfolios as China moves toward upper-middle-income status. They argue that China's international balance sheets are extremely lopsided at present, with assets being mostly low-yielding foreign reserves and liabilities mostly high-yielding foreign direct investments. Such a lopsided international balance sheet has important macroeconomic and financial stability implications—self-fulfilling expectations of currency appreciation and bubble-prone domestic financial markets.

Opponents, on the other hand, see no compelling evidence that capital flow liberalization contributes to economic growth or welfare, and point instead to signs that openness to increasingly volatile capital flows is detrimental to domestic

[17]These arguments are summarized in a collection of essays titled "Capital Account Liberalization: Strategy, Timing and Roadmap" (Chen and Qian 2014).

monetary and financial stability. They further argue that liberalization is self-destructive because capital controls are the last line of defense against financial crises. Specifically, China weathered the Asian financial crisis well because it had a largely closed capital account. They also emphasize that capital flow liberalization should happen only after domestic financial reforms (including interest rate liberalization) have been completed and exchange rate flexibility has been achieved. In addition, some recent literature argues that monetary policy is constrained when capital flows have been liberalized (Rey 2016).

While the arguments in opposition have some merit, it is difficult to imagine that one of the world's largest economies and trading nations will maintain tight controls on capital flows indefinitely as it becomes an upper-middle-income economy. Most, if not all, upper-middle- to high-income economies have ultimately liberalized capital flows. At the same time, persuasive arguments have been made against hasty or premature liberalization, and an emerging consensus in the literature sees an open capital account as beneficial when certain conditions have been met. Eichengreen, Gullapalli, and Panizza (2011) show that benefits are limited to countries with relatively well-developed financial systems, good accounting standards, and strong creditor rights and rule of law. Similarly, IMF (2012b) finds that capital flow liberalization is positively correlated with economic growth, and the result is more pronounced for countries with an income level above a certain threshold. Klein and Olivei (2008) also find that capital flows can benefit growth and increase financial depth for countries with adequate institutions and sound macroeconomic policies.

Perhaps reflecting the lack of consensus on the desirability and pace of further liberalization, the government has not published any comprehensive road map or timetable, while reiterating that capital account convertibility remains the objective. Nevertheless, the authorities have continued to implement incremental liberalization of specific transactions (Box 8.2) and announced plans for further liberalization. These more recent plans include the liberalization of individual investments of residents and nonresidents and further two-way opening of capital markets. Some liberalization of inflows in derivatives transactions is also envisaged, together with establishment of a unified bank account system for both local and foreign currencies. A sweeping revision of the regulatory framework for foreign exchange and cross-border transactions is also foreseen. The revision aims at establishing a unified framework for international payments and transfers in renminbi and foreign currencies, simplifying the approval requirements, and establishing and reinforcing balance of payments reporting and statistical surveillance of cross-border capital flows. The new framework would include a negative list (transactions related to money laundering and the financing of terrorism, tax evasion, national security, and international obligations), a strengthening of the macroprudential management of capital flows, and provision for a crisis response mechanism (Liu 2015).

Based on the track record, the authorities seem likely to push forward with capital flow liberalization, although the pace will be fine-tuned according to the prevailing domestic and international macroeconomic and financial conditions and the experiences with specific liberalization measures. The "going global" strategy, confirmed at the Third Plenary Session in November 2013, will probably lead to more liberalization of outward FDI and transactions related to the operation of Chinese companies abroad.[18] More recently, China's 13th Five-Year Plan reiterates its commitment to an orderly transition toward capital account convertibility, including steady internationalization of the renminbi (see also Chapter 9 on RMB internationalization), improving the prudential regulatory framework, and further two-way opening of capital markets.[19]

The authorities' plans appear to be largely in line with the integrated approach to capital flow liberalization (IMF 2012a). The integrated approach is made up of successive and often overlapping phases, accompanied or preceded by supporting legal, accounting, financial, and corporate reforms, and a strengthening of financial regulation and supervision. In general, FDI inflows would be liberalized first, followed by FDI outflows and long-term portfolio flows. Finally, controls on short-term portfolio flows would be removed. Within this general framework, the integrated approach stresses that the path taken and the extent of liberalization need to be based on a country's circumstances.

THE WAY FORWARD: POSSIBLE OPTIONS

Given the size of the Chinese economy and the potential global effect of liberalization, it is generally agreed that the removal of controls should be gradual and sequenced with supporting policies. Missteps can have significant consequences for China and the global financial system. Therefore, the process should be carefully designed to avoid backtracking that could undermine both the credibility of the authorities' policies and confidence in the liberalization strategy.

The Role of Supporting Policies

A domestically oriented and independent monetary policy is a desirable goal for a large economy like that of China. In this case, capital flow liberalization needs to be supported by greater exchange rate flexibility. Indeed, the removal of capital controls will reduce the authorities' ability to control the exchange rate and monetary policy simultaneously. New arrangements for monetary and exchange rate policies will be needed. The authorities recognized this and have moved toward greater exchange rate flexibility. In August 2015 China adopted a more market-based approach to the exchange rate by setting the central parity of the yuan to the U.S. dollar with stronger reference to the closing spot rate of the previous day. However, depreciation pressures and capital outflows intensified

[18]"Decision of the Central Committee of the Communist Party of China on Some Major Issues Concerning Comprehensively Deepening the Reform," November 12, 2013. The going global strategy was included in both the 10th and the 11th Five-Year Plans, with emphasis on SOE investments abroad in strategic sectors, such as energy (oil and gas) and minerals.

[19]See http://ghs.ndrc.gov.cn/ghwb/gjwngh/201605/P020160516532440059919.pdf.

during the ensuing months and, in late 2015, China indicated that it would aim to keep the renminbi stable through reference against a basket of currencies.

Moving to greater exchange rate flexibility would require development of a credible monetary framework. A new policy target is needed to replace the exchange rate anchor, and the instruments used to achieve this target would need to be clearly defined before abandoning the current de facto soft peg.[20] The new monetary and exchange rate policy framework would help market participants understand the overall direction of policy and also underpin their expectations about the exchange rate. The authorities have already started the transition from the use of direct levers by removing the ceiling on de jure interest rates and enhancing short-term management of the rate. However, further decisions are needed to prevent reliance on directed lending and other nonmarket tools to firmly establish a market-based monetary framework that uses interest rates effectively. Increased operational independence of the People's Bank of China (PBC) in the conduct of monetary policy would be another important component of the new framework, with the government continuing to set the key medium-term monetary policy goals (see Chapter 7 on the monetary policy framework).

Although a flexible exchange rate can act as a shock absorber to volatile capital flows, excessive exchange rate movements may produce adverse economic effects. The onshore foreign exchange market is relatively deep and liquid, and capital flow liberalization may stimulate further deepening and enhance the ability of the market to safely cope with capital flow volatility. However, there is a risk that increased capital flows after controls are removed may prove too large for the market to absorb and could lead to high exchange rate volatility or misalignments. If liberalization is followed by depreciation pressures and the exchange rate is allowed to adjust, currency risk on the balance sheets of firms and banks may materialize. Firms may be unable to honor debt denominated in foreign exchange, nonperforming loans may increase, and banks' capital may shrink. Depreciation may also trigger a shift in corporate borrowing as firms may be inclined to refinance their external loans with domestic renminbi loans, resulting in additional outflows and further depreciation. In 2015 corporates have repaid part of their external debt in light of depreciation and increased volatility in the exchange rate. International reserves are still ample, but they are not unlimited, and this imposes a constraint on the authorities' ability to intervene in the longer term. Accordingly, the removal of capital controls needs to be tailored to the economy's ability to deal with the potential effects on the exchange rate.

Capital flow liberalization may also pose risks to the financial sector, especially for countries with insufficiently developed institutional capacity. Cross-country experience suggests that in most cases where financial crises coincided with or followed capital flow liberalization, financial sector policies were inadequate (Ishii

[20]The IMF has classified China's de facto exchange rate regime as a crawl-like arrangement since June 21, 2010, and as "other managed" since December 24, 2014.

and others 2002). Hence, the sophistication and effectiveness of the domestic financial prudential framework and financial sector policies need to match the pace of capital flow liberalization.

Capital and liquidity buffers and other macroprudential measures to increase the resilience of the financial system are particularly important—and should be in place before controls on cross-border capital transactions are liberalized. Once capital controls have been removed, macroprudential tools can help deal with the risks associated with surges in inflows and their reversals. Some of these macroprudential tools may at the same time be capital flow management measures (IMF 2012a, 2013).

To ensure that macroprudential policy is effective, China needs to build a strong institutional framework. The current institutional framework for financial stability in China has multiple layers, involving the State Council at the top, the PBC and financial regulatory commissions in the middle, and communication between the regulators and the regulated institutions below (IMF 2011b; Wang and Sun 2013). In addition, the sector-based regulatory and supervisory framework in China requires strong coordination to limit supervisory "blind spots" (IMF 2011b). One important and desirable feature of any institutional framework is its ability to overcome the bias in favor of inaction that reflects, among other things, difficulties in quantifying the benefits of macroprudential action (IMF 2013). Put differently, the framework needs to foster the *ability* to act so that a macroprudential policymaker has access to information; include instruments with appropriate range and reach; define a clear objective; and provide strong accountability, including through clear communication. It is also important that the macroprudential mandate be clearly assigned, say to a specific institution or a committee, preferably with the central bank playing an important role.

In addition to macroprudential policy, contingency plans are needed in the event that liberalization triggers large and destabilizing capital flows. In many countries, the central bank has authority to introduce temporary emergency measures when there are threats to macrofinancial stability. In China, the establishment of the Financial Crisis Response Group and the Joint Ministerial Committee to assess and act on systemic risks is a significant move toward developing a coherent macroprudential and crisis management framework. To further strengthen the framework, the PBC could be authorized to introduce temporary measures to address the destabilizing effects of inflows or outflows.

How Should Controls Be Removed?

China is in the second phase of liberalization, according to the IMF's integrated approach (IMF 2012a). FDI has been largely liberalized and some long- and short-term portfolio investments partially liberalized. The next steps in the approach would involve gradual further easing of controls on these investments, moving to transactions that typically imply greater volatility in capital flows (see Table 8.3). The supporting policies related to this phase include modernizing the frameworks for monetary and exchange rate policies; strengthening systemic liquidity arrangements and related monetary and exchange operations; enhancing prudential regulation, supervision, and risk management; restructuring the financial and corporate sectors; and developing capital markets and long-term investors, including pension funds. These supporting policies need to be adequately sequenced with liberalization of controls to prevent macroeconomic and systemic risks. Key reforms also include addressing high corporate sector debt, reforming SOEs, and establishing hard budget constraints (IMF 2012a, 2015a).

Generally, any given control should be eased only when the conditions for its removal have been met. This approach helps reduce the risk of destabilizing flows and also reduces the potential need to reverse earlier liberalization steps: reversals tend to hurt investor confidence and should be avoided if at all possible. Policies should generally seek to enhance macro-financial resilience to capital flow volatility. However, in some cases the temporary reimposition of controls may be necessary if a premature liberalization step leads to instability (see IMF 2012a).

China's current quota system appears to provide a suitable framework for gradual and well-sequenced liberalization. Quotas can be increased incrementally to give the authorities some control over total inflows and outflows until they are eventually removed. On the inflow side, as part of the recent liberalization steps, the PBC abolished the quota for qualified foreign financial institutions to enter the domestic bond markets in February 2016. Looking forward, similar steps could be implemented for equity investments, and the range of institutions eligible for investments could be gradually expanded by lowering the qualification thresholds (by allowing retail investors), while maintaining an overall quota. It is unlikely that such easing would expose China to significantly more risk. In fact, large institutional investors (qualified investors under the current regime) may be able to move significantly larger amounts than retail investors, and they are often bound by prudential or industry-specific regulations that require them to limit certain country positions. By contrast, retail investors do not face such limits on their positions. Managing quotas for a large number of small investors can, however, give rise to a higher administrative burden.

Since the quotas are currently biased toward inflows, it would be advisable to increase quotas on outflows to achieve greater balance. That said, any significant easing of outflow controls would need to account for the effect of the ensuing outflows on the exchange rate and the financial system. Removing the ceiling on interest rates on deposits was an important step toward establishing the conditions for easing outflow controls. However, outflows may initially be large even if domestic interest rates are higher than foreign rates, owing to pent-up portfolio rebalancing pressures. Over the longer term, once the stock adjustments are completed, investment decisions will be mostly motivated by risk-return considerations (Box 8.3). The outflows may result in depreciation pressures, which the authorities may want to smooth with intervention, provided that reserves are adequate.[21] The global implications of portfolio rebalancing by Chinese residents following liberalization may also be significant.

---

[21]Garber (2013) suggests that the proper response would be for the authorities to accommodate the outflows and accept the loss imposed by the preliberalized regime.

Table 8.3. Potential Sequence of Capital Flow Liberalization with Supporting Policies

Capital Flow Liberalization	Supporting Policies	Financial Sector Policies
(1) Gradual increase of quotas and relaxing qualification requirements on inflow and outflow of foreign direct investment and portfolio investment Gradual increase of yearly limit on individuals' investments abroad Selective liberalization of cross-border derivative transactions Relaxing controls on external loans	Modernizing the monetary and exchange rate policy framework: • Establishing new monetary target, increasing flexibility of exchange rate • Strengthening systemic liquidity arrangements and related monetary and exchange operations Establishing hard budget constraints Reforming state-owned enterprises Addressing the high debt of the corporate sector Revision of the legal, accounting, financial, and corporate frameworks to the extent necessary	Deepening domestic financial markets by introducing new financial instruments Strengthening financial regulation and supervision in advance of liberalization to improve the financial sector's ability to withstand the effect of volatile capital flows Building up capital and liquidity buffers before controls are liberalized Introduction of macroprudential tools on credit, liquidity, and exchange rate risk (for example, sectoral capital requirements on specific loans, constraints on lending, liquidity tools—separate or tighter liquidity requirements on foreign currency liabilities) Implementing adequate investment regulations on pension funds' and other institutional investors' investments abroad Designing a contingency plan to address potential threats to macro-financial stability
(2) Replacing quotas and qualification requirements with price-based controls such as unremunerated reserve requirement (URR) or tax. Adjusting the calibration of the URR/tax to changing conditions. Removal of mandatory holding period on nonresidents' portfolio equity and fixed-income investments Relaxing controls on resident and nonresident individuals' investments Further relaxing controls on external loans	Further strengthening of the monetary and exchange rate policy framework Continued reform of state-owned enterprises and the corporate sector Enhancing the monitoring of capital flows	Continued deepening of the financial markets Introducing net stable funding ratio and/or liquidity charges on noncore funding Implementing higher risk weights on foreign exchange loans Eliminating directed lending Expanding the regulatory perimeter to shadow banking and the corporate sector

(continued)

Table 8.3. Potential Sequence of Capital Flow Liberalization with Supporting Policies *(continued)*

Capital Flow Liberalization	Supporting Policies	Financial Sector Policies
(3) Gradual move from preapproval to registration and notification requirement followed by reporting requirement. As a first step, the ex ante approval requirements could be replaced by a registration requirement under which the transaction is deemed to have been registered (and thus allowed) if the authorities do not object to it in a certain and relatively short time (for example, three or four days) Replacing residency-based controls with currency-based controls, if possible	Continued improvement of the monetary and exchange rate policy framework Adequate capital flow monitoring framework in place	Continued deepening of the financial markets Further strengthening of the supervisory and financial sector regulatory framework
(4) Removal of most of the controls	Track record of well-defined credible monetary policy and full exchange rate flexibility	Adequate supervisory and micro- and macroprudential framework in place

Source: IMF, *Annual Report on Exchange Arrangements and Exchange Restrictions*; and IMF staff.

In addition to the easing and rebalancing of quotas, the administration of controls could gradually be shifted away from ex ante approval to ex post monitoring. As a first step, ex ante approval requirements could be replaced by a registration requirement under which the transaction is deemed to have been registered and allowed if the authorities do not object to it in a relatively short time (for example, three or four days). This change would significantly ease the administrative burden on investors and the authorities and increase the predictability and transparency of the control system. Several countries that liberalized their foreign exchange regimes in the past 20 years (Korea, for example) took a similar route by gradually replacing preapproval with registration, followed by simple reporting requirements. Such reports allow for close monitoring of capital flows, and are generally prepared by financial intermediaries participating in the cross-border transactions for their clients.

In the process of gradual relaxation of controls, the current administrative and quantity-based controls could be replaced with price-based controls. Since high volatility in capital flows could result from the removal of administrative and quantitative controls, the switch to price-based controls would be an appropriate intermediate step. For example, a mandatory holding period for specific portfolio and FDI investments is a useful tool for reducing capital flow volatility. However, both could be changed over time to a price-based instrument such as an unremunerated reserve requirement (URR) or a tax. Given that FDI is more stable than other capital flows, its mandatory holding period could be removed first, followed by portfolio equity and fixed-income investments.

Box 8.3. Domestic and International Impact of China's Capital Flow Liberalization

The impact on global financial markets of liberalizing capital flows will likely depend on the speed with which it is undertaken. The IMF (2011a) examined the spillover and external effects of policies in China from various aspects, including savings, its financial flows to emerging markets, and the potential impact on global bond markets from the reallocation of reserves. It noted that gradual liberalization would likely lead to offsetting effects on inflows and outflows. The size of these flows will depend on the sequencing and timing of reforms. One scenario estimates that even a relatively large outflow from China would not offset the reallocation of global assets from non-S5 countries to China.[1] As a result, net flows into China could lead to declining asset valuations in the rest of the world. The IMF study also found that if China rebalances its reserve assets away from U.S. assets into emerging markets, say by US$100 billion, U.S. yields could increase by as much as 12 basis points and emerging market yields drop by as much as 48 basis points.

Experience from other countries shows that capital flow liberalization has led to large capital flows in both directions. However, the net direction of capital flows after liberalization depends on many factors and is difficult to predict. Bayoumi and Ohnsorge (2013) find that gross flows both into and out of China would be substantial, and the likely direction of net flows would be outward, with significant repercussions for global financial markets, resulting in Chinese investors accumulating net international assets of about 11–18 percent of GDP. Saadi Sedik and Sun (2012) estimate a 2–3¼ percentage point increase in inflows and outflows, with outflows dominating in 2012–16. He and others (2012) show that China's gross international investment position would grow significantly, and inflows and outflows would be more balanced, following a stock adjustment, particularly in outward portfolio investments. A similar exercise by Hooley (2013) concludes that full liberalization would lead the capital account balance to turn negative, with net capital outflows. Smaller reserves accumulation would be associated with this swing. He and Luk (2013) construct a two-country general equilibrium model to predict the portfolio choice of Chinese residents after capital flow liberalization, with outcomes broadly in line with those in the empirical literature.

It is unlikely that China's liberalization would have any parallels to past experience, given the size of potential capital flows following liberalization. According to Hooley (2013), China's international investment position could increase from about 5 percent to 30 percent of world GDP by 2025. In contrast, the change in the international investment position following liberalization has been quite modest in previous episodes (see Table 8.3.1). Considering the advancements in financial instruments and technology and the increased interconnectedness of global markets today, the potential for volatile capital flows from liberalization in China affecting global markets cannot be ruled out. The IMF 2011a study also showed the potential for China's capital flow liberalization to affect global asset prices. Given the potential magnitude of flows, even a gradual liberalization may have significant effects on global markets.

Overall, studies indicate that outflows may dominate in the short term as a result of liberalization. However, caution is advised in interpreting these results as they are sensitive to assumptions, including those about the speed of liberalization.

---

[1]The S5 (Systemic 5) includes China, the euro area, Japan, the United Kingdom, and the United States.

Box 8.3. Domestic and International Impact of China's Capital Flow Liberalization *(continued)*

Table 8.3.1. Average of External Assets (excluding reserves) and Liabilities

(Percent of global GDP)

	Year of Liberalization[1]	Five Years after Liberalization
Chile (1998)	0.1	0.2
Finland (1989)	0.2	0.3
France (1990)	3.1	4.5
Germany (1981)	1.9	3.0
Italy (1992)	1.8	2.6
Norway (1988)	0.2	0.2
Spain (1992)	0.8	1.0
Sweden (1989)	0.6	0.7

Sources: IMF, International Financial Statistics and World Economic Outlook databases.

[1] As shown in parentheses next to the country; based on Kaminsky and Schmukler 2003.

Price-based controls may have advantages over administrative or quantity-based controls, notably in more-transparent and less-arbitrary implementation. The literature suggests that such controls can tilt capital flows toward the longer term even if they do not appreciably reduce their overall volume.[22] Price-based controls are also more flexible than administrative controls because the "tax rate" can be adjusted relatively easily to changes in interest rate differentials or global liquidity conditions. However, it is often difficult to calibrate price-based measures appropriately, as shown by the frequent adjustments of such measures (in Brazil and Chile, for example).

The most frequently used price-based measures are URRs (in Chile and Thailand) and taxes (Brazil). While implementation is different, the two measures are economically similar given that each URR has a tax equivalent (a function of the URR as a proportion of the investment and the opportunity cost of those funds). However, they also differ in that the URR—in contrast to the tax—has an effect on domestic liquidity if deposited in local currency, and may give rise to appreciation pressures; conversely, it may reduce appreciation pressures if deposited in foreign exchange.[23] Legal issues can be a factor in the choice: in many countries the central bank cannot impose taxes, and the measure out of necessity has to be a URR.

[22]For Brazil, see Ariyoshi and others 2000, Baba and Kokenyne 2011, and Cardoso and Goldfajn 1998. For Chile, see De Gregorio, Edwards, and Valdes 2000. For Colombia, see Cardenas and Barrera 1997 and Clements and Kamil 2009. For Malaysia, see Goh 2005. For Thailand, see Jittrapanum and Prasartset 2009.

[23]The tax is usually paid in local currency and thus further increases appreciation pressures when the foreign exchange is converted to local currency.

Currency-based controls are often preferable to residency-based controls. They can be equally effective and less distortionary,[24] and IMF advice has favored them (IMF 2012a).[25] In recent years, emerging market economies, including OECD countries, have increasingly used currency-based measures, especially to manage capital inflows (De Crescenzio, Golin, and Ott 2015). Cross-country studies show that currency-based controls are effective at reducing domestic financial risks and helped countries improve their economic resilience during the 2007 global financial crisis (Ostry and others 2012). Currency-based controls could therefore gradually replace residency-based controls as part of China's liberalization process.

Addressing Risks from Capital Flow Liberalization

Following capital flow liberalization, macroeconomic and financial sector risks often increase. Inflow surges may heighten macroeconomic volatility through rapid currency appreciation, leading to a loss of competitiveness, distortions in money markets, disruptions in monetary policy transmission, asset price bubbles, credit booms, and loose fiscal discipline (IMF 2011a, 2012a). Surges can be followed by sudden stops or reversals. When reversals of inflows (or outflows) are large or sustained, they pose macroeconomic policy challenges—even absent a crisis—through their effects on exchange rates, interest rates, credit, and output.

Risk of Inflow Surges

Inflow surges typically require adjustments in the policy mix.[26] Appropriate macroeconomic policy responses include rebalancing the monetary and fiscal policy mix consistent with inflation and growth objectives, allowing the currency to strengthen if it is not overvalued, and building foreign reserves if they are not more than adequate. Capital flow management measures are also warranted in certain circumstances (IMF 2012a). During liberalization, structural reforms can increase the capacity to absorb inflows and channel them toward productive investments, although such reforms typically have a long lead time.

Inflow surges may also result in systemic financial instability (IMF 2015b):

- Capital inflows can contribute to *a credit boom and increases in local asset prices*, which can erode lending standards and raise credit risks. Tian and Gallagher (2015) show a link in China between short-term capital flows and rising house prices. Channels include the effect of capital inflows on the domestic banking system, and foreign investors pushing up local asset pric-

[24]Not all currency-based measures are capital controls or capital flow management measures in the most recent terminology of the IMF. They are often prudential measures, such as a net open foreign exchange position limit.

[25]The preference for nondiscriminatory measures mainly reflects a regard for the general standard of fairness and equal treatment that IMF members expect their nationals will enjoy as a result of members' participation in a multilateral framework like the IMF (IMF 2012c).

[26]See IMF 2011c for country experiences with capital inflows.

es, forcing domestic investors to borrow larger amounts to keep up with increasing prices for local real estate.

- Easier access to foreign capital can lead to *increases in short-term wholesale funding of the financial system.* During credit booms, banks often face difficulties finding domestic retail funding and turn to lower-cost foreign funds. This tendency was observed ahead of many financial crises, including the Asian crisis in 1997 (Ishii and others 2002; Lane and others 1999) and the global financial crisis of 2007. As banks increasingly resort to short-term wholesale funding, the system becomes exposed to funding and liquidity shocks. Currently, in China, this type of risk is mitigated by ceilings on banks' borrowing and ample retail deposits, supported by controls on outflows by individuals. However, even though China's regulations reduce risk, they also produce other costs and distortions.
- Cross-border funding often carries *foreign exchange risk, which can create procyclical feedback between exchange rates and domestic credit.* In emerging market economies that have liberalized these flows, wholesale funding is often denominated in foreign currency. When capital flows reverse, rollover and currency mismatch risks may materialize because of incomplete hedging. Capital inflows can also lead to local currency appreciation and strengthen the banking sector's local currency balance sheet, which in turn allows more risk taking by banks and creates procyclical feedback between domestic credit and exchange rates.
- Foreign-currency-denominated loans may involve *high currency mismatch and credit risks.* The corporate or household sector may borrow without sufficient hedging when their borrowing is motivated by large interest rate differentials from global rates, or when the local currency is expected to appreciate. In addition, incentives and skills to manage currency risks may not be present when exchange rate flexibility has been limited or is nonexistent. When capital flows reverse and a currency depreciates, unhedged borrowers may be unable to service their foreign exchange loans, impairing banks' capacity to lend and aggravating the effects of the initial shocks.

A number of these systemic risks can be addressed by well-designed macroprudential measures, some of which may also be considered capital flow management measures (IMF 2013, 2014).[27] For example, risks from excessive credit growth and asset price appreciation could be mitigated by macroprudential tools targeted at specific credit categories, including sectoral capital requirements on specific loans or constraints on lending.[28] Macroprudential liquidity tools, notably minimum

[27]In this case, the use of such measures needs to be appropriate under both frameworks (macroprudential and capital flow management [IMF 2012a]).

[28]In fact, China implemented several macroprudential tools in 2010–12 to contain excessive growth in credit and house prices (Wang and Sun 2013). The measures include lowering the loan-to-value ratio, prohibition of mortgages for third homes, and adjustments in provisioning requirements and the reserve requirement ratio.

standards for the liquidity coverage ratio and the net stable funding ratio in the Basel III framework, can promote both longer-term and more-stable funding. Liquidity charges on noncore funding can be useful for promoting more-stable funding and to reduce the risk of capital flow reversals.[29] Increases in foreign currency funding can be contained by macroprudential policy measures, such as separate or tighter liquidity requirements in foreign currency, constraints on open foreign exchange positions, or measures targeting foreign-currency-denominated funding. Risks stemming from foreign currency loans can be addressed by targeted tools on foreign exchange exposures, including higher risk weights.

Such policies and measures will be particularly important, as the Chinese authorities have abolished the quota restrictions for qualified foreign institutional investors to participate in domestic bond markets and have initiated measures to promote their investments in the stock markets. These may raise asset prices and lead to appreciation pressures. In addition, regulatory arbitrage can motivate credit provision to move to the nonbank sector or to foreign banks. Hence, there is a need to ensure that the regulatory perimeter of macroprudential policy extends to important providers of credit and liquidity other than banks.

Risk of Outflow Surges

Capital outflows are among the natural consequences of capital account openness. In many cases, outflows are moderate and benign and do not require significant policy action. However, given China's unbalanced international investment position, outflows are expected to be significant for some time as residents diversify their portfolios.

Outflows, absent a crisis, should be primarily managed with sound macroeconomic policies, strong financial supervisory frameworks, and structural reforms to deepen financial markets, taking into account country-specific circumstances (IMF 2012c, 2015c). For instance, macroeconomic policy responses could include allowing the exchange rate to absorb the external shock by letting it depreciate. However, if the exchange rate adjustment would be excessively damaging to balance sheets, and if reserve levels allow, foreign exchange intervention may be helpful. The still-sizable official reserves in China would permit such interventions if necessary, while still maintaining adequate reserve coverage. If necessary, monetary or fiscal policy could also be tightened (for instance, if outflows were fueled by macroeconomic imbalances).

Other policies and measures can also help countries prepare for large outflows and weather their impact. Stronger financial regulation (such as liquidity requirements) and supervision can be implemented in advance of liberalization to strengthen the financial sector's ability to withstand the effect of large capital outflows, for example, if depositors withdraw their deposits to invest abroad.

---

[29]For example, Korea introduced a levy on banks' noncore foreign currency liabilities (macroprudential stability levy) in 2011 to mitigate systemic risks from short-term foreign borrowing (IMF 2013, 2014).

Expanding the regulatory perimeter to the shadow banking and corporate sectors could further reduce the negative effect of capital outflows. Deepening the domestic financial markets by introducing new financial instruments could reduce the incentive for residents to invest their deposits abroad. Adequate regulations on overseas investments by pension funds and other institutions would also reduce outflows.[30]

When outflows threaten to lead to a crisis, capital controls may also be needed. However, experience shows such measures are unlikely to have the expected results unless they are part of a broader policy package that addresses the fundamental causes of capital outflows.[31] Capital controls can help provide breathing space until more fundamental policies take effect, but they should not substitute for warranted macroeconomic adjustments. Implementation of outflow measures should also avoid the accumulation of external payment arrears or default, and the least discriminatory measures that are effective should be preferred.

CONCLUSIONS

Even as China has made significant progress in liberalizing its capital account, capital transactions remain largely controlled. The country's preeminent role in global trade indicates room for more significant integration into the global financial system. In light of the potentially large global effects, it is important that liberalization be well managed and not give rise to undue volatility in capital flows.

While the authorities have specific plans to liberalize capital flows as set out in the 13th Five-Year Plan, coordinated actions are needed to ensure the safe removal of controls without increasing the risk of reversal.

In particular, liberalization needs to be coordinated with supporting macroeconomic, financial, and structural policies to create a virtuous circle for continuing safe liberalization. A new monetary policy framework and a more flexible exchange rate regime will be essential to dampen the effect of larger and more volatile capital flows on the economy, and to anchor market expectations. Existing structural rigidities may prevent the financial sector from making smooth adjustments to a liberalized environment and may lead to excessive risk taking. Upgrading the regulatory and supervisory framework, including enhanced macroprudential policies, will be essential to mitigating the risks that capital flow liberalization can pose to the financial sector.

China's liberalization has broadly followed the advised sequence for removing controls laid out in the IMF's "integrated approach." However, the gradual removal of capital controls in China has displayed several unique features not often seen in other countries: (1) the combination of quotas and specific investor groups (qualified institutional investors), (2) the removal of specific controls in

---

[30]For example, if future pension payments are in yuan, the investment of the pension funds' assets should not be overwhelmingly in U.S. dollars, or at least should be properly hedged.

[31]See IMF 2012b for country experiences with capital flows during a crisis.

parts of the country (that is, location-specific policy experiments) to test liberalization before more general implementation, and (3) efforts to expand the international use of a heavily controlled currency. This unique approach to liberalization allows the authorities to liberalize gradually and adjust the pace flexibly to match prevailing conditions, but also poses challenges owing to the existence of a large offshore deliverable renminbi market and the several channels through which the offshore renminbi market is connected to the onshore market.

Liberalization needs to ensure a balanced approach to inflows and outflows. Existing controls appear largely effective, although there is evidence of leakages, which are likely to increase as liberalization advances. Orderly liberalization will thus require an effort to maintain the effectiveness of controls until they are removed. To this end, capital flows need to be closely monitored during the liberalization process, and policies adjusted as needed. There would also be advantages to changing the methods used to manage the capital account: replacing administrative and quantitative controls with price-based controls, gradually shifting to registration and ex post monitoring of transactions instead of preapproval, and using currency-based measures instead of residency-based controls.

The effects of China's capital flow liberalization on the global economy and financial system are uncertain. That said, there appears to be broad agreement in the literature that in the short term, outflows will dominate as a result of residents' pent-up demand for portfolio rebalancing. Over the longer term, capital flows are likely to become more balanced, although gross capital flows will increase significantly.

REFERENCES

Alon, Ilan, Hua Wang, Jun Shen, and Wenxian Zhang. 2014. "Chinese State-Owned Enterprises Go Global." *Journal of Business Strategy* 35 (6): 3–18.

Ariyoshi, Akira, Karl Habermeier, Bernard Laurens, Inci Ötker-Robe, Jorge Ivan Canales-Kriljenko, and Andrei Kirilenko. 2000. "Capital Controls: Country Experiences with Their Use and Liberalization." Occasional Paper 190, International Monetary Fund, Washington.

Baba, Chikako, and Annamaria Kokenyne. 2011. "Effectiveness of Capital Controls in Selected Emerging Markets in the 2000s." Working Paper 11/281, International Monetary Fund, Washington.

Bayoumi, Tamim, and Franziska Ohnsorge. 2013. "Do Inflows or Outflows Dominate? Global Implications of Capital Account Liberalization in China." Working Paper 13/189, International Monetary Fund, Washington.

Beja Jr., Edsel L. 2008. "Estimating Trade Mis-invoicing from China: 2000–2005." *China & World Economy* 16 (2): 82–92.

Cardenas, Mauricio, and Felipe Barrera. 1997. "On the Effectiveness of Capital Controls: The Experience of Colombia during the 1990s." *Journal of Development Economics* 54 (1): 27–57.

Cardoso, Eliana, and Ilan Goldfajn. 1998. "Capital Flows to Brazil: The Endogeneity of Capital Controls." *IMF Staff Papers* 45 (1): 161–202.

Chen, Yuan, and Qian Yingyi, eds. 2014. *Capital Account Liberalization: Strategy, Timing and Roadmap*. China Finance 40 Forum Books, Social Sciences Academy Press (in Chinese).

Cheung, Yin-Wong, and Risto Herrala. 2014. "China's Capital Controls: Through the Prism of Covered Interest Differentials." *Pacific Economic Review* 19 (1): 112–34.

Clements, Benedict J., and Herman Kamil. 2009. "Are Capital Controls Effective in the 21st Century? The Recent Experience of Colombia." Working Paper 09/30, International Monetary Fund, Washington.

Craig, R. Sean, Changchun Hua, Philip Ng, and Raymond Yuen. 2013. "Development of the Renminbi Market in Hong Kong SAR: Assessing Onshore-Offshore Market Integration." Working Paper 13/268, International Monetary Fund, Washington.

De Crescenzio, Annamaria, Marta Golin, and Anne-Christelle Ott. 2015. "Currency-Based Measures Targeting Banks: Balancing National Regulation of Risk and Financial Openness." OECD Working Paper 2015/03, Organisation for Economic Co-operation and Development, Paris.

De Gregorio, José, Sebastian Edwards, and Rodrigo O. Valdes. 2000. "Controls on Capital Inflows: Do They Work?" *Journal of Development Economics* 63 (1): 59–83.

Eichengreen, Barry. 2013. ADB Distinguished Lecture–Renminbi Internationalization: Tempest in a Teapot? *Asian Development Review* 30 (1): 148–64.

———, R. Gullapalli, and U. Panizza. 2011. "Capital Account Liberalization, Financial Development and Industry Growth: A Synthetic View." *Journal of International Money and Finance* 30 (6): 1090–106.

Funke, Michael, Chang Shu, Xiaoqiang Cheng, and Sercan Eraslan. 2015. "Assessing the CNH-CNY Pricing Differential: Role of Fundamentals, Contagion and Policy." BIS Working Paper No. 492, Bank for International Settlements, Basel.

Garber, Peter. 2013. "China Sequencing." In *IMF and PBC Joint Conference on Capital Flows Management: Lessons from International Experience*, edited by Markus Rodlauer and Papa N'Diaye, 258–60. Washington: International Monetary Fund and People's Bank of China.

Goh, Soo Khoon. 2005. "New Empirical Evidence on the Effects of Capital Controls on Composition of Capital Flows in Malaysia." *Applied Economics* 37 (July): 1491–503.

He, Dong. 2014. "The Internationalization of the Renminbi." In *The Oxford Companion to the Economics of China*, edited by S. Fan, R. Kanbur, S.-J. Wei, and X. Zhang. Oxford: Oxford University Press.

———, Lillian Cheung, Wenlang Zhang, and Tommy T. Wu. 2012. "How Would Capital Account Liberalization Affect China's Capital Flows and the Renminbi Real Exchange Rates?" *China & World Economy* 20 (6): 29–54.

He, Dong, and Paul Luk. 2013. "A Model of Chinese Capital Account Liberalization." Working Paper 12/2013, Hong Kong Institute for Monetary Research, forthcoming in *Macroeconomic Dynamics*.

He, Dong, and Robert McCauley. 2010. "Offshore Markets for the Domestic Currency: Monetary and Financial Stability Issues." BIS Working Paper 320, Bank for International Settlements, Basel.

———. 2012. "Eurodollar Banking and Currency Internationalization." *BIS Quarterly Review* (June) 33–46.

Hooley, John. 2013. "Bringing Down the Great Wall? Global Implications of Capital Account Liberalisation in China." Bank of England, *Quarterly Bulletin* 53 (4): 304–16.

International Monetary Fund (IMF). 2010. "Measuring Capital Account Restrictiveness: A Survey of the Literature." In *2010 Annual Report on Exchange Arrangements and Exchange Restrictions*. Washington: International Monetary Fund.

———. 2011a. "People's Republic of China Spillover Report for the 2011 Article IV Consultation and Selected Issues." Country Report 11/193, International Monetary Fund, Washington.

———. 2011b. "People's Republic of China: Financial System Stability Assessment." Country Report 11/321, International Monetary Fund, Washington.

———. 2011c. "Recent Experiences in Managing Capital Inflows—Cross-Cutting Themes and Possible Policy Framework." Policy Paper, International Monetary Fund, Washington.

———. 2012a. "The Liberalization and Management of Capital Flows—An Institutional View." Policy Paper, International Monetary Fund, Washington.

———. 2012b. "Liberalizing Capital Flows and Managing Outflows: Background Paper." Policy Paper, International Monetary Fund, Washington.

———. 2012c. "Liberalizing Capital Flows and Managing Outflows." Policy Paper, International Monetary Fund, Washington.

———. 2013. "Key Aspects of Macroprudential Policy." Policy Paper, International Monetary Fund, Washington.
———. 2014. "Staff Guidance Note on Macroprudential Policy." Policy Paper, International Monetary Fund, Washington.
———. 2015a. "People's Republic of China 2015 Article IV Consultation." Country Report No. 15/234, International Monetary Fund, Washington.
———. 2015b. "Macroprudential Policy and Capital Flow Management." Paper delivered to the ASEAN Plus Three Finance and Central Bank Deputies' Meetings, International Monetary Fund, Washington.
———. 2015c. "Managing Capital Outflows: Further Operational Considerations." Policy Paper, International Monetary Fund, Washington.
Ishii, Shogo, Karl Habermeier, Jorge Iván Canales-Kriljenko, Bernard Laurens, John Leimone, and Judit Vadasz. 2002. "Capital Account Liberalization and Financial Sector Stability." Occasional Paper 211, International Monetary Fund, Washington.
Jittrapanum, Thawatchai, and Suthy Prasartset. 2009. "Hot Money and Capital Controls in Thailand." *TWN Global Economy Series* 15. Penang: Third World Network.
Kaminsky, Graciela, and Sergio Schmukler. 2003. "Short-Run Pain, Long-Run Gain: The Effects of Financial Liberalization." NBER Working Paper No. 9787, National Bureau of Economic Research, Cambridge, MA.
Klein, Michael W., and Giovanni P. Olivei. 2008. "Capital Account Liberalization, Financial Depth, and Economic Growth." *Journal of International Money and Finance* 27: 861–75.
Lane, Philip R., and Gian Maria Milesi-Ferretti. 2003. "International Financial Integration." *IMF Staff Papers* 50: 82–113.
———. 2007. "The External Wealth of Nations Mark II: Revised and Extended Estimates of Foreign Assets and Liabilities, 1970–2004." *Journal of International Economics* 73: 223–250.
Lane, Timothy, Atish Ghosh, Javier Hamann, Steven Phillips, Marianne Schulze-Ghattas, and Tsidi Tsikata. 1999. "IMF-Supported Programs in Indonesia, Korea, and Thailand. A Preliminary Assessment." Occasional Paper 178, International Monetary Fund, Washington.
Liu, Xiangmin. 2015. "China's Strategy toward Capital Flow Liberalization." Presentation by the Chinese delegation at the OECD.
Ma, Guonan, and Robert N. McCauley. 2008. "Efficacy of China's Capital Controls: Evidence from Price and Flow Data." *Pacific Economic Review* 13 (1): 104–23.
Maziad, Samar, and Joong Shik Kang. 2012. "RMB Internationalization: Onshore/Offshore Links." Working Paper 12/133, International Monetary Fund, Washington.
Ostry, Jonathan D., Atish R. Gosh, Marcos Chamon, and Mahvash S. Qureshi. 2012. "Tools for Managing Financial-Stability Risks from Capital Flows." *Journal of International Economics* 88 (2012): 407–21.
Prasad, Eswar, and Shang-Jin Wei. 2007. "The Chinese Approach to Capital Inflows: Patterns and Possible Explanations." In *Capital Controls and Capital Flows in Emerging Economies: Policies, Practices and Consequences*, edited by Sebastian Edwards. Chicago: University of Chicago Press.
Rey, Helene. 2016. "International Channels of Transmission of Monetary Policy and the Mundellian Trilemma." NBER Working Paper No. 21852, National Bureau of Economic Research, Cambridge, MA.
Saadi Sedik, Tahsin, and Tao Sun. 2012. "Effects of Capital Flow Liberalization—What Is the Evidence from Recent Experiences of Emerging Market Economies?" Working Paper 12/275, International Monetary Fund, Washington.
Tian, Yuan, and Kevin P. Gallagher. 2015. "Housing Price Volatility and the Capital Account in China." GEGI Working Paper, Boston University, Boston.
Wang, Bin, and Tao Sun. 2013. "How Effective Are Macroprudential Policies in China?" Working Paper 13/75, International Monetary Fund, Washington.
Yi, Gang. 2015. "The Future of China's Foreign Exchange Liberalization." *China Finance* 2015 (19).

Yu, Yongding. 2014. "How Far Can RMB Internationalization Go?" ADBI Working Paper 461, Asian Development Bank Institute, Tokyo.

Zhang, Ming. 2015. "Internationalization of the Renminbi, Developments, Problems and Influences." CIGI New Thinking and the New G20 Series Paper No. 2, Centre for International Governance Innovation, Waterloo.

CHAPTER 9

Renminbi Internationalization

Malhar Nabar and Camilo E. Tovar

The current role of emerging market currencies in the international monetary system is limited. However, the increasing importance of emerging markets in the global economy suggests that these currencies could become a vehicle for greater reserve currency diversification and the production of reserve assets in the future.

In recent years, the growing importance of China in the global economy (Figure 9.1), the policies and reforms implemented by the Chinese authorities, and the increasing interconnectedness of the global economy have set the stage for a greater role for the renminbi (RMB) in the international monetary and financial system. In November 2015 the IMF's Executive Board recognized the increasing use in economic and financial transactions and wide trading of the RMB by deciding to include the RMB in the special drawing right (SDR) basket of currencies, effective on October 1, 2016 (IMF 2015a, 2015b). The decision is another milestone in the integration of the Chinese economy into the global financial system and an acknowledgment of China's progress in reforming its monetary and financial system.

This chapter examines RMB internationalization. It briefly discusses what drives currency internationalization, looks at the existing literature, reviews key developments in offshore RMB use and trading, summarizes underlying policy measures that have promoted RMB internationalization, and discusses the implications of RMB internationalization for the international monetary system.

This chapter draws on material prepared by the authors for the 2015 SDR Valuation Review (IMF 2015a, 2015b). We are greatly indebted to IMF staff involved in the review. In particular, we thank Siddharth Tiwari, Andrew Tweedie, Sean Hagan, Andreas Bauer, Tom Krueger, Bernhard Steinki, Donal McGettigan, Ceyda Oner, and Andrew Swiston for their detailed comments and suggestions. We also thank Alfred Kammer, Kristina Kostial, Alfred Schipke, W. Raphael Lam, and Mark Milford for their comments and encouragement to prepare the chapter. Finally, we acknowledge the excellent assistance of Frank Wallace, Yang Hao, Ji Jiang, and Arshia Karki.

Figure 9.1. China's Share in Global GDP
(Percent)

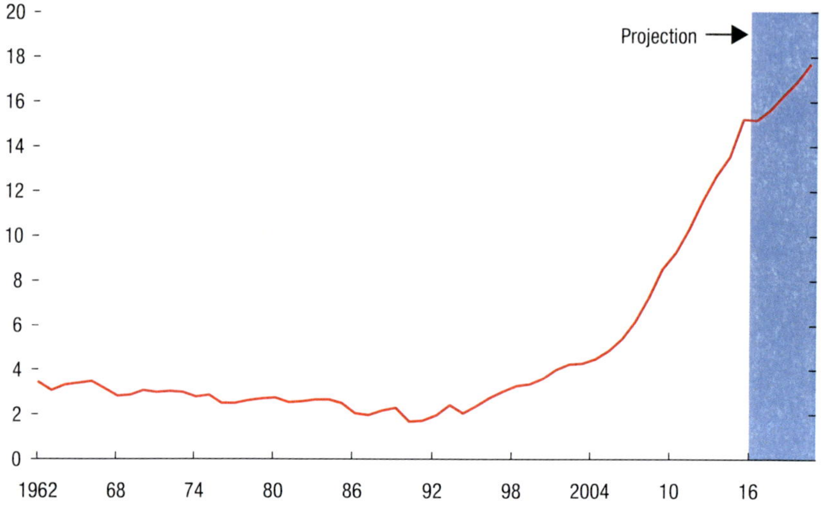

Source: IMF, World Economic Outlook database.

CURRENCY INTERNATIONALIZATION: A LITERATURE OVERVIEW

An international currency is usually one used and held beyond the borders of the issuing country, not merely for transactions with residents, but also for transactions between nonresidents (Kenan 2009). Moreover, an international currency performs several tasks—and in line with those of a currency used solely domestically—as a unit of account, medium of exchange (means of payment), and store of value. This allows the private sector to use the currency as a vehicle for transactions (invoicing or financial transactions), and the official sector for interventions, as an anchor (a peg, for example), or as reserves (Krugman 1984).

While the internationalization of a currency is ultimately market driven, supporting policies can facilitate it. Historical evidence and the existing literature suggest that a number of factors drive currency internationalization (Chinn 2015; Frankel 2011; Maziad and others 2011). To start with, the issuer has to be eager to internationalize the currency, with the authorities promoting its use and trading—rather than deliberately choosing not to—as Germany did with the deutsche mark in the 1970s (Eichengreen 2011). Policies can support the international use of a currency as a unit of account and medium of exchange by encouraging the establishment of trade networks and invoicing in a country's own currency. For this, both the size and structure of the economy matter. Increasing trade and financial integration is also likely to foster currency internationalization. The development of deep and liquid financial markets onshore and offshore,[1] especially for sovereign debt trading, has also been identified as a key feature of successful currency internationalization. However, this requires a certain degree of openness of the capital account. Moreover, the international use of a currency—in particular as a reserve asset—will depend on its stability, which in turn hinges on the creditworthiness of the sovereign, as captured by stable, sustainable, and predictable macroeconomic outcomes; strong institutions; and the integrity of markets (including a reliable rule of law). Finally, policymakers should have the capacity to respond to unexpected shocks and to influence expectations, and the central bank must be able and willing to provide liquidity to support financial institutions (both foreign and domestic) if the market for its currency dries up.

While policies can help support currency internationalization, the process is not straightforward and is subject to a number of caveats. First, it is essential to determine the right pace, sequencing, and prioritization of reforms and to design a process consistent with a country's institutional and financial development. For instance, given that financial deepening and capital account liberalization are important drivers of currency internationalization, considerations regarding the appropriate sequencing of these reforms apply here as well; for example, liberalization of more stable inflows first, followed by the liberalization of long-term and short-term portfolio flows (IMF 2012). Similarly, countries will need to manage trade-offs that may arise during internationalization (such as balancing the need for deepening sovereign debt markets to enhance market liquidity with the need to ensure fiscal soundness and debt sustainability).

Second, the relative importance of specific policies to support the process will likely vary across countries. For example, the size of financial markets—rather than the size of the economy—has been fundamental to supporting the international use of the Swiss franc or the British pound (Maziad and others 2011). Similarly, the development of a cross-currency swap market (such as for liquidity funding) has played a key role in increasing the international use of the Australian dollar (McCauley 2006).

Third, countries should also take into account the benefits and risks associated with currency internationalization. While they are likely to benefit from lower transaction costs, greater ability to issue debt at more favorable terms, and increased seigniorage, they are also likely to face risks—such as larger and more volatile capital flows, and heightened volatility in asset prices—and more complex policy trade-offs for monetary and financial stability. Recent experiences with some safe-haven currencies in small open economies have been a reminder of these challenges—Switzerland, for example (Jordan 2016). Finally, countries whose

[1]When non-U.S. residents use the U.S. dollar to settle trade and make investments, they do not transact onshore through banks and in financial markets in the United States. On the contrary, they concentrate transactions in international financial centers such as the eurodollar market in London. It is for this reason that many consider that without offshore markets the U.S. dollar would not have attained the dominant position in international trade and payments it has today. See He and McCauley 2010.

currencies are used as reserves may be called on to support global liquidity in periods of stress and may need to coordinate policies with other reserve-currency-issuing countries in some circumstances.

TAKING STOCK OF RMB INTERNATIONALIZATION

Growth in the international use of the RMB has traced several of these features of currency internationalization.

Offshore Use

The use of RMB in cross-border payments has grown rapidly in recent years along with its status as an increasingly actively traded currency in global financial markets. This movement reflects the growth and increasing interconnectedness of the Chinese economy with the rest of the world, which has resulted in a growing interest and willingness among nonresidents to settle cross-border trade and direct investment payments in RMB, to invest in RMB-denominated securities, and to obtain funding in the currency.

RMB Trade Settlement

Since its accession to the World Trade Organization in 2001, China's swift rise up the ranks of trading nations has positioned it as the single-largest trading partner for Asia and sub-Saharan Africa, and the second-largest trading partner for the European Union, the United States, and Latin America. It is now the largest source of imports for the United States, the European Union's 28 members, and Japan, which together account for nearly 50 percent of world GDP.

The use of RMB for cross-border trade invoicing and payment has grown rapidly since its introduction in 2009. In 2014 close to 20 percent of China's goods trade was settled in RMB, and nearly 25 percent of other current account transactions—services, income, and dividend payments (IMF 2015a). In 2015 the RMB settlement portion of China's goods trade rose nearly 10½ percent over the previous year, while that of other current account transactions rose close to 28½ percent (PBC 2016). Among the factors cited for the rapid rise are mutual benefits, such as better pricing for nonresident buyers; more security against currency risk for Chinese entities; and more efficient cash flow management and lower transactions costs for both sides.

RMB Direct Investment Settlement

Since 2011 direct investment payments—inward foreign direct investment (FDI) and outward direct investment—have been permitted in RMB. The RMB is rapidly advancing as the currency of choice for settling direct investment payments in both directions. Nearly 30 percent of FDI transactions were settled in RMB in 2014, up from 13 percent in 2012. Reflecting a growing willingness of nonresident counterparties to accept RMB in settlement, close to 16 percent of China's outward direct investment was settled in RMB in 2014, up from just 4

Figure 9.2. Offshore Deposits in RMB
(RMB billion)

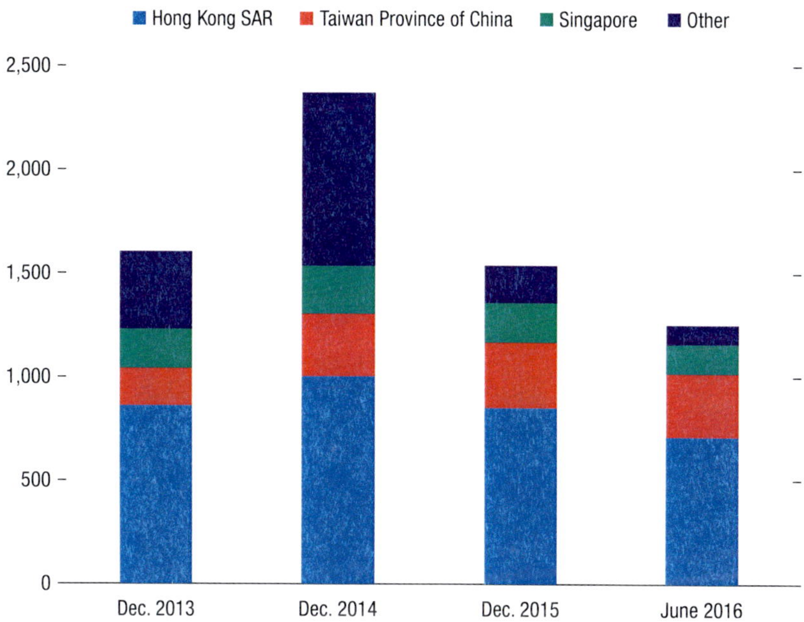

Sources: CEIC; and IMF staff calculations.

percent in 2012 (IMF 2015a). In 2015 the RMB settlement portion of China's FDI and outward direct investment increased 65.2 percent and 228.1 percent over the previous year (PBC 2016).

Offshore RMB Deposits

Licensed banks in Hong Kong Special Administrative Region (SAR) began accepting RMB deposits in February 2004, initially primarily to support mainland tourism and remittances. The pace of accumulation began to accelerate after cross-border trade settlement in RMB was permitted in 2009, driven by corporate deposit growth. Offshore RMB deposits rose to RMB2.3 trillion in 2014 (from about RMB100 billion in 2010) as the RMB appreciated against major currencies over this period. The volume of offshore RMB deposits has since dropped to around RMB1.3 trillion in mid-2016 (Figure 9.2).

Offshore RMB Bonds

Providing foreign investors with a deep and liquid pool of high-quality RMB assets is crucial to China's goal of boosting international use of its currency. The issuance of offshore RMB bonds—usually referred to as "dim sum" bonds by traders—was initially restricted to mainland policy and commercial banks, starting with China Development Bank listing in July 2007 in Hong Kong SAR. China's own sovereign issuance in Hong Kong SAR has been an important driver of the market since the first auction took place in September 2009, and further boosted by foreign investors' perceptions of the RMB as a safe bet to rise in value or at least hold steady.

Several corporate issuers have tapped RMB funds in the offshore market, including foreign firms such as McDonald's, Volkswagen, and Caterpillar. Issuance has since spread, including to centers outside Asia such as London, where HSBC issued the first RMB-denominated bond in April 2012.

Overseas agencies and governments have also been active in tapping offshore RMB funds. In September 2014 the International Finance Corporation issued what was then the largest London-listed RMB bond, worth RMB1 billion. In October 2014 the United Kingdom issued its first RMB-denominated sovereign bond (raising RMB3 billion) and indicated the proceeds would be held as foreign exchange reserves. A month later the Canadian province of British Columbia issued its second RMB-denominated bond, for RMB3 billion.

Instruments that allow hedging of interest rate and currency risk have accompanied the growth of the offshore debt market. Market participants note the large volumes in cross-currency swaps involving offshore RMB and the emergence of the cross-currency swap curve as a key offshore RMB benchmark interest rate curve.

While these developments have possibly facilitated the growth of the dim sum bond market, regression analysis by Law (2016) confirms that the net issuance of dim sum bonds has been mainly driven by expectations of RMB appreciation from CNY nondeliverable forwards and the CNH-CNY basis, a measure for ease of RMB hedging (where CNY and CNH are the internationally recognized codes for trades in the Chinese currency onshore and offshore). By contrast, the interest rate differential between onshore and offshore and credit spreads in both onshore and offshore markets are found to be statistically insignificant factors determining the issuance of dim sum bonds.

Foreign Holdings in RMB

Sparse data on central bank holdings of RMB-denominated assets preclude a definitive judgment of how widespread the practice is. As of April 2015 the People's Bank of China estimates the total offshore holding of bonds, stocks, deposits, and other RMB assets by foreign central banks and monetary authorities amounted to RMB666.7 billion—slightly more than US$100 billion.[2]

Offshore Trading

The 2016 Bank for International Settlements Triennial Central Bank Survey on Foreign Exchange and Derivatives Market Activity shows that the RMB's share

[2]Starting in October 2016 the IMF identifies the RMB in its official foreign exchange reserves database. This provides a better picture of official reserves holdings of RMB.

of global foreign exchange turnover over the past few years has increased rapidly from a low base. These developments were already evident in the 2013 survey, which showed a considerable increase in the RMB's share of trading volumes since 2010, to 1.1 percent of total global turnover (daily average turnover of $120 billion) and 0.8 percent of spot global turnover ($34 billion). In 2016 these shares had increased to 2.0 percent in both instances ($202 and $68 billion, respectively). This amount places global turnover in the RMB behind the other reserve currencies in the world (that is, the U.S. dollar, the euro, the Japanese yen, the pound sterling, the Australian dollar, the Canadian dollar, and the Swiss franc). IMF analysis using SWIFT data—based on interbank messages used to confirm foreign exchange transactions—also shows that total RMB turnover increased by 108 percent from the first quarter of 2013 to the second quarter of 2015 (IMF 2015b).

Foreign exchange market activity by region shows RMB trading is most common in Asia, constitutes a small but growing share in Europe, and is still thin in North America. Since electronic trading is now widespread, the association between the location of the foreign exchange transaction and that of the underlying clients has weakened, as trades booked in a particular market could be executed on behalf of clients elsewhere. Therefore, data on foreign exchange turnover by trading center are best analyzed by aggregating trades across three broad time zones (Asia, Europe, and the Americas) and can indicate overall liquidity in each. Doing so confirms that the RMB is one of the most-traded currencies in Asia. The 2016 BIS Triennial Survey also confirms that, and mainland China, Hong Kong SAR, and Singapore account for almost three-quarters of global RMB turnover. RMB trading has also increased rapidly in London and now averages more than $40 billion per day (15 percent of total offshore trading). Trading in North America remains very thin, but there has been substantial growth relative in other markets (such as Korea).

Data on hourly foreign exchange transactions from the Electronic Broking Services (EBS) platform confirm this trading profile, with a significant volume in the offshore renminbi bond market (CNH) during Asian trading hours, which also overlap with the first hours of the European trading day (Figures 9.3 and 9.4).[3] The profile of hourly CNH turnover is similar to that of the Swiss franc against the U.S. dollar on the EBS platform. Turnover in the major currency pairs tend to remain higher during off-peak hours, even as turnover in those currency pairs drops substantially from late in North American trading hours until Asian trading picks up.

Detailed data from the EBS trading platform can be used to obtain an additional perspective on the relative stance of the USD/CNH currency pair

[3]This chapter uses in its analysis the following currencies and international codes for them: Australian dollar (AUD), euro (EUR), British pound (GBP), Canadian dollar (CAD), Chinese renminbi (RMB), Swiss franc (CHF), Hong Kong dollar (HKD), Japanese yen (JPY), Mexican peso (MXN), Russian ruble (RUB), Singapore dollar (SGD), the South African rand (ZAR), and the United States dollar (USD).

Figure 9.3 Daily Trading Volumes
(Index)

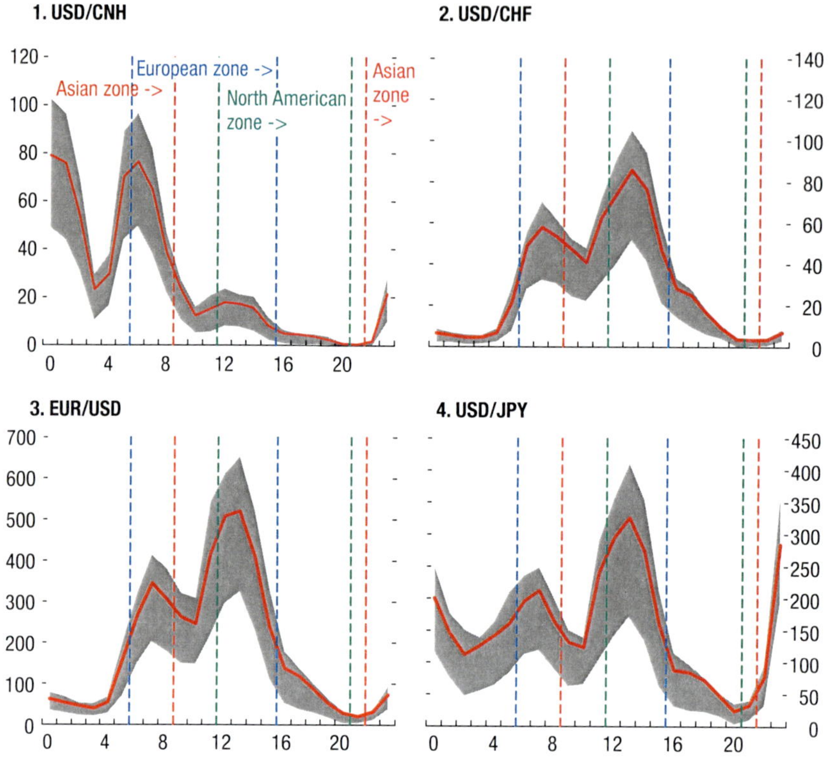

Sources: Electronic Broking Services (EBS); and IMF staff calculations.
Note: The horizontal axis displays the Greenwich Mean Time. The shaded area displays the 25th and 75th interquartile range. Vertical lines denote trading zones. The index is calculated by taking the daily average of the volumes traded of the four currencies to equal 100.

market liquidity status relative to other major currency pairs (Annex 9.1). Specifically, several indicators are constructed to capture the cost of executing trades (bid-offer spreads and effective trading costs) and measure market resilience to order flow (order-flow price impact and order-flow price return reversal). The costs of executing trades in the USD/CNH currency pair are on average nearly as low as those for the USD/JPY and USD/EUR currency pairs, albeit with a wider distribution across transactions and more variation across time zones, while in this sample comparing favorably to a number of other currency pairs (Figures 9.5 and 9.6). Similarly, USD/CNH market resilience was found to be among the strongest of the currency pairs analyzed. While exchange rates are affected by a variety of factors, the analysis found the price impact and return reversal of the USD/CNH currency pair less sensitive to net

Figure 9.4. Traded Volumes by Currency and Principal Exchange Markets

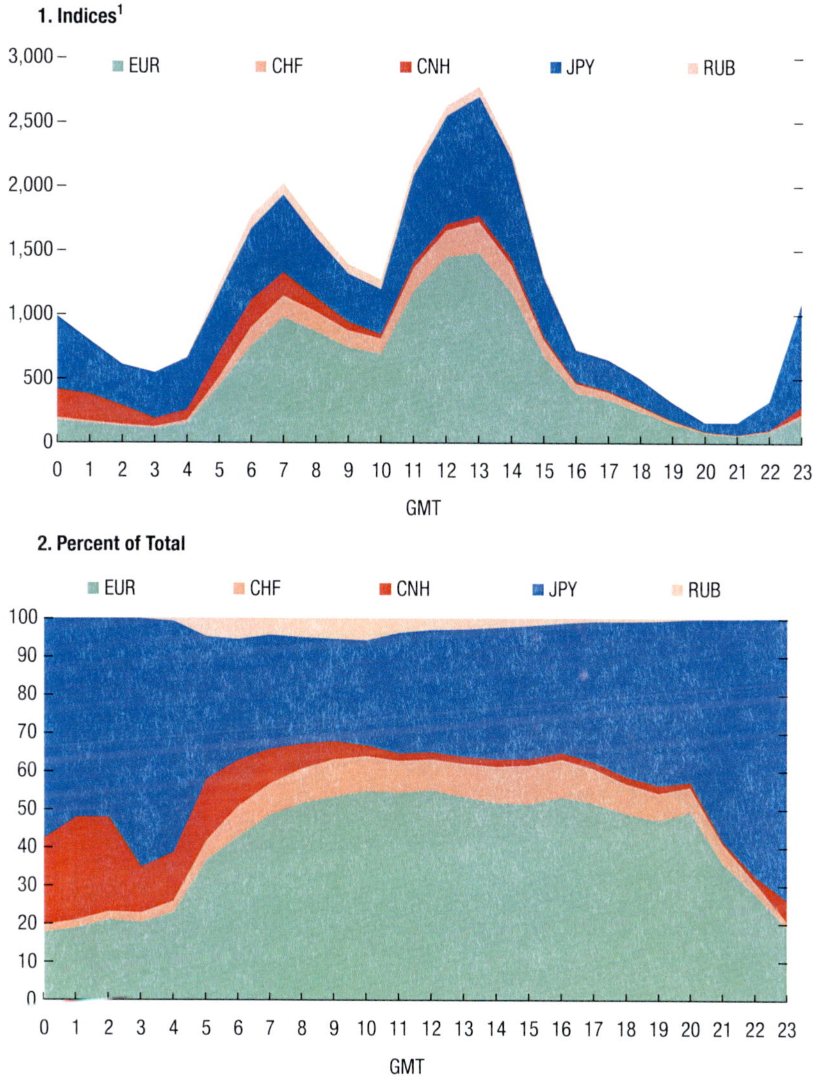

Sources: Electronic Broking Services (EBS); and IMF staff calculations.
Note: GMT = Greenwich Mean Time.
[1] The indices are calculated by taking the daily average of the volumes traded across all currency pairs equal to 100.

buying/selling pressures than those of other major currency pairs. These results should be interpreted with caution, given that data coverage varies across currency pairs and the EBS platform represents only a portion of the global foreign exchange market.

Figure 9.5. Liquidity Indicators by Currency Pair
(Daily averages, basis points)

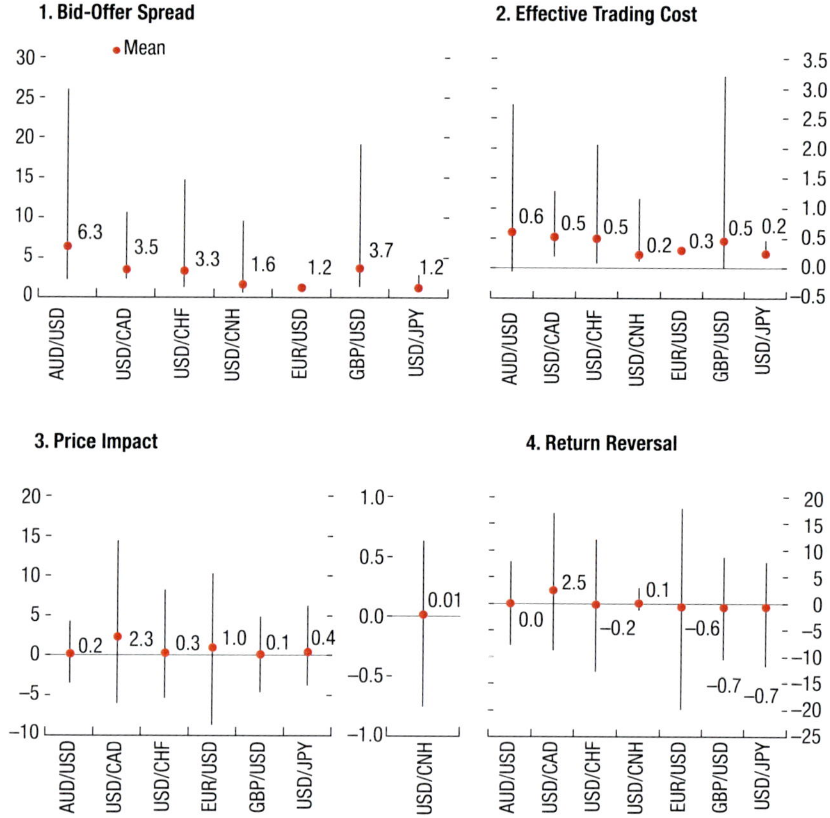

Sources: Electronic Broking Services (EBS); and IMF staff calculations.
Note: Vertical lines show the 25th percentile and 75th percentile range.

Overall Progress

The RMB globalization index, which measures growth in offshore RMB usage—by taking into account the four areas covered in our analysis, CNH deposits, trade settlement and other international payments, dim sum bonds and certificates of deposit issued, and foreign exchange turnover—shows a sustained increase in RMB internationalization over the past few years (Figure 9.7). However, most of this progress since 2009 has been in its use for trade settlement and direct investment purposes. The use of the RMB as an international funding and reserve currency, while growing, remains in its early stages. Evidence also shows that the RMB is widely traded offshore and its liquidity is comparable to that of other major currency pairs.

Figure 9.6. Bid-Ask Spread and Effective Cost of Transaction by Time Zone
(Basis points)

1. Bid-Ask Spread

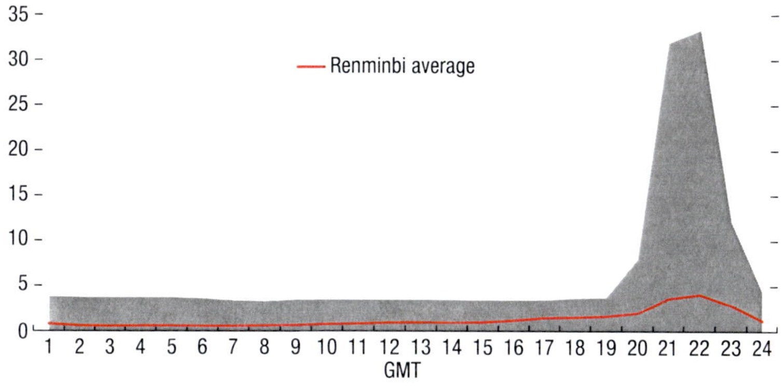

2. Effective Cost

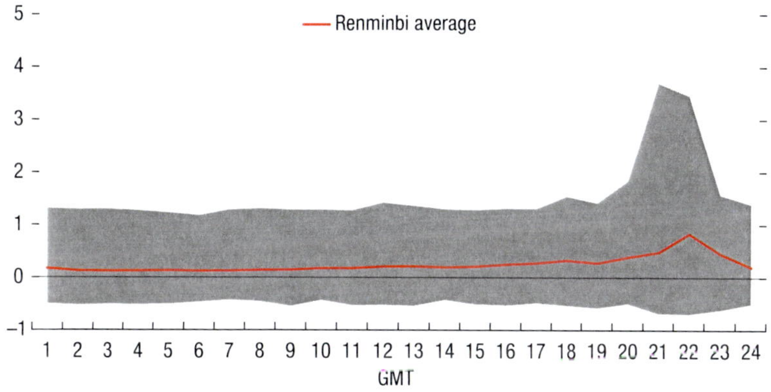

Sources: Electronic Broking Services (EBS); and IMF staff calculations.
Note: Shaded areas display the 10th and 90th percentile range for the following currency pairs vis-à-vis the USD: AUD, CAD, CHF, EUR, GBP, and JPY. GMT = Greenwich Mean Time.

Furthermore, progress made so far suggests prospects for the internationalization of the RMB remain strong, particularly as policies and reforms continue to support the process (as we discuss next). These structural supporting factors will likely more than compensate for any transitory developments that can affect the attractiveness of the RMB—such as the RMB's depreciation on August 2015 that affected the RMB yield (see Box 9.1).[4]

[4]Yields are important determinants of internationalization. Evidence shows that one of the most important factors in explaining the growth of the euromarket was the dollar yield (McCauley 2005).

Figure 9.7. RMB Globalization Index

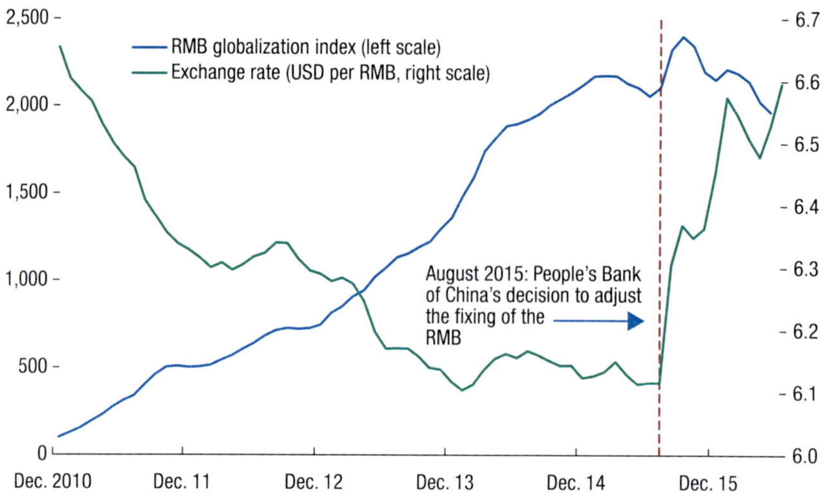

Sources: Bloomberg L.P.; and Standard Chartered.

UNDERLYING POLICY MEASURES TO PROMOTE RMB INTERNATIONALIZATION

While the internationalization of a currency is market driven, policies and reform can play a key supporting role. In this regard, the Chinese authorities have implemented policy reforms to encourage RMB internationalization and strengthen macro-financial stability by taking gradual steps to develop functioning markets, move to market-determined prices and interest rates, and put in place sound policy frameworks.

Policy measures to promote RMB internationalization, particularly its use as an investment and funding currency, have covered three main areas: gradual opening of the capital account, steps to strengthen the domestic financial system, and offshore liquidity support through improvements to cross-border payments infrastructure and central bank swap lines. Table 9.1 provides a timeline with the policy measures implemented to support RMB internationalization. The progress made in each of these areas will be discussed next.

Gradual Opening of the Capital Account

While China allowed RMB convertibility on the trade accounts nearly two decades ago, capital account transactions remain in varying degrees under control. Capital account transactions with China are generally subject to restrictions, preapprovals, and quotas, as summarized in the IMF's 2016 *Annual Report*

Table 9.1. Key Measures Supporting RMB Internationalization

Date	Agency	Key Development	Notes
Jul-09	PBC/MOC/GACC/SAT/CBRC	Pilot program for cross-border trade RMB settlement was launched in Shanghai and four cities in Guangdong province. The program was subsequently expanded to 20 cities in June 2010 and nationwide in July 2011.	PBC Document [2010] No. 186 PBC Document [2011] No. 203
Sep-09	MOF	Ministry of Finance issued RMB treasury bonds for RMB6 billion in Hong Kong SAR, the first issuance outside mainland China.	
Aug-10	PBC	Offshore central bank or monetary authority, offshore RMB clearing banks, and other offshore participants allowed to invest in the interbank market (China Interbank Bond Market).	PBC Document [2010] No. 217
Aug-10	CFETS	Initiated direct currency trading with Malaysian ringgit and eventually added other currencies such as RUB, JPY, AUD, NZD, GBP, EUR, SGD, CHY, ZAR, and KRW as of June 2016.	
Jan-11	PBC	Domestic institutions were allowed to use RMB for outward foreign direct investment.	PBC Announcement [2011] No. 1
Oct-11	PBC	Foreign Institutions were allowed to use RMB for inward foreign direct investment.	PBC Announcement [2011] No. 23
Oct-11	PBC	Onshore banks can make RMB loans for offshore projects.	PBC Announcement [2011] No. 255
Dec-11	CSRC/PBC/SAFE	Renminbi qualified foreign institutional investor (RQFII) scheme was officially launched. Expanded to RMB200 billion for Hong Kong SAR in November 2012. Expanded quota and broadened eligibility requirements on investor type in March 2013. As of end-June 2016 granted quota to 19 countries/regions. The total quota ceiling is RMB1,460 billion, of which RMB508 billion has been approved.	CSRC Order No. 76 CSRC Order No. 90
Dec-12	PBC	Authorized Bank of China Taipei Branch as RMB clearing bank in Taiwan Province of China. Having agreed on clearing settlements with 20 countries/regions.	
Mar-13	PBC	Granted Qualified Foreign Institutional Investor access to onshore interbank bond market.	PBC Document [2013] No. 69
Jul-13	PBC	Simplified the procedures for various cross-border businesses.	PBC Document [2013] No. 168
Sep-13	PBC	Foreign investors can use RMB to invest in domestic financial institutions.	PBC Document [2013] No. 217
Sep-13		Launched the first Free Trade Zone (FTZ) in Shanghai. In February 2014 cross-border RMB cash-pooling scheme allowed companies within the Shanghai FTZ for two-way flows of cash with their parent companies and affiliates.	
Dec-13	PBC	Adjusted the quota management to macroprudential management for the RMB purchases and sales.	PBC Document [2013] No. 321
Nov-14	CSRC/PBC	Hong Kong-Shanghai stock connect was officially launched as well as Renminbi Qualified Domestic Institutional Investor (RQDII).	PBC Document [2014] No. 336 PBC Document [2014] No. 331 RQDII new quota suspended in January 2016

(continued)

Table 9.1. Key Measures Supporting RMB Internationalization ***(continued)***

Date	Agency	Key Development	Notes
Nov-14	PBC	Cross-border RMB cash-pooling schemes were expanded to multinational corporations across the rest of China with cap of RMB cash inflows and no limit for outflows. Relaxed the requirements for qualified corporations and increased the cap in September 2015.	PBC Document [2014] No. 324 PBC Document [2014] No. 279
Jun-15	PBC	Open interbank repo market to qualified foreign banks.	PBC Document [2015] No. 170
Jul-15	PBC	Plan to price and settle China's first crude oils in RMB.	PBC Announcement [2015] No. 19
Jul-15	PBC	Lifted the cap for foreign central banks, sovereign wealth funds, and international financial institutions in the interbank market. By end-September 2015 granted them to the onshore foreign exchange market on a registration basis. In February 2016 further expanded the scope by permitting most types of foreign institutional investors (deemed as medium or long-term by PBC) into the China Interbank Bond Market.	PBC Document [2015] No. 220
Aug-15	PBC	Reformed RMB fixing mechanism to make it more market driven.	
Oct-15	PBC	Launched Cross-Border Interbank Payment System in Shanghai. The current system (Phase I) adopts real-time gross settlement approach.	
Nov-15		IMF announced the inclusion of RMB in the special drawing right basket by October 2016.	
Nov-15	PBC/SAFE	Securities regulators in China and Hong Kong SAR announced first batch of approval for mutual fund recognition, allowing recognized funds in Hong Kong SAR to be distributed in China and vice versa. The scheme was launched in July 2015.	PBC and SAFE Announcement [2015] No. 36.
Dec-15	PBC/CFETS	CFETS published CFETS CNY index, shifting focus from USD/CNY bilateral exchange rate to a trade-weighted index.	
Jan-16	PBC/CFETS	PBC lengthened interbank foreign exchange trading hours from 9:30–16:30 to 9:30–23:30.	
Feb-16	SAFE	Relaxed Qualified Foreign Institutional Investor quotas, with maximum allocations now linked to assets under management and subject to a ceiling of $5 billion.	PBC Announcement [2011] No. 3

Source: National authorities.

Note: CBRC = China Banking Regulatory Commission; CFETS = China Foreign Exchange Trading System; CSRC = China Securities Regulatory Commission; GACC = General Administration of Customs of the People's Republic of China; MOC = Ministry of Commerce; PBC = People's Bank of China; SAFE = State Administration of Foreign Exchange; SAT = State Administration of Taxation.

on Exchange Rate Arrangements and Restrictions (AREAER).[5] As part of a broader financial reform agenda, however, the authorities have been gradually easing restrictions, widening channels of access, and increasing quotas for two-way flows (for example, the U.S. dollar "Qualified Foreign Institutional Investor—QFII" program that from 2003 has given foreign asset managers access to the mainland securities markets, and the U.S. dollar "Qualified Domestic Institutional Investor—QDII" program, established in 2006, through which Chinese asset managers can invest in overseas securities markets, both subject to approval and quotas).

Lower Regulatory Barriers

Steps have also been taken to facilitate cross-border transactions, including by reducing the costs associated with regulatory approval. For certain direct investment transactions in the capital account, the regulations have already shifted from preapprovals to registration and ex post monitoring. The State Administration of Foreign Exchange (SAFE) tracks each transaction and follows up with banks on aberrant transfers. The IMF reports in its 2016 Article IV that the authorities take the view that capital account liberalization will proceed with a broad rationale to minimize disruptive short-term capital flows, contain currency and maturity mismatches, and exercise tight supervision to curb money laundering, terrorist financing, and tax evasion.

Easier Market Access for Official Institutions and Long-Term Private Investors

Over the past year, the authorities have introduced specific measures to ease access to onshore markets for overseas official institutions and private institutions, by removing restrictions on the type of instruments and amounts authorized for investment. However, the authorities expect these institutions to act as long-term investors and the PBC will regulate their trading in accordance with reciprocity principles and macroprudential requirements. The timeline for these measures was as follows:

- In July 2015 the authorities announced that foreign central banks, sovereign wealth funds, and international financial institutions registered with the PBC could choose their own size of investment in the onshore China Interbank Bond Market (CIBM), repurchase agreements (repos), bond lending, bond forwards, interest rate swaps, and forward rate agreements. The guidelines permitted these overseas official institutions to select either the PBC or a settlement agent registered with the PBC to conduct trading and settlement on their behalf.
- In September 2015 official sector reserve managers and their agents were allowed to take part in the onshore foreign exchange market through any of

[5]See AREAER at http://www.elibrary-areaer.imf.org/Pages/YearlyReports.aspx.

Box 9.1. Currency Trading following the RMB Depreciation

On August 11, 2015, the RMB had its largest single-day depreciation since the People's Bank of China (PBC) resumed its exchange rate reform on July 21, 2005. The weakening of the RMB reference rate against the U.S. dollar by 1.9 percent (from 6.12 to 6.23 CNY per USD), was described by the central bank as a "one-off adjustment" and followed the PBC decision to modify the fixing of the exchange rate to better reflect market forces. As shown in this chapter, the RMB's use and trading has increased substantially since 2010, becoming one of the most traded currencies in the Asian time zone, and displaying reasonably deep liquidity during the first part of the European trading day. This box examines how the 2015 depreciation influenced the trading and liquidity conditions of the USD/CNH along with 11 other major currency pairs across the world (AUS/USD, EUR/USD, GBP/USD, USD/CAD, USD/CHF, USD/HKD, USD/JPY, USD/MXN, USD/RUB, USD/SGD, and USD/ZAR). Specifically, we use high-frequency intraday (one-second basis) data from Electronic Broking Services (EBS) to gauge liquidity conditions in foreign exchange markets by calculating quantity-based indicators, such as trading volumes, as well as price-based indicators, such as bid-ask spreads, effective cost of transactions, and the price impact effect from order flows (see Annex 9.1).

Results—reported on a weekly basis for tractability purposes—indicate that PBC's decision led to a temporary decoupling of the RMB offshore market (CNH) from the onshore market (not shown), and induced a transitory tightening of liquidity conditions in the trading of the USD/CNH. Furthermore, there is evidence that PBC's decision triggered comovements (a phenomenon known in the finance literature as "commonality") in the trading of some Asian currency pairs (mainly the USD/SGD and the USD/HKD) at the time of the depreciation, but only across some liquidity dimensions (as we discuss below). However, evidence of commonality with other currency pairs outside Asia are not evident.

Specifically, the analysis shows evidence of liquidity strains in the USD/CNH market following the RMB's depreciation:

(1) the distribution for the size of trades in the USD/CHN market widened and shifted slightly upward in the three weeks following August 11 (Figure 9.1.1, panel 1);

(2) USD/CNH bid-ask spreads widened on average 2.2 basis points (bps) on the week of the depreciation, about three times those quoted in the four weeks before the event, 0.66 bps (Figure 9.1.2, panel 1);

(3) the distribution of the effective cost of transactions market widened and shifted upward (Figure 9.1.3, panel 1); and, finally,

(4) the response of foreign exchange returns to order flows (price impact response) increased.

While results confirm the USD/CNH market experienced liquidity strains in the days following the RMB depreciation, trading in USD/CNH was resilient enough to recover from the overshoot. Indeed, the price impact of order flows was reversed in the three days following the event.

The analysis also confirms that because of the steady internationalization of the RMB and its growing importance, shocks in China have commonality effects on the trading of other Asian currency pairs. This is evident in the tightening of liquidity across Asia following the RMB's depreciation.

Particularly, we find an upward shift in the distribution of deals sizes and bid-ask spreads of the Hong Kong dollar (USD/HKD) and the Singapore dollar (USD/SGD). However, we find no evidence of comovements in the transaction costs or price impact in the trading of other currency pairs.

Box 9.1. Currency Trading following the RMB Depreciation *(continued)*

While the analysis reported here gauges only liquidity conditions, it constitutes a first step toward better understanding the functioning of the limitedly transparent, highly heterogeneous, and decentralized foreign exchange market and its spillover effects. Understanding such liquidity conditions can also help assess funding costs in financial markets, rollover risks, and the ability of agents to hedge foreign exchange strategies—all key aspects in assessing the importance of an international currency.

Figure 9.1.1. Deal Size—Four-Week Window around the August 11, 2015, RMB Depreciation

(Hourly average—index, sample average = 100)

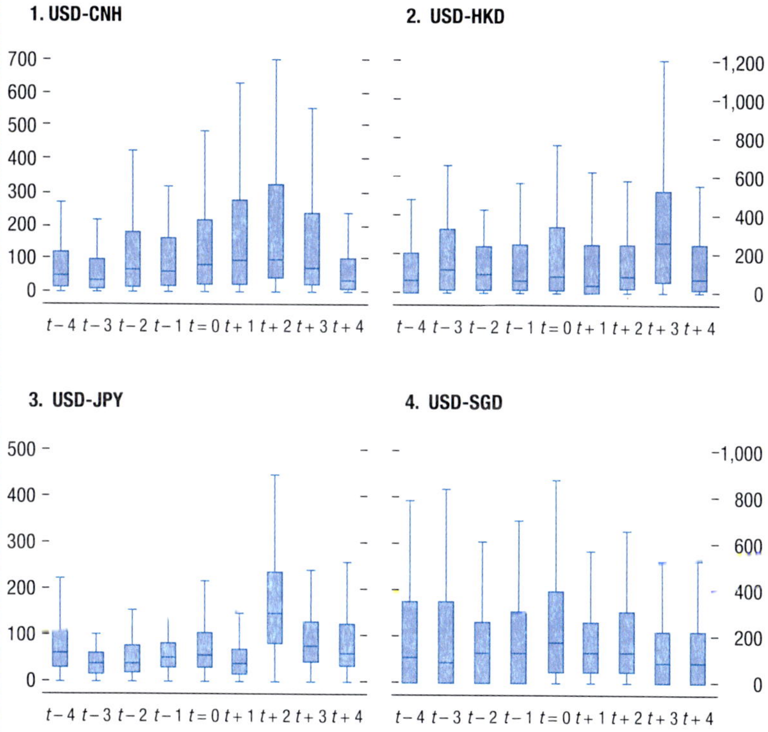

Sources: Electronic Broking Services (EBS); and IMF staff calculations.

Box 9.1. Currency Trading following the RMB Depreciation *(continued)*

Figure 9.1.2. Bid-Ask Spreads—Four-Week Window around the August 11, 2015, RMB Depreciation
(Basis points)

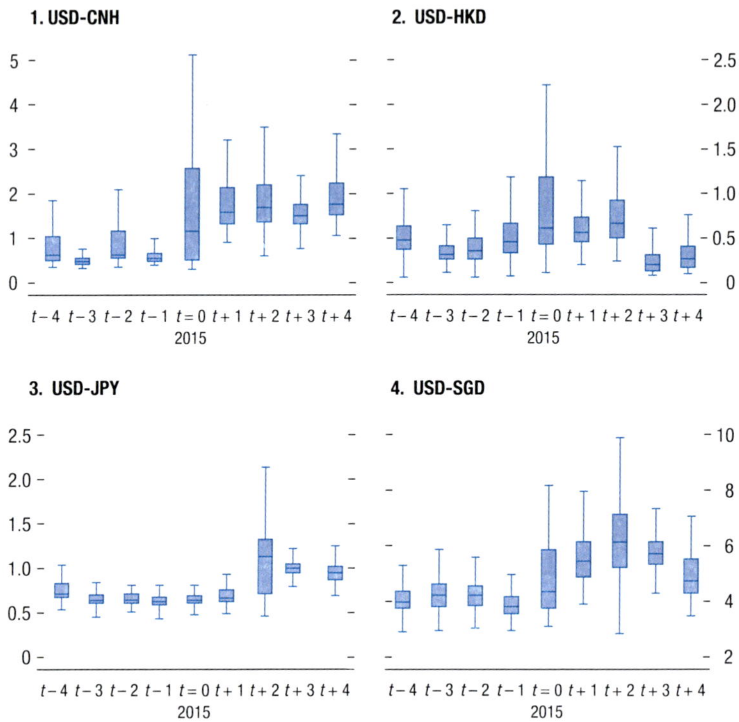

Sources: Electronic Broking Services (EBS); and IMF staff calculations.

Figure 9.1.3: Effective Transaction Costs, Price Impact, and Return Reversal Four Weeks before and after the August 11, 2015, RMB Depreciation
(Basis points)

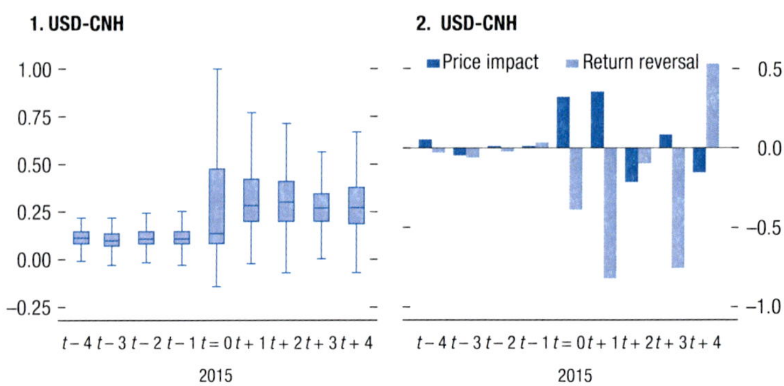

Sources: Electronic Broking Services (EBS); and IMF staff calculations.

three channels, including entrusting the PBC as their agent, using interbank foreign exchange market members as their agents, or participating in the interbank market as foreign members. They can execute foreign exchange trades and hedge risk across all maturities, without prior requirement to hold an underlying RMB asset or demonstrate their need for using the instrument.

- In December 2015 the PBC approved RMB convertibility on the capital account with a prescribed limit of $10 million for the Tianjin, Guangdong, and Fujian free trade zones.
- In February 2016 the authorities announced that overseas commercial banks, insurance firms, pension funds, and other foreign fund managers the PBC considered to be long-term investors would have quota-free access to the onshore CIBM. Under this new regime, foreign institutional investors have to first register with the PBC before they can trade bonds in the CIBM. As such, the PBC is unlikely to grant hedge funds and other short-horizon investors access to the CIBM.

Channels for Repatriating RMB Funds

Amid gradual opening of the capital account, nonresident interest in RMB as a funding and investment currency has been supported by specific steps to allow RMB funds to flow onshore.

- The "Renminbi Qualified Foreign Institutional Investor (R-QFII)" program, introduced in 2011, allows foreign asset managers to channel offshore RMB funds into mainland securities markets, subject to approval measures from two agencies: a license from the China Securities Regulatory Commission and a quota from the State Administration of Foreign Exchange. Market participants note that restrictions on remittances of dividends, minimum holding periods, and "soft" barriers to holding cash onshore deter entry (about 50 percent of overall approved quotas have been used). Nevertheless, familiarity with market conditions seems to mitigate these obstacles in some cases (the Hong Kong SAR R-QFII quota has been fully taken up).
- Since November 2014 individuals and institutional investors with a brokerage account in Hong Kong SAR can trade stocks on the Shanghai stock exchange under the North-bound corridor of the "Shanghai–Hong Kong Stock Connect" scheme, while a South-bound corridor permits trades in the reverse direction (Hong Kong SAR stocks traded via a Shanghai brokerage account). Although take-up from Hong Kong SAR has been significant (about 50 percent of the RMB300 billion North-bound quota has been used as of May 2015), a lack of clarity on the legal framework governing ownership and voting rights for onshore stock appears to have deterred large international institutional investors. Plans are underway, however, to expand the program to cover Shenzhen.

- In May 2015 the PBC announced that offshore clearing banks and nonresident banks with quotas to access the CIBM could borrow in the onshore interbank repo market to fund offshore RMB business. The limit on financing through repos is tied to the bonds held onshore. Greater access to the onshore market should enhance the efficiency of offshore RMB liquidity management, facilitate participation in the Stock Connect program and offshore RMB securities issuance, and more generally advance the cross-border use of RMB.
- In July 2015 a new channel for two-way flows between Hong Kong SAR and the mainland (Mutual Recognition of Funds) was launched with mutual funds in either location permitted to mobilize investments from the other jurisdiction, subject to regulatory approval and an overall quota.
- In September 2015 the PBC approved onshore issuance of RMB securities by foreign financial institutions in the CIBM. Previously only nonfinancial firms were allowed to borrow onshore through the interbank bond market.
- A sequence of measures has also been introduced to facilitate regional corporate treasury operations. Since February 2014 firms registered in the Shanghai Free Trade Zone have been allowed onshore–offshore RMB and U.S. dollar cash transfers between their parent company, subsidiaries, and affiliates. In November 2014 the program was extended to firms registered in pilot cities across the country. These "cash-pooling" or "cash-sweeping" arrangements are intended to help firms centralize and standardize risk management, debt servicing, and working capital transfers. In September 2015 the PBC relaxed the eligibility criteria and thresholds for participation in these arrangements (based on annual sales turnover and how long the firms have been in operation), to give a larger number of firms the option of streamlining intragroup cash transfers and liquidity management. This move permits greater ease of two-way cross-border flows by enabling closer integration of treasury operations among firms in the same corporate group.

Domestic Financial Reforms

The international appeal of RMB securities ultimately rests on the stability of the domestic financial system along with other attributes such as overall macroeconomic performance and access to information on corporate issuers. As part of a broader structural reform agenda to transition China onto a safe and sustainable growth path, the authorities have initiated financial reforms aimed at achieving more market-based pricing, better alignment of risks with returns, and greater efficiency of credit allocation. Key elements have included the liberalization of interest rates, the introduction of a deposit insurance program, measures to strengthen liquidity management, directives to rein in shadow banking, and steps to ensure the RMB exchange rate better reflects market forces. We describe these measures as follows:

- ***Interest rate liberalization.*** Over the past decade, the PBC has gradually dismantled controls over commercial bank interest rate settings. Lending rates were completely liberalized in 2013. Starting in 2012 commercial banks were given greater control over pricing deposits through an increasingly wider band of flexibility above the benchmark. In June 2015 nine large banks were permitted to issue negotiable certificates of deposits to households and nonfinancial corporations at market rates, subject to an annual target balance quota. Deposit rates were formally liberalized in October 2015.
- ***Deposit insurance.*** A nationwide deposit insurance program was established in May 2015. It covers all deposit-taking banking institutions, excluding branches of foreign banks. Deposits up to RMB500,000 (about $80,600) per depositor per bank are insured, which covers 99.6 percent of depositors.
- ***Reserve averaging.*** The authorities have introduced reserve averaging to facilitate liquidity management. From September 2015 compliance with reserve requirements is based on average ratios over a 10-day period. In addition, banks' reserve ratios are not allowed to fall more than 1 percent below their reserve requirements on a daily basis. Because the averaging period is relatively short, this measure is unlikely to have much immediate effect on liquidity management, but the period could be lengthened in the future.
- ***Measures to rein in shadow banking.*** Over the past two years the authorities have taken steps to tighten the regulation and supervision of securities and trust firms, activity in the interbank market, the issuance of high-yield wealth management products, and lending to high-risk sectors of the economy. These measures appear to have had an impact on the composition of credit: the share of intermediation that has been brought back on to bank balance sheets (and is therefore subject to capital and provisioning requirements) has increased significantly in recent months, while off-balance-sheet activity has decelerated sharply.
- ***Toward a more market-determined exchange rate.*** In August 2015 the PBC modified RMB fixing to make it more market driven. Specifically, this decision aimed at correcting the discrepancy between the reference rate exchange rate (also known as the daily fixing or the central parity) and the market spot rate. In December 2015 the PBC announced that the RMB exchange rate would henceforth reference a basket of currencies in an attempt to de-emphasize the de facto link to the U.S. dollar and introduce greater flexibility in bilateral exchange rates.

Cross-Border Payments Infrastructure and Offshore Liquidity

The third set of measures that have supported the growing international use of the RMB (accompanying capital account liberalization and reforms to strengthen macro-financial stability) has focused on cross-border payments. Starting 2003 the PBC has designated close to 20 "clearing banks" (overseas subsidiaries or branches of Chinese banks in the mainland) to provide RMB settlement services. From 2003 to end-2012 there were just two offshore clearing banks, located in Hong Kong SAR and Macao SAR. Since then, clearing banks have been opened in major cities and international financial centers across the world, including most recently in New York.

Clearing banks have access to RMB liquidity from the PBC or through their headquarters in China. In addition, they have access to the onshore interbank lending and bond market, and the foreign exchange market. They thus provide liquidity to the offshore markets, while also allowing the PBC to monitor the RMB flows.

A new RMB Cross-Border Interbank Payment System was launched in October 2015. This vehicle provides a streamlined platform for clearing and settling cross-border RMB payments, and will eventually also provide access to offshore participants and thereby support wider international use of the currency.

Bilateral swap lines provide a liquidity backstop to counterpart central banks. Since 2008 the PBC has signed bilateral swap lines with over 30 foreign central banks, cumulatively worth over RMB3 trillion (Table 9.2). The PBC notes that the purposes of each bilateral currency swap arrangement include promoting bilateral trade and direct investment for economic development of the two countries, supporting domestic financial market stability, and other purposes agreed upon by both parties. Although the purpose of foreign exchange intervention is not explicitly included, a counterpart can convert RMB into other currencies in the offshore market and use the funds for purposes it deems appropriate. Swap agreements are effective for a three-year period from the effective date of agreement and the drawing/usage period is up to 12 months.

Inclusion of the RMB in the SDR Basket

In November 2015 the Executive Board of the IMF concluded that the RMB met all the existing criteria to be included—effective October 1, 2016—in the SDR currency basket (Box 9.2.1 in Annex 9.2). With this decision the RMB joined the U.S. dollar, the euro, the Japanese yen, and the British pound, which until then were the currencies in the basket. This decision meant that the IMF's Board deemed the RMB to be freely usable—that is, used by international members in international transactions and backed by active foreign exchange markets, thus providing some degree of diversification (IMF 2015b). This was a recognition of the progress made not only with RMB internationalization, but also in reforming the Chinese economy. As stated by the IMF's Managing Director, Christine Lagarde, after the completion of the SDR review "to include the RMB in the SDR basket is an important milestone in the integration of the Chinese economy into the global financial system. It is also a recognition of the progress that the Chinese authorities have made in the past years in reforming China's monetary and financial systems. The continuation and deepening of these efforts will bring about a more robust international monetary and financial system, which in turn will support the growth and stability of China and the global economy" (IMF 2015c).

RMB INTERNATIONALIZATION AND THE INTERNATIONAL MONETARY SYSTEM

We now consider the implications of the RMB's internationalization for the international monetary system (IMS) (Annex 9.2 discusses implications for the IMF's SDR).

RMB Internationalization and the IMS

Since World War II the IMS has been dominated by a few currencies, with the U.S. dollar playing a leading role. Many see in the lack of diversification of global reserve currencies a source of weakness and vulnerabilities for the IMS (IMF 2011, 2016b; Zhou 2009). However, others argue that the dominance of a few currencies has served the IMS well, for instance by providing reliable and high-quality safe haven assets in times of financial stress.

Proponents of the more critical view about the current IMS argue that the drawbacks associated with the lack of reserve currency diversification are evident, in, among other things, (1) the liquidity shortages of U.S. dollars at the height of the global financial crisis, which triggered systemic stress in the international banking system with well-known real and financial effects (McGuire and von Peter 2009); (2) the advantage enjoyed by reserve currency issuers in the form of seigniorage revenue and access to cheaper external financing, which in turn allows them to run larger external deficits (Farhi, Gourinchas, and Rey 2011); (3) the spillover effects, excess capital flows, and excessive risk-taking behavior resulting from policies implemented in reserve-issuing currencies; (4) the uphill capital flows resulting from the excess demand for safe global reserve assets in emerging market and developing economies, which undermine fiscal discipline in major reserve currency issuers—a modern manifestation of Triffin's dilemma (Farhi, Gourinchas, and Rey 2011; Landau 2013); or (5) the use of the reserve currency status to pursue objectives unrelated to the proper functioning of the IMS such as the use of the payments system to enforce economic sanctions, and anti-money-laundering and counterterrorist (AML/CFT) regulations (Katzenstein 2015).

For the proponents of these views, a more diversified system with multiple reserve currencies could ease some of the tensions arising in the current IMS. Such a system would spread the advantages enjoyed by few reserve-issuing countries across competing currencies, strengthen incentives for fiscal discipline in reserve-currency-issuing countries, and mitigate systemic vulnerabilities arising from global spillovers and spillbacks of shocks or policy decisions in reserve currency issuers. Thus, a multiple-currency system could facilitate the adjustment of global imbalances and help diversify risks. It is in this context that some believe sustained RMB internationalization could support the stability of the IMS.

However, proponents of the more supportive view of the current IMS express doubts about whether a multiple-currency system would be more robust. For instance, they consider that the financial turmoil in 2008–09 was not just a problem of flight to quality, but rather a flight away from a number of credit markets

Table 9.2. PBC Bilateral Swap Lines with Foreign Central Banks and Monetary Authorities

Country	Size (RMB billion)	Original Start Date	Duration
Total (32)	**3,139**		
Asia (13)	**1,678**		
Hong Kong SAR	400	27-Nov-14	3 years
Korea	360	11-Oct-14	3 years
Singapore	300	7-Mar-13	3 years
Australia	200	8-Apr-15	3 years
Malaysia	180	18-Apr-15	3 years
Indonesia	100	1-Oct-13	3 years
Thailand	70	22-Dec-14	3 years
New Zealand	25	25-Apr-14	3 years
Mongolia	15	21-Aug-14	3 years
Pakistan	10	23-Dec-11	3 years
Sri Lanka	10	16-Sep-14	3 years
Kazakhstan	7	14-Dec-14	3 years
Uzbekistan	0.7	9-Apr-11	3 years
Other (19)	**1,482**		
European Central Bank	350	9-Oct-13	3 years
United Kingdom	200	22-Jun-13	3 years
Canada	200	8-Nov-14	3 years
Brazil	190	26-Mar-13	3 years
Russia	150	13-Oct-14	3 years
Switzerland	150	21-Jul-14	3 years
Argentina	70	18-Jul-14	3 years
United Arab Emirates	35	17-Jan-12	3 years
Qatar	35	3-Nov-14	3 years
South Africa	30	10-Apr-15	3 years
Chile	22	25-May-15	3 years
Ukraine	15	15-May-15	3 years
Turkey	10	21-Feb-12	3 years
Hungary	10	9-Sep-13	3 years
Belarus	7	10-May-15	3 years
Iceland	3.5	11-Sep-13	3 years
Albania	2	12-Sep-13	3 years
Suriname	1	18-Mar-15	3 years
Armenia	1	25-Mar-15	3 years

Source: People's Bank of China.

(such as the interbank market) that would have occurred, independently of the number of currencies in the system. Policy spillovers from reserve currency issuers and the difficulties in managing volatile capital flows in non-reserve-issuing countries are seen mostly as a consequence of poor policies across the world rather than a systemic failure. Moreover, in the context of unconventional monetary policies, any negative spillovers are more than compensated by the positive impact of these policies on domestic and therefore global growth. Skeptics of a multicurrency system also question whether a larger number of reserve currencies would reduce the extent of spillovers and spillbacks, or help improve global risk sharing and enhance the resilience of the current IMS. In their view, a system of multiple reserve currencies could fragment global financial markets and liquidity, and increase global trade and settlement costs, thus undermining the stability and efficiency of the IMS. Therefore, a multiple-currency system could be less efficient and more unstable, as the close substitutability of reserve currencies could result in higher financial volatility.

Irrespective of these views, the increasingly multipolar structure of the global economy—of which China and the RMB internationalization are at center stage—and the ongoing structural shifts, such as the rapid expansion and increasing interconnectedness of global trade and financial markets, could provide conditions for a more diversified system of reserve currencies in the future. In this context, it is important to mitigate risks that could arise under such a system. For sure, the potential for instability highlights the importance of sound and stable policies, especially in reserve-currency-issuing countries. It may also require international coordination to facilitate a smooth transition to a more diversified reserve currency system, including efforts to dampen any accompanying volatility in foreign exchange markets, and ensuring that the global financial safety net is large and broad enough to mitigate potential spillover effects on bystanders (IMF 2016c). In this respect, as we discussed in the previous section, bilateral swap lines similar to the ones put in place between China and other countries provide an important liquidity backstop to counterpart central banks.

CONCLUSIONS

The internationalization of the RMB has advanced substantially over the past decade. Expanding through the offshore market in Hong Kong SAR, the RMB is now widely used as a payment currency for settling China's cross-border trade and direct investment transactions. While the internationalization of the RMB has been supported through broad reforms, all of which will help move China onto a sustainable growth path, the internationalization of the currency is ultimately market driven. Even as RMB use and trading is increasing, it still has a long road ahead before it becomes an international funding currency and acquires the attributes associated with a global reserve currency. Progress in these areas will ultimately determine its broader role in the international monetary and financial system.

ANNEX 9.1. THE ANALYSIS OF CURRENCY TRADING

This annex provides background on currency trading. The analysis relies on high-frequency trading data (one-second basis) provided by the Electronic Broking Services (EBS), a leading platform for spot interdealer trading for most of the currencies in our analysis. EBS reports the best bid and ask quotes, volume indicators, and the direction of trade. All quotes in the database are transactable, and therefore represent the prevalent spot exchange rate. Moreover, since all dealers on the platform are prescreened for credit and bilateral credit lines and are monitored continuously, counterparty risk is negligible when analyzing the data set. These features of the EBS data set make it ideal for an accurate estimation and analysis of liquidity in the foreign exchange market. Although we present results for a large number of currencies, the focus is on the relative characteristics of the CHN.

The analysis covers 12 currency pairs: AUD/USD, EUR/USD, USD/CAD, USD/CHF, USD/CNH, GBP/USD, USD/HKD, USD/JPY, USD/MXN, USD/RUB, USD/SGD, and USD/ZAR from June 5, 2014, to June 5, 2015. This sample was extended to October 6, 2015, for the analysis in Box 9.1.

Since the information for each exchange rate is irregularly spaced and to ensure comparability across currencies, the data are processed to construct second-by-second data and volume series, and then aggregated into minute-by-minute data. For every minute, the transaction price of a deal is used to construct one-minute log returns. Observations between 10 p.m. Fridays and 10 p.m. Sundays Greenwich Mean Time are excluded, since only minimal activity is observed during these nonstandard hours. The data are filtered to eliminate any observation that does not reflect the market activity from the ultra-high-frequency data. This information is then used to construct quantity- and price-based liquidity indicators, which capture the extent of currency trading and the costs of executing trades (that is, *bid-ask spreads* and *effective trading costs*), and gauge the resilience of a currency (*price impact* and *return reversal*).[6,7] Liquidity indicators are constructed using the methodology proposed by Mancini, Ranaldo, and Wrampelmeyer in 2013. Returns in turn are multiplied by 10,000 to obtain basis points as the unit of measurement.

ANNEX 9.2. STRENGTHENING THE ROLE OF THE IMF'S SPECIAL DRAWING RIGHTS

The RMB can also help strengthen the IMS by enhancing the attractiveness of the IMF's official SDR (Box 9.2.1). Specifically, the inclusion of the RMB in the SDR currency basket—effective October 2016—diversifies the basket and makes its composition more representative of the world's major currencies.

The IMF is currently engaged in a broader analysis of the role of the SDR and whether its use can help smooth the functioning of the IMS (IMF 2016a). In addition to examining the broader role of the official SDR, the IMF is also examining alternative SDR concepts, in particular the role of SDR-denominated financial market instruments, or "M-SDRs," which could be both issued and held by any parties; and that of the SDR as a unit of account.

[6]The "return reversal" is the reversal to the "fundamental value" of an exchange rate after a large transaction causes the exchange rate to deviate temporarily from its fundamental value.

[7]Order flow captures the net buy/sell pressure but is not synonymous to trading volume. Order flow refers to *signed* volume. Trades can be signed depending on whether the deal is initiated by the buyer or the seller. The dealer posting the quote is the passive side of the trade. For example, a sale of 10 units by a trader acting on a dealer's quotes represents an order flow of –10, while the volume is 10.

Box 9.2.1. Official Special Drawing Rights

Special drawing rights (SDRs) are a reserve asset created in 1969 and defined under the IMF's Articles of Agreement. It is not a currency, but a potential claim on the holdings of freely usable currencies of participants in the SDR Department (currently all IMF members). SDRs are allocated by the IMF to these participants according to their quotas. Allocations are not targeted based on need or any other consideration, but aim to supplement existing reserve assets. These characteristics imply that it is neither a direct liability of any single economy nor accumulated through a balance of payments surplus.

The SDR can be held on the balance sheets of participant countries in the SDR Department or used unconditionally to obtain a freely usable currency to meet a balance-of-payments need (or for other reserves management purposes). Transactions and holdings are limited to participants in the SDR Department, the General Resources Account within the General Department of the IMF (as a result of transactions between participants and the IMF), and prescribed holders (some international financial institutions and regional central banks; prescribed holders can hold official SDRs (O-SDRs) but do not receive allocations). SDRs are primarily exchanged for freely usable currencies through voluntary exchanges between members, typically mediated by the IMF through the system of Voluntary Trading Arrangements. The designation mechanism remains as a backstop by ensuring that participants with a balance-of-payments need can exchange on demand their SDRs with participants with a strong external position (such participants cannot be obligated to increase their holdings of O-SDRs to more than twice their cumulative allocation), but this mechanism has not been used since 1987.

Since 1974 the O-SDR has been valued based on a basket of currencies, which currently includes the U.S. dollar, euro, Japanese yen, pound sterling, and effective October 1, 2016, the Chinese renminbi. The recent inclusion of the RMB reflects its rising international use and trading. The SDR carries an interest rate determined by the yields on three-month Treasury bills of the component currencies, making its return comparable to that of an asset of the highest credit quality. The SDR mechanism is self-financing and levies charges on allocations, which are then used to pay interest on SDR holdings. If the SDR holdings of a participant are equal to its allocation, the charges are equal to the interest received. If a participant's holdings rise above its allocation, it effectively earns interest on the excess. Conversely, if it holds fewer O-SDRs than allocated, it pays interest on the shortfall.

In its initial analysis, the IMF has highlighted that M-SDRs reduce foreign exchange and interest rate risk relative to single-currency instruments, but there are some drawbacks and challenges (IMF 2016a).[8] The basket nature of M-SDRs would allow the volatility of returns to be lower than for a similar single currency instrument. However, the SDR represents only one of many possible sets of portfolio weights, and issuers or investors could use existing instruments to replicate their preferred weights at a relatively low cost. There are also challenges to market development, including settling and clearing of M-SDR transactions, dealing with potential basket redefinition, and fostering secondary market trading in order to generate liquidity and market depth.

[8]The need for an IMS that relies on an international reserve currency with a stable valuation is one of the key arguments for PBC Governor Zhou's support for the SDR (Zhou 2009).

Taking advantage of the potential benefits of the M-SDR the Chinese authorities have been supporting the issuance of M-SDR bonds, which they also expect will support the process of global reserve diversification and the stability of the IMS. In August 2016 the People's Bank of China (PBC) approved a program for the issuance of SDR 2 billion in SDR-denominated bonds by the World Bank. These bonds, which are tradable in the Chinese interbank market, had an initial offering for SDR 500 million and a maturity of three years, and are payable in yuan upon maturity. This offering is the first in the past 35 years in the world and is expected to be the first step to set an M-SDR bond market in China.

In addition, the Chinese authorities have been supporting the SDR as a unit of account for economic statistics, financial statements, and pricing of transactions. In April 2016 PBC announced the release of foreign reserve data denominated in SDRs. This should help reduce valuation changes caused by large fluctuations in major currencies (IMF 2016a). In this manner the Chinese add to the handful of instances in which the SDR is used as a unit of account. Data are published in SDR terms in the International Financial Statistics, a number of international and regional institutions use the SDR as a unit of account for their balance sheets, and the lending of some multilateral development banks is denominated in SDRs. The SDR is also used to price some transactions with a multinational character—Suez Canal fees and damages, such as lost baggage claims, incurred by air carriers under the Montreal Convention.

REFERENCES

Chinn, Menzie. 2015. "Emerging Market Economies and the Next Reserve Currencies." *Open Economies Review* 26 (1): 155–74.

Eichengreen, Barry. 2011. *Exorbitant Privilege: The Rise and Fall of the Dollar and the Future of the International Monetary System.* Oxford: Oxford University Press.

Farhi, Emmanuel, Pierre-Olivier Gourinchas, and Hélène Rey. 2011. *Reforming the International Monetary System.* Centre for Economic Policy Research.

Frankel, Jeffrey. 2011. "Historical Precedents for Internationalization of the RMB." Council on Foreign Relations, November, New York.

He, Dong, and Robert N. McCauley. 2010. "Offshore Markets for the Domestic Currency: Monetary and Financial Stability Issues." BIS Working Paper 320, September, Bank for International Settlements, Basel.

International Monetary Fund (IMF). 2011. "Strengthening the International Monetary System: Taking Stock and Looking Ahead." Policy Paper, IMF, Washington.

———. 2012. "The Liberalization and Management of Capital Flows: An Institutional View." Policy Paper, International Monetary Fund, Washington.

———. 2015a. "Review of the Method of Valuation of the SDR—Initial Considerations." International Monetary Fund, Washington.

———. 2015b. "Review of the Method of Valuation of the SDR." Policy Paper, International Monetary Fund, Washington.

———. 2015c. "IMF's Executive Board Completes Review of SDR Basket, Includes Chinese Renminbi." Press release of November 30, 2015, International Monetary Fund, Washington. http://www.imf.org/external/np/sec/pr/2015/pr15540.htm

———. 2016a. "Staff Note for the G20: The Role of the SDR—Initial Considerations." July, International Monetary Fund, Washington.

———. 2016b. "Strengthening the International Monetary System—A Stocktaking." Policy Paper, March, International Monetary Fund, Washington.

———. 2016c. "Adequacy of the Global Safety Net." March, International Monetary Fund, Washington.

Jordan, Thomas. 2016. "The Impact of International Spillovers on Swiss Inflation and the Exchange Rate." *Journal of International Money and Finance*, forthcoming.

Katzenstein, Suzanne. 2015. "Dollar Unilateralism: The New Frontline of National Security." *Indiana Law Journal* 90 (1): Article 8.

Kenan, Peter B. 2009. *Currency Internationalization—An Overview*. Princeton, NJ: Princeton University.

Krugman, Paul. 1984. "The International Role of the Dollar: Theory and Prospect." In *Exchange Rate Theory and Practice*, edited by J. Bilson and R. Marston. Chicago: University of Chicago Press.

Landau, Jean-Pierre. 2013. "Global liquidity: Public and Private." Federal Reserve Bank of Kansas City, Proceedings Economic Policy Symposium, Jackson Hole.

Law, Daniel. 2016. "Determinants of Dim Sum Bonds." Working Paper. International Monetary Fund, Washington, forthcoming.

Mancini, L., A. Ranaldo, and J. Wrampelmeyer. 2013. "Liquidity in the Foreign Exchange Market: Measurement, Commonality, and Risk Premiums." *Journal of Finance* LXVIII (5): 1805–41.

Maziad, Samar, Pascal Farahmand, Shengzu Wang, Stephanie Segal, and Faisal Ahmed. 2011. "Internationalization of Emerging Market Currencies: A Balance between Risks and Rewards." SDN/11/17, International Monetary Fund, Washington.

McCauley, Robert. 2005. "Distinguishing Global Dollar Reserves from Official Holdings in the United States." *BIS Quarterly Review*, September, Bank for International Settlements, Basel.

———. 2006. "Internationalising a Currency: The Case of the Australian Dollar." *BIS Quarterly Review*, December, Bank for International Settlements, Basel.

McGuire, Patrick, and Goetz von Peter. 2009. "The U.S. Dollar Shortage in Banking." *BIS Quarterly Review*, March.

People's Bank of China (PBC). 2016. "RMB Internationalization Report." PBC, Beijing.

Zhou, Xiaochuan. 2009. "Reform the International Monetary System." BIS Review 41.

CHAPTER 10

A Rapidly Changing Financial System

NAOMI N. GRIFFIN AND JAMES P. WALSH

China's historically high rate of economic growth has gone hand in hand with even faster financial sector development, and its financial system now contains the world's largest banks, second-largest stock market, and third-largest bond market. Ten years ago the system was relatively conservative and almost completely dominated by banking, but major fiscal stimulus after the global financial crisis and an innovative and competitive financial sector have changed that picture.

Yet, with the wide range of financial products that has emerged, the system has become much harder to understand. And the increasingly complex financial system calls for constant effort to upgrade financial sector regulation and supervision.

This chapter reviews the financial system overall, scrutinizes the banking sector, and looks at the rapidly growing nonbank sector and products. It then discusses the equity, bond, and insurance sectors, in that order. The chapter concludes with policy recommendations.

OVERVIEW OF THE FINANCIAL SECTOR

Despite the changes of recent years, China's banking sector continues to dominate the financial system. Credit is still primarily channeled through banks. In addition, many years of high economic growth, a high savings rate, and a closed capital account (see Chapter 8), have supported the sector's rapid expansion. Between 2010 and 2015 the size of banking sector assets doubled from RMB95 trillion (234 percent of GDP) to RMB199 trillion (295 percent of GDP) (Figure 10.1). By asset value and Tier 1 capital, China's banks now include four of the world's five largest.

Within the sector, large, state-owned commercial banks dominate, while state-owned commercial banks' dominance has declined amid ever-increasing competition for funding. The following are the main types of institution:

Thanks to Simon Gray, Alfred Schipke, and Alison Stuart for comments. Zhe Qi, Angelin Oey, and Naixi Wang provided excellent research assistance.

Figure 10.1. Financial System Structure

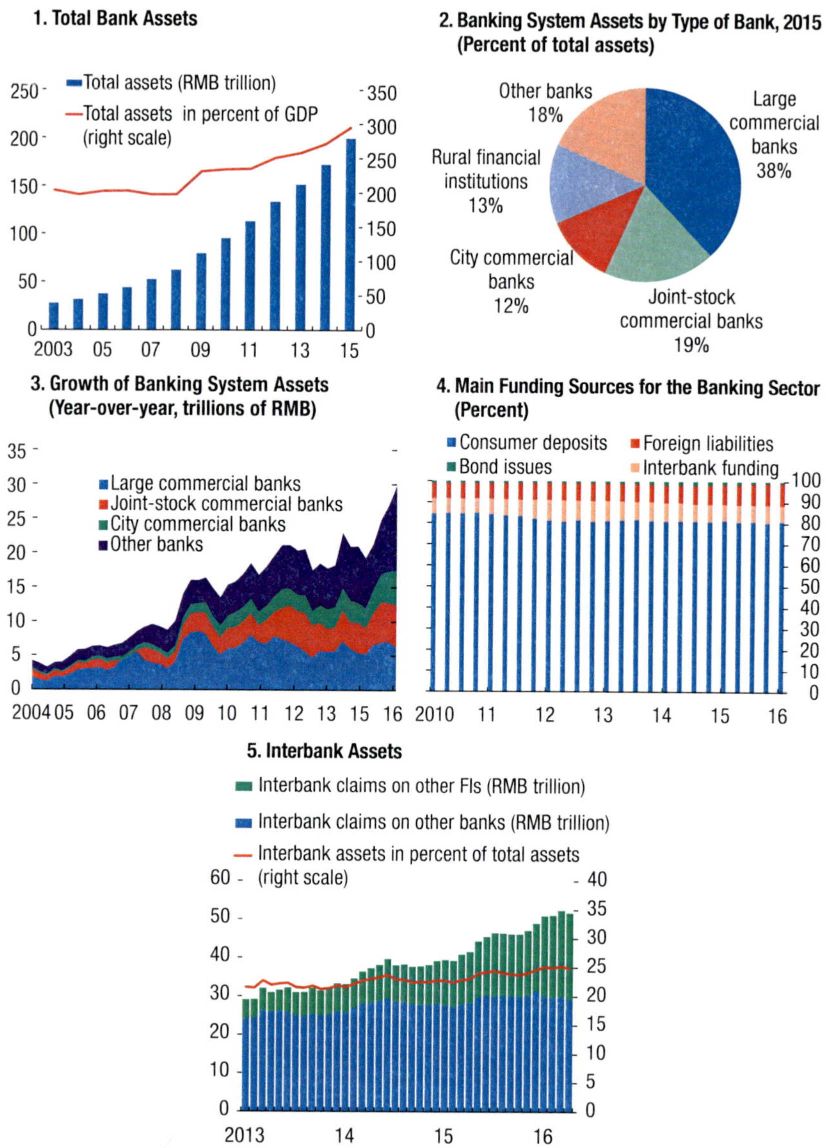

Sources: CEIC; China Banking Regulatory Commission; Morgan Stanley Research; People's Bank of China; WIND; and IMF staff calculations.

- *State-owned banks.* The big four (four largest banks) are the Industrial and Commercial Bank of China, China Construction Bank, Agricultural Bank of China, and Bank of China. The big four continue to dominate the banking sector, although their combined share of total sector assets declined from 50 percent at the end of 2010 to 40 percent at the end of 2015. All four are publicly traded onshore and in Hong Kong SAR, but the Chinese government—through either the Ministry of Finance or Central Huijin Investment, a state-owned investment company—remains the majority shareholder in all of these institutions. In addition, the Bank of Communications is structurally similar, but given its somewhat smaller size, observers normally refer to the big four, rather than the big five.
- *Joint-stock commercial banks (JSCBs).* JSCBs constitute the next tier down. Twelve such banks jointly accounted for 18.6 percent of total bank assets at the end of 2015.[1] JSCBs, with a wider range of controlling shareholders, have a more distant relationship to the central government than the big four. Most of these banks have expanded beyond their initial regional home bases to operate nationally.
- *Development and policy banks.* China Development Bank and two policy banks—Agricultural Development Bank and the Export-Import Bank of China—accounted for roughly 10 percent of total bank assets at the end of 2015. These banks provide loans to rural and urban areas on projects related to economic, trade, and infrastructure development. They are fully state owned.
- *City-commercial and rural banks.* The banking system includes an array of smaller, third-tier city-commercial and rural banks. The 145 city-commercial, 468 rural, and 122 rural cooperative banks have assets amounting to 25 percent of the banking sector. Except for those in big cities, such as the Bank of Beijing and Bank of Shanghai, they are generally small but have strong local networks. The ownership of these banks also varies: many have extensive, or even majority, private ownership, but local governments often play a key role through key ownership stakes or indirect influence.
- *Foreign banks.* Forty-two locally incorporated foreign banking institutions operate in China, but their combined assets are small, accounting for less than 5 percent of total bank assets.

Meanwhile, nonbank financial intermediaries—trusts, fund management companies, and fund subsidiaries—have also grown rapidly in number and assets in recent years. These intermediaries have collaborated with banks to channel credit to sectors or borrowers that usually face difficulty gaining credit through bank loans. The ownership of these firms varies, with many privately and some

[1]The 12 JSCBs are China Merchants Bank, Industrial Bank, Shanghai Pudong Development Bank, China CITIC Bank, China Minsheng Bank, China Everbright Bank, Hua Xia Bank, China Guangfa Bank, Ping An Bank, Evergrowing Bank, Zhe Shang Bank, and Bo Hai Bank.

publicly owned or with controlling shares held by local or provincial governments. They include the following forms:

- *Trusts.* Sixty-eight trust companies collectively managed RMB16 trillion in assets as of the end of 2015 (KPMG 2015). They offer three main products: single fund trusts, assembled or collective trusts, and property management trusts.[2] Trust companies still dominate nonbank financial activities, although the growth of their assets under management moderated recently (Figure 10.2).
- *Securities companies.* As of the end of 2015, 125 securities companies collectively managed RMB6 trillion in assets, mostly on behalf of clients, and with relatively small balance sheets. Aside from their normal brokerage activities, they also provide credit to the financial system through two types of asset management plans (directed or collective). The size of directional asset management plans, in particular, has grown in recent years.
- *Fund management companies.* Also as of the end of 2015 the 101 fund management companies provided products that are largely divided into two types: public offering funds (mutual funds), with RMB8 trillion under management, and special accounts, with RMB4 trillion.
- *Fund management subsidiaries.* First established in 2012, fund management companies' subsidiaries have expanded rapidly, with 78 fund management subsidiaries having RMB8.6 trillion by the end of 2015, up from less than RMB1 trillion in 2013. Fund management subsidiaries offer one-to-one (directional) and one-to-many (multiclient) products.
- *Asset management companies.* The four asset management companies (AMCs)—Cinda, Huarong, Great Wall, and Orient—were established in 1999 to purchase nonperforming loans from large banks. They have expanded on their core business managing distressed assets to provide a wide range of financial products. In addition, concerns about rising nonperforming loans have led the government to issue provincial-level AMC licenses in more than 20 provinces (Box 10.1).

The links among these entities have become increasingly tight and complex. Competition for deposits and regulatory arbitrage have motivated banks to cooperate with nonbank financial institutions in search for higher yields.[3] Accordingly, banks directly or indirectly finance a large portion of investment products created by nonbank financial intermediaries. Midtier listed banks and smaller unlisted

---

[2]Single trust funds match single investors (normally banks or wealth management products, which can themselves have one or many investors) with specific projects, whereas collective trust funds raise funds from multiple investors and allocate them to multiple projects.

[3]Originally, banks used trust companies to invest in restricted, high-risk, and high-return projects, but the landscape has changed continuously in response to various regulatory measures aimed to control shadow banking activities. In recent years, securities companies, fund management companies, and fund management companies' subsidiaries have expanded in size to channel funds from banks and other investors to high-risk projects, equity, and bonds.

Figure 10.2. Financial System Structure

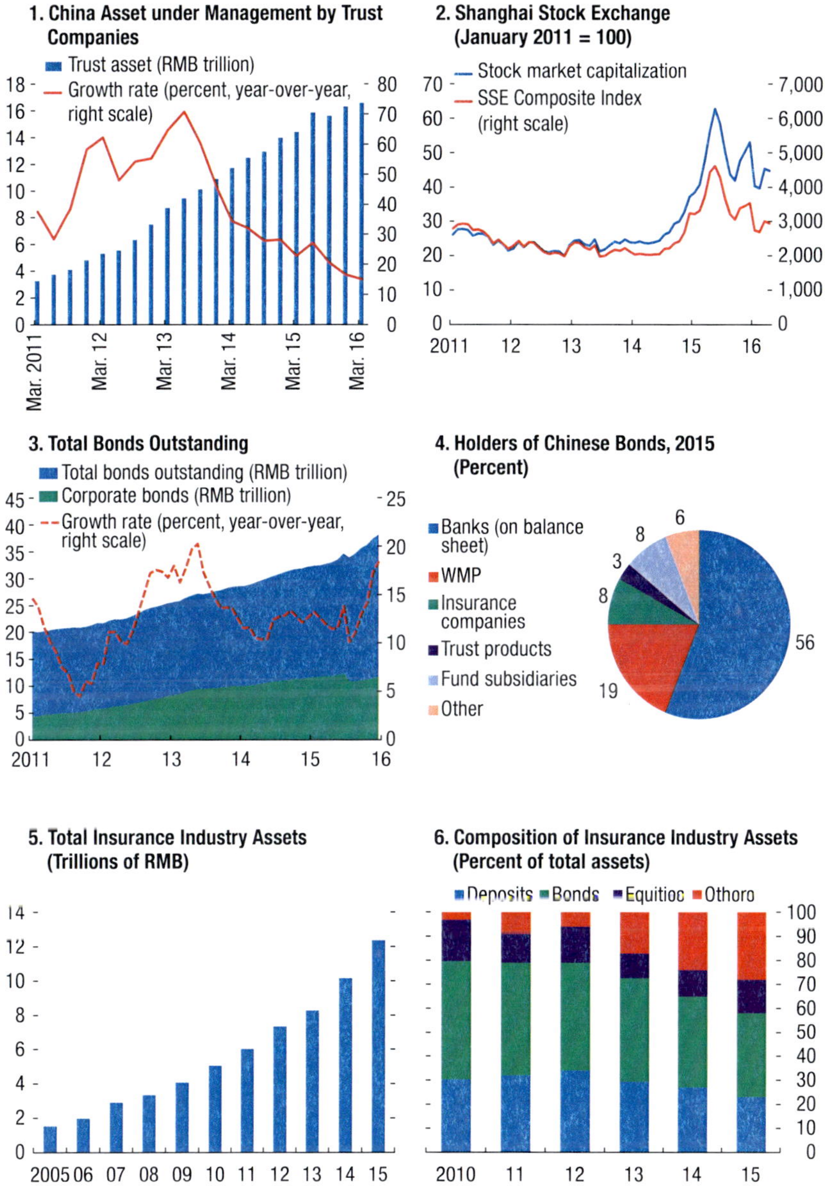

Sources: CEIC; China Banking Regulatory Commission; China Insurance Regulatory Commission; Morgan Stanley Research; People's Bank of China; WIND; and IMF staff calculations.
Note: SSE = Shanghai stock exchange; WMP = wealth management product.

Box 10.1. Bad Loans in China

Not all troubled debt in China is eventually classified as nonperforming. Chinese banking supervision recognizes several categories of loan quality, with nonperforming being the lowest, though these categories are to some extent qualitative. In addition to nonperforming loans, some loans with credit risk are described as "special mention" loans, some of which are eventually reclassified as nonperforming loans (NPL). Loans to companies for which recovery is deemed to be impossible are classified as NPL, but this is the end of a long process, and not all loans remain on the balance sheet for this classification.

To avoid this process, banks employ various techniques for minimizing at-risk exposures on their balance sheets. Regulations on bank lending are relatively strict, but those on trust companies and some other lenders are significantly looser. In some cases, banks will set up a single-unit trust that lends money to the company. The bank can then invest itself in the trust, booking it as an investment. While regulations forbid this procedure with a bank's own loans, banks can invest through wealth management products in collective trusts, which they can then buy.

Once a loan is nonperforming, banks have limited options. But over the past decade, an important option has been selling NPLs to asset management companies (AMCs). During the banking crisis beginning in the 1990s, China established the four large AMCs discussed earlier in this chapter. These companies still buy troubled assets from bank balance sheets, but are reluctant to do so at face value, while banks are reluctant to recognize losses, reducing the flow of assets into AMCs. To cover their own cost of capital and operations absent the influx of new troubled assets, AMCs have increasingly moved into other industries, such as fund management. The perception that competition in this sector is insufficient is one reason why provincial AMCs have been established in recent years. The ownership and capitalization structure of these AMCs differ across provinces, with some having large ownership shares by local governments or their holdings companies, and others having more private sector participation. While flows so far have been small, these AMCs increasingly bid against the four national AMCs for troubled debt, but the long-term viability of their business model is not yet clear.

Two more transparent methods for addressing at-risk debt gained increasing prominence in 2016. First, while it is illegal for banks to directly hold shares of companies, this rule has been relaxed in an increasing number of cases in which debt has been swapped for equity. In other countries this has been a successful way to improve the management of companies and work out the stock of debt. In China's case, however, many potential participants are state-owned enterprises (SOEs); changing management would thus have to be part of overall SOE reform. Second, official securitization of troubled loans has been discussed, though there are fewer cases as yet. Successful securitization depends on transparent pricing and finding a market to purchase such debts. The experience of securitized low-quality mortgage debt in the United States before the global financial crisis shows that this process carries substantial risks.

banks have particularly high exposure to investment products issued by trust companies (such as trust beneficiary rights), as well as asset management plans (such as directional asset management plans) issued by securities companies and fund management companies and their subsidiaries. Banks also have exposure to shadow investment products through their off-balance-sheet wealth management products (WMPs)—investment vehicles that offer fixed rates of return well above deposit rates (that were previously regulated). WMPs also allow banks to get around "window guidance," which restricts banks from extending loans to certain risky sectors.

Capital markets have grown in recent years, although their role in the financial sector is still relatively small compared with other major countries. Bond and equity markets have undergone recent phases of rapid growth and their importance in the financial sector has increased over time. The total combined market capitalization of China's mainland exchanges more than doubled between 2010 and 2015, from RMB26 trillion to RMB53 trillion, and is now the world's second largest. Similarly, the outstanding balance of corporate bonds increased from RMB4 trillion in 2010 to RMB14 trillion in 2015. Banks hold the majority of bonds, both on balance sheet and through WMPs.

Finally, insurance companies are also growing rapidly—total insurance industry assets increased from RMB5 trillion in 2010 to RMB12 trillion by the end of 2015. In addition, insurance companies have been shifting their assets from bank deposits or bond investment to equity or other investments.

New forms of lending—such as peer-to-peer (P2P) lending platforms and internet banking (called fintech)—are emerging rapidly. Development of these new lending platforms has stirred technological innovation while alarming regulators after a number of large failures. Each platform is discussed below:

- *P2P*. P2P platforms have grown very rapidly since 2007, although growth has slowed recently due to a number of fraud cases and stricter regulations. The number of P2P platforms increased from 10 in 2010 to more than 2,500 in 2015. The loan balance increased from RMB100 billion at the end of 2014 to RMB440 billion at the end of 2015. Borrowers include both small and medium-sized enterprises (SMEs) and retail customers. Aside from interest charges, P2P platforms also charge borrowers a transaction fee, which depends on the borrower's credit risk. P2P lenders have offered very high returns—initially above 20 percent—to attract investors. However, yields on offer have fallen since mid-2013, and reached about 10 percent by the end of 2015. While some P2P platforms have institutional investors, most platforms work with retail investors. The average duration of P2P loans was about seven months at the end of 2015. Most P2P platforms, in principle, do not take any credit risk (as they simply match borrowers with lenders), although they have often worked with guarantee companies and other lenders to protect investors' interests.
- *Internet banking*. Several leading e-commerce companies have created subsidiaries to provide financial services to their consumers and SMEs that provide products. Chinese e-commerce giant Alibaba has created its financial subsidiary—Ant Financial—to provide internet and mobile-phone banking services. Alipay—a commonly used payment service in China—allows consumers to shop online, transfer money, buy services, and even make investments with a small amount of money through Yu'ebao, a wealth management fund affiliated with Alipay. The growth of Yu'ebao demonstrates the speed China's financial system can develop. Following its inception in mid-2013, within

one year Yu'ebao had 85 million customers. Today, Alipay overall has more than 450 million users (the largest in the world), and Ant Financial was valued (after a private fundraising round) at about $40 billion in early 2016. Similarly, Chinese e-commerce company JD.com established a financial subsidiary—JD Finance—to extend financial services including consumer finance for online purchases; loans to the suppliers of products, which are often SMEs; crowdfunding; and wealth management. JD Finance had raised RMB7 billion in financing as of early 2016.

BANKS: LENDING AND DEPOSITS

The composition of assets and loans varies among different types of banks:[4]

- *State-owned banks.* The big four banks have a larger share of mortgage and corporate loans and a smaller share of interbank loans than other types of banks (Figure 10.3). These banks have traditionally provided loans to large and medium-sized enterprises, especially state-owned enterprises (SOEs) (see Chapter 11). A large share of loans goes to the transportation and utilities sectors and the manufacturing industry. Industrial Commercial Bank of China's loans are particularly highly concentrated in the transportation and utility sectors (roughly a quarter of its loan portfolio).
- *JSCBs.* These as a whole have a smaller share of corporate and mortgage loans than the big four banks, but have a larger share than city-commercial and rural banks. The shares of consumer loans and investment in securities have increased. These banks generally provide a larger share of their corporate loans to SMEs compared with the big four banks. The loan portfolio of JSCBs seems to be more evenly distributed across industries than that of the big four banks—JSCBs generally a provide a higher share of loans to the real estate and construction sectors, and wholesale and retail trade.
- *City-commercial and rural banks.* City-commercial and rural banks have a smaller share of corporate, mortgage, and consumer loans than their bigger counterparts. Instead, they hold a larger share of their total interest-generating assets—roughly one-third—in securities. City-commercial banks, in particular, have invested more aggressively than their larger counterparts in nonstandard credit assets to expand their businesses amid fierce competition. These banks play a more vital role than their bigger counterparts in making loans to local micro and small enterprises. Having an advantage in knowing local businesses, their loan portfolios have a relatively high exposure to wholesale and retail trade.

Several other salient considerations deserve attention:

---

[4]In all cases, however, foreign currency exposure tends to be small. Even among the big four, which are globally systemic banks, assets are overwhelmingly in domestic currency and overseas operations are relatively small.

Figure 10.3. Bank Funding

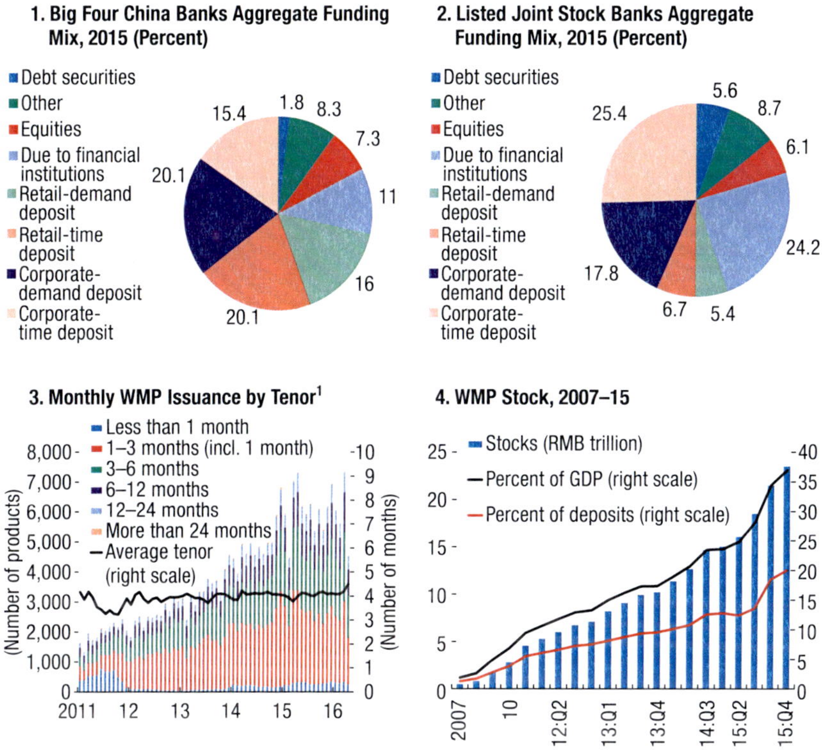

Sources: CEIC; China Banking Regulatory Commission; Morgan Stanley Research; People's Bank of China; WIND; and IMF staff calculations.
Note: WMP = wealth management product.
[1] Sample covers all products issued by banks covered in WIND.

The average rate of return on assets is higher for smaller banks. In the first half of 2015 average return on assets ranged from 1.1–1.3 percent for the big four banks, and was about 1 percentage point higher for a select group of JSCBs and city-commercial banks. Higher average return on assets for these banks are produced by several factors: (1) higher rate of return for loans, (2) higher rate of return on investment (including financial assets held under resale agreement and receivable investment), and (3) lower share of deposits at the central bank (which has the lowest yield).

Bank funding depends heavily on deposits, supported by high domestic savings, although the share of deposits in total bank funding has declined recently. China's share of deposits in total banking liabilities is high, at above 70 percent at the end of 2015, or 185 percent of GDP, and is among the highest in the Group of Twenty countries. Total deposits in the banking system increased from RMB68 trillion in 2010 to RMB125 trillion in 2015. At the same time, the share of deposits in banking liabilities declined from 80 percent in 2010 to 73 percent in 2015. In particular, interbank funding, including nonbank financial intermediaries, increased from 12 percent of total funding in 2010 to 17 percent in 2015, concentrated mostly in JSCBs and other smaller banks. This has been supported by the rapid development of an interbank market, discussed below.

Large state-owned commercial banks generally have an advantage over joint stock and city-commercial banks in securing lower-cost demand deposits. The funding sources for the big four banks are largely retail and corporate deposits, while JSCBs rely less on retail deposits and more on corporate and interbank and nonbank funding. The access to cheaper retail funding sources has allowed the funding costs for the big four banks to remain below the costs for JSCBs and other smaller banks.

Because the big four are able to attract deposits at lower cost, joint-stock and some other banks have relied on WMPs to fund growing balance sheets. To compete with the big four, JSCBs and city-commercial and rural banks have used WMPs to attract funding. Before the formal liberalization of deposit rates, WMPs allowed those smaller banks to offer rates above deposit ceilings on their short-term investments. Those banks, in turn, have targeted higher-yielding and often unsecured lending to offset the higher cost of funding. Even though the liberalization of bank deposit rates in late 2015 allowed banks to compete for deposits more freely, banks seem to continue to take advantage of WMPs to invest in high-risk and high-return sectors, since window guidance and higher capital and provisioning requirements work to discourage direct lending.

NONBANK LOANS AND OTHER PRODUCTS

The 2008–09 global financial crisis saw the volume of nontraditional financial assets explode in China. Shifts in regulatory and supervisory priorities, caps on interest rates, and regulatory arbitrage as the authorities clamped down on risky products and excessive credit growth in nonfavored sectors had the effect of shifting the financial system away from traditional lending (Figure 10.4).[5] This has accelerated more recently as banks have become more concerned about the rising number of defaults in the bond market and restructurings of bank loans, further driving weaker firms toward the nonbank financial sector. For these reasons, much of the new debt created in China in recent years has either come from nontraditional lenders or is bank lending that has been transformed through financial engineering into investment assets. These assets are held either directly on bank balance sheets or on the balance sheets of special purpose vehicles financed by investment products sold by banks.

[5]"Traditional lending" in this case refers to loans held on the loan book of banks' balance sheets. Lending has instead been shifting toward loans repackaged and held in the investments book of balance sheets, held in off-balance-sheet special purchase vehicles, or moved away from the banking sector entirely.

Figure 10.4. Nonstandard Lending and the Nonbank Financial System

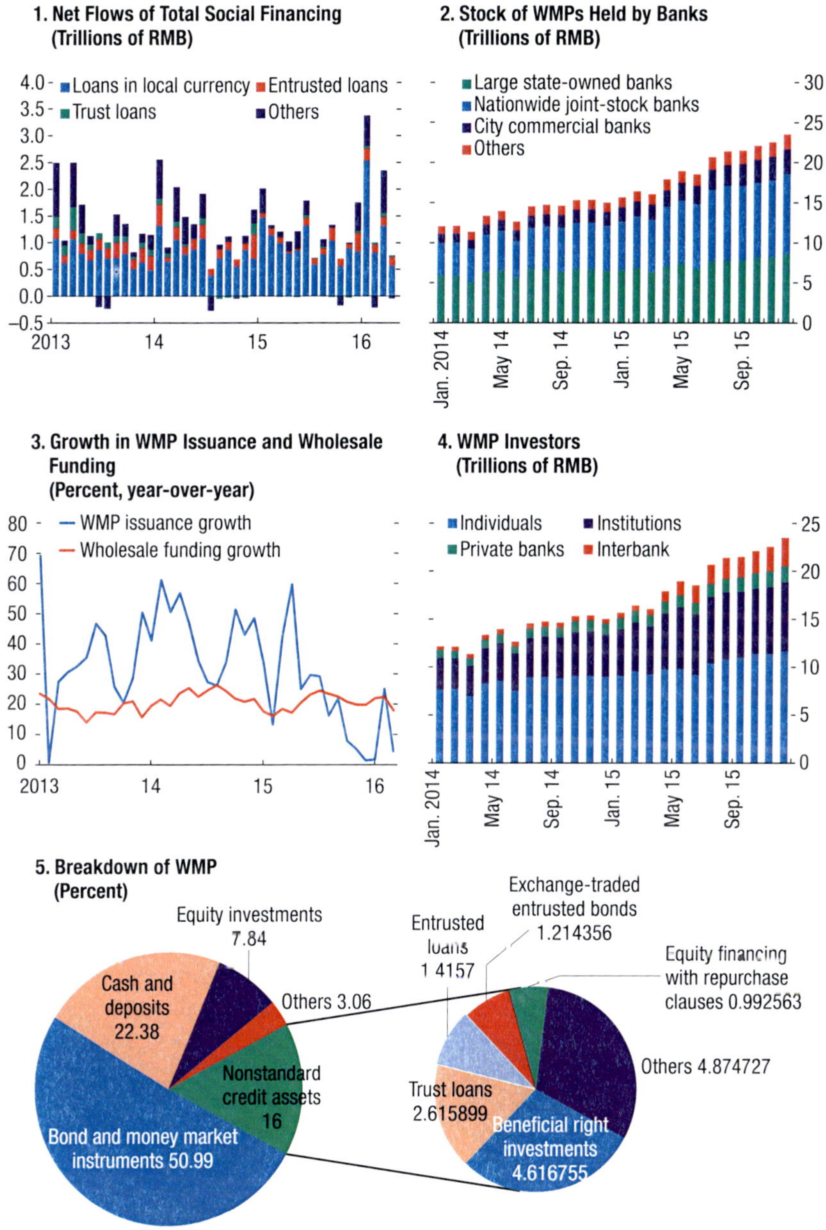

Sources: Bloomberg L.P.; CEIC; national authorities; WIND; and IMF staff calculations.
Note: WMP = wealth management product.

The result is a complex and opaque system linking borrowers and lenders. Much of the borrowing under this system has gone to local government investment projects, overcapacity sectors, and real estate. These borrowers are generally rationed from direct bank lending, due to either restrictions on lending to unfavored sectors, capital, or provisioning requirements, or (in the past) limits on loan-to-deposit ratios. These incentives have pushed lending to these industries off of banks' loan books. In many cases, loans to these industries have been repackaged into investments, which banks either sell to clients or keep on their own balance sheets. Funds for these investments until recently largely came from WMPs, but wholesale funding through China's rapidly growing interbank market has grown in recent years. Between borrowers and lenders are a web of complex intermediaries, whose financial links to banks and borrowers vary widely.

An important systemic vulnerability of this arrangement is its direct link to the banking sector. Banks are estimated to have as much as RMB16 trillion of these nonstandard assets on their balance sheets, almost one-third of their overall assets, and off-balance-sheet exposures are also very large. While supervisory rules require banks to treat these assets for most purposes as carrying the same risks as the underlying products, this is not always straightforward (for example senior tranches of products with minimal credit history or assets with implicit guarantees). In some cases, this can result in underprovisioning or inadequate capital coverage. Liquidity risks from such products are also a serious concern, as the nontransparency of the system, widespread perception of implicit guarantees, and the strong presence of retail investors, who do not expect losses, raise the risk of runs. Deposit insurance can mitigate this risk to bank balance sheets,[6] but a loss of confidence in WMPs or other products indirectly linked to banks could lead to a run in these areas, with unforeseeable results. Finally, the complexity and opacity of these products present a serious challenge for bank supervisors, who must ensure that increasingly complex structured products are adequately provisioned for.

Lower-quality creditors appear to be the main borrowers under this system. As in many countries, the highest-quality borrowers issue bonds and tend to rely on larger banks. In China, state-owned and other very large enterprises are seen as the highest-quality borrowers, with joint-stock and city-commercial banks instead lending to local government SOEs and private companies with good records. Nonbank borrowers tend to be companies rationed away from this system, either due to credit quality or due to regulations that limit lending to unfavored sectors, such as real estate, overcapacity industries, or infrastructure. These form the bulk of borrowers in the nonbank system.

A key group of borrowers under this system is special purpose vehicles established by local governments to finance infrastructure projects. A major part of China's stimulus package during the global financial crisis was infrastructure investment pursued at the local government level. China's local governments have

[6]China's deposit insurance system was formally established on May 1, 2015.

the main spending responsibility, but the central government has the main authority for collecting taxes (see Chapter 6 on local governments). As a result, during the global financial crisis, local governments were forced to find new ways to mobilize resources for infrastructure investment. So-called local government financing vehicles (LGFVs) were a primary tool. These included many variations, but the most common was special purpose vehicles, which raised funds through bank WMPs and lent the funds to an infrastructure firm that paid off the loans after being paid by the government. Regulations gradually clamped down on this system beginning in 2014, and some provisions of the 2015 Budget Law (aimed at eliminating local government guarantees of special purpose vehicles and at shifting infrastructure investment toward public-private partnerships that take their risks) were intended to end this practice.

Many types of firms have moved into this disintermediated financial system. As deposit rate liberalization squeezed bank margins and the slowing economy reduced profits elsewhere, firms looked to the rising equity market and continued rapid growth of credit, and more firms began to move into financial services. The expanding availability of wholesale funding has reduced the importance of bank deposits in financial intermediation, catalyzing this process. The range of firms now involved in the system includes the following:

- Fund subsidiaries of banks, which have about 10 percent of GDP under management, and issue WMPs to investors and then purchase various products.
- Trust companies, which establish entities that invest in the securities market. These exposures are largely off the balance sheets of trust companies and are financed through wealth management products set up by banks.
- National AMCs, which have moved into asset management as the profitability of their traditional business of disposing of troubled bank assets has declined.
- Insurance companies, which invest in complex products to increase returns.

Despite this diversity and range of financial entities engaging in lending, a number of common threads emerge:

- *Nonbank intermediaries in general assume no credit risk for the loans they make.* Most intermediaries act only as channels for investment, taking funds from institutional investors, banks, or high-net-worth individuals and investing them in products. However, some high-risk products are directly sold to retail investors, or are repackaged or tranched into assets that can then be sold, with senior tranches going on bank balance sheets and equity tranches to high-net-worth individuals or institutional investors. Some (for example, trust companies and securities companies) have their own balance sheets, but these tend to be dwarfed by off-balance-sheet exposures that the nonbank financial institutions do not guarantee.
- *Complexity and opacity add to regulatory challenges.* Banks' WMPs in many cases turn over rapidly; banks' on-balance-sheet investment products can include a wide range of direct loans, restructured fixed-income products, or equity investments in special purpose vehicles; and interbank borrowing is

short term, over the counter, and complex. While supervision aims to minimize maturity mismatches and ensure adequate capital coverage for banks' risks, this complexity is highly challenging.

- *Mispricing of credit risk.* Companies with weak profitability or in overcapacity sectors and local governments constrained by the 2015 Budget Law would still like to (or need to) borrow. The expectation that the central government will bail out local governments creates a perception that they are low-risk borrowers. Moreover, companies deemed strategic by local governments can also continue to borrow, despite poor financial prospects.
- *Regulatory arbitrage is an important motivation.* As banks move from investing deposits in loans to investing funds raised through WMPs or the wholesale market into investment products, the regulatory framework can shift. In some cases, capital or provisioning coverage may be insufficient, or, for off-balance-sheet WMPs, perceived guarantees can raise reputational risks that may lead to losses. Even in cases where banks do not carry these exposures on balance sheet, as in the case of WMPs or assets held by bank subsidiaries, the fact that retail investors are almost never made to bear losses can create a self-fulfilling equilibrium where banks, for reputational purposes, may feel obligated to bail out investors in nonguaranteed products.

Supervisors in China are aware of these risks, and have moved to contain them (Table 10.1). These measures have aimed to improve risk management by banks, reduce leverage and complexity in structured products, limit the risks from WMPs, reduce maturity mismatches, and eliminate the implicit guarantees (perceived or otherwise) that pervade the sector. But the sector is extremely innovative and keeping up with the constant pace of transformation, and creative exploitation of loopholes has been challenging.

Intermediating Products

Trust Loans and Products

Trust companies are important providers of loans. They began to grow rapidly following the global financial crisis, as banks' ability to lend was constrained and concerns rose about infrastructure investment. Trusts were seen as a way to conserve bank capital but continue to support investment.

Trusts were a crucial link to the first phase of shadow banking in 2013. They often were established to support LGFVs and other special purpose entities that allowed financial activity to migrate off bank (or trust) balance sheets. These items, generally financed by banks' wealth management products, could invest in infrastructure, equity, bad loans, or other products, and often provided guaranteed rates of return well above regulated deposit rates. Many of the excesses of these products were quickly reined in, however: guaranteed products are now required to be on banks' balance sheets,

Here, too, supervisors have moved to rein in risks. Beginning in 2013 regulations on capital requirements for trust companies—even on assets for which they

Table 10.1. Supervisory Measures Aimed at Reducing Shadow Banking Risks

Date	Measure
July 2014	The China Banking Regulatory Commission (CBRC) sets tighter rules on wealth management products (WMPs); establishment of department for supervising WMPs; new rules on trading.
December 2014	CBRC encourages banks to invest WMP funds directly, rather than through nonbank financial institutions.
	CBRC and the Ministry of Finance announce plans to establish an insurance fund for the trust sector, financed through funds from trust companies.
	Asset Management Association of China announces draft proposals to discourage securitization of local government debt.
January 2015	CBRC tightens rules on entrusted loans by disallowing firms' onlending of bank loans and prohibiting borrowers from investing in financial assets such as WMPs, bonds, and equity.
April 2015	China Securities Regulatory Commission (CSRC) bans brokerage firms from using "umbrella trusts" (considered high leverage) for margin trading in the stock market.
May 2015	Deposit insurance scheme implemented May 1. Seen as prerequisite for interest rate liberalization, which reduced demand for WMPs.
June 2015	CSRC proposes cap of margin trading and short selling business conducted by each securities firm at four times their net capital.
July 2015	CSRC eases margin rules on collateral of borrowers, and expands the permissible range of securities firms' funding channels.
September 2015	CSRC intensifies crackdown on less-regulated margin financing activities such as umbrella trusts and private financing.
January 2016	CBRC steps up scrutiny of banks' bill finance operations, which had been misused to circumvent regulatory requirements.
March 2016	CBRC steps up scrutiny of asset management companies to discourage concealment of banks' credit risks through, for example, repurchase agreements.
	CBRC issues a directive to improve risk management at trust companies, including by limiting leverage on stock market products.
April 2016	CSRC proposes modifications to risk-control indicators of securities firms to help address emerging risks in the industry.
May 2016	CBRC issues guidance on banks' loan-beneficiary rights transfers, to curb banks' transferring loans off balance sheet without full risk transfer, and to enhance transparency of nonperforming loans on their books.

Source: Moody's Investors Service.

assume no formal credit risk—began to fully bind. Additional regulations on trust companies' liquidity have further reduced their ability to lend. This, unfortunately, occurred as the stock market began to surge rapidly, encouraging trust companies to shift their investments into equities.

Nevertheless, trusts are still important players in the nonbank lending system. With balance sheets increasingly tightly supervised, most trust-related exposures are off-balance-sheet products. These are generally single-unit trusts, which match a single investor (a high-net-worth investor or institutional investor, though WMPs are often classified as institutional investors) with a pool of loans. These account for about 57 percent by value of total trust company products. In these cases, credit risks may be high if the quality of the portfolio is low, but with only a single investor, the risks of contagion are contained. On the other hand, trusts also sell collective trusts, in which many investors buy into a pool of loans or other assets. These products—constituting about 32 percent of trust company products—may also carry high credit risk, but here liquidity risk is more salient than with single-investor trusts, since investors in a nontailored product may not roll over funding, or if permitted, may withdraw their investments in a stress episode. The trust company may then have to step in, which, if such withdrawals were widespread, could lead to systemic liquidity problems.[7]

Investment Receivables

Investment receivables is a broad category that includes many products for which the owner has residual profit rights. These are normally held as an "investment" item on banks' balance sheets, but are occasionally held and classified as securities repurchased through the interbank market or as reverse repos, with bankers' acceptances used as collateral. Two of the most common investment receivable items are trust beneficiary rights and directed asset management plans. These products are similar, but trust beneficiary rights are investment products sold by trusts, while directional asset management plans are sold by securities companies.

To construct these products, a trust company or other nonbank financial intermediary makes a loan to a borrower, occasionally with credit enhancement provided by a bank. The nonbank financial institution packages these loans into an investment product and sells it to a bank, potentially the same one that provided credit enhancement for the original underlying. If the resulting trust beneficiary right/directional asset management plan is entered on a bank's balance sheet, supervisory rules require it to carry the same risk weight as the underlying product, though provisioning requirements are significantly lower. Investment products also did not count against the implicit quota set by loan-to-deposit ratios; these are now gone, but it is not yet clear how new liquidity requirements will affect incentives to hold them.

However, a second step of financial innovation with investment receivables can further reduce capital coverage. By structuring receivables and having the tranches rated, nonbank financial institutions can sell the banks products with a lower risk weight than a package of unstructured corporate loans. Corporate loans themselves—and thus under supervisory rules, any asset composed of such loans—would attract a risk weight of 100 percent on banks' balance sheets. But a nonbank financial institution can repackage the loans into trust plans, asset management plans, or other innovative financial products. If the senior tranche of these repackaged products can be rated at AA- or higher, the resulting investment receivable can be brought on banks' balance sheets at a risk weight of only 20 percent. This may be a reasonable level of capital coverage, but the experience of subprime loans in the United States shows that even products with a long history of default can be underpriced. In China, there is no such history, and a growing role for market forces means that defaults should rise in the future. The equity tranche can then be sold to banks' off-balance-sheet WMPs—which do

[7]About 10 percent of trust company assets fit into neither category; these assets are highly varied.

not have capital requirements—with a high return and no explicit guarantee by the bank, to high-net-worth, or to risk-seeking institutional investors.

Beyond trust beneficiary rights and directional asset management plans, similar products can be sold by other financial institutions. Insurance companies and fund management companies increasingly engage in direct lending or invest funds in structured products with underlying loans, while banks operate increasingly important fund subsidiaries that hold equities and invest in such products. The proliferation of direct lending and asset management by almost the full range of financial firms in China raises the stakes for supervisors, who not only have to understand complex products held on balance sheets, but also must assess the potential risk from off-balance-sheet products that could be covered by entities if there is a run or contagion from liquidity or credit shocks.

Entrusted Loans

Since companies in China cannot generally provide loans to each other, banks sometimes broker "entrusted" loans between firms. In China these loans are generally made to companies that have been somehow rationed out of the formal banking system, either because they are in overcapacity or otherwise troubled industries or because they are perceived to be too high risk. The stock at the end of March 2016 was RMB11.6 trillion, up by 19.6 percent from March 2015. Much entrusted lending happens between firms in the same conglomerate, but about one-quarter is between unrelated firms. In general, loans between unaffiliated enterprises tend to bear higher interest rates.

Evidence exists that some entrusted lending comes from firms borrowing from banks, only to onlend to unrelated firms through entrusted loans. Analysis conducted by the Hong Kong Monetary Authority shows that Chinese firms' financial assets tend to be positively correlated with their financial liabilities, rather than negatively, which one would expect if firms borrowed only to finance investment, rather than to finance lending of their own. This relationship is particularly strong among SOEs, but the China Banking Regulatory Commission (CBRC) has become increasingly concerned about this practice, and is working to reduce it.

Bankers' Acceptances

Chinese banks also use bankers' acceptances to provide credit to borrowers. In most countries, bankers' acceptances provide borrowers with financing in a manner analogous to working capital.[8] In China, supervisory rules require them to be tied to a real underlying transaction, such as an international trade transaction or an investment. However, as the cash position of Chinese corporations has deteriorated but the web of implicit guarantees surrounding many sectors has remained, bankers'

[8]The difference is that while working capital is a short-term loan provided to a borrower, bankers' acceptances are promises of future payment by a borrower and guaranteed by the bank drawn on a deposit made by the borrower to the bank providing the banker's acceptance.

acceptances have become a way for banks to finance the continued operation of firms with low profits but that are nevertheless seen as unlikely to go out of business.

The growth of bankers' acceptances in China was partly motivated by regulatory arbitrage. Since recipients of bankers' acceptances must place a deposit (generally for a significantly smaller amount) at the issuing bank, they become a way for banks to increase deposits while also providing credit to high-risk enterprises; bankers' acceptances thus took up less space under banks' loan-to-deposit limits. In the past, bankers' acceptances were valued at a discount close to benchmark one-year loan rates. However, as the practice has become more widespread, and as bankers' acceptances have come to be traded among banks and companies, discounts have grown and differentiated based on issuers and borrowers.

As with other products, financial innovation and speculation have led to increased demand for bankers' acceptances. Banks will provide bankers' acceptances to firms, which then sell the acceptance to a nonbank financial institution at a discount for cash. The company can then invest the cash in a trust product, earning the spread between the rate of return on the trust product and the rate implied by the discounting. In these cases, while the original bankers' acceptance may have been priced at a relatively high level to cover a low-risk trade transaction, the actual underlying transaction—nonbank financial institution purchase of potentially speculative assets—can be substantially riskier.

Bankers' acceptances are also occasionally repackaged by nonbank financial institutions to evade supervisory requirements. Bankers' acceptances themselves are categorized as loans for supervisory purposes. However, if a bank discounts a bank bill and sells it to a nonbank financial institution, that institution can in turn sell the bank a structured product with the acceptances as an underlying asset. This product, since it contains loans, carries the same risk weight as loans, but, since it is classified as an investment, does not count against the bank's loan quota or loan-to-deposit ratio, so the transaction frees loan quota for the bank.

Other Products

Beyond these products, there are other forms of nonbank finance that are generally of less importance. Finance companies, leasing, and consumer credit companies are formal parts of the nonbank financial system that also provide financing either for consumers or investment projects. Beyond the formal financial system are pawnshops, informal lending, and traditional forms of lending, which are still used in some circumstances by SMEs or firms rationed out of the formal financial sector. Finally, emergent growth areas such as P2P and Internet banking are increasingly important.

Nonstandard Funding Sources

Wealth Management Products

When China still had ceilings on deposit rates, banks established WMPs to invest in riskier projects that could pay a higher rate of interest to investors. Following the publication of the CBRC's Regulation #8 in 2013, which limited the ability of WMPs to invest in shadow bank products, and the full lifting of deposit ceilings in 2015, their role began to diminish. However, the infrastructure remains convenient for banks (and other financial institutions) to channel savings into particular investments. They are thus analogous to the money market mutual funds that developed in the United States to circumvent interest rate ceilings, capital charges, and Federal Deposit Insurance Company fees in the 1970s, but have remained an important part of the financial system.

CBRC regulations state that guaranteed-principal WMPs must go on bank balance sheets, while nonguaranteed ones (where owners take the credit risk) can be put off balance sheet. As recently as the end of 2013 guaranteed products accounted for slightly less than half of the total, but by the end of 2015 this had fallen to only one-quarter, with floating return products now accounting for 73 percent of the total stock. Nevertheless, most WMPs are held on balance sheet, and many hold relatively low-risk assets, such as bank deposits and bonds. However, the stock of off-balance-sheet WMPs is large, and these do raise important concerns. In practice, investors have in some cases been compensated by the banks that issue the WMP for losses on such products. Here too there are similarities with the U.S. financial system, where reputational risks pushed banks to compensate investors in nonguaranteed products during the global financial crisis. The share of off-balance-sheet items (including non-WMP items) in total liabilities is particularly large for joint-stock banks.

Despite the lifting of deposit ceilings, WMPs continue to grow very strongly. At the end of 2015 there were nearly 61,000 WMPs in China, with a total value of RMB23.5 trillion. WMPs are issued by all types of banks, but the largest and fastest-growing share is from joint-stock banks, which account for 42 percent of the total stock.

Traditionally, a majority of WMP investments came from retail investors, but the share has been gradually falling (to half of December 2015 flows), with "interbank" investments becoming more and more important (to about 12 percent), and institutional investors comprising about one-third. Traditionally, WMPs were "closed," with a time-specific payoff, which was generally linked to a particular investment. However, "open" WMPs, where buyers can buy in and out with fewer restrictions, now account for slightly less than half of the total.

At the same time, the average maturity of WMPs has been increasing, but remains short term. Products with maturities greater than one year account for only about 10 percent of the outstanding stock. Since some WMPs are invested in longer-term assets, this can lead to mismatches. While such mismatches are an inherent part of the banking business, banks can direct income from one maturing asset to cover liabilities invested in another. WMPs, however, match investors' funds to specific investments, meaning that funds have to be rolled over each time to avoid illiquidity, raising the risk of a potential default on WMPs. So far, no WMP has failed to repay investors, however, as banks or other investors have stepped in to cover potential losses. But this blurs the line between on-balance-sheet guaranteed products and off-balance-sheet products that are not explicitly guaranteed, but for which investors may expect the same treatment that others have received.

WMPs invest in a wide range of products. About half of WMP assets at the end of 2015 were bonds, with another 22.4 percent in bank deposits and cash. Equity accounts for another 7.8 percent of WMP assets, a total of which has been depressed both by the sharp stock market decline in 2015 and by the reallocation of investors away from equities toward fixed-income assets. Following concerns about excessive risk concentration in WMPs, investment in nonstandard credit assets, which can include distressed or suspect debt, is capped at 35 percent and now accounts for 15.7 percent of total assets.

However, not all fixed-income products held by WMPs are innocuous. As the stock market boomed in 2014, some WMPs bought equities, but offered high fixed returns to shareholders based on expected dividend income. These WMP investments were in some cases categorized as fixed income. In addition, private placement notes, which are cash bonds issued by companies (potentially including weak companies in overcapacity sectors or local SMEs with poor profitability) on the interbank market to qualified investors, have risen in popularity due to recent regulatory shifts. Private placement notes are both less transparent and less liquid than regular bonds, but since they are classified for supervisory purposes as bonds, they are not subject to the ceilings on nonstandard credit assets that would apply if, for example, trust loans directly made to those companies were put on WMPs' balance sheets.

Finally, nonstandard credit assets held by WMPs now total RMB3.7 trillion and are in many cases complex and nontransparent. Among these, RMB1.1 trillion are in structured products such as trust beneficiary rights/asset management plans, while another RMB620 billion are trust loans. Other items—such as entrusted loans, repos, and other assets banks classify as "interbank market assets"—are smaller. These products are often repackaged corporate loans. In some cases, they are nonperforming loans restructured by nonbank financial institutions and then bought by WMPs, but many are simply corporate loans that banks have removed from their balance sheets to free space for lending under loan-to-deposit restrictions, to reduce provisioning requirements, or for other reasons. In some cases, these products are structured; this allows risks to be diversified, but undermines transparency. Senior tranches, as highly rated investments, are easily sold, but WMPs aimed at high-net-worth investors or risk-seeking institutional investors will also buy junior tranches. With poor risk pricing in the corporate sector, and the number of defaults rising, these tranches are particularly risky. Investors may not fully understand the potential downside risks, but since WMP investors have often been compensated by issuing banks, this may not be a concern for many.

Wholesale Market and Interbank Finance

The WMP infrastructure built up while deposit rates were regulated is gradually being supplemented with a more sophisticated system of wholesale funding through the interbank market. While China's banks remain less dependent on wholesale funding than banks in other regions, this is gradually changing as the repo and bond markets deepen. Interbank borrowing in China happens largely on the China Foreign Exchange Trade System platform, which is also used for bond trading. The bond market is discussed in more detail later in the chapter, which focuses on bank liabilities incurred in the interbank market.

Banks and other financial intermediaries can easily access short-term finance through repo on the interbank market. The key link to the nonbank lending sector comes through collateralized repo, which constitutes the majority of trading in the interbank market. The terms of repos in this market are set bilaterally between buyers and sellers; that is, haircut, yield, and eligibility of collateral are determined largely on a case-by-case basis. Tenors on this market tend to be very short: the average tenor at the end of 2015 was 2.7 days, down from 4.2 days at the end of 2010. Interest rates on overnight repo in early 2016 were about 2.1 percent, about 100 basis points above three-month certificate of deposit rates. The range of accepted collateral has also widened in recent years, as occurred in the United States in the years before 2008, raising concerns about adequate valuation, though discounting (haircuts) are widespread. In addition, much interbank borrowing at short tenors is uncollateralized; this raises the same potential maturity mismatch risk—from banks that invest repo'ed funds in longer-term assets—as collateralized borrowing, but raises counterparty risks. Uncollateralized short-term borrowing is particularly common among those smaller banks most invested in unconventional products.

As in all wholesale funding markets, there are potential collateral and counterparty risks. In most cases, public sector bonds (including policy banks) are used as collateral, lowering potential risks. Counterparty risks, however, are a more serious concern, as are risks from the valuation of collateral underlying over-the-counter repo transactions. All these risks can be contained under tight supervision, but the rapid growth of the market itself is a strain on resources.

Repos and uncollateralized short-term borrowing are only one part of a very diverse spectrum of assets banks can buy and sell through the interbank market. In addition to short-term lending to other bank and nonbank financial institutions, banks sometimes classify as "interbank investments" holdings of special purpose vehicles invested in nonstandard credit assets. If financial intermediaries have their products structured and then rated, they become standardized assets and can be sold on the interbank market. These carry more favorable risk weights than the underlying products might attract if they were held without being repackaged, analogous to the highly rated senior tranches of structured mortgage products in the United States before 2008.

Nonbank financial intermediaries also use the repo market to add leverage. Banks can invest WMPs—or even reinvest investment receivables—with nonbank financial intermediaries. These nonbank financial intermediaries can invest in bonds, which can then be repo'ed out, with the proceeds further repurchased (haircutting, of course, reduces the amount that can be repo'ed out with each step). The resulting product can be tranched, with very high risk resulting for the equity tranche, but with senior tranches having sufficiently low leverage that they can gain high ratings. As corporate defaults rise, in a context of widespread underpricing of risk, uncertainty about bankruptcy proceedings, and a lack of clear methods for valuing firms and collateral, this structure carries substantial risks, for both credit and liquidity.

Other Sources of Finance

Many formal participants in the disintermediated financial system raise their own funds. For example, insurance companies collect premiums and securities firms invest funds on behalf of their clients; funds from both of these sources are occasionally invested in nonstandard credit assets. Entrusted loans are made by corporates, though in some cases, companies in less profitable industries that are still perceived as low risk are able to borrow from banks, and then onlend to riskier companies through entrusted loans. Trust companies also have off-balance-sheet clients' accounts that do not use WMPs. In some cases, these are single-fund trusts, where a single investor is tied to a single product. In others, these are collective trusts, where numerous investors are brought together on a portfolio of projects. While all of these businesses are growing rapidly, their contribution to the market for nonstandard credit assets has not dramatically increased in recent years.

Other nonbank entities—P2P lenders, pawnshops, and so on—also make loans to companies or individuals. However, they generally intermediate directly, and are discussed in detail below.

BOND MARKET

China's bond market has grown rapidly in recent years and is now the third largest in the world. In reality, there are two markets: the exchange-traded market and the so-called interbank market.

China's significantly larger interbank market is much more than a straightforward bond market. Participants in the interbank market include not only banks, but also trusts, insurance companies, and money market funds. Banks are net borrowers from the system, while investors seeking high returns, including high-net-worth individuals, institutional investors, and retail investors investing through WMPs and other intermediary products, are net lenders to the market. The disintermediated nature of the market makes it very difficult to avoid mismatches between banks' short-term interbank borrowing and longer-term lending, and to accurately price credit and liquidity risk.

Most of the issuance in the bond market is by large companies and public sector entities. Bonds issued by the government and policy banks account for a large share of the bonds outstanding (about 54 percent). More recently, however, local governments have been allowed to issue bonds. Established only in 2014, over RMB3.8 trillion in municipal bonds was issued in 2015. During 2016 almost all provincial-level entities issued debt. These are subject to strict ceilings, but have added a new aspect to the market (see Chapter 6 on local governments).

The municipal bond market was established to reduce the overhang of LGFV debt as uncertainty about the ability and willingness of local governments to pay these debts rose. In 2013 the National Audit Office estimated about RMB18 trillion in outstanding debt either directly owed or contingent liabilities of local governments. The government planned to address the flow problem through the National Budget Law passed in 2015, mentioned above, which established a municipal bond market for local governments to issue debt, up to an annual quota, to finance infrastructure projects. The stock problem was to be addressed through a swap program under which LGFV debt could be swapped off bank balance sheets for new municipal bond issuance. However, the greater risk accruing to LGFV debt, with only a nontransparent potential implicit guarantee, than to municipal bonds meant that the former carried higher interest rates. Encouraging banks to participate in the swap thus required adding sweeteners to the deal. A key sweetener was determining that municipal bonds were eligible collateral for the various People's Bank of China liquidity operations, such as the Medium-Term and Standing Lending Facilities, and the Pledged Supplementary Lending facility.

Corporate bonds now account for 27 percent of the outstanding volume of the bond market. In general, and as in most countries, bond yields are lower for large companies than bank lending rates, which has encouraged disintermediation. State-owned enterprises have traditionally dominated the market. In recent years, however, a wider variety of firms have issued bonds, encouraged to do so by falling yields, increased secondary market turnover, and greater appetite among investors, particularly following the stock market correction in mid-2015.

There are three classes of corporate bonds with maturities greater than one year, each supervised differently. So-called enterprise bonds, issued by state-owned firms, normally at maturities of three to 10 years, and under the supervision of the National Development and Reform Commission. Corporate bonds, mostly issued by nonfinancial corporates that are not national SOEs, are supervised by the China Securities Regulatory Commission (CSRC). Finally, medium-term notes, issued by nonfinancial corporates, are self-regulated by the National Association of Financial Market Institutional Investors, under the guidance of the People's Republic of China. The term "corporate bonds" is generally used interchangeably for all three types.

Medium-term notes have certain advantages over the other two. These are effectively corporate loans from banks that are repackaged into bonds and can then be sold. This program was designed to relieve pressure from bank balance sheets, but it is not clear how much of this has happened: much of the stock of new bonds has been bought either by banks (which may reduce large exposure risks and help liquidity management, but retains the credit risk on banks' balance sheets under different capital coverage and provisioning requirements), by WMPs (which may also be on balance sheet), or by trust beneficiary rights/directional asset management plans (which themselves may be held by WMPs).

Aware of perceptions of guarantees in the financial system, the authorities have gradually allowed more defaults in the bond market, where previously there had been very few. The pace of defaults, particularly among SOEs, began to rise in 2014, though so far, bankruptcies have remained extremely rare. This has made investors aware of potential risks within the market. By mid-2016 this had raised the overall yield curve, but also led to an improvement in risk pricing, with more differentiation by credit quality.

At the shorter end of the interbank market, collateralized repos dominate the interbank bond market, with around RMB2.1 trillion in daily trading in the first quarter of 2016, compared with less than RMB150 billion in uncollateralized repo. Some of this is bank lending but much is also between investors. Many investors repo out their bonds and use the proceeds to lever up their corporate bond portfolios. This maturity mismatch raises sensitivity to interest rate risk. This leverage is primarily taken by institutional investors (insurers, fund managers, securities firms). Individuals and corporates are often the lenders in such cases. The CSRC has tightened the haircut on the corporate bond repo to try to curtail this behavior, along with other measures.

EQUITY MARKET

China's stock markets are now the world's second largest. By both market capitalization and trading volume, the Shanghai and Shenzhen stock markets lag behind only the United States' New York Stock Exchange and NASDAQ markets. As with other areas of the financial system, growth has been very fast and volatility is high. Share turnover—which in China is unusually fast, for reasons discussed below—on the Shanghai exchange passed London in 2007; at that time the market capitalization of the Shenzhen exchange was smaller than that of Johannesburg, while it is now larger than Toronto's.

A wide range of companies are listed, but market capitalization is dominated by state-owned firms. Some of China's companies—such as China National Petroleum Corporation, China Petrochemical Corporation (Sinopec), and China State Construction Engineering Corporation, and China's large public banks—are among the largest companies in the world by market capitalization. However, in many of these cases, the government (or other large investors) share of equities is very high, leaving only a small share for free float. This adds to price volatility.

The dominance of retail investors in Chinese stock markets has amplified volatility. While less than 10 percent of Chinese people own stocks (compared with a majority of Americans), in 2014 about 80 percent of tradable shares were held by individual investors. During 2015, as the stock market rose rapidly before peaking midyear, 38 million new accounts (many opened by investors who already held at least one account) were opened. Many, though by no means all, were held by small investors who held shares for only a brief time. The importance of these investors in daily trading volumes increased during the boom, amplifying volatility.

The market is also largely closed to foreign investors. Chinese companies can, and do, list in foreign markets and in Hong Kong SAR. Foreign investors are subject to quotas under China's Qualified Foreign Institutional Investor program (see Chapter 8 on the capital account). While these quotas have gradually been expanded, they remain binding in many cases. Concerns about these restrictions were one reason behind the decision in June 2016 to postpone inclusion of onshore Chinese equities in the MSCI Emerging Markets Index.

The rapid run-up of equity prices and subsequent correction in mid-2015 also raises questions about the stock market. A perception among investors, to some extent encouraged by the government, that China's stock market was a one-way bet on the country's future led to a 112 percent increase in the Shanghai Composite Index between January 2013 and June 2015. As prices began to correct in July, the authorities became very concerned about potential fallout. While direct linkages between the equity market and the real economy were believed to be small, widespread leverage among investors and uncertain risks from complex products were a serious concern. The authorities embarked on a wide-ranging effort to stabilize the market, which included a moratorium on initial public offering, large purchases of equities by the government entity China Securities Finance Corporation, and a lockup of shares held by large investors. The market correction continued for a few months after, but in a more orderly fashion. However, the measures taken at the time have not yet been fully unwound, underscoring the lack of a predictable framework for investors.

High returns in the equity market also attracted a large pool of risk capital, which has subsequently moved on. WMPs are not allowed to invest directly in equities, but can invest through asset management plans. Securities firms also grew rapidly as new investors moved their savings into the stock market. The stock market provided a cheap source of equity finance for firms as well, some of which took advantage of the rise in prices to raise equity finance to pay off debts. Insurance companies' limits on equity investment were raised in mid-2015, and their funds also moved into equity markets. As prices fell in 2016, many firms liquidated these positions, with one of the main beneficiaries being the bond market.

Regulations on leveraged trading have continued, but remain a concern. The high degree of leveraged trading in China has aggravated price swings in a market already dominated by retail investors and momentum investing. There are a few mechanisms for leveraged investing in Chinese equity markets:[9]

- *Securities companies.* Formal leveraged trading is allowed up to certain margin requirements (generally 50–80 percent of assets net of haircuts).
- *Umbrella trusts.* These are tranched trusts in which junior investors (largely high-net-worth investors or institutional investors) borrow from senior investors (WMPs). This is more informal.
- *Over-the-counter fund matching.* Fund providers set up and monitor stock accounts that investors use for leveraged trading.

[9]Taken from HKMA 2015.

The use of equities as collateral also raises risks. Most bank-loan collateral is in the form of real estate, and interbank trading, when collateralized, normally uses government debt. But equity is used in some cases. Haircuts on collateral are generally large, and supervisors in recent years have raised them. Nevertheless, this remains a potential concern for equity investors and for lenders' stability.

INSURANCE

China's insurance industry, like the rest of the financial sector, has grown very rapidly in recent years. Total assets of the insurance sector reached RMB12 trillion at the end of 2015, with 32 percent of the Chinese population having access to insurance products in one form or another. About 80 percent of assets are held by life insurers. Around two-thirds of insurance company assets are in deposits or fixed-income securities.

Seeking return, China's insurers have moved away from fixed-income and liquid investments. In 2010 bonds and cash accounted for nearly 80 percent of insurers' assets. The China Insurance Regulatory Commission loosened rules on insurance investment in 2104, after which insurance companies began to actively move into the booming equity market. As noted above, in mid-2015, as equity prices began to fall, insurers were allowed to raise their equity exposure from 30 to 40 percent of assets if the difference was invested in blue chip stocks. By the end of 2015 the share of insurance company assets in cash and bonds had fallen to 58 percent. The biggest share of this shift, however, came from alternative assets. The composition of this part of the portfolio is not easy to assess, but investments in infrastructure projects—which generally carry implicit guarantees from local governments—have risen in recent years.

This rising riskiness in asset portfolios is matched by shifts in liabilities. A rising share of products have promised high guaranteed returns. Much of the rapid rise in premium income seen in 2015 came from universal life insurance products. Until February 2015 the return on such products was guaranteed at 2.5 percent. After this ceiling was lifted, average premiums rose to about 5 percent, with smaller companies selling products at even higher returns.[10] Many of these products were also of very short duration, raising concerns about asset-liability mismatches and rollover risks.[11]

The China Insurance Regulatory Commission has responded to these risks. In March 2016 the commission required insurance companies to stop selling products in which most policies would have a duration of less than one year and assigned ceilings based on capital levels to limit the exposure of insurance companies to other short- and medium-term products. China's new China Risk Oriented Solvency System supervisory framework is also being implemented to bring supervision closer into line with global norms.

[10]The ceiling was initially raised to 3.5 percent, but in September 2016 it was reduced to 3 percent.

[11]Short- and medium-term insurance products in China are products with a duration of less than five years.

CONCLUSIONS AND POLICY PRESCRIPTIONS

Ensuring China's financial system remains up to the task of underwriting rapid growth will require continued effort to ensure stability.[12] Certain key areas of emphasis emerge:

- The increasing complexity of financial systems makes supervisory coordination important. Increasing linkages of banks, insurance companies, trusts, securities firms, and other companies mean that systemic risk can jump rapidly from one sector to another.
- The dispersion of credit risks across the financial systems, from transparent and closely supervised bank loans to more opaque investment portfolios, WMPs, and nonbank financial firms that may still have linkages back to banks, is also a concern. In the case of banks, supervision should ensure that capital coverage and provisioning are sufficient to cover credit and liquidity risks on bank balance sheets, whether these are in the loan book or in complex structured products in the investment book. In other cases, such as WMPs, insurance companies, or asset management plans, the issue is less clear cut, but ensuring a level supervisory playing field that does not allow credit risks to collect in one sector will be crucial.
- The deepening of interbank and other funding markets also raises potential risks. As the funding models for banks and other firms diversify, ensuring sufficient systemic liquidity becomes more complex. In the case of banks, the move toward Basel III liquidity rules by mid-2017 is an important step. But better understanding of the linkages between banks and other financial firms and ensuring that collateral standards are high are also essential.

Overall, continued development of China's financial system represents an important opportunity to support growth in what is now the world's largest economy in purchasing power parity terms. But ensuring this growth is managed in a safe and sustainable way is equally important.

REFERENCES

China Insurance Regulatory Commission (CIRC). 2015. *Annual Report of the Chinese Insurance Market 2015.* Beijing.

Hong Kong Monetary Authority (HKMA). 2015. *Monetary and Financial Stability Report.* Hong Kong SAR.

———. 2016. *Monetary and Financial Stability Report.* Hong Kong SAR.

KPMG Huazhen LLP. 2015. "2015 China Trust Survey." Hong Kong SAR.

Morgan Stanley Research. 2016. "Asia Insight: Primer—Demystifying China's Financial System." Hong Kong SAR.

[12]The ongoing work of the joint IMF-World Bank Financial Sector Assessment Program will provide additional detailed recommendations.

CHAPTER 11

State-Owned Enterprise Reform

W. Raphael Lam and Alfred Schipke

Tackling the rising vulnerabilities and low efficiency of state-owned enterprises (SOEs) is crucial to China's transitioning toward a more sustainable growth path. The need now for bold SOE reforms is similar to the reforms at the end of the 1990s, which, after steadfast implementation, helped unleash the country's growth potential and secure rapid development in the early 2000s. Successful SOE reform can improve resource allocation, create space for the private sector to flourish, and address major vulnerabilities.

SOEs continue to play a large role in the economy and cover a wide range of sectors, including heavy industries and utilities, financial institutions, media, and cultural services. Of the 10 largest companies listed on the Shanghai stock exchange, eight are SOEs, ranging from banks to energy and infrastructure sectors.[1] This chapter focuses on nonfinancial and non-cultural SOEs. Although their share in output and employment has declined over the past decades, China still has some 150,000 nonfinancial SOEs. The urgent need to implement reforms is reflected in significantly less-efficient SOE performance compared to their private counterparts, while rising leverage and deterioration of repayment capacity adds to increasing vulnerabilities.

Unlike reforms in the financial, monetary, and fiscal areas, SOE reform has been lagging, reflecting the magnitude and complexity of the problem and strong interest groups resisting change. For example, less than half of the provinces have completed the classification of SOEs for respective reforms. Current draft proposals still lack sufficient detail and are not always consistent with maximizing potential economic benefits.

The chapter examines current proposals and identifies key elements of SOE reforms that can improve resource allocation and facilitate China's transition toward sustainable growth. It then provides an illustration of the role and recent

We are grateful for comments by Nick Lardy, DONG Chaohui, SHENG Hong, CHEN Long, Cyril Lin, ZHANG Chunlin, ZHAO Luan, Hoon Soh, Mona Haddad, Paul Hubbard. MENG Jingzhou, TAN Yuyan, and WU Yuchen provided excellent assistance.

[1]Of the top 10 listed companies on the Shanghai stock exchange, and based on market capitalization, China National Petroleum Corporation, Industrial and Commercial Bank of China, Bank of Agriculture, China Construction Bank, Bank of China, China Life Insurance, China Petroleum & Chemical Corporation (Sinopec), and Bank of Communications are SOEs.

performance of SOEs, analyzes vulnerabilities emanating from high and rising leverage, and estimates the implicit support to SOEs that has contributed to resource misallocation. The chapter summarizes the government's SOE reform initiatives and current progress and presents policy recommendations and assesses potential growth benefits from SOE reforms based on international good practices.

SOEs' ROLE AND PERFORMANCE: NUMEROUS, LARGE, BUT LESS EFFICIENT

SOEs have played an important role in China's overall development strategy and have been used to smooth business cycles and support growth through changes in investment spending, in particular during the global financial crisis (see also Batson 2016). SOEs also fill social functions, including to stabilize employment, provide social services that in other countries often either belong to or are supported by the government, and pursue other noneconomic national strategies.

About 110 central, state-owned conglomerates are supervised by the State-Owned Assets Supervision and Administration Commission of the State Council (SASAC),[2] and each has layers of subsidiaries (sometimes six or nine levels). This implies as many as 50,000 central SOEs. In addition, some 100,000 local nonfinancial SOEs exist nationwide, and with the implementation of the revised budget law, some financing vehicles funded by local governments may also be classified as SOEs (see Chapter 6). Multiple line ministries and agencies, such as SASAC, the Ministry of Finance, and the National Development and Reform Commission, are responsible for SOEs and their policies.

While SOEs account for declining shares of output and employment, they continue to take up a large share of resources (Figure 11.1). The SOE share of industrial value-added has dropped from about 40 percent to 16 percent over the past two decades, and SOEs now account for only about 12–15 percent of urban employment, reflecting previous reforms and the remarkable growth of private enterprises (Figure 11.2 and Table 11.1). Despite the decline, SOE assets still accounted for 180 percent of GDP in 2015.

SOEs underperform, however, with low returns and widening losses. Following the late-1990s reforms, returns improved and were catching up with those in private enterprises, but have deteriorated to 2–3 percent since 2008, well below private firms.[3] SOE productivity is about 30–40 percent of that of private enterprises (Hsieh and Song 2015 and Table 11.1).[4] Interest expenses in turn are relatively high and account for one-quarter of net profits on average, much higher

[2]SASAC was established in 2003 to better manage SOEs' assets and improve governance. It has been involved heavily in SOE operations, including key personnel decisions and asset allocation.

[3]The comparison is at the aggregate level. Since SOEs concentrate in capital or resource-intensive industries, direct comparison is difficult between private and SOEs that fully controls for size and sector.

[4]Average productivity was 1.5 percent for SOEs and 4.6 percent for private enterprises (Brandt and Zhu 2010).

Figure 11.1. SOEs Dominate Resource Use and Operate Less Efficiently
(SOEs' share of total unless otherwise stated[1])

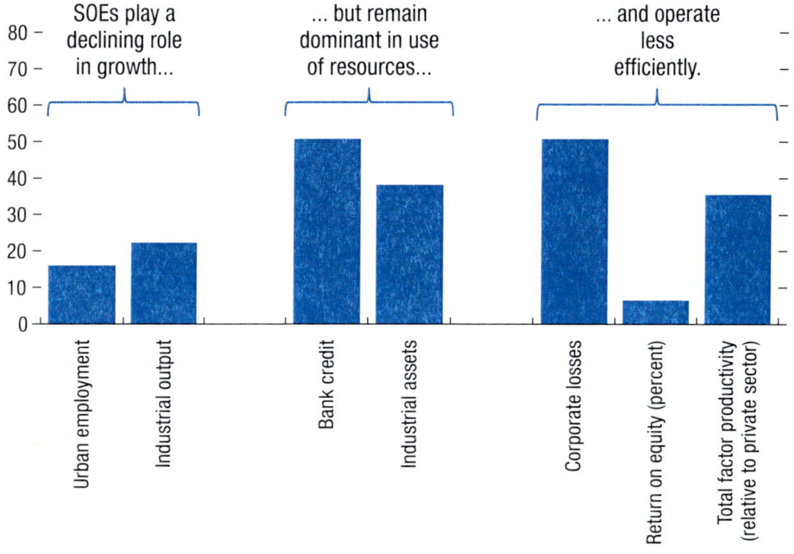

Sources: CEIC; Ministry of Finance; National Bureau of Statistics; People's Bank of China; WIND; and IMF staff estimates.
Note: SOE = state-owned enterprise.
[1] Sample period as of end-2015 where data are available. Bank credit and total factor productivity are average between 2011 and 2015.

than in private enterprises. Many SOEs also suffered sizable losses in 2015, mostly in resource-intensive industries with low capacity utilization (Figure 11.2).

Compared to other large emerging market economies, Chinese SOEs appear to be an outlier. Chinese SOEs are more dominant—measured by sales revenue and assets in percent of GDP (Table 11.2)—while on average their returns on assets are lower (about 2 percent) than those in other emerging economies (about 4 percent), underscoring the need for reform.

HIGH AND RISING CORPORATE LEVERAGE LARGELY DRIVEN BY SOEs

In recent years, one of China's key vulnerabilities has been excessive corporate credit growth. Nonfinancial corporate credit grew about 20 percent on average per year between 2009 and 2015, much higher than nominal GDP (Maliszewski and others 2016; IMF 2016). The corporate debt-to-GDP-ratio (broadly defined) rose from about 100 percent of GDP in 2009 to about 145 percent of GDP in 2015, and is now significantly higher than in countries at a similar level of development, and even exceeding that typical for developed economies

Figure 11.2. SOE Share of Output Has Shrunk and Efficiency Has Declined

1. Share of SOE in Total Industrial Sector (Percent)

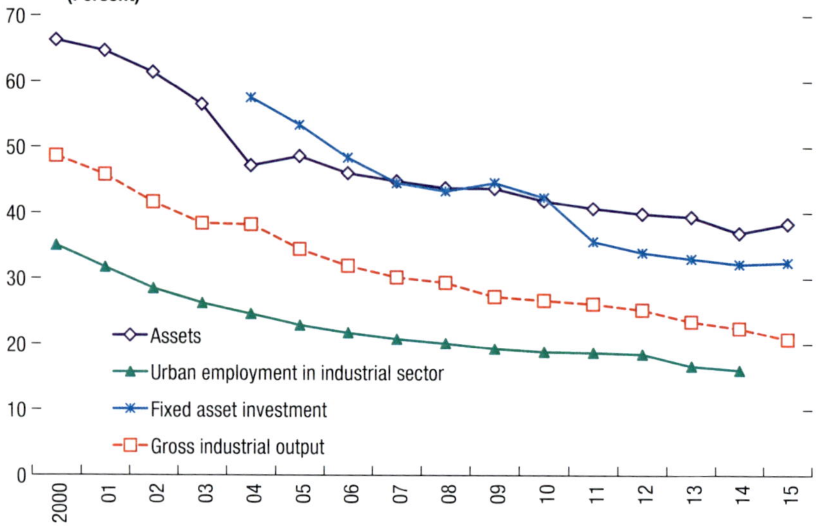

Sources: CEIC; National Bureau of Statistics; and IMF staff estimates.

2. Still Numerous and Sizable Assets (Number of SOEs and percent of GDP)

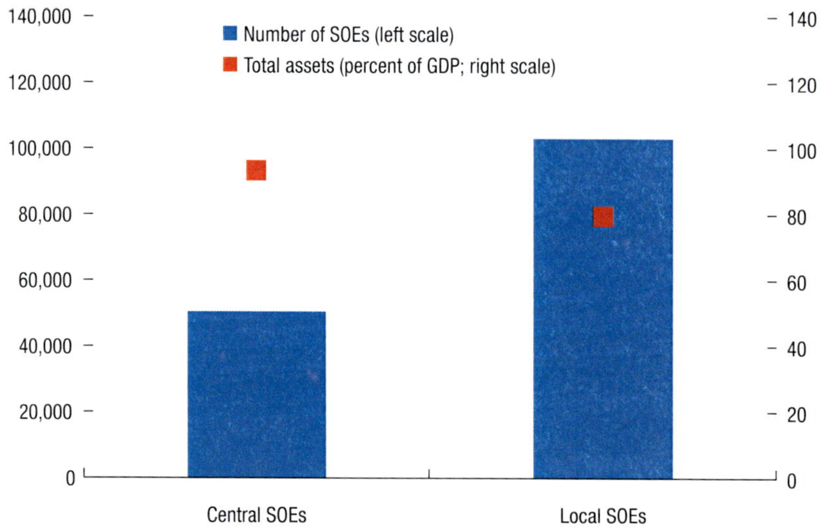

Sources: CEIC; Dragonomics; and Ministry of Finance.
Note: SOE = state-owned enterprise.

Figure 11.2. SOE Share of Output Has Shrunk and Efficiency Has Declined *(continued)*

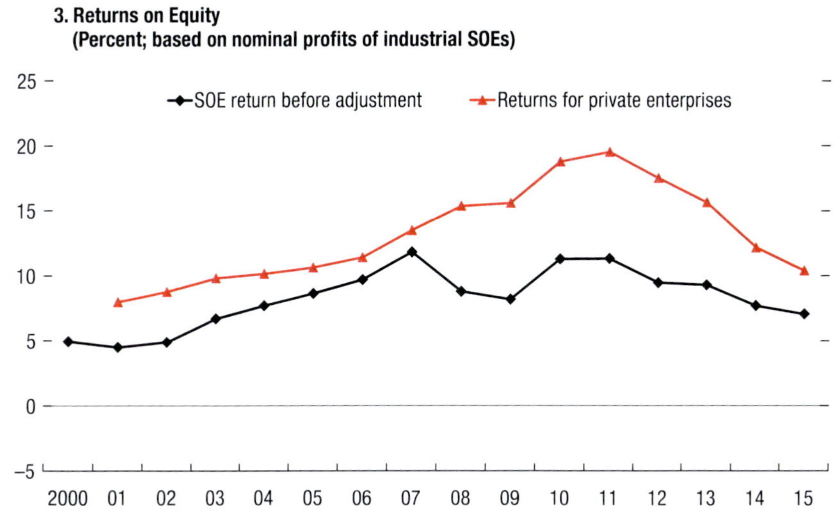

Sources: *Statistical Yearbook* 2015; Unirule Institute of Economics 2015; and IMF staff estimates.
Note: SOE = state-owned enterprise.

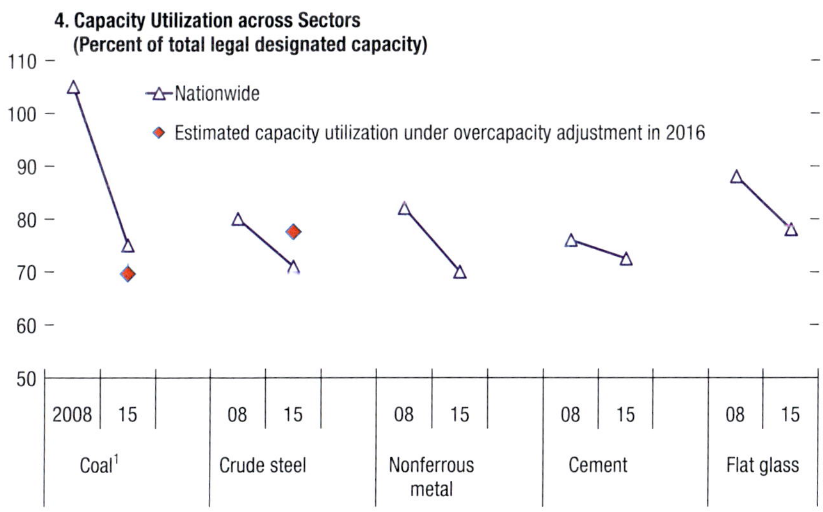

Sources: European Chamber of Commerce; Goldman Sachs; and IMF staff estimates.
[1] Coal capacity exceeds 100 percent because coal mines produced more than the legal designed capacity level in earlier years.

Table 11.1. Comparative Indicators between SOEs and Private Enterprises

	State-Owned Enterprises			Private Enterprises		
	2000–07	2013–15	Direction	2000–07	2013–15	Direction
	(Share of total in percent unless otherwise indicated)					
Industrial Sector						
Total assets	54	38	Down	46	62	Up
Urban employment	35	16	Down	65	84	Up
Gross industrial output	37	22	Down	63	78	Up
Loss-making enterprises (amount)	46	52	Up	54	48	Down
Fixed asset investment	51	33	Down	49	67	Up
Bank credit to nonfinancial corporate	62	51	Down	38	49	Up
Leverage (percent of owners' equity)	125	192	Up	144	101	Down
Return on equity (percent)	8.4	6.6	Weaken	10.3	12.7	Improve
Efficiency relative to private enterprise (measured by gross output by each unit of credit)	54	43	Weaken	...		
Total factor productivity in percent	1.6			4.5		
Total factor productivity of SOEs relative to private enterprises	35.6			...		

Sources: CEIC; Ministry of Finance; National Bureau of Statistics; People's Bank of China; WIND database; and IMF staff estimates.

[1] Some data are not available for the whole sample period. Estimates are based on where data are available.

Table 11.2. Key Indicators of SOEs

	Percent of GDP				
	Sales Revenue	Net Profit	Asset	Market Value	Share in the Top 10 Firms
China	**35**	**3**	**176**	**45**	**88**
Brazil	12	2	51	18	50
India	16	4	75	22	59
Indonesia	3	0	19	12	69
Russian Federation	16	3	64	28	81
South Africa	2	2	3	1	2

Sources: Kowalski and others 2013; and IMF staff estimates.

(Figure 11.3). The credit boom, in turn, has led to falling investment efficiency, weakening debt servicing capacity, and rising economic and financial risks.

Much of the rise in corporate leverage has been driven by SOE borrowing. At the end of 2015, SOEs accounted for over half of bank outstanding credit, and by some estimates, about two-thirds of overall corporate debt was related to SOEs (Li 2016). Acting as a conduit for policy-driven investment to support growth, SOEs have higher and rising leverage[5]—reaching 180 percent on average (with a fat tail in the distribution at the 90th-percentile SOEs of about 350 percent) (Figure 11.4).

[5]Ratio between total liabilities and owners' equity.

Figure 11.3. SOEs Contributing to High and Rising Corporate Credit

1. A Proxy of Credit Intensity
(Number of times; Change in total debt to change in net operating revenue)

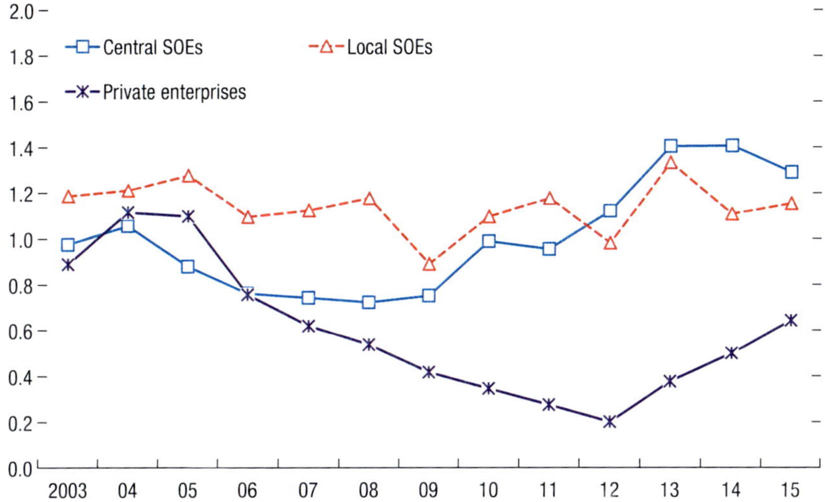

Sources: WIND; and IMF staff estimates.
Note: SOE = state-owned enterprise.

2. Distribution of Leverage Ratios
(Total liabilities in percent of total equity)

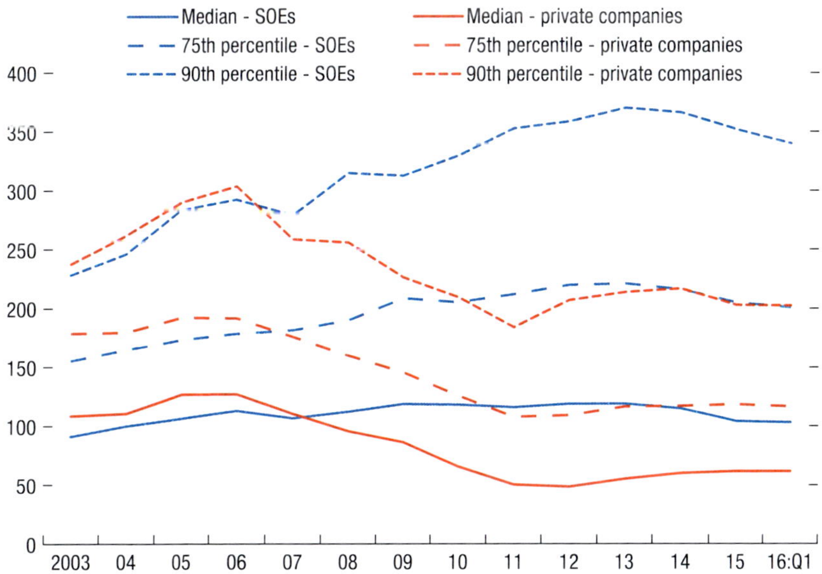

Sources: WIND database; and IMF staff estimates.
Note: SOE = state-owned enterprise.

Figure 11.4. Rising Average Leverage Ratios
(Total liabilities as percent of total owners' equity based on listed companies)

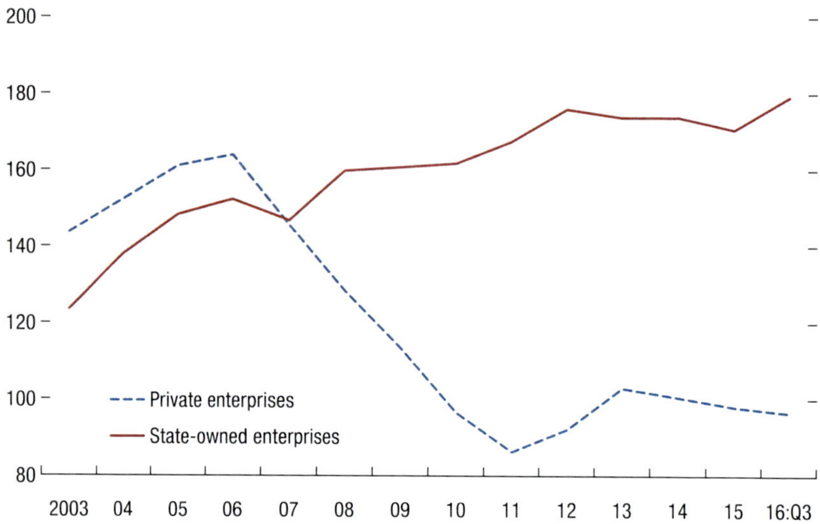

Sources: WIND database; and IMF staff estimates.

Alongside the rising leverage, SOEs' credit efficiency has deteriorated. At the same time, and despite the weaker corporate performance, SOEs' nonperforming loan ratios have been much lower than those of private companies, possibly related to implicit support and soft budget constraints (see next section). The accumulated nonperforming loan ratio (including historical write-offs) since 2010 was only 1.3 percent of total loans for SOEs, relative to 12.6 percent for private firms as of June 2016. At the same time, debt servicing capacity, measured by earnings before interest and tax relative to interest expenses, was three times lower for SOEs on average relative to private firms (Deutsche Bank 2016).

RESOURCES MISALLOCATION ARISING FROM IMPLICIT SUPPORT

SOEs tend to enjoy significant implicit support on factor inputs, such as land, credit, and natural resources. This implicit support has contributed to resource misallocation and an uneven playing field with private firms, further reinforced by protected markets and monopolistic and oligopolistic rights.[6] It partly crowds

[6]Empirical research finds a statistically significant negative relationship between SOE ownership and corporate efficiency and productivity, and the efficiency (measured in returns and sale revenues) tends to improve after introducing private ownership (Unirule Institute of Economics 2015).

out private investment and impedes competition and innovation. The implicit support includes:

Land use. Before 2002, SOEs received land from the state based on allocations or negotiated sales at book value. Although the current guidelines require SOEs to pay for land use, it is not clear if such land rental is appropriately charged. Exemptions also exist from land use taxes in selected sectors (for example, thermal power stations). More importantly, SOEs can use endowed land as collateral and are hence often able to borrow at favorable interest rates.

Credit. Financing costs for listed SOEs tend to be about 40–50 basis points below the benchmark lending rate, even as banks increasingly differentiate among SOEs in their lending policy (for example, those in overcapacity sectors). Some studies conclude that SOEs are more likely to get bank financing and undertake fixed investment than private firms, despite having lower average returns on capital, while others note that the spread between comparable SOEs and private enterprises has turned much narrower (Lardy 2014).[7] Widespread implicit guarantees imply that SOEs have credit ratings about two to three notches higher than comparable private firms (Moody's 2015), allowing SOEs to access financing in capital markets at low costs. Some SOEs can also access cheaper funds through their own financing companies by borrowing directly in the interbank market (Chun, Chu, and Liao 2010).

Input prices. Some studies suggest that SOEs may have paid for natural resources below market value (equivalent to about 7–12 percent of SOE profit during 2003–13) but quantifying this is difficult (Unirule Institute of Economics 2015).[8] For example, SOEs tend to enjoy lower resource taxes and fees for petroleum, natural gas, and coal. Dominance in natural resources also encourages SOEs to diversify to upstream and downstream industries, potentially further adding distortions in resource allocation.[9]

Fiscal support. Direct fiscal subsidies to cover SOE losses have been largely phased out since 2007, although a few exemptions remain for oil and fuel industries.[10] Ad hoc fiscal support was provided to SOEs in oil, aviation, and other industries in 2007–09 and later took the form of capital injection (National Development and Reform Commission 2016). Indirect fiscal support takes place more often through local governments, such as through tax deductions. For

[7]Also see Dollar and Wei 2007 and Brandt and Zhu 2010.

[8]An indirect estimation can be based on the difference in tax levied on resources based on the price differential with global prices. Unirule Institute of Economics (2015) estimates the extent in a few sectors, including petroleum, natural gas, and coal sectors.

[9]In some sectors, the government sets prices above those in world markets supporting profitability, often in sectors dominated by SOEs (for example, in oil and natural gas).

[10]Consumption tax is exempted or fully refunded for oil consumed by manufacturers of refined oil for own use since 2009. A preferential tax rate is levied for value-added tax on coal and gas. While these are available for all enterprises, they tend to favor SOEs, given their dominant role in these sectors.

instance, the average effective tax rate for listed local SOEs was about 10 percent, much lower than the 24 percent rate for private firms.[11]

Market access. In addition to implicit support, SOEs often operate as monopolies or oligopolies, especially in the natural resource sectors (for example, petroleum and coal). Also, there are significant barriers to entry, or, in the case of a number of service sectors, outright entry restrictions (for example, telecommunications).

Estimates of Implicit Support

Overall the implicit support to SOEs in recent years is estimated at about 3 percent of GDP (Figure 11.5).[12] Adjusting for the estimated implicit support shows that SOE return on equity would have fallen from an average of 8 percent to about −1.3 percent during 2011–15. In particular, the rapid buildup of SOE leverage after the global financial crisis suggests credit misallocation is increasing and accounts for half of the estimated implicit support (or 1½ percent of GDP).

Estimating implicit support is subject to caveats due to data limitations. First, the estimates cover only the data of industrial SOEs published in the *Statistical Yearbooks*, excluding SOEs in the services sector.[13] Second, the estimates rest mostly on lower pricing. Some implicit support could have been reflected in the amount of credit rather the lower cost. Third, estimates do not account for SOE legacy cost and social functions (about 0.9 percent of GDP in 2015) such as excess labor, complying with better regulatory standards, and paying for retiree pensions and payroll.

CURRENT SOE REFORM PLANS

Faced with these challenges, the government has identified SOE reform as a main pillar of its reform efforts. The broad objectives are outlined in the Third Plenum reform blueprint and the latest Five-Year Plan (2016–20), as well as a number of reform proposals (Table 11.3). Faced with SOEs' deteriorating

[11]Significant variation existed in the effective tax rates of SOEs, with an effective tax rate at 31 percent for the largest 50. On average, taxes paid by SOEs are about 8 percent of their total revenue, higher than private enterprises, at 3 percent of total revenue.

[12]For the land use, the quantity of land endowed to SOEs is taken from Unirule, while land prices are taken from the annual *Statistical Yearbook* published by National Bureau of Statistics. With respect to credit, the credit component, the average spread of effective interest payments is estimated between listed individual SOEs and private firms, controlling for firm characteristics (Chivakul and Lam 2015). Estimates on input prices are based on Unirule, while the fiscal support component is based on periodic releases by the Ministry of Finance. From 2007 to 2014, incomplete estimates based on Ministry of Finance capital contributions suggest ad hoc fiscal subsidies were about RMB274 billion (0.4 percent of 2015 GDP). Distortions arising from protected market access are excluded. As a result, the estimated implicit support could be considered a lower bound.

[13]While data of the Ministry of Finance have broader coverage, they do not contain subcategory information.

Figure 11.5. Implicit Support to SOEs Contributing to Resource Misallocation

1. Adjusting Return on Equity based on Implicit Support to SOEs
(Net return on total owners' equity; percent)

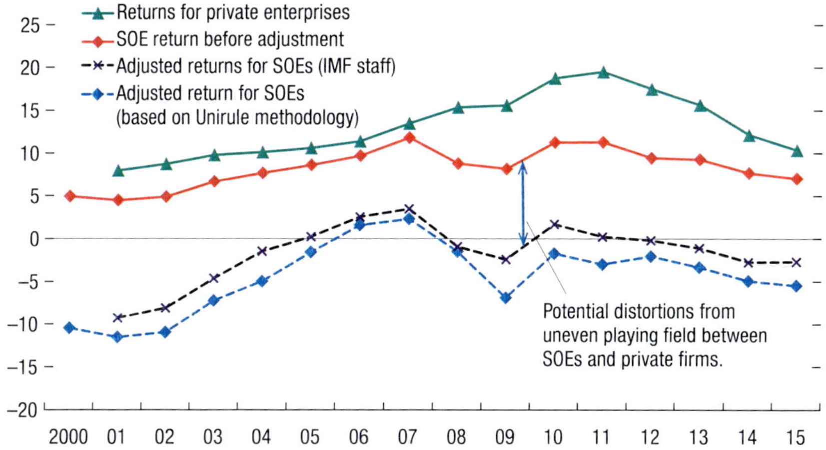

Sources: *Statistical Yearbook* 2015; Unirule Institute of Economics 2015; and IMF staff estimates.
Note: SOE = state-owned enterprise.
[1] Based on nominal profits of industrial SOEs net of fiscal subsidies, implicit support through the use of land and natural resources, and lower implicit financing cost.

2. Implicit Support to SOEs
(Percent of GDP)

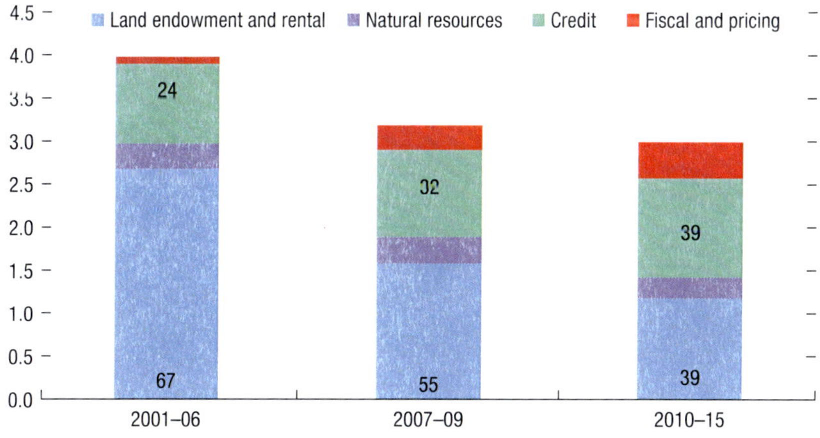

Sources: CEIC; Unirule Institute of Economics 2015; and IMF staff estimates.
Note: SOE = state-owned enterprise.
[1] Numbers in the bar chart refer to the share of total implicit support.

performance and overcapacity, the reform plan focuses on modernizing corporate governance, improving the supervision of state assets, and phasing out excess capacity. The Five-Year Plan also calls for "diverse forms of ownership and private participation in SOEs," as well as "restructuring zombie enterprises." At the same time, it stresses "keeping state ownership as the mainstay of the economy" and "making SOEs bigger and stronger to strengthen the influence and to serve national strategies." Current plans envisage the following:

- **Classifying SOEs into several categories,** each with specific ownership structures, reform plans, and assessment criteria (Table 11.4). Specifically,
  - *Commercial strategic SOEs* (such as defense, telecommunications, and major energy companies) will be entrusted to pursue national strategies such as "going global" and "creating global champions," possibly through merger and acquisition. The state will continue to hold majority ownership;
  - *Commercial nonstrategic SOEs* will compete directly in the market; and
  - *SOEs with social functions* will be tasked to provide quality public services with better efficiency.
- **Improving SOE efficiency** through repositioning the state as a capital investor rather than operator. Mixed-ownership reforms envisage a spectrum of ownership structures (for example, cross-shareholdings and public listings) and greater private sector participation.[14] The reforms envisage professional management and better alignment of respective rights and responsibilities between owners (the respective government agency) and the board, with checks and balances. State capital investment and operation corporations would be established to exercise state ownership rights (Annex 11.1). Social SOE functions such as the provision of hospitals, schools, and some fringe benefits for employees and retirees are to be gradually phased out. At the same time, SOEs are required to contribute more dividends to the government budget (a target of 30 percent by 2020) and allocate part of their capital to replenish social security funds.
- **Resolving nonviable SOEs.** Broad guiding principles on resolving debt were announced, including the use of debt-equity swaps and creditor committees. Sectors with overcapacity (such as the coal industry) often overlap with highly leveraged SOEs. The State Council committed to reducing overcapacity by 10–15 percent over 3–5 years, cutting aggregate losses by 2017, and expediting the exit of nonviable "zombie" SOEs through asset transfer, consolidation, and closure. Currently, the list of zombie SOEs includes over 2,000 subsidiaries of central and near 7,000 local SOEs, and a few central SOEs are assigned pilot plans for potential debt-equity swaps.
- **Institutionalizing the leadership role of the Communist Party.** The core political role in SOEs will be institutionalized, for example, the board chair

[14]Capital reforms for SOEs provide for more diverse ownership, including SOE listings on stock exchanges, preference shares, cross-shareholdings, equity swaps, joint ventures, and franchises.

Table 11.3. Strategic Principles of Current SOE Reforms

Strategic Principles	Measures	Recent Developments and Progress
1. Classifying SOEs for respective reforms	- SOEs to be classified into commercial competitive, commercial strategic, and social functions.	About 20 provinces have identified SOEs into various categories for respective reforms. All central SOEs to be incorporated by 2017.
2. Improving SOE efficiency		
• Mixed-ownership reform	- Encourage private capital participation	Pilot program initiated; about two-thirds of SOEs plan to diversify equity base but few in strategic industries.
	- Allow employee stock ownership	Pilot program initiated but without details.
• State asset management	- Focus on ownership rather than management	About 11 SOEs were chosen as pilot state capital management/ operation companies.
• Professional management	- Link remuneration to management performance; salary cap; professional recruitment and board of directors	Salary structure reviewed for 72 central SOEs, while pilot programs on corporate governance rolled out.
• Separate social functions	- Separate fringe benefits for employees (utilities and other public services) from SOEs	Social functions on utilities and real estate management fees to be separated from SOEs by 2018, while other public services will be gradually phased out.
3. Resolving overcapacity and meeting national strategies	- Eliminate excess capacity	Reduce coal and steel capacity by 10–15 percent over 3–5 years (meeting 38–47 percent of 2016 target as of end July). A restructuring fund established to minimize social cost.
	- Exit of nonviable "zombie" firms	About 345 central SOEs identified as zombies (about 7,000 at local level) to be resolved in 2–3 years. However, the focus appears to be on mergers and consolidation of SOEs.
	- Prepare broad guiding principles on resolving overindebtedness	Guidelines made available on creditor committee and debt-equity swaps to advance debt restructuring.
	- Encourage strategic SOEs to "go global"	An SOE Adjustment Fund was established to facilitate restructuring and facilitate investment.
4. Institutionalizing the Communist Party's control of SOEs	- Prevent the loss of state assets	Pilot program initiated but details not disclosed.

Sources: Chinese Communist Party and State Council 2015; Ministry of Finance and State-Owned Assets; State Council 2015a, 2015b, 2015c; State-Owned Assets Supervision and Administration Commission of the State Council, Ministry of Finance, and National Development Reform Commission 2016; Supervision and Administration Commission of the State Council 2015.

Note: SOE = state-owned enterprise.

Table 11.4. Classification of SOEs under the Reform Plans

	Commercial SOEs		
	Competitive SOEs	**Strategic SOEs**	**Social Function SOEs**
Objectives	Commercial-oriented with capital appreciation	Meeting national strategy	Provide quality social services and improve living standards.
Reform Plan	Turn these SOEs into joint-stock corporations; improve corporate governance.	Separate state involvement from daily management; specific measures vary across industries.	Introduce market mechanism to improve efficiency of public services
Ownership Structure	Encourage a diverse ownership structure, including state majority holding, private sector capital.	Maintain state's majority ownership, while allowing some minority nonstate capital.	Can maintain full state ownership but can allow diverse private capital base. Private participation can take the form of agency, purchasing, and franchises.
Assessment Criteria	Asset returns; capital gains; market competitiveness	Ability to meet national security and strategic goals; reasonable returns on capital	Ability to meet social functions (service quality, social feedback, operation efficiency); less priority on returns of capital

Source: Ministry of Finance and State-Owned Assets Supervision and Administration Commission of the State Council 2016.
Note: SOE = state-owned enterprise.

will also be designated as the corporate party secretary and management will have greater mobility between party and corporate ranks. Strategic SOEs will be strengthened to become global champions to meet national strategies. President XI Jinping highlighted that this feature of political leadership in SOEs would be integrated into modern corporate governance.[15]

ASSESSMENT OF CURRENT REFORM PLANS

Parts of the reform proposals are in line with international good practices[16] and have the potential to increase efficiency and create the conditions for a more level playing field. However, the current proposals also contain competing objectives, while important details still need to defined. At the same time, implementation—as acknowledged by the government itself—has been an uphill battle.

During the SOE reforms in the late 1990s, the government implemented bold and far-reaching reforms, including through restructuring excessive debt, reducing redundancy, and opening up the economy to greater competition (notably

[15]Reported in *China News*, October 11, 2016 (in Chinese). http://news.china.com/domestic/945/20161011/23747105_1.html.

[16]According to the Organisation for Economic Co-operation and Development (OECD), the proposed governance reform could be broadly consistent with their Guidelines on Corporate Governance of SOEs if there is sufficient transparency on the role of state (OECD 2009, 2015a, 2015b, 2016).

Table 11.5. Selected SOE Reform Pilot Programs

1	Clearly define the role of the board of directors
2	Market-based personnel recruitment
3	Institutionalizing professional management in SOEs
4	Corporate wages and salary compensation
5	Establishing State-Capital Investment Operation Company
6	Consolidation and restructuring
7	Key areas on mixed-ownership reforms
8	Employee stock holdings
9	Information disclosures
10	Separation of social functions and legacy issues

Sources: SASAC; and media reports.

through World Trade Organization accession) (Annex 11.2).[17] Compared to the challenges then, today's SOEs problems seem less challenging in economic terms (such as employment).

In recent years, SOE reform implementation has been lagging other reforms (financial, monetary, external, and fiscal). For example, less than half of the provinces have completed the classification of SOEs for respective reforms. Ten pilot programs, each with a few selected SOEs, started in 2016 (Table 11.5). The State Council announced that it would reduce a significant part of SOE social services in providing utilities and property management (*Sangongyiye*) to employees by 2018. Greater discretion is given to local governments on local SOE reform (Annex 11.3). Nonetheless, substantial SOE reform has proved difficult—as reflected by government statements—reflecting vested interests and the lack of consensus. The announced pilot plans to reform a few central SOEs seem focused more on financial restructuring through merger and consolidation without concrete steps to raise efficiency. Progress has been slow in regions where SOEs play an outsized role in the local economy and have complex, multilayer subsidiary structures.

A key issue is continuing ambiguity about the role of the market and the government. While highlighting greater market discipline, reform proposals emphasize the strengthening of state influence (Naughton 2016). The same is true for the creation of a more "arms-length relationship" between the government as an owner and corporate management. While reforms envisage better delegation to professional management and boards of directors, the more institutionalized role of the Communist Party could lead to greater political influence and misaligned incentives for managers, and undermine the ability of company management to make decisions based on commercial considerations (Leutert 2016). Also, while the government might want SOEs to pursue more than just economic objectives, there is the risk that too many objectives will undermine its ability to evaluate performance, invite shirking, and, in the end, lead to continued misallocation of resources. Instead, the government could pursue noneconomic and social

[17]Reform in the 1990s led to a temporary wave of layoffs of some 35 million workers.

functions more efficiently and directly on-budget. Also, even under the mixed-ownership concept, the prospects for private sector participation might be more limited except, for example, in cases where the private investor wants to benefit from SOE's monopoly rents. The recent establishment of an equity fund (RMB350 billion or ½ percent of GDP) financed by SOEs has the potential to facilitate debt restructuring, but there is also the risk of supporting ailing industries and delaying needed restructuring.

STEPS TO ADVANCE SOE REFORMS

Successful SOE reform is critical to reduce vulnerabilities from rising indebtedness and foster a more efficient resource allocation. It should leave China with a more dynamic set of SOEs that compete on a level playing field with the private sector, and feature modern corporate governance with professional boards and management. Nonviable SOEs would be restructured or allowed to exit.

Empirical estimates support this conclusion. A two-sector model with reasonable parameters—including SOEs' share of the economy, productivity, and cost of capital differentials—suggests that successful SOE reforms could improve growth prospects significantly over the medium term. Illustrative scenarios show that a better allocation of capital and labor, as well as narrowing the productivity gap between SOEs and private enterprises, could lift output by 3–9 percent (relative to baseline projections), or about 0.3–0.9 percentage points of growth per year if the effect is spread across a decade (Annex 11.4). Other research supports the estimates, although they vary, suggesting that growth could improve by 2–13 percent of GDP (Dollar and Wei 2007; Hsieh and Song 2015; Unirule Institute of Economics 2015).

China's SOE reform strategy, based on international experience, should focus on the following:

- Act early to tackle both SOEs' stock and flow problems of excessive debt through financial and operational restructuring.
- Harden SOE budget constraints and strengthen corporate governance.
- Reduce barriers to entry and create a level playing field.
- Strengthen safety nets to support temporarily displaced workers and to facilitate the restructuring process.
- Establish a high-level steering committee to deal with the complexity of the reforms and to overcome strong interest groups.

In particular, this strategy should imply the following:

Restructuring or resolving nonviable SOEs. Triage the universe of SOEs to (1) identify those that are fundamentally sound; (2) liquidate nonviable SOEs (which does not necessarily mean closure); (3) establish a restructuring plan for viable SOEs that encounter losses or low returns. Expedited out-of-court restructuring for priority distressed companies that would use independent experts may complement the existing insolvency framework. Given the size and complexity, progress could usefully be kick-started with a few high-profile pilot cases of over-indebted SOEs (IMF 2016). Successful pilot restructuring in a controlled manner can help build up experience in advancing further SOE reforms (such as the experience of restructuring large chaebols in Korea [Darrow and others 2006]). Noncore objectives such as social functions (hospitals, schools, and provision of utilities) should be transferred to the budget with related assets and expenses accounted for.

Hardening budget constraints. Gradually resolving implicit guarantees through greater tolerance of defaults and carefully allocating losses to firm owners and creditors will improve the markets' assessment of credit risks in the financial system unaccustomed to defaults. Removing implicit SOE support through credit, land endowment, and natural resources would not only help address the existing debt overhang, but also improve the efficiency of new credit allocation. In addition, increasing the transfer of individual SOE profits, which is now mostly reinvested and well below the target, to the fiscal budget (the target of 30 percent by 2020)[18] and allocating SOE capital to social security funds would help harden budget constraints (Figure 11.6).

Introducing greater competition to level the playing field. Reducing entry barriers and phasing out restrictions that give SOEs a privileged role will send a clear signal (Kitzmuller and Licetti 2012). Analysis of firm-level data suggests that partial reforms of ownership change do not bring significant gains (Hao 2016). In that regard, allowing entry of private firms in the state-dominated services sector (currently more stringent than in OECD markets) (Figure 11.6) such as logistics, finance, and telecommunications; breaking up administrative monopolies; and promoting the growth of dynamic small and medium-sized enterprises would foster competition and promote growth (Kovaic, Lin, and Morris 2016).[19]

Increasing measures to support the restructuring. To minimize social costs during the restructuring, the government can mobilize on-budget fiscal support to minimize the adverse effects of layoffs, retraining, and relocation of workers The recently established RMB100 billion (0.15 percent of GDP) restructuring fund for coal and steel industries is an important step in this direction. Complementary reforms on the household residency system, rural land property rights, and framework for insolvency and resolution will facilitate the process. Fiscal reforms to improve social security portability and align intergovernmental finances by matching expenditure responsibilities with revenue sources will help address SOE legacy issues.

---

[18]This would bring Chinese SOEs more in line with other countries where SOEs transfer one- to two-thirds of profits to the budget (Zhang 2009).

[19]In 1999, the plenum tried to define the functions of state ownership by listing four areas of SOE ownership—state safety, natural monopolies, public goods provision, and important pillar and high-tech sectors. In 2006, SASAC declared the state should have full control in seven sectors and strong influence in another nine. Classification of SOEs should withdraw SOEs from contestable markets, while state ownership can focus on the provision of public goods.

Figure 11.6. SOE Reforms to Unleash Growth

1. Transfer of SOE Dividend to Fiscal Budget
(Percent of SOEs' profit)

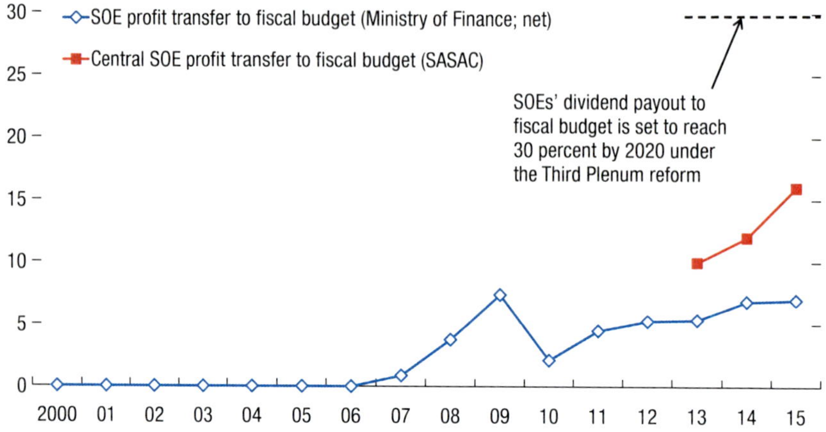

Sources: Ministry of Finance; Unirule Institute of Economics; and IMF staff estimates.
Note: SOE = state-owned enterprise.
[1] SOEs were required to contribute their profits to fiscal budget since 2007. Data for 2007 did not cover all SOEs. The Third Plenum reform required the transfer 30 percent of SOE profits to fiscal budget by 2020.

2. Further Room to Open Up Services Sector
(Index between 0 and 1; higher index reflects more restrictive)

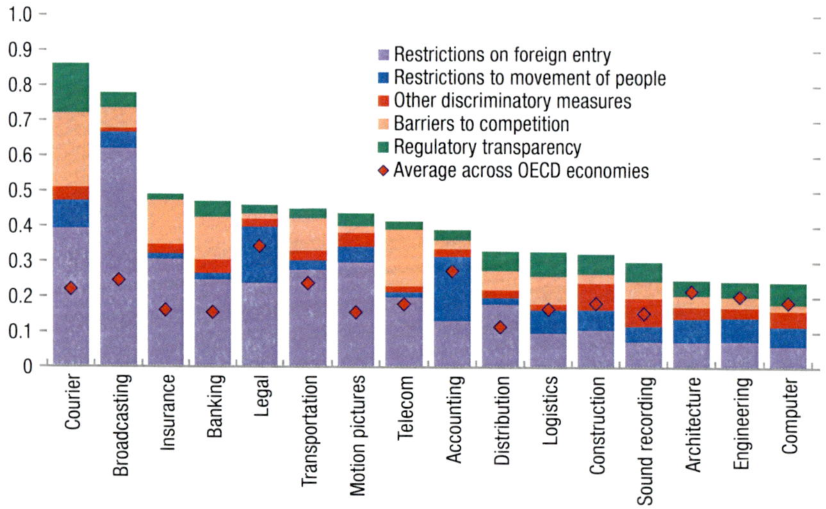

Source: Organisation for Economic Co-operation and Development (OECD) 2015c.

Establishing a high-level committee. Structural reforms are difficult to implement in any country because of strong vested interests to maintain the status quo. It is even more challenging in China's case given the large number of SOEs and the fact that reforms straddle many government agencies. There are therefore merits in establishing a well-staffed, high-level steering group with a clear mandate to promote and implement practical SOE restructurings. Strong coordination between the central and local governments, as well as financial regulators and development ministries, will facilitate the process.

CONCLUSIONS

SOEs continue to play a key role in the Chinese economy and have served as key players in countering the slowdown after the global financial crisis. While SOEs' share of output and employment has declined, they still take up an outsized portion of resources and operate at low efficiency. Implicit support to SOEs (about 2–3 percent of GDP)—such as preferential access to finance, land, protected market access, and cheaper use of natural resources—has contributed to resource misallocation.

SOE reform is a main pillar of the government's overall reform agenda. Broad objectives were outlined in the Third Plenum reform blueprint and the latest Five-Year Plan (2016–20). Key strategic principles include classifying SOEs for respective reforms, improving SOE efficiency by repositioning the state as a capital investor rather than operator, resolving overcapacity and nonviable zombie SOEs, and institutionalizing the leadership role of the Communist Party. Important details still need to be defined and it is less clear if the current reform will be as bold as that in the late 1990s, which transformed the economy.

Although SOE reforms were rightly featured prominently in the overall reform strategy, objectives are often competing and implementation has proven difficult. So far the implementation has been uneven. The announced plans for several central SOEs seem to focus more on financial restructuring without concrete steps to raise efficiency. Progress is particularly slow in regions where SOEs play an outsized role in the local economy and complex multilayer subsidiary structure.

Successful SOE reforms can help reduce vulnerabilities and raise growth potential. The overarching strategy is to address both the stock and flow problems of SOEs' excessive debt and to strengthen corporate governance. This requires prompt action to restructure SOEs and allow exit of nonviable zombie firms, harden budget constraints, and open up state-dominated sectors to a level playing field. These could significantly lift growth potential over the medium term. In the process, the government could mobilize on-budget fiscal support to minimize temporary social costs. To overcome vested interests and to foster the coordination among the many government agencies that need to be involved, a strong mandate to promote and implement SOE restructuring will be critical.

ANNEX 11.1. STATE CAPITAL INVESTMENT AND OPERATION COMPANIES TO MANAGE STATE ASSETS

Annex Figure 11.1.1. State Capital Investment and Operation Companies to Manage State Assets

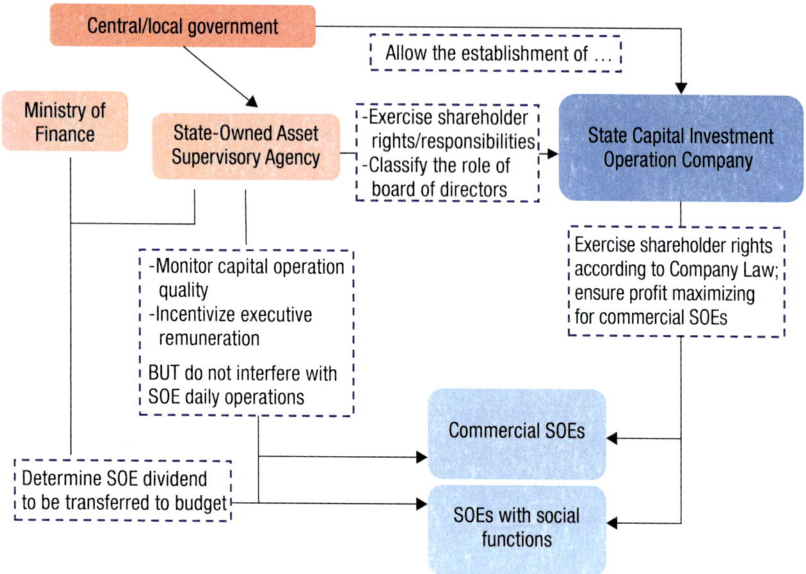

Sources: Chinese Communist Party and State Council 2015; Ministry of Finance and State-Owned Assets; State Council 2015a, 2015b, 2015c; State-Owned Assets Supervision and Administration Commission of the State Council, Ministry of Finance, and National Development Reform Commission 2016; Supervision and Administration Commission of the State Council 2015.

ANNEX 11.2. WILL CURRENT SOE REFORM BE AS BOLD AS THE LAST ROUND?

SOE reform has traditionally lagged behind other economic reforms in China. SOEs were often a policy tool to stabilize macroeconomic shocks, at times when the government advanced on other economic reforms. Since the mid-1990s, SOE reform has been a priority. The 14th Third Plenary meeting in 1993 set the agenda to modernize SOE corporate governance.[20] Later, in the Fifth Plenum in 1995, the strategy of "Grasp the large, let go the small"

[20]The "modernization of the enterprise system" consisted of four main pillars, including the clarification of property rights, rights and responsibilities of SOE management, separation of political bureaucracy and business, and professional management.

Annex Figure 11.2.1 Layoffs from the Previous SOE Reform
(Millions of workers unless otherwise stated)

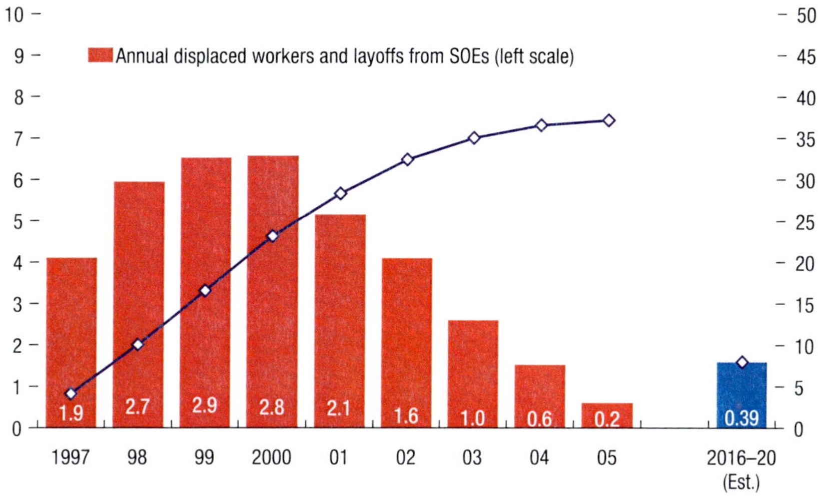

Sources: *Labor Statistics Yearbook*, National Bureau of Statistics; and IMF staff estimates.
Note: SOE = state-owned enterprise. Numbers in the chart are annual displaced workers in percent of urban employment.

concentrated these efforts in revitalizing large SOEs, while small SOEs would be boldly restructured.

It was not until SOE finances had deteriorated markedly that policymakers took bold reform action. Although progress was made on ownership reforms during the mid-1990s, SOEs faced intense competition and one-third of them incurred severe losses. In 2001, the central government decided to resolve SOE difficulties. Restructuring policies were accelerated by then-Premier Zhu Rongji's reform plan in 1998. Measures such as financial support, layoffs, buy-outs, debt-equity swaps, and corporate insolvency were implemented. Millions of SOE workers were laid off—with subsidies provided for some periods (Annex Figure 11.2.1; Cao, Qian, and Weingast 1999). Unemployment, by some estimates, rose to double-digit rates. Excess workers were quickly absorbed in the private sector, driven by strong growth from reform dividends and the accession to the World Trade Organization. Unprofitable SOEs were rehabilitated, with some nonviable ones eventually going bankrupt. A new agency, the State Administration of State-Owned Assets Commission, was established in 2003 to manage state assets and exercise ownership rights on behalf of the state.

While the SOE reform in late 1990s brought near-term costs, it has set China on a strong and sustained growth path for the next decade. The role of the SOEs was scaled back significantly following the reform (Figure 11.2.). The number of SOEs also declined from 262,000 in 1997 to 116,000 a decade later, even though the number of central SOEs was unchanged. As a result, the share of total industrial assets of SOEs dropped from 90 percent in 2000 to about 40 percent in 2006, of which central SOEs' asset share rose from 40 to 50 percent of all SOE assets. Although SOEs have a declining share in the economy, they still matter.

ANNEX 11.3. SHADES OF GREY OF STATE-OWNED ENTERPRISES REFORMS

Progress in SOE reforms has been limited. Some local governments have taken incremental steps to expand mixed-ownership (Chongqing from 47 percent to two-thirds and Guangdong to at least 70 percent by 2017) and transfer equity stakes to provincial social security fund (Shandong). Among local SOEs, some entered payment difficulties and began to enter restructuring through consolidation, while others diversified to noncore businesses.

Case Studies

Local SOEs in the coal industry. Longmay Group, a local SOE in Heilongjiang, is the largest coal company in northeast China. The group was formed by consolidating across four local areas with the legacies of these zombies, but incurred sizable losses (more than half of registered capital) when coal prices plummeted. It has a staggeringly large payroll of 0.24 million workers (60 percent of total cost) and fringe payments for another 0.18 million retired workers. The group has taken steps, including cutting wages by nearly half and restructuring debt by extending maturity and lowering interest rates. Plans to divert 30–40 percent of workers will be implemented in steps, first through vocational training; layoffs are not considered.

Steel industry.

- *Local SOE.* The Dongbei Special Steel Company allowed several debt defaults since 2015. Initial debt restructuring attempts through debt-equity swaps failed to reach a broad agreement among creditors and shareholders and the company has filed for bankruptcy procedures. It is likely to be a lengthy process and creditors are less certain of the recovery rate on claims.
- *Central SOEs.* Sinosteel Company has delayed the redemption of claims since October 2015. The latest debt restructuring consists of refinancing through lower interest rates and extending maturity, as well as a debt-equity swap of 30–90 percent of claims. The ratio varies depending on the nature of the claims. At the same time, the merger between Baosteel Group and Wuhan Steel is underway and it is uncertain to what degree the merger will significantly improve efficiency.

Local SOE in the textiles industry. A medium-sized textile SOE in Hebei has faced headwinds in its core business on cotton yard and textile cloth. The company employed about 8,000 workers in 2014, down from the peak of 30,000 in 2010. The local SOE bears social responsibility for its workers, guided by local governments. Employees were made redundant with a lump-sum package (about one-third of the total workforce), reemployed in nearby services with comparable wages, and offered a buy-out package (80 percent of the minimum wage for five years). The SOE also holds sizable land resources (with substantial unrealized gains), which were pledged to finance losses, leased, or sold to generate revenue.

ANNEX 11.4. GROWTH IMPACT OF SOE REFORMS

SOE reforms can improve growth broadly through two channels: better resource allocation and catching up productivity with the private sector. The following illustrates a simple two-sector production model to examine the efficiency gains associated with SOE reforms based on Dollar and Wei (2007).

Model

Assume the output in a given year is the sum of value-added from the SOEs and private firms. A standard Cobb-Douglas production function will imply: $Y = Y_s + Y_p = A_s K_s^{\alpha} L_s^{1-\alpha} + A_p K_p^{\alpha} L_p^{1-\alpha}$ in which Y is the GDP output, A is the total factor productivity (TFP), K and L are capital and labor inputs, and s and p denote SOEs and private firms.

Narrowing the productivity gap between SOEs and private firms will mean the difference between A_s and A_p becomes smaller. A reallocation of resources of capital from SOEs to private firms (leaving the labor input fixed), would result in a change of GDP by

$$Y' - Y = \left(A_s'\left(K_s - X\right)_s^{\alpha} L_s^{1-\alpha} + A_p\left(K_p + X\right)_p^{\alpha} L_p^{1-\alpha}\right) - \left(A_s K_s^{\alpha} L_s^{1-\alpha} + A_p K_p^{\alpha} L_p^{1-\alpha}\right)$$

in which A_s' is larger than A_r and X is positive representing the resource reallocated from SOEs to private firms. The optimal reallocation of capital will satisfy the marginal equilibrium conditions that the marginal returns to capital will be identical across state and private firms. As a result, using the representation in Dollar and Wei (2007), the increment in GDP (in percent) will become the following with d_p and d_s representing the output to capital ratios for respective firms:

$$\%\Delta GDP = \frac{(1 + \frac{K_p}{K_s})^{\alpha}\left[1 + (\frac{K_p}{K_s})^{1-\alpha}(\frac{d_p}{d_s})^{\frac{1}{1-\alpha}}\right]}{1 + \frac{K_p}{K_s}(\frac{d_p}{d_s})}$$

This is a one-off improvement of GDP in level terms. Under the assumption that the benefits are gradually (and linearly) released over a decade, one could infer the annual increase of the growth rate each year through geometric means.

Annex Table 11.4.1. SOE Reforms to Unleash New Sources of Growth
(Percent)

	Scenarios								
Scenarios	**1A**	**1B**	**1C**	**2A**	**2B**	**2C**	**3A**	**3B**	**3C**
Reduction of credit spreads between SOEs and private sector	1.5	1.5	1.5	2.0	2.0	2.0	2.5	2.5	2.5
SOEs' share of total capital inputs	20	33	40	20	33	40	20	33	40
Increase in growth rate	0.3	0.5	0.6	0.4	0.6	0.7	0.5	0.7	0.9
Direct effect from total factor productivity improvement	0.1	0.2	0.2	0.1	0.1	0.1	0.1	0.1	0.1
Indirect effect from resources reallocation	0.2	0.3	0.4	0.3	0.5	0.6	0.4	0.7	0.8
Total implied GDP level change	3.3	4.8	5.7	3.9	5.9	7.0	4.8	7.6	9.0
Direct effect from total factor productivity improvement	1.2	1.7	2.1	0.7	1.0	1.3	0.7	0.9	1.1
Indirect effect from resources reallocation	2.1	3.2	3.6	3.1	4.9	5.7	4.2	6.7	7.9

Sources: Dollar and Wei 2007; Hsieh and Song 2015; Unirule Institute of Economics 2015; and IMF staff estimates.

Parameterization

Data suggest that capital ratios between state and private firms are about 38 percent (based on total industrial assets). This uses parameters of 20, 33, and 40 as illustration.

One cannot directly observe the capital reallocated (X) and improvement of TFP (A'_s) but it can be inferred from the equilibrium condition of marginal returns of capital between SOEs and private firms. As illustrated previously, credit cost for SOEs are lower due to implicit support. With SOE reforms, the credit spreads are likely to narrow as capital reallocated and implicit guarantees being resolved. It uses the parameters of reduction of credit spreads by 1.5, 2.0, and 2.5 percent, respectively.

REFERENCES

Batson, A. 2016. "Villains or Victims? The Role of SOEs in China's Economy?" In *The State Sector's New Clothes, GaveKal China Economic Quarterly* 20 (2).

Brandt, L., and X. D. Zhu. 2010. "Accounting for China's Growth." IZA Discussion Paper No. 4764, Institute for the Study of Labor, Bonn. http://ssrn.com/abstract=1556552.

Cao, Y., Y. Qian, and B. Weingast. 1999. "From Federalism, Chinese Style, to Privatization, Chinese Style." *Economics of Transition* 7: 103–31.

Chinese Communist Party and State Council. 2015. "Guiding Principles on Deepening SOE Reforms." September 14. http://www.sasac.gov.cn/n85881/n85921/c2051975/content.html.

Chivakul, M., and W. R. Lam. 2015. "Assessing China's Corporate Sector Vulnerabilities." Working Paper No.15/72, International Monetary Fund, Washington.

Chun, Y., J. Chu, and G. M. Liao. 2010. "State Ownership Corporate and Unsecured Loan: Government Intervention, Implicit Collateral or Information Advantage?" *Accounting Research* 10: 49–54 (in Chinese).

Darrow, D., C. Lewis, Y. M. Shin, and Y. S. Park. 2006. "The Debt Restructuring Process in South Korea." Orrick, Herrington & Sutcliffe and Shin & Kim.

Deutsche Bank. 2016. "Transition between Two Credit Cycles: Private vs State." Deutsche Bank Markets Research, September 19.

Dollar, D., and S. J. Wei. 2007. "Das (Wasted) Kapital: Firm Ownership and Investment Efficiency in China." Working Paper No. 07/09, International Monetary Fund, Washington.

Hao, Y. 2016. "Can Mixed-Ownership Reform Improve SOE Efficiency? Firm-Level Analysis Based on Ownership Change." Unpublished, Peking University.

Hsieh, C. T., and Z. Song. 2015. "Grasp the Large, Let Go of the Small: The Transformation of the State Sector in China." *Brookings Papers on Economic Activity*, Spring.

International Monetary Fund (IMF). 2016. "The People's Republic of China—Selected Issues." Country Report No. 16/271, Washington.

Kitzmuller, M., and M. M. Licetti. 2012. "Encouraging Thriving Markets for Development." *Viewpoint*, World Bank Policy Note 331, World Bank, Washington. http://siteresources.worldbank.org/EXTFINANCIALSECTOR/Resources/282884-1303327122200/VP331-Competition-Policy.pdf.

Kovaic, W., C. Lin, and D. Morris. 2016. "China's Competition Policy and Legal Framework." Unpublished, forthcoming.

Kowalski, P., M. Buge, M. Sztajerowska, and M. Egeland. 2013. "State-Owned Enterprises: Trade Effects and Policy Implications." OECD Trade Policy Paper No. 147, OECD Publishing, Paris.

Lardy, N. 2014. *Markets over Mao: The Rise of Private Business in China*. Washington: Institute for International Economics.

Leutert, W. 2016. "Challenges Ahead in China's Reform of State-Owned Enterprises." *Asia Policy* 21 (January): 83–99.

Li, Y. 2016. "Deleveraging Requires an Integrated Solution." Unpublished.

Maliszewski, W., S. Arslanalp, J. Caparusso, J. Garrido, S. Guo, J. S. Kang, W. R. Lam, T. Law, W. Liao, N. Rendak, P. Wingender, J. Yu, and L. Zhang. 2016. "Resolving China's Corporate Debt Problem." IMF Working Paper 16/203, International Monetary Fund, Washington.

Ministry of Finance and State-Owned Assets Supervision and Administration Commission of the State Council. 2016. "Notice to Strengthen the Evaluation Criteria Based on Classification of Central State-Owned Enterprises." Guozifa 2016/No.252.

Ministry of Finance of the People's Republic of China. "On the Issuance of the 'Implementation Plan on Improving the Central Corporate Functions Classification Assessment.'" http://www.mof.gov.cn/zhengwuxinxi/zhengcefabu/201609/t20160927_2427520.htm [in Chinese].

Moody's. 2015. *Government-Related Issuers: Rating Methodology*. Moody's Investors Services.

National Development and Reform Commission. 2016. "G20 Voluntary Peer Review by China and United States on Fossil Fuel Subsidies." Unpublished.

Naughton, B. 2016. "State Enterprise Reform: Missing in Action." In *The State Sector's New Clothes: Will SOEs Save China's Economy or Drag It Down. China Economic Quarterly* 20 (2).

Organisation for Economic Co-operation and Development (OECD). 2009. "State Owned Enterprises in China: Reviewing the Evidence." OECD Working Group on Privatization and Corporate Governance of State Owned Assets, OECD Occasional Paper, Paris.

———. 2015a. *State Owned Enterprises in the Development Process*. Paris. OECD Publishing.

———. 2015b. *OECD Guidelines on Corporate Governance of State Owned Enterprises, 2015 Edition*. Paris: OECD Publishing.

———. 2015c. Service Trade Restriction Index. Paris. http://www.oecd.org/tad/services-trade/services-trade-restrictiveness-index.htm.

———. 2016. *Policies for Sound and Effective Investment in China*. Better Policies Series. Paris: OECD Publishing.

State Council. 2015a. "Comments on State-Owned Enterprise Mixed-Ownership Reforms." September 24. http://www.sasac.gov.cn/n85881/n85921/c2111460/content.html.

———. 2015b. "Comments on Strengthening the Mechanism of National Asset Management." November 4. http://www.sasac.gov.cn/n85881/n85921/c2111356/content.html.

———. 2015c. "Comments on Measures to Prevent a Loss of National Assets." November 11. http://www.sasac.gov.cn/n85881/n85921/c2111374/content.html.

State-Owned Assets Supervision and Administration Commission of the State Council, Ministry of Finance, and National Development Reform Commission. 2015. "Guidelines for Classification of State-owned Enterprises." December 29. http://www.sasac.gov.cn/n85881/n85921/c2169765/content.html.

Unirule Institute of Economics. 2015. *The Nature, Performance, and Reform of the State-Owned Enterprises.* Unirule Institute of Economics, Beijing.

Zhang, C. 2009. "Effective Discipline with Adequate Autonomy: The Direction for Further Reform of China's SOE Dividend Policy." Policy Note, World Bank, Washington. http://www.wds.worldbank.org/external/default/WDSContentServer/WDSP/IB/2010/03/02/000333038_20100302031054/Rendered/PDF/532540ESW0P11310final0Nov27020090En.pdf.

CHAPTER 12

Upgrading Macroeconomic Statistics

ZHAO XIUZHEN AND ROBERT DIPPELSMAN

China has achieved tremendous progress in modernizing its economy and is increasingly integrated into the global economy. As the market plays a more decisive role in economic and financial developments, the Chinese government and market participants need accurate and timely information for sound policymaking and investment and consumption decisions. New requirements for data call not only for a broader range of indicators, involving all sectors, but also for more frequent release of timely and high-quality macroeconomic data. China's economic and financial integration with the rest of the world (Figures 12.1–12.4) also suggests the need for cross-country comparable data to support comparative analysis, the coordination of global economic policies, and informed decision making.

Along with these developments, the Chinese authorities have continued efforts to modernize the statistical framework; particularly measures to strengthen the statistical system and enhance data transparency. This culminated with China's subscription in October 2015 to the Special Data Dissemination Standard (SDDS) of the IMF, which positioned its statistical practices at a higher tier of the IMF's data dissemination standards, an important step in the dissemination of more timely and comprehensive statistics. Box 12.1 summarizes key dimensions and elements of the SDDS.

As a member of the Group of Twenty (G20) nations, meanwhile, China has been involved in the G20 Data Gaps Initiative (DGI) (Box 12.2) and has made important progress in several key areas of the DGI framework.

This chapter reviews recent developments in China's statistical system for producing and disseminating macroeconomic statistics and highlights statistical challenges facing the rapidly growing economy.

The authors would like to thank Michael Stanger, Marco Marini, Antonio Galicia-Escotto, Gary Jones, Longmei Zhang, Evrim Bese Goksu, Greta Butaviciute, and Lina Yu for their contributions and comments. This chapter also benefited from general guidance and valuable suggestions from Johannes Mueller and Alfred Schipke.

Figure 12.1. Share of World GDP
(Percent, 2015)

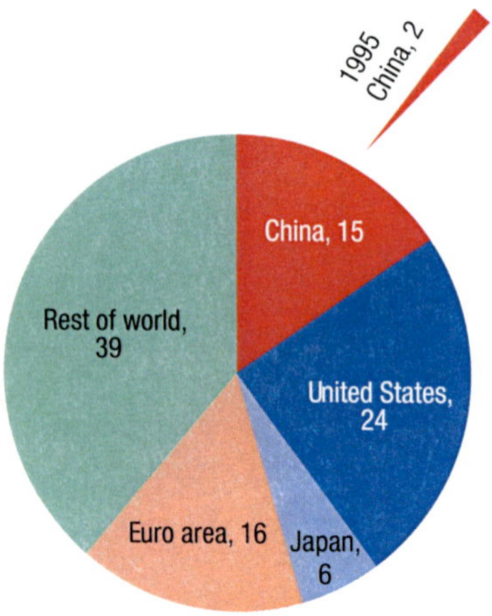

Sources: IMF, World Economic Outlook database; and IMF 2016.

Figure 12.2. Share of Foreign Exchange Reserves
(Percent, 2015)

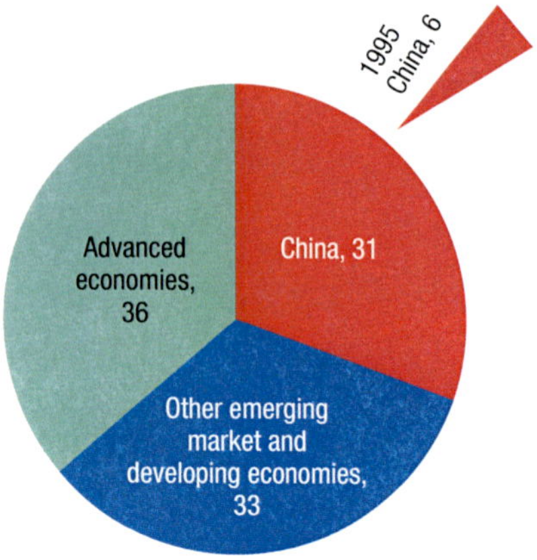

Source: IMF, International Financial Statistics database.

Figure 12.3. Contribution to Global Growth
(Percentage points)

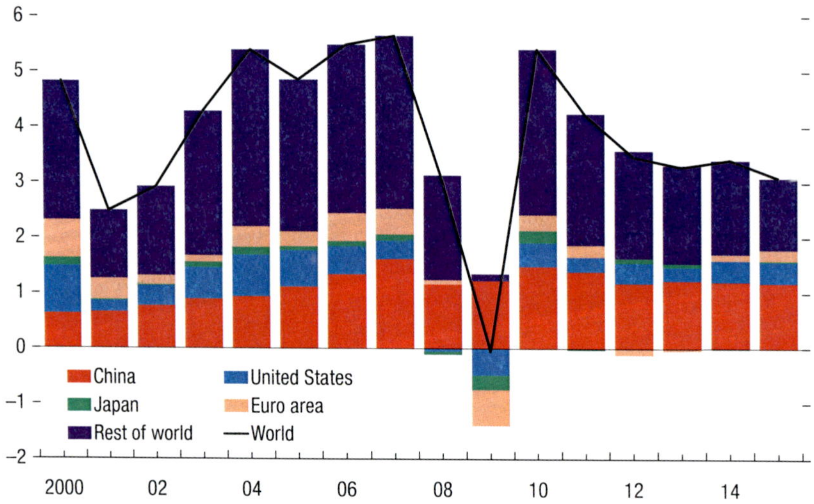

Sources: IMF, World Economic Outlook database; and IMF staff calculations.

Figure 12.4. Share of World Exports and Imports
(Percent)

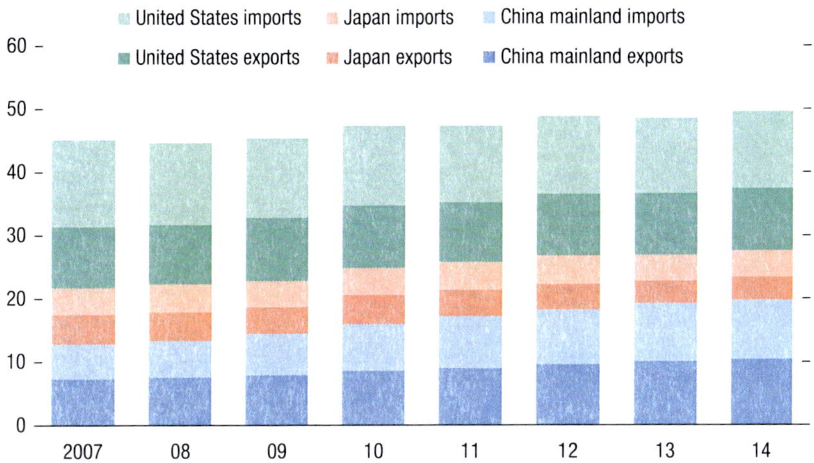

Source: IMF 2015.

RECENT DEVELOPMENTS IN CHINA'S STATISTICAL SYSTEM

Macroeconomic statistics have one broad purpose: to serve decision making. The availability of comprehensive, reliable, timely, and high-quality statistics is essential for the formulation of appropriate macroeconomic and financial policies. Discussion here focuses primarily on the following macroeconomic data sets: real sector statistics (national accounts, labor market statistics, and prices), government finance statistics, external sector statistics, and monetary and financial statistics.

Real Sector Statistics

The National Bureau of Statistics (NBS) is responsible for compiling real sector data in China and has come a long way toward the adoption of the System of National Accounts (SNA) as a comprehensive framework.[1] The first official accounts were compiled in 1952 in accordance with the Material Product System

[1]The SNA is the internationally agreed standard set of recommendations on how to compile measures of economic activity in accordance with strict accounting conventions based on economic principles. Other macroeconomic data sets also follow the SNA as their respective underlying framework: government finance, external sector, and monetary statistics. The latest edition is the 2008 SNA.

Box 12.1. IMF Data Standards Initiatives

These initiatives are designed to promote the dissemination of timely and comprehensive statistics. The standards have almost universal coverage and are intended to contribute to the formulation of sound macroeconomic policies and the efficient functioning of financial markets. Three tiers currently comprise the initiatives:

- The Special Data Dissemination Standard (SDDS) was established in 1996 to guide members who have, or might seek, access to international capital markets in providing their economic and financial data to the public (IMF 2013a). SDDS identifies four dimensions of data dissemination: (1) data coverage, periodicity, and timeliness; (2) access by the public; (3) integrity of the disseminated data; and (4) quality of the disseminated data. As of November 2016, 63 jurisdictions were SDDS subscribers. China subscribed to the SDDS in October 2015.[1]
- The General Data Dissemination System (GDDS) was created in 1997 to guide countries in providing to the public comprehensive, accessible, timely, and reliable economic, financial, and sociodemographic data (IMF 2013b). From May 2015, an enhanced GDDS (e-GDDS) superseded the GDDS, emphasizing the data dissemination aspect under the initiative. As of November 2016, 110 countries were e-GDDS participants. China participated in the GDDS until 2002, when it graduated to the SDDS.[2]
- The SDDS Plus was created in 2012 as the third and highest tier of the IMF's Data Standards Initiatives to help address data gaps identified during the global financial crisis, including in the context of the G20 Data Gaps Initiative (IMF 2013c). As of November 2016, 11 countries were SDDS Plus adherents.[3]

[1]See http://dsbb.imf.org/pages/sdds/home.aspx.

[2]See http://dsbb.imf.org/pages/gdds/home.aspx.

[3]See http://dsbb.imf.org/pages/SDDS/Home.aspx?sp=y.

(MPS),[2] with official SNA estimates produced from 1985. Accounts were compiled from 1985 to 1992 using both the MPS and the national accounts, although the latter were essentially derived from the MPS accounts using a conversion system developed by the United Nations Statistics Division. In 1992, the SNA replaced the MPS as the official accounts system. Since then, the NBS has concentrated on developing data sources and refining its procedures to directly estimate national accounts according to the SNA (OECD 2000). China's participation in the IMF's General Data Dissemination System in 2002 and subscription to SDDS in 2015 facilitated NBS efforts to improve the compilation of real sector data by doing the following:

- Conducting surveys on small industrial and commercial enterprises
- Assessing regional GDP data compiled by provincial statistical agencies

[2]The MPS was developed in the Soviet Union and used by most countries with centrally planned economies. The main difference between the MPS and SNA is that the former excluded "non-material services" from the production boundary. The MPS statistical system was oriented to monitoring central plans and therefore put little emphasis on time-series data.

Box 12.2. G20 Data Gaps Initiative

In April 2009, the G20 Finance Ministers and Central Bank Governors called on the IMF and the Financial Stability Board (FSB) to identify major financial and economic information gaps. As a result, in September 2009, the IMF and the FSB presented a report to launch the Data Gaps Initiative (DGI), along with a set of recommendations to be implemented in years to come (IMF and FSB 2009). Given the significant progress made in implementing the DGI recommendations, in September 2015 the G20 Finance Ministers and Central Bank Governors endorsed the completion of the first phase of the DGI and the start of its second phase (DGI-2). DGI-2 aims to strengthen and consolidate the progress to date, achieve the potential for data provision embodied in the initiative, and promote the regular flow of high-quality statistics for policy use. The Sixth Progress Report on the Implementation of the G20 Data Gaps Initiative (prepared by IMF and the Financial Stability Board) provides the latest status of the DGI progress and outlines the recommendations of DGI-2.[1]

DGI-2 maintains the continuity of DGI-1 while also reflecting on the evolving policy needs. Work on DGI-2 started in 2016 with particular focus on (1) finishing uncompleted work (sectoral accounts, government finance statistics); (2) starting regular collection of data under the new conceptual frameworks; (3) strengthening collection of data already covered by the DGI recommendations; (4) promoting the comparability of data sets; and (5) improving the quality, completeness, timeliness, frequency, and general robustness of data.

Monitoring risk in the financial sector remains central, but DGI-2 also raises the emphasis on the inter-linkages across the economic and financial system, reflecting the evolving policy needs to provide a complete picture of the economic and financial system.

The Principal Global Indicators website, hosted by the IMF, was launched as part of the DGI, which collects and disseminates comparable data for all G20 economies and selected non-G20 member economies.[2]

China, as a G20 country, has made important progress under the first phase of the DGI framework, and continues efforts to fully implement the DGI recommendations during its second phase. In particular, the country has been working through the G20 DGI to address some data gaps relevant for surveillance of financial sector risk and interconnectedness. These efforts created synergies with the authorities' work programs for improving macroeconomic statistics. Annex 12.1 presents a heat map showing the DGI implementation status of all G20 countries. China assumed the G20 presidency in 2016 and its close involvement in the G20 DGI, which entered its second phase in 2016, will be critical to the continued success of the initiative.

[1]See http://www.imf.org/external/np/g20/pdf/2015/6thprogressrep.pdf.

[2]See http://www.principalglobalindicators.org.

- Compiling growth rates on a trial basis for industrial and agricultural production using the price deflator approach
- Introducing sampling survey methods for estimating output of agricultural products, other than grain crops, such as cotton and animal stocks
- Compiling price indices using a fixed reference base (2010) to bring them closer to international good practices
- Enhancing the implementation of the Statistical Law by conducting an annual nationwide inspection of statistical law compliance and publishing outcomes of the inspection

- Taking measures to improve data dissemination formats through regular publications, including the *China Statistical Yearbook*, *China Statistics Abstract*, *China Economic Indicators*, and the NBS website
- Expanding compilation of the producer price index (PPI), using a fixed base period
- Establishing procedures for collecting, compiling, and disseminating data on the labor market
- Improving the integrity and accessibility of data dissemination by publishing advance calendars and information on data revisions
- Compiling and disseminating quarterly data for discrete GDP (by production approach) at both current and constant prices
- Improving transparency in the dissemination of the consumer price index (CPI) and PPI

Despite progress, real sector statistics remain weak and have not kept pace with the emerging needs of the larger, more sophisticated, more market-oriented economy. The NBS and public commentators have identified shortcomings. Labor market and high-frequency data are often unavailable to the public. These data weaknesses might be better understood in association with the unique institutional arrangements under which China's statistical system operates. The statistical system is highly decentralized, with a large network of statistical offices in local and provincial governments and closely linked to their structures, including planning activities. The system operates with less transparency than in many other countries, although data collection initiatives across several areas have improved in recent years.

National Accounts

The main gap in availability of national accounts is the lack of quarterly GDP by expenditure at constant prices. Expenditure data are available only annually and only at current prices. This gap is an obstacle in monitoring the planned shift from growth driven by exports and investment to growth driven by consumption.

External criticism has suggested that data are not always consistent within the system or with other indicators, and that national accounts still have a long way to go to align with international standards and best practices. Structural issues in the economy include a switch from state-owned industrial enterprises to market-oriented private service firms, emphasis on household consumption over investment, and the role of the small-scale and informal sectors for services. These developments present challenges for statistical measurement, requiring additional data sources, and revision of techniques and ratios. At the same time, the decentralized structure of the Chinese statistical system adds obstacles to making changes. Important gaps remain for domestic demand, especially private consumption and investment spending. One major problem with constant price GDP data by industry is the use of the single deflation method, which leads to significant over- or underestimation of GDP growth when movements in input and output prices are significantly different.[3] Shortcomings exist in the deflation methodology, as price indices are often missing or incomplete, and they frequently do not match the related activity or expenditure category. Detailed breakdown of GDP (for example, GDP by industry of nine economic activities) is more limited than other G20 economies. The sources and methods used for compiling the national accounts are not very transparent and differences in trends shown by GDP and compared to some published quarterly and monthly indicators are not generally explained.

In recent years, China has published annual and quarterly GDP estimates in line with the revisions policy set by the authorities. Based on the recent history, the first estimate of GDP growth—published just two or three weeks after the end of each quarter—was not changed substantially in later estimates. Small revisions in quarterly GDP growth appear related only to seasonal adjustment factors and do not incorporate revisions to data sources. Box 12.3 details the recent history of China's GDP revisions.

Although balance sheet data are lacking, the authorities are committed to producing a national balance sheet by 2020. Compilation of the national balance sheet would also contribute to China's implementation of the G20 DGI recommendation on sectoral accounts, which is aimed at promoting the compilation and dissemination of sectoral balance sheets, flow of funds, and sectoral data more generally, starting with the G20 economies.[4] These data are particularly suited for analysis of financial interlinkages and vulnerability of the households and nonfinancial corporate sectors.

Price Statistics

The NBS has recently improved transparency in the dissemination of consumer and producer prices. The National Summary Data Page contains monthly series of the CPI and PPI,[5] with 2010 as the reference year, in line with SDDS requirements. More information about the coverage and compilation methodology, in particular CPI weightings, is needed to understand the characteristics of these data.

Since February 2012, three monthly residential property price indices (RPPI) for China have been available on the website of the Bank for International Settlements. No commercial real estate price indices are currently available. The NBS plans to expand the cities covered in the compilation of

[3]The effect could be significant and would tend to mask fluctuations in GDP. In a simulation with data from one developing country, Dippelsman, Josyula, and Métreau (2016) found the distortion in GDP growth rates caused by single deflation peaked at about 1.5 percent in 2009, a period of lower commodity prices.

[4]Countries that adhere to the SDDS Plus are required to disseminate a minimum set of internationally comparable sectoral financial balance sheets.

[5]See China's National Summary Data Page at http://www.stats.gov.cn/english/Statisticaldata/nsdp/201508/t20150819_1232260.html.

Box 12.3. China—An Assessment of GDP Revisions

GDP Revisions Policy

The official revision policy of China's GDP is outlined in the metadata posted on the National Summary Data Page.[1] The preliminary estimate for a given year is published 15 days after the end of the year. This is made as the sum of quarterly estimates of the year. The preliminary verification is published 9 months after the end of the year, and final verification comes three months later. Quarterly data are revised in accord with the annual GDP revision cycle. The GDP revisions policy strictly adheres to the timeliness of source data received after 10 days, 8 months, and 11 months after the end of the year. Benchmark revisions are made to incorporate census data, changes in the calculation methods, international standards, and classification criteria. Many other countries have larger revisions because additional information becomes available over time, such as late identification of new enterprises, more complete data from detailed surveys and administrative systems, and reconciliation processes such as supply and use balancing.

The release calendar of recent GDP publications is aligned with the current revisions policy. Table 12.3.1 shows the GDP press releases published on the National Bureau of Statistics (NBS) website (in English) during January 2014–September 2015. The average timeliness of the preliminary GDP estimate was 19 days (slightly above the 15-day target). The preliminary verification and final verification for the year 2013 were replaced by the benchmark revision published in December 2014, which was based on the results of the 2013 Economic Census.

Revisions of Annual GDP

In recent years, China has not made substantial revisions to the preliminary estimates of annual GDP growth (Table 12.3.2). Small, downward revisions are noted in the second estimate (the preliminary verification) for 2012 and 2014, both signaling a reduction of GDP growth by 0.1 percentage points compared with the preliminary estimate. On the other hand, GDP growth for 2013 has remained unchanged at 7.7 percent.

Table 12.3.1. China: GDP Press Releases Published from January 2014 to September 2015

Preliminary Estimate	
January 21, 2014	Annual GDP in 2013
April 17, 2014	Quarterly GDP in 2014:Q1
July 17, 2014	Quarterly GDP in 2014:Q1–14:Q2
October 22, 2014	Quarterly GDP in 2014:Q1–14:Q3
April 20, 2015	Quarterly GDP in 2015:Q1
July 16, 2015	Quarterly GDP in 2015:Q1–15:Q2
January 22, 2015	Annual GDP in 2014
Preliminary Verification	
September 8, 2015	Annual GDP in 2014
Final Verification	
January 9, 2014	Annual GDP in 2012
Benchmark Revision	
December 19, 2014	Benchmark revision of GDP for year 2013 (based on economic census)

Source: National Bureau of Statistics.

[1] http://dsbb.imf.org/Pages/SDDS/CtyCtgList.aspx?ctycode=CHN.

Box 12.3. China—An Assessment of GDP Revisions *(continued)*

Table 12.3.2. China: Annual GDP Estimates for the Years 2012, 2013, and 2014

(Annual rates in percent, Constant prices)

Year	PE	PV	FV
2012	7.8	7.7	7.7
2013	7.7	7.7	7.7[1]
2014	7.4	7.3	...

Source: National Bureau of Statistics.

Note: ... = none; FV = final verification ($t + 12$ months); PE = preliminary estimate ($t + 15$ days); PV = preliminary verification ($t + 9$ months).

[1] Benchmark revision released in December 2014, based on 2013 economic census results.

Figure 12.3.1. Quarterly GDP—Revisions to 2013 and 2014 Quarters

(Quarterly rates in percent, seasonally adjusted in constant prices)

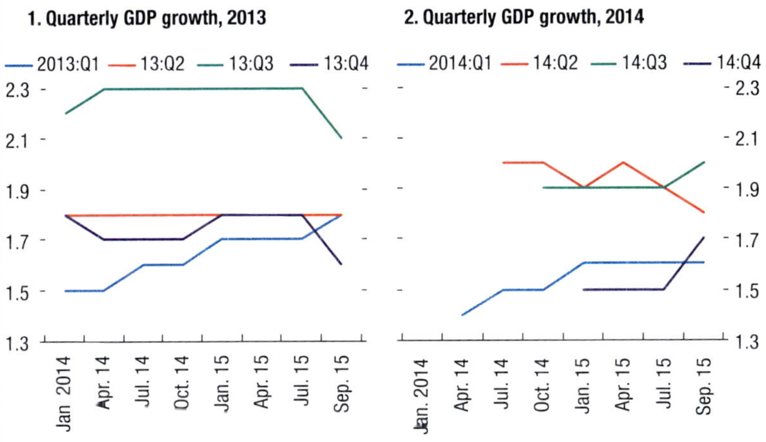

Source: National Bureau of Statistics website and publications.

The 2013 benchmark revision altered the GDP estimates at current prices. The benchmark revision increased nominal GDP in 2013 by 3.4 percent. The nominal growth for 2013 was revised up, to 10.1 percent from 9.5 percent. Therefore, the 0.6 percent upward revision was due to an upward revision of the GDP deflator.

Revisions of Quarterly GDP

As for annual data, no revisions are made to unadjusted quarterly GDP data. However, revisions to seasonally adjusted data are generated by seasonal adjustment techniques. Table 12.3.3 presents the quarterly GDP growth series published between January 2014 and September 2015. The quarterly revisions during this period appear of limited size, unsystematic (see Figure 12.3.1), and comparable with revisions due to seasonal adjustment in other countries.

Box 12.3. China—An Assessment of GDP Revisions (*continued*)

Table 12.3.3. Quarterly GDP Growth by Month of Release

(Period: 2013:Q1–15:Q2. Quarterly rates in percent, seasonally adjusted in constant prices)

Quarter	Jan-14	Apr-14	Jul-14	Oct-14	Jan-15	Apr-15	Jul-15	Sep-15
2013:Q1	1.5	1.5	**1.6**	1.6	**1.7**	1.7	1.7	**1.8**
Q2	1.8	1.8	1.8	1.8	1.8	1.8	1.8	1.8
Q3	2.2	**2.3**	2.3	2.3	2.3	2.3	2.3	**2.1**
Q4	1.8	**1.7**	1.7	1.7	**1.8**	1.8	1.8	**1.6**
2014:Q1		1.4	1.5	1.5	**1.6**	1.6	1.6	1.6
Q2			2.0	2.0	**1.9**	**2.0**	**1.9**	**1.8**
Q3				1.9	1.9	1.9	1.9	**2.0**
Q4					1.5	1.5	1.5	**1.7**
2015:Q1						1.3	**1.4**	**1.3**
Q2							1.7	**1.8**

Source: National Bureau of Statistics.

RPPI. Progress here should also contribute to China's implementation of the Phase II G20 recommendation on RPPI, which also encourages production of long time series, development of a list of other housing-related indicators, and dissemination of the headline RPPI data through the Principal Global Indicators website (Box 12.2).

Labor Market Indicators

Major data gaps remain for labor market indicators. Employment data are compiled annually and disseminated within two months of the end of the year. The NBS has conducted a monthly labor force survey since 2009, but it is not publicly available. If publicly disseminated, survey data could provide timely information on both employment and unemployment. The registered unemployment rate for urban areas is available quarterly but these do not appear to truly measure unemployment because of the limited scope of the registration process. Wage data are compiled annually and disseminated within four to five months after the end of the year. To increase coverage and timeliness of wage statistics, the NBS is planning to add a survey of small establishments to an online quarterly survey of large establishments.

Reforms Under Way to Improve Real Sector Statistics

The NBS is aware of the shortcomings in the real sector statistics and has been taking steps to address some of the main problems. Reforms of official statistical systems are currently focused on four areas that the NBS has identified as shortcomings (Xu 2016): (1) compilation of GDP, for owner-occupied housing valuation, household final consumption, and valuation of research and development expenditure;[6] (2) fixed-asset investment; (3) lack of integration of urban and rural household surveys; and (4) services sector statistical methodology and procedures.

To improve the statistical process, the NBS plans to undertake 10 measures to enhance data reliability (Xu 2016). These are (1) strengthening the business/institution registry system, (2) establishing integrated reporting forms for enterprises, (3) adopting unified data processing software, (4) establishing an internet-based direct data reporting system, (5) integrating urban and rural household surveys, (6) adopting a comprehensive and standardized statistical survey for the services sector, (7) adopting a methodology to compile chain-linked indices, (8) raising the threshold of enterprises for the fixed investment and industrial enterprise surveys, (9) conducting data validation of basic information for enterprises with assets above a threshold value, and (10) establishing a data quality assessment and evaluation system.

External Sector Statistics

The State Administration of Foreign Exchange is responsible for compiling external sector statistics for China. Balance of payments and international investment position are compiled with reference to the sixth edition of the IMF's *Balance of Payments and International Investment Position Manual* (BPM6).[7] These data are disseminated on China's National Summary Data Page. Overall, balance-of-payments transactions are recorded on an accrual basis. However, due to some limitations in sources, parts of the transactions data are recorded on a cash basis. Although the International Transactions Reporting System—which collects data on a cash basis—is still used as a data source, the State Administration of Foreign Exchange plans for extra surveys that will move collection to a full accrual basis.

Although China's presentation of items for external sector statistics is in line with international standards, there is room for improvement in recording the international investment position, and no breakdown exists for foreign direct investment by equity and debt instrument in these data. As for the Coordinated Direct Investment Survey, inward data are reported consistent with the requirements of the survey, but further efforts are needed on the compilation of outward data. The Coordinated Portfolio Investment Survey was reported for the first time in December 2015, but further efforts would be welcome to report additional information (as specified in the "encouraged tables").

---

[6]Research and development expenditure was included in capital formation in revised national accounts data released in July 2016, better covering this growing aspect of the economy and bringing the data more closely into line with international statistical standards.

[7]BPM6 is the internationally agreed standard set of recommendations on how to compile measures of international transactions and positions based on economic principles. It uses concepts harmonized with the SNA and other statistical manuals. It is supported by a compilation guide and specialized guides on other aspects such as reserve assets and remittances.

The Reserves Data Template is disseminated monthly. It covers the monetary authorities that manage and hold the international reserves and the central government, which together with the monetary authorities, accounts for most of the official foreign currency obligations. Predetermined net drains on foreign currency allow for consistency checks with short-term external debt data as the former also includes debt for residents that is denominated in foreign exchange. Partial figures for currency composition of foreign exchange reserves were reported for the first time in September 2015, with data from June 2015 onward for inclusion in world aggregates published on the IMF's website.

Government Finance Statistics

The Ministry of Finance is the official agency responsible for compiling and disseminating government finance statistics for China. The ministry compiles government operations data with monthly, quarterly, and annual periodicity. The annual series consolidate central government, provincial, local governments, and social security funds, while the monthly and quarterly data exclude social security funds. The data are compiled following the methodology in the *Government Finance Statistics Manual* (GFSM) 1986,[8] and so are on a cash-basis only, which limits the analytical usefulness of the data. GFSM 1986 focuses primarily on a single balancing item, the deficit/surplus, and the government's financing requirement, where the liquidity constraint rather than the sustainability of policy choices is seen as the most binding priority. Among the many shortcomings of the cash-based GFSM 1986 system, some key elements are (1) the lack of alignment with other macroeconomic statistical systems; and (2) the lack of accounting for arrears, interest on discounted bonds, in kind transactions, and consumption of fixed assets ("depreciation").

The Ministry of Finance has recognized these shortcomings and has taken some initial steps to begin compiling and reporting to the IMF general government revenue data following the GFSM 2001 methodology. Detailed revenue data for 2003–13 as well as data on outlays by function have been compiled. However, to date no data are available on the economic classification of expenses, and this limits fiscal analysis. While the functional classification of expense provides information on the purpose for which an expense was incurred, a well-structured economic classification identifies the types of expense incurred according to the economic process involved. For example, compensation of employees, use of goods and services, and consumption of fixed capital all relate to the costs of producing nonmarket (and, in certain instances, market) goods and services by government. Subsidies, grants, social benefits, and transfers

[8]The GFSM is the internationally agreed standard set of recommendations on how to compile measures of transactions and stock positions for government finance statistics based on economic principles. It uses concepts harmonized with the SNA and other statistical manuals. The latest edition is the GFSM 2014.

other than grants relate to transfers in cash or in kind, and are aimed at redistributing income and wealth. Such measures would support improved fiscal analysis in China.

The current GFSM 2001-based series lack data on transactions in assets and liabilities, gross debt, and balance sheet stock positions. Data about general government off-budget fiscal activities are also lacking on a monthly or quarterly basis, especially for local governments, including credit to local government financing vehicles. This limits fiscal analysis aimed at determining the net worth of general government (and public sector) units, which can be viewed as a stock position resulting from the transactions and other economic flows stemming from policy actions in all previous periods. Given China's increasing exposure to the global economy and the resulting risks of changes in asset and liability positions owing to changes in currency composition, maturity breakdown, and counterparty exposures, developing these data should be a priority. Improvements in these areas of China's government finance statistics would better facilitate fiscal analysis, while also supporting China's efforts in implementing the G20 DGI recommendations.

Concurrent with the need to further improve the fiscal data, the availability of debt data that are internationally comparable for the general government and public sector could be enhanced. Because they carry obligations to make future payments, debt liabilities have the potential to create circumstances that render not only government and public corporations, but also the entire economy, vulnerable to solvency and liquidity problems. Moreover, as experience has shown—most recently by the international financial crisis that started in 2007—these vulnerabilities can have widespread economic costs, and not just for the initially affected economy. To this end, China, under the G20 DGI, has been reporting to the IMF/World Bank Public Sector Debt Statistics database following internationally agreed guidance on (1) the concepts, definitions, and classifications of public sector debt statistics; and (2) the sources and techniques for compiling these data.[9] While the series provided currently only cover the central government, the provision of enhanced institutional coverage will further improve fiscal analysis in China.

Monetary and Financial Statistics

The People's Bank of China (PBC) is the official data compiling agency for China's monetary and financial statistics. It also compiles a wide range of other macroeconomic data and financial stability indicators.

Over past years, the PBC has made continual progress in monetary and financial statistics in accordance with the IMF recommended methodology in the *Monetary and Financial Statistics Manual 2000*.[10] The most notable include the following:

---

[9]See http://worldbank.org/qpsd.

[10]The *Monetary and Financial Statistics Manual* is the internationally agreed standard set of recommendations on how to compile measures of transactions and stock positions for monetary

- Expanding coverage of other depository corporations to include foreign-funded banks operating in China, and other financial institutions such as policy banks, postal savings bank, and finance firms that accept deposits or issue liabilities included in broad money
- Improving classification of financial firm subsectors in accordance with the *Monetary and Financial Statistics Manual* into central bank, other depository corporations, other financial corporations (consisting of insurance and pension funds, other financial intermediaries, and financial auxiliaries), leading to improved data on linkages between subsectors of the financial sector
- Regular reviewing and updating the "all accounts" reporting system for use by financial institutions in China to report data in standardized format for compilation of monetary statistics as well as other macroeconomic and financial stability indicators
- Improving data dissemination by releasing monetary data on a timely and regular basis on the PBC website in addition to publication of these data in *PBC Statistics Bulletin* (quarterly), and the *PBC Annual Report*

To meet emerging data needs arising from the recent developments in China's financial system, the PBC also took initiatives in compiling new indicators. A major one is the compilation of the total social financing (TSF) indicator (Box 12.4). The TSF is not an internationally commonly used broad credit measure, but takes into consideration recent developments in China's financial systems and some unique features of the economy.

Rapid developments in China's economy and financial system have led to increasingly diverse channels of financing for the real sector, while traditional measures of credit volumes—for example, banks loans—have become of increasingly limited use to reflect the full size of financing to the real sector. In light of this, the PBC based the TSF indicator on a series of empirical studies and broad consultation with Chinese government agencies. The indicator is now closely monitored and analyzed for macroeconomic management and is also widely followed by the private sector and the general public.

Going forward, continued efforts would be needed for improving China's monetary and financial statistics, particularly the adoption of the Standardized Report Forms for reporting monetary data to the IMF. The forms embody the IMF-recommended methodology for compiling monetary statistics and present data in a manner that facilitates cross-country comparison and the application of the balance sheet approach to vulnerability analysis. Compilation of data for other financial corporations in the format of the Standardized Report Form would also contribute to China's implementation of the G20 DGI

---

and financial statistics based on economic principles. It uses concepts harmonized with the SNA and other statistical manuals. The latest edition is the *Monetary and Financial Statistics Manual and Compilation Guide.*

Box 12.4. Total Social Financing Indicators

The People's Bank of China (PBC) began compiling the total social financial (TSF flow data) series of indicators and release of data on a quarterly basis in 2011. Since 2012, the TSF has been published monthly.[1]

The TSF (flow data) is defined as the total amount of financing obtained by the real economy from the financial system monthly, quarterly, or annually. The real economy refers to nonfinancial corporations and households. The financial system refers to the entire domestic financial system, covering financial sectors and financial markets (Sheng 2014).

The TSF consists of bank loans in renminbi and in foreign currencies, entrusted loans,[2] trust loans,[3] undiscounted bankers' acceptance, net issuance of corporate bonds, funds raised from the domestic stock market by nonfinancial enterprises, and other forms of financing. The indicator (TSF flow data) is intended to provide a broad measure of new funding from the financial system to the domestic economy during the reference period.

In February 2015 the PBC also released TSF stock data for 2002–14 on an annual basis. TSF stock data are defined as the outstanding funding provided by the domestic financial system to the real economy (nonfinancial corporations and households) at the end of the reference period. The domestic financial system has similar coverage as TSF flow data. TSF stock data cover four broad categories: (1) balance-sheet-related items of financial institutions, consisting of renminbi and foreign currency loans; (2) off-balance-sheet items of financial institutions, consisting of entrusted loans, trust loans, and undiscounted bankers' acceptances; (3) direct financing (market-based) items, consisting of corporate bonds, nonfinancial corporations shares, and other equity financing; and (4) others.

---

[1]The indicator is also known as "Aggregate Financing to the Real Economy."

[2]Entrusted loans are lending between nonfinancial entities facilitated by banks, whose existence is due to regulation prohibiting nonfinancial firms from making loans. The terms of lending are decided by the lender rather than the bank.

[3]Trust loans are between nonfinancial entities facilitated by trust firms, and follow a similar operational mechanism as entrusted loans.

recommendation on cross-border exposures of nonbank corporations. These data provide useful information for analysis of cross-border exposures of nonbank financial institutions.

To support macroprudential data collection, the PBC coordinates with the China Banking Regulatory Commission in compiling financial soundness indicators and reports these data to the IMF for dissemination (Box 12.5). China's financial soundness indicators cover all core and two other indicators for deposit takers, and are produced semiannually. Continued efforts would be needed for improving the compilation of financial soundness indicators (FSIs), including, in particular, (1) compilation of FSIs for sectors other than deposit takers and (2) compilation of FSIs with the preferred quarterly frequency.

Box 12.5. Financial Soundness Indicators

The IMF developed financial soundness indicators (FSIs), together with the international community, to support macroprudential analysis and assess the strengths and vulnerabilities of financial systems. FSIs provide insight into the financial health and soundness of a country's financial institutions and its corporate and household counterparts. The IMF's Statistics Department disseminates data reported by national authorities at the FSI website.[1] As of November 2016, 117 countries and jurisdictions regularly report FSIs (data and metadata) to the IMF, including all G20 countries.

As of November 2016, the FSIs data set comprises 12 core and 28 encouraged indicators. The revised list of FSIs, reported to the Executive Board in November 2013, for future implementation includes 17 core FSIs and 35 encouraged FSIs, which resulted from IMF staff's review of the current list of FSIs in response to users' needs and financial sector developments.[2]

[1]See http://data.imf.org/?sk=9F855EAE-C765-405E-9C9A-A9DC2C1FEE47.

[2]See http://www.imf.org/external/ns/cs.aspx?id=158.

China also takes part in a financial access survey conducted by the IMF, which collects annual data on several important indicators that are aimed at measuring inclusive development in financial sector service.[11]

CHALLENGES FOR MEETING DATA NEEDS IN A RAPIDLY EVOLVING ECONOMY

China's economic reforms have accelerated over the past few years and the 13th Five-Year Plan (2016–20) has reaffirmed the country's commitment to move its ambitious reform agenda forward. This will continue to challenge statistical systems to meet ever-emerging data needs for policymakers and market participants. These challenges relate mainly to the following areas:

- New data needs arise from continued structural reforms in the economy and financial system. For instance, as financial sector reform deepened, interest rate controls were fully removed in 2015. The full liberalization of interest rates in China calls for a set of comprehensive, indicative, and timely rate data. Also, the rapid development of the debt securities market requires

[11]The financial access survey is carried out every year and managed by the IMF's Statistics Department. The survey collects and disseminates comparable time-series data on the geographical outreach and use of basic financial services provided by resident financial corporations to resident customers within a country. The survey identifies separately the following users of financial services: households and small and medium enterprises. As of November 2016, it contains data and metadata for 189 jurisdictions from 2004 onward in 152 underlying series and 47 indicators. The data can be accessed at http://data.imf.org/?sk=E5DCAB7E-A5CA-4892-A6EA-598B5463A34C.

more comprehensive, detailed, and timely data that are consistent with international methodologies and best practices.

- As China moves toward a market economy, it may become increasingly difficult to have direct access to source data, as was the case for data collection from state-owned entities under the centrally planned economy. Comprehensive and effective source data collection will require application of more techniques (for example, sample surveys) as well as more direct data reporting (through census).

The SDDS Plus as the highest tier of IMF's data standards (Box 12.1) includes rigorous data dissemination practices designed to further improve transparency and strengthen the international financial system and is open to all SDDS subscribers, especially those with systemically important financial sectors. After China has gained more experience with SDDS subscription and improved the compilation and dissemination of macroeconomic and financial statistics,[12] it may be prepared to aim for the SDDS Plus.

CONCLUSIONS

China's efforts to move toward international standards and best practices in its statistical system have accelerated the progress made in improving statistical capacity. In particular, the country's participation in IMF's GDDS from 2002 has led to the following:

- The dissemination for the first time of a comprehensive set of documentation on compilation practice of China's macroeconomic statistics
- The formulation and dissemination of plans for improvements in macroeconomic statistics
- Much improved interagency coordination and cooperation in addressing statistics-related issues

China's subscription to SDDS in 2015 was a major advance in data compilation and dissemination. Under the SDDS, the country now disseminates a comprehensive set of macroeconomic data in accordance with prescribed coverage, periodicity, and timeliness. In particular, several important data sets have become publicly available under the SDDS. These include: (1) quarterly data for discrete GDP by the production approach (at current and constant prices); (2) data on

[12]As an SDDS subscriber, China uses flexibility options for periodicity of labor market data, which are annual instead of the quarterly data that are the norm for SDDS; and timeliness for general government operations data, which are available with a lag of seven months, instead of the two quarters the SDDS normally requires. The authorities plan to make improvements in these areas.

general and central government operations, and central government debt; (3) official reserves assets; and (4) reserve data template.[13]

China's statistical capacity developments have benefited from its cooperation with international and regional organizations and bilateral agencies over many years of capacity development. International cooperation will continue to contribute to the development of China's statistical system and its integration with the rest of the world through familiarizing the authorities with internationally agreed statistical standards and best practices and assisting the authorities' efforts to align China's statistical system more closely with international standards. Box 12.6 summarizes the IMF's technical cooperation with China in macroeconomic statistics.

As China has evolved into a major force in the global economy, interest has increased in monitoring domestic economic developments that carry global impact. Policymakers, business leaders, and foreign observers are all digging deeper into Chinese data to understand its complex and influential economy and keep informed of the effects of large structural transformation and policy reforms. With growing complexity and continued change, some of the conventional economic gauges have become less indicative, while additional data on the fast-changing "new economy" are needed to better understand it. Chinese data will need to evolve and continue to improve as the economy changes and grows.

Emerging data needs will drive continued progress in the statistical system. This progress applies to the scope of data compiled, the underlying methodologies adopted, and the data dissemination practices adopted. For macroeconomic analysis, management, and surveillance, particular effort should be taken to close data gaps in the following areas:

- GDP data at constant prices for expenditure components, which are critical for more accurate macroanalysis and prediction
- Industrial structure: that is, the breakdown of data on the industrial sector in national accounts, which is crucial to understand structural changes and the evolving relationship between conventional economic gauges and GDP growth
- High-frequency indicators of the labor market (especially in the private sector), which are important to better understand labor market dynamics and set macroeconomic policies
- High-frequency indicators of the services sector, which are key to tracking growth in the "new economy"
- Borrowing by local government financing vehicles with monthly frequency, which is essential to monitor off-budget fiscal and quasi-fiscal activities

[13]The link to these data under the SDDS is http://dsbb.imf.org/Pages/SDDS/CtyCtgList.aspx?ctycode=CHN.

Box 12.6. IMF's Technical Cooperation with China in Macroeconomic Statistics

The emerging data needs arising from China's economic reforms and developments and its integration into the world economy have motivated the authorities to reform the statistical system and establish infrastructure for macroeconomic data collection, compilation, and dissemination in accordance with international best practices. To facilitate this, the authorities continuously expand their technical cooperation with the international community. The IMF's Statistics Department, among others, has been involved in China's capacity development in macroeconomic statistics for many years.[1] Figure 12.6.1 summarizes the Statistics Department's capacity development during 2000–15.

The Statistics Department's capacity development focuses on the review of current practices in data compilation, identifying areas for improvement in line with international methodologies and standards. The main source documents for these methodologies and standards are summarized in Table 12.1.[2]

In recent years, the Chinese authorities and the Statistics Department have developed new modalities of technical cooperation, including the joint International Conference on New Statistical Challenges Facing Central Banks with the People's Bank of China (PBC),[3] an on-the-job training program for one PBC staff and four National Bureau of Statistics staff to join the Statistics Department for six months,[4] and PBC staff visits to IMF headquarters to attend seminars on data compilation and uses.

Figure 12.6.1. IMF's Statistics Department Missions and Training Courses, 2000–15

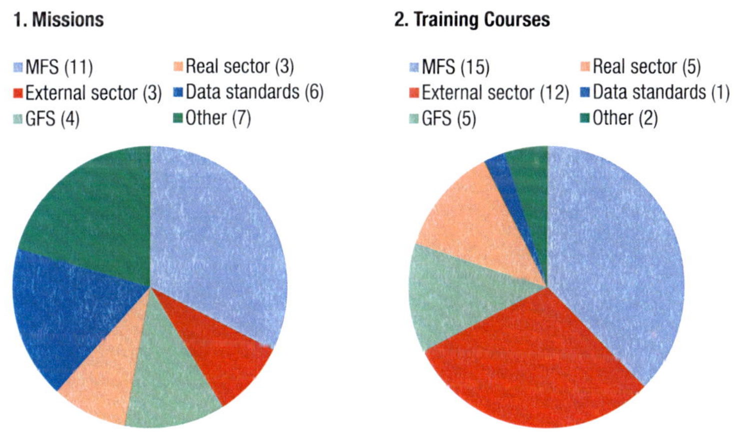

Source: IMF Statistics Department.
Note: GFS = government finance statistics; MFS = monetary and financial statistics.

---

[1]In statistical capacity development and technical cooperation, the Chinese authorities have widely engaged with other international, regional, and bilateral agencies. This chapter focuses only on IMF's engagement with China in statistical capacity development.

[2]Accessed at http://www.imf.org/external/data.htm#manuals.

[3]The first such conference on New Statistical Challenges Facing Central Banks was held in Dalian, China, and was attended by 14 representatives from 10 international, regional, and national agencies outside China, and 33 representatives from Chinese government agencies and academia and think tanks.

[4]NBS staff members were funded under a United Nations Statistics Division cooperation program with China.

Box 12.6. IMF's Technical Cooperation with China in Macroeconomic Statistics *(continued)*

Table 12.6.1. Manuals and Guides on Macroeconomic and Financial Statistics

Real Sector Statistics	Brief Description
System of National Accounts (SNA) 2008	Provides a comprehensive analytical framework for compiling national accounts data. The 2008 SNA, the fifth version of the SNA, updates the 1993 SNA.
Quarterly National Accounts Manual—Concepts, Data Sources, and Compilation	Provides guidance to help countries establish or strengthen quarterly national accounts that meet user needs (currently being updated).
Export and Import Price Index Manual	Contains detailed, comprehensive information and explanations for compiling the manuals
Consumer Price Index Manual	Provides guidance on compilation of the consumer price index, which measures the rate at which the prices of consumer goods and services are changing over time.
Producer Price Index Manual	Provides guidance on compilation of producer price data, which measures the rate at which the prices of producer goods and services are changing over time.
Practical Guide to Producing Consumer Price Indices	Targets developing countries and focuses on practical solutions to the problems facing compilers of consumer price data in the developing world.
Handbook on Residential Property Price Indices	Provides guidelines for the compilation of residential property price indices and explains the methods and best practices used to calculate this index.
Government Finance Statistics	**Brief Description**
Government Finance Statistics Manual (GFSM) 2014	Provides an analytical framework for compiling government finance statistics to support fiscal analysis. GFSM 2014 updates GFSM 2001.
Quarterly Government Finance Statistics—Guide for Compilers and Users	Serves as a reference for compilers and users of government finance statistics.
Public Sector Debt Statistics—Guide for Compilers and Users	Provides guidance for the measurement, compilation, analytical use, and presentation of public sector debt statistics.
Government Finance Statistics: Compilation Guide for Developing Countries	Provides detailed information and guidance on how to gradually introduce the guidelines of the GFSM 2001 and best practices into the compilation and dissemination of fiscal statistics.
External Sector Statistics	**Brief Description**
Balance of Payments and International Investment Position Manual, sixth edition (BPM6)	Provides analytical framework and guidance for collecting and compiling balance-of-payments and international investment position data. BPM6 published in 2009 updates the fifth edition that was released in 1993.
BPM6 Compilation Guide	Provides guidance on how the conceptual framework described in the BPM6 may be implemented in practice. BPM6 Guide updates the Balance of Payments Compilation Guide released in 1995.
International Reserves and Foreign Currency Liquidity: Guidelines for a Data Template	Provides operational advice to IMF members that subscribe to the Special Data Dissemination Standard regarding how to complete the prescribed (mandatory) monthly data template on international reserves and foreign currency liquidity.
2013 External Debt Statistics: Guide for Compilers and Users	Provides guidance for the measurement, compilation, analytical use, and presentation of external debt statistics.
International Transactions in Remittances: Guide for Compilers and Users	Provides practical guidance on the compilation of remittances based on the concepts set out in BPM6.
2015 Coordinated Portfolio Investment Survey Guide	Provides guidance to assist economies in participating in the Coordinated Portfolio Investment Survey.
Monetary and Financial Statistics	**Brief Description**
Monetary and Financial Statistics Manual and Compilation Guide (2016)	Updates *Monetary and Financial Statistics Manual* (2000) and *Monetary and Financial Statistics Compilation Guide* (2008), and combines the two documents into one volume (prepublication draft now available).
Financial Soundness Indicators Compilation Guide (2006)	Provides analytical framework and guidance for the compilation and dissemination of financial soundness indicators.
Handbook on Securities Statistics (2015)	Develops a conceptual framework for presenting statistics to improve information on securities markets. Updates *Handbook on Securities Statistics* 2015 and combines the previous three separate volumes of this handbook.

ANNEX 12.1. HEAT MAP OF DGI RECOMMENDATIONS

Annex Figure 12.1.1. Heat Map of DGI Recommendations

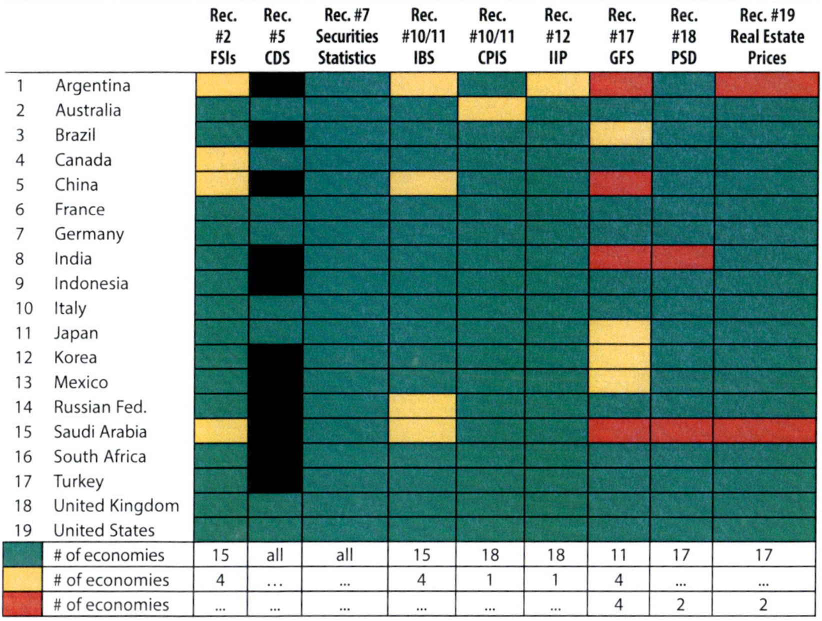

Source: Inter-Agency Group on Economic and Financial Statistics.

Note: Recommendations #1, #3, #4, #6, #8, #9, #13, #14, #15, and #16 are not included in the table as provision of data for these areas was not requested under DGI Phase One due to ongoing developmental work. ... = none; BIS = Bank for International Settlements; CDS = credit default swap; CPIS = Coordinated Portfolio Investment Survey; FSI = financial soundness indicator; GFSM = Government Finance Statistics Manual; IBS = international banking statistics; IIP = international investment position.

Rec. #2 (FSI = Financial Soundness Indicators)

indicates economies that report the seven FSIs expected from SDDS Plus adherent economies.

indicates economies that report most of the seven FSIs.

Rec. #5 (CDS = Credit Default Swaps)

indicates economies (with significant CDS markets) that report to the BIS semiannual over-the-counter derivatives survey.

indicates economies that do not have significant CDS markets, and so are not expected to participate in the data collection.

Rec.#7 (Securities Statistics)

indicates economies that participate in the BIS securities statistics.

Rec. #10/11 (IBS = International Banking Statistics)

indicates economies that participate in BIS IBS statistics with regular reporting.

indicates economies that provided test data for IBS statistics.

indicates economies that do not participate in the IBS.

Rec. #10/11 (CPIS = Coordinated Portfolio Investment Survey)

indicates economies that provide semiannual CPIS data to the IMF.

indicates economies that provide annual CPIS data to the IMF.

indicates economies that do not participate in the CPIS.

Rec. #12 (IIP = International Investment Position)

indicates economies that disseminate quarterly IIP data with a time lag of one quarter or less.

indicates economies that disseminate annual IIP data.

Rec. #17 (GFS = government finance statistics)

indicates economies for which quarterly general government data are disseminated under the GFSM framework.

indicates economies for which quarterly central government data and/or annual general government data are disseminated under the GFSM framework.

indicates economies for which general government or central government data are not disseminated under the GFSM framework.

Rec. #18 (PSD = public sector debt)

indicates economies that participate in World Bank/IMF/OECD Quarterly Public Sector Debt Database.

indicates economies that do not provide data to the database.

Rec. #19 (Real Estate Prices)

indicates economies that provide residential real estate price index (RPPI) for dissemination at the BIS website.

indicates economies that do not provide RPPI data to the BIS.

REFERENCES

Dippelsman, R., J. Josyula, and E. Métreau. 2016. "Fixed Base Year vs. Chain Linking in National Accounts: Experience of Sub-Saharan African Countries." IMF Working Paper 16/133, International Monetary Fund, Washington.

International Monetary Fund (IMF). 2013a. *The Special Data Dissemination Standard Guide for Subscribers and Users.* Washington.

———. 2013b. *The General Data Dissemination System Guide for Participants and Users.* Washington.

———. 2013c. *The Special Data Dissemination Standard Plus Guide for Adherents and Users.* Washington.

———. 2015. *Balance of Payments Statistics Yearbook.* Washington.

———. 2016. *Asia and Pacific Regional Economic Outlook: Navigating the Transition: Trade and Financial Spillover from China.* Washington, April.

——— and Financial Stability Board (FSB). 2009. "The Financial Crisis and Information Gaps." Report to the G-20 Finance Ministers and Central Bank Governors, Washington.

Organisation for Economic Co-operation and Development (OECD). 2000. *National Accounts for China Sources and Methods.* Paris.

Sheng, Songcheng. 2014. *The Theory and Practice of the Aggregate Financing to the Real Economy.* Beijing: China Finance Publisher.

Xu, Xianchun. 2016. *Research on China's Official Statistics Issues.* Beijing: Social Science Literature Publisher.

Index